What People Are Saying About

Yo Tookie, I've been bangin' since I was eight. And I Really Wanted To Thank You For Settin' Me Free, Cuz. I Mean You Were My Idol, And Now I See All Tha Pain I've Caused People Who Never Deserved It, Over A Color And What It Stood For. Thanks To You, I Now See How Wrong I Was. I Needed To Get My Life Back, And You Gave It To Me.

I would like to share the effect your books, movie and website are having on the juveniles in my rehabilitation program.

1) Dictionaries are going off the shelf faster than I can buy them.
2) More books are borrowed from the library than before.
3) Juveniles are telling me and writing me that they are changing their ways, that they are working harder at school.

Here is a sample, from a sixteen-year-old juvenile serving time in an adult prison.

"Thank you for writing me about Tookie Williams and sending me information about him. It encouraged me to pay attention to my school work while it lasts and get my mind focused on my weak points. My teacher tells me I'm the fastest worker in class. My comprehension skills are above average."

Thank you for changing lives. You may be saying the same things I tell the inmates, but when you say something, it reaches so many more.

—*Juvenile Rehabilitation Officer, Florida*

If the creator of the Crips can turn it around, why can't I? I know I'm going to stumble on my path. Old habits are easy to come by and hard to break. But one day at a time. Your example saved my life. I thank God for you every day.

Mr. Tookie, wut'up? I seen your movie and read your books. I really learned a lot. I see being a gangbanger is really lots of evilness. I had wanted to be one like that at first, because I seen how people was living large. But at the same time dying over crazy stuff. Like money, girls, cars and whose gang is bigger and better. I took the wrong path trying to fit in with others. But it didn't get me anywhere but in trouble and behind bars. None of them write me or come and see me, send me money or accept my phone calls or anything. I sit in my cell writing poems or drawing things. I wrote a poem in here on my birthday about being in here. I come from a place where people sat on their porch selling and smoking drugs in front of little kids and around babies. Thank you for showing me the light.

Tookie, your work has convinced six members of my family to not involve themselves in gang activities. Thank you for everything that you've done to help stop the violence that is tearing not only the Black community to pieces but other communities around the world.

Mr. Williams, I am an eighth-grade history teacher in California. I have read each of your books to over three hundred students. We were the first school group to ever speak to a death-row inmate—you—over a speakerphone. Your books have had a positive effect on my students, many of whom would be classified as "at risk."

Tookie, I was a member of a Los Angeles street gang. I would just like to let you know how big of an impact your story had on my life. Your works have made me realize the self-destruction that my involvement in a gang was causing. I love you for that. Thank you for saving my life.

---

i just want to let you know the impression you have made on my life. i have lost several friends to gang violence, one whom was particularly close to me. i wanted revenge, i wanted to join up with my friends and go after the people that killed her. then i stumbled upon your book "life in prison." i read it, and looked at myself and decided that i did not want to do that. after all, if i had tracked them down and hurt them, or worse, what good would that do? i'd probably have ended up incarcerated, and it would not have brought my friend back. YOU are my HERO. thank you for all that you have done for the countless other teenagers all over the world who you have touched. you are in my prayers.

I used ta be a crip but I watched tha movie. It helped me a lot in seeing that bangin blue aint nuthin. I can do without the trouble. Tookie kept me from bein behind barz. I'm stayin out of jail and keepin my head up all cuz of him. He deserves to live. He helped people live and stay off the streets.

---

hello tookie. i ran with the crips for thirteen yrs. after what you said from that day you changed my life for the best. i ran with the westside mafia. i have been shot and lived. no one can touch me but the words you said helped out for the best thank you. i am twenty-four yrs old. you saved my life. much love, your friend.

Also by Stanley Tookie Williams

Redemption

Life in Prison
(with Barbara Cottman Becnel)

Tookie Speaks Out Against Gang Violence Book Series
(with Barbara Cottman Becnel)
Gangs and the Abuse of Power
Gangs and Wanting to Belong
Gangs and Weapons ✓
Gangs and Self-Esteem ✓
Gangs and Violence
Gangs and Drugs ✓
Gangs and Your Friends
Gangs and Your Neighborhood

STANLEY TOOKIE WILLIAMS

BLUE RAGE, BLACK REDEMPTION

A Memoir

 DAMAMLI PUBLISHING COMPANY

PUBLISHED IN CONJUNCTION WITH DAMAMLI PUBLISHING

A TOUCHSTONE BOOK
PUBLISHED BY SIMON & SCHUSTER
NEW YORK   LONDON   TORONTO   SYDNEY

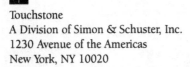

Touchstone
A Division of Simon & Schuster, Inc.
1230 Avenue of the Americas
New York, NY 10020

First Touchstone trade paperback edition November 2007

TOUCHSTONE and colophon are registered trademarks of Simon & Schuster, Inc.

For information about special discounts for bulk purchases,
please contact Simon & Schuster Special Sales at
1-800-456-6798 or business@simonandschuster.com

Designed by Jan Pisciotta

Manufactured in the United States of America

20 19 18 17 16 15 14 13 12 11

Library of Congress Cataloging-in-Publication Data

Williams, Stanley Tookie, 1953–2005.
   Blue rage, black redemption : a memoir / Stanley Tookie Williams.
      p.   cm.
   1. Williams, Stanley Tookie, 1953–2005.   2. Crips (Gang)—Biography.   3. Gang
members—California—Los Angeles—Biography.   I. Title.
HV6439.U7L7885 2007
364.152'3092—dc22
[B]   2007011583

ISBN-13: 978-1-4165-4449-4
ISBN-10:   1-4165-4449-6

To poor people, prisoners, slaves, and the disenfranchised everywhere—through faith and theories put into practice, *you can bend the most oppressive circumstances to your will, to make the impossible possible.*

—*Stanley Tookie Williams*

Contents

Part 2: BLACK REDEMPTION

"[President Nixon] emphasizes that you have to face the fact that the *whole* problem is really the Blacks. The key is to devise a system that recognizes this, while not appearing to."

—*H. R. Haldeman,*
The Haldeman Diaries:
Inside the Nixon White House

Foreword

It started out as a gray Friday morning, and as I rushed into a West Oakland McDonald's to grab a breakfast sandwich, I heard the commotion coming from a table of older black gentlemen in the back of the restaurant. "If he killed those people, he ought to die," said one. "Well, whether he did it or not, if he stays locked up for the rest of his life, that ain't living," said another. "He might as well be dead." Although I tried to avoid this breakfast-table debate, as soon as I was spotted I was summoned to the table.

"Tavis Smiley, what are you doing here?" One brother yelled out. "We're talking about that gang leader Tookie Williams who is supposed to be executed for killing those people in L.A. back in the day." "So, Smiley," asked another, "what do you think? Should he die?"

The whole scene was surreal. I had just flown into Oakland International Airport that morning and, ironically, my radio producer and I were on our way to San Quentin to meet with Stanley Tookie Williams. He asked to meet me in person before doing an interview that would be aired on both my radio and television shows. It was November 25, 2005, the day after Thanksgiving, and I was already riding a sea of emotions long before being confronted by the breakfast club. Of all the McDonald's we could have chosen.

The truth is, at that moment, I wasn't sure how to respond to the brother's question. All I knew for sure is that I am vehemently opposed to the death penalty and, as a person of faith, I believe in the scripture where God says, "Vengeance is mine." So, without going into too much more detail, that was my answer as I wished the brothers a good day.

As I got back in the car, I started thinking about the morning ahead. Although unfortunately I've visited friends or family members in jail over the years, fortunately I had never been to death row. I wasn't sure what to expect. But as for Stanley, I had a little bit of insight. When Jamie Foxx came on my television show, he talked about what it was like to portray Stanley in the television movie *Redemption: The Stan Tookie Williams Story.* Jamie also told me that in spite of Stanley's imposing figure—a massive chest and bulging arms and legs from bodybuilding—Stanley was very gentle and soft-spoken.

When we arrived at San Quentin a short while later, I found all of that to be true. After going through two metal detectors and security doors, we waited in a small visitors' cell that held an old table, a few chairs, and a small barred window that looked out onto the bay. A few minutes later, a guard escorted the shackled, gentle, soft-spoken bodybuilder with glasses and gray hair to the cell. After his cuffs were unlocked, he reached out, shook my hand, and said, "I'm Stan, and I've been waiting to meet you."

As we sat down, Stan immediately opened the window and we began to talk. We talked briefly about the childhood he discusses at length in this book. We talked about what it was like to be in prison for nearly twenty-five years—what an average day was like—and how he had coped for all that time. We talked about his children's books and his Nobel Peace Prize nomination. Then I asked some of the tough questions.

I asked him about his life as a gang leader, and how he felt about all the death and destruction caused in the black community by gang violence in Los Angeles, where I live, as well as many other parts of the country. I asked him about the murders for which he was convicted, and how he felt about the victims' families. I also asked him about the fact that he reportedly refused to assist law enforcement with information in their efforts to arrest, prosecute, and convict other gang members.

Stan solemnly and candidly answered all my questions. He told me that he was sorry for his gang involvement and for the havoc he had personally wreaked in the community. He said that he was sorry for the losses suffered by the Owens and Yang families, but maintained that he was innocent of the murders. He told me that he believes God allowed him to go to prison to pay for some of the horrible things he had done in his life, although ultimately he was being punished for crimes he did not commit. Regarding his cooperation with law enforcement, Stan gave me a somewhat more complicated explanation: he said that it was a violation of a prison code for him to discuss certain gang-related matters because of broader implications that could lead to more violence for him and other prison members.

Then we talked about the power of redemption. Stan told me that prison had afforded him the time to read and learn and grow. He shared how through prayer, reflection, and discipline he had changed from a young, violent man filled with rage to a man whose life revealed redemption. Throughout our conversation, Stan held my gaze and his calm never wavered. And then we talked about his impending death. He told me that he had already told the prison that he had chosen to deny his last meal and, with the exception of Minister Louis Farrakhan, he would deny last rites or counsel with any clergy. I told him about the brothers at McDonald's and the questions that I had been asked. In particular, I wanted to know how he felt about fighting to spend the rest of his life—which could be another twenty-five plus years—behind bars. Death or life in prison? What does it feel like to face that inevitability?

Stan smiled as he told me that his ability to influence young people to stay out of gangs was reason enough to want to live. He said that in spite of the soul-stripping regimens of prison, he had learned how to create and experience his own *joie de vivre,* the French term for joy of life. As our conversation ended we stood, shook hands, and, as I patted him on the back in a brief embrace, he reminded me to "keep the faith." I realized that this could be the first and last time I would see him. It was.

Three weeks later, Stan was executed by lethal injection by the State of California. The night before he died I couldn't sleep. I stayed awake past midnight, and after he was pronounced dead I felt numb. Even after such a brief encounter I felt a connection to another black man whose life, through bad circumstances and bad choices, like so many others, had ended way too soon. I also felt sorrow for all the mothers and fathers and communities that have lost loved ones to gang violence. After wrestling with these thoughts, I realized that Stan's legacy can be one of tragedy and triumph. It is also a legacy that helped me grapple with the power of redemption.

I believe that Stan reminded our society that we send people to prison to rehabilitate them, and we have to believe that process is real and possible for even some of the worst offenders. Ultimately, if we don't believe in redemption, we don't believe in America.

For many reasons, meeting Stan was a life-changing experience that reminded me that but for the earnest prayers of my mother, and the grace of God, as a black man, I too could have been one of the four black men in prison, on probation, or on parole.

I was blessed to have the personal encounter with Stan, but for all those who will never be able to witness his courage, conviction, and commitment to prevent young people from taking the same path he did, you can experience some of that pain and passion throughout this book, *Blue Rage, Black Redemption*. I sincerely hope that for many young men and women in Los Angeles and throughout the country, Stan's death will reaffirm the importance of life.

—Tavis Smiley
Los Angeles, 2007

Introduction

The title of this book represents two extreme phases of my life.

"Blue Rage" is a chronicle of my passage down a spiraling path of Crip rage in South Central Los Angeles. "Black Redemption" depicts the stages of my redemptive awakening during my more than twenty-three years of imprisonment on California's death row. These memoirs of my evolution will, I hope, connect the reader to a deeper awareness of a social epidemic that is the unending nightmare of racial minorities in America and abroad as well.

Throughout my life I was hoodwinked by South Central's terminal conditions, its broad and deadly template for failure. From the beginning I was spoon-fed negative stereotypes that covertly positioned black people as genetic criminals—inferior, illiterate, shiftless, promiscuous, and ultimately "three-fifths" of a human being, as stated in the Constitution of the United States. Having bought into this myth, I was shackled to the lowest socioeconomic rung where underprivileged citizens compete ruthlessly for morsels of the American pie—a pie theoretically served proportionately to all, based on their ambition, intelligence, and perseverance.

Like many others I became a slave to a delusional dream of capitalism's false hope: a slave to dys-education (see Chapter 5); a slave to nihilism; a slave to drugs; a slave to black-on-black violence; and a slave to self-hate. Paralyzed within a social vacuum, I gravitated toward thughood, not out of aspiration but out of desperation to survive the monstrous inequities that show no mercy to young or old. Aggression, I was to learn, served as a poor man's merit for manhood. To die as a street martyr was seen as a noble thing.

In 1971, I met Raymond Lee Washington (may he rest in peace) and we ultimately decided to unite our homeboys from the west and east sides of South Central to combat neighboring street gangs. (An erroneous grapevine suggests that the Crips formed in 1969, or even as early as the 1950s.) Most Crips themselves are unaware that the original name for our alliance was "Cribs," a name selected from a list of many options. But the short-lived label of "Cribs" was carelessly mispronounced by many of us and morphed into the name "Crips," our permanent identity.

Most of us were seventeen years of age.

The Crips mythology has many romanticized, bogus accounts. I never thought it would be necessary to address such issues. But I can set the record straight—for Raymond Washington, for me, and for others who fought and often died for this causeless cause.

I assumed that everyone in South Central knew that Raymond was the leader of the East Side Crips, and that I was the leader of the West Side Crips. A few published chronicles have Raymond attending Washington High School and uniting the neighborhood west side gangs where he supposedly resided. In fact, Raymond attended Fremont High School on the east side, where he lived. A fundamental inquiry would have revealed that I lived on the west side, where I attended Washington High and rallied our homeboys and groups of local gangs. Even our former rivals have a better understanding of the Crips' origins than many social historians.

Most of the public misinformation has been fostered by academics, journalists and other parasitical opportunists, stool pigeons, and wannabe Crip founders who shamelessly seek undue profit and recognition for gang genocide. There is no honor in insinuating yourself as a player in this legacy of bloodletting where your feet have never trod.

Another version incorrectly documents the Crips as an offshoot of the Black Panther Party. No Panther Party member ever mentioned the Crips (or Cribs) as being a spin-off of the Panthers. It is also fiction that the Crips functioned under the acronym C.R.I.P., for Community

Resource Inner-City Project or Community Revolutionary Inner City Project. (Words such as "revolutionary agenda" were alien to our thuggish, uninformed teenage consciousness.) We did not unite to protect the community; our motive was to protect ourselves and our families.

There are people who say it was karmic justice that Raymond and I, who impinged on society in 1971 with a violent pact, deserved our exit from society in 1979—Raymond to the grave and myself to San Quentin State Prison. They cry out that I am incapable of redemption. My detractors' attitude toward my redemption is driven largely by my open apology (see the apology at www.tookie.com) to black folks and others whom I have offended by my helping to create the Crips over thirty-three years ago. My detractors argue that I could not be redeemed because I have not apologized to the family members of the victims I was convicted of killing.

Please allow me to clarify.

I will never apologize for capital crimes that I did not commit—not even to save my life. And I did not commit the crimes for which I was sentenced to be executed by the State of California.

Being a condemned prisoner, I am viewed among the least able to qualify as a promoter of redemption and of peace. But the most wretched among society can be redeemed, find peace, and reach out to others to lift them up. Real redemption cannot be faked or intellectualized. It must be subjective: experienced, and then shared.

In the past, redemption was an alien concept to me. But from 1988 until 1994, while I lived in solitary confinement, I embarked on a transitional path toward redemption. I underwent years of education, soul-searching, edification, spiritual cultivation, and fighting to transcend my inner demons.

Subsequently the redeeming process for me symbolized the end of a bad beginning—and a new start. In time I developed a conscience that empowered me to think beyond the selfish "I" principle. Armed with new insight, I discovered the means to control my ego, which enabled me to reunite with God; to reclaim my humanity; to discover inner peace; and to find my raison d'être—my reason to be.

Since then, I have written nine antigang and antiviolence books for children, created the Internet Project for Street Peace—an international peer mentoring program that links high-risk youth in other countries to their counterparts in the United States—and wrote a Local Street Peace Protocol that provides guidance on how to initiate a gang truce and is available to anyone who chooses to download it from my website at www.tookie.com.

Yes, redemption has resurrected me from a spiritual and mental death. And whether people are able to accept my redemption or not, they can never take it away. God chooses to redeem, not the laws of the government, the media, the sanctimonious, or the vindictive.

To be redeemed, I have learned, is to be at peace with oneself. In fact, true virtue is self-victory by a path of redemption to peace.

To avoid damaging others, certain names, nicknames, and quite a few well-known incidents have been excluded from *Blue Rage, Black Redemption*. For the same reason I have used pseudonyms for some of the people I include in this book. Otherwise, the story I tell is true.

Part II

BLUE RAGE

Born in the Bayou

On December 29, 1953, in New Orleans Charity Hospital, I entered the world kicking and screaming in a caesarean ritual of blood and scalpels. Because this was the 1950s, in pre–civil rights Louisiana, my seventeen-year-old mother, a "colored woman," was deprived of anesthetics as her torso was slit from sternum to pubic bone. Over and over again, she sang the Christmas carol "Silent Night" to distract her from the pain.

I was christened Stanley Tookie Williams III, but mostly referred to as Tookie.

Perhaps my laborious birth—and a seizure I experienced before the age of two, requiring a spinal tap—foreshadowed more tragic things to come. But I've always felt that the real adversity fell on my teenage mother because of her station in life: a black woman living in the South, and with very little money. Morbid conditions of poverty were eager to devour us. Being exposed to this apocalyptic society, as I grew to adolescence my thin skin of innocence began to peel slowly away.

In my life, the natural progression from maternal weaning to paternal guidance was absent. My father was the weak link in the family equation. He had abandoned us before I reached my first birthday. My memories of him were so remote that I could not have recognized him in a jailhouse line-up. He was like a stranger showing up once in a blue moon bearing gifts and an uncertain smile. His attempts at playing part-time Santa Claus and spreading good cheer failed to win me over. As far as I was concerned, my father was an unwelcome visitor whom I watched carefully until he vacated the premises.

My mother was the true backbone of the family. She was hardworking, serious, tough, and soft-spoken and had the foot-speed of a cheetah. I can attest to that quickness through my many failed attempts to escape punishment. Prior to my mother's pregnancy, she was well known as a track star. Her genes were passed down to me; I could outrun my peers and many older youths. Standing at five feet two inches, she was a vision of loveliness with chocolate-hued skin, a shapely physique, and long, silky black hair.

But my mother's beauty attracted a lot of unwanted male attention. Though her no-nonsense expression held most men at bay, a few boldly approached. Their foolhardy advances compelled me, for a while, to carry a sharpened seven-inch butter knife concealed in my waistband. To protect my mother, I would have happily become a Ninja mercenary.

Unknown to my mother, I later stashed that knife beneath a slab of rock in the backyard. Had she discovered it, I would have been severely beaten, or "disciplined," as she called it. My mother adhered religiously to the Judeo-Christian Bible, in particular Proverb 13:24: "He who spareth his rod hateth his son. But he that loveth him chastiseth him betimes (whips him quickly)." Yes, my mother loved me deeply, and I regularly felt her love's sting. But compared to the beatings some of my friends received from their parents, I got off easy. I will admit the biblically-inspired beatings did make me tougher. On the other hand, her punishments failed to derail my misbehavior.

The frequency of beatings aged me considerably. I became more unruly, distant, and indifferent to the predictable consequence of my actions. By no means was I born a criminal. I understood the penalties for my actions all too well. Though my mother tried to instill in me the fundamentals of right and wrong, the development of my conscience was shaded with different meanings. I learned from the street culture that criminal activity was an economic necessity and violence a means to a desired end. Plain and simple, in my neighborhood, if you wanted something, you had to take it—and then fight to keep it. I clashed often with my mother over my mindset and incorrigible behavior.

Whatever was physically possible for a mischievous youth my size to do, I did. Motivated by greed and envy, I took to stealing little food items and toys from stores. If my mother happened to discover any item unaccounted for, she would march me back to return the item, or would destroy it. Although I didn't completely understand this, my philosophy was hardening: adapt and survive. That was the street rule.

Sometimes my partner in crime was Rex, my brown and white mutt dog. The entire neighborhood was in an uproar over my letting Rex run through flower beds and chase chickens and roosters. Time and time again I was warned about unleashing Rex, but it was all fun and games to me. Eventually I had to watch teary-eyed as Rex was hauled away to the dog pound. If there was a lesson to be learned, I didn't grasp it.

Being mischievous, hyperactive, and with a short attention span, I had to find something to do. My older cousin Walter and I used to slide and tumble on a gunnysack down a nearby dirt hill. Too poor to afford baseball equipment, we liked playing stickball with rocks and would play stickball for hours before dinner. That was stopped after Walter hit a rock that smashed into my forehead. Blood gushed everywhere! My grandmother, "Momma," simply patched me up with some Beechnut chewing tobacco, a trusted home remedy, and I was good as new. But my stickball days were over.

I believe it was the lingering racist effects of Jim Crow—systematic discrimination against Southern blacks during the period following the Civil War—as well as my incorrigible behavior that fueled my mother's desire to migrate to California. She first planned to leave me behind and then send for me after she got settled. But I was too hyperactive for my aunts and my aging grandmother. If you recall *The*

Beverly Hillbillies and the woman called Granny, you will have a pretty good notion about Momma's stature and style of dress. A beautiful Cherokee Indian, she was five feet tall, about ninety pounds, with whitish-gray shoulder-length hair and a copper-penny skin tone. She was a devout Baptist who had served as a deaconess for seventeen years in the New Salem Baptist Church in New Orleans. Momma spoke softly, her melodic voice often issuing quotations from Biblical scriptures. Her religious influence was evident in each of her sixteen children—nine daughters and seven sons.

Momma's gospel sermons of fire and brimstone held my attention for hours. I enjoyed sitting on the porch with her, drinking ice-cold lemonade, listening to her preach. Afterward, I would bombard her with questions. But I could not fathom why the religious figures in drawings and paintings were all white—and most of them *glowed*. I remember trying to sneak a peek whenever I saw white men, women or children, just to see if they really did glow. They did not.

In all of the religious children's literature I was given to read, there was an obvious absence of black people. Everybody was white: angels, Jesus, Adam, Eve, Cain, Abel, Moses, and Noah. Only the devil was red. I'd ask Momma: Where were the black people like us? Did God only make white people? Momma always seemed to be holding back. The more I'd ask race-based questions, the more she would say, "Boy, you're tiring me out with all your questions!" Though I never did get a straight answer, I still believed something was not right with all those pictures depicting white figures as divine. Decades would pass before I'd be able to uncover the answers to those questions.

I relished Momma's home-cooked meals, especially her gumbo and sweet potato pie. The gumbo consisted of crabs, shrimps, oysters, clams, crawdads, chicken, mild and hot link sausages, okra, and gumbo filé. The taste was heavenly, etched forever in my taste buds. Her sweet potato pies were better than any store pies I ever tasted.

There were rare times when Momma would fall silent—the mention of my grandfather inevitably stopped her. He was a huge, muscular, loving, pensive man who worked tirelessly on the railroad and held other jobs to support his large family. He died from overexhaustion; he worked himself to death. He left behind no pictures of himself. He didn't like taking them. My mother said he would fight if you tried to take a picture of him. Often my mother would tell me, "If you want to know what your grandfather looked like, just look in the mirror." Since he loved Momma as I did, there is no doubt I would have loved him too.

I guess I didn't realize how much I loved Momma until my mother and I were on the Greyhound bus waving good-bye to her and our other relatives. Fear and curiosity had me wondering what was in store for us in California. I could see the sadness in Momma's expression mirroring the tears streaming down my face.

South Central

My mother and I were silent throughout most of that long bus ride to Los Angeles in 1959. Neither of us talked that much, anyway. It was difficult for us to express our feelings, probably one of the reasons we weren't in tune with one another. Still, our bond was evident. My mother struggled hard to clothe, feed, and provide for me. She was a fighter who had to wade through incredible obstacles to her progress. In more ways than she cared to admit, we were alike: determined, stubborn, demanding, quick-tempered, and fastidious. Besides our characteristically serious expression, each of us had a black mole on the upper left side of the nose.

I adored my mother, and I regret never voicing those feelings to her.

As she slept on the bus, a beam of sunlight shone through the window onto the smooth dark brown skin of her face, and I wondered if my mother was as worried as I was about our destination.

After several days the Greyhound bus finally reached the bus terminal in downtown Los Angeles, California. The ambience was strange. It was like being on another planet. People dressed differently, talked fast, and moved fast, as did the cars and trucks. I saw a small crowd of men who seemed to mirror comedian Red Skelton's portrayal of hoboes. It was the first time I had ever seen a hobo close up. This was the so-called City of Angels, where my mother hoped to achieve prosperity. If she could have foreseen the path I would follow, no doubt we would have quickly reboarded the bus to return to New Orleans.

After several days and nights in a motel, my mother located an affordable, furnished place to stay. It was a white duplex apartment on 43rd and Kansas on the west side, the area called South Central, or "South Los Angeles," as it was recently renamed. The apartment was positioned far in the back, behind two larger duplexes. The front door of the duplex was set up high, about three feet, with three rickety steps up to the door. Immediately inside was the kitchen. To the left was a small living room, where I slept on a couch that unfolded into a bed. To the right in the middle of the living room was a door leading into my mother's bedroom. Inside her room, to the left, was a tiny bathroom. The entire place was smaller than a tiny classroom. But it was home.

We lived in a predominantly black area of private homes, apartments, and duplexes. As I grew older, I realized that it wasn't the typical urban ghetto—it had a deceptive look of prosperity. It was a west side colony of poverty behind a façade of manicured lawns and clean streets, of Cadillacs, Fords, and Chevys. The neighborhood was a shiny red apple rotting away at the core.

I was the new six-year-old on the block, soon to undergo the ritual that would determine my position in the pecking order. The scenario was no different than one between nations, corporate executives, siblings, animals, or anyone else vying for status. The first day, outside the duplex, I was presented with a fight-or-flight option. Monroe, a stocky black youth about my height, strolled up and asked my name. I was about to say "Stan" when Monroe suddenly rained a barrage of punches on my head. Caught off guard, out of panicked anger I began to swing wildly in defense. Whether it was a lucky punch or a slip, Monroe fell to the ground. Spurred by fear and instinct, I jumped on top of Monroe and started whaling away at his head. Then, abruptly, I was snatched up by Monroe's heavyset mother, smelling of cheap wine and cursing as bad as any man. She held me by the head with one arm, viselike, while holding in her free hand a jug of wine that was spilling all over me. Mrs. Monroe marched me down the narrow walkway to the duplex and knocked on the door. When my mother opened the door, I could see the puzzled look on her face. Rocking back and forth, Mrs. Monroe released me and began to complain loudly about how I beat up her son for nothing.

The evidence against me seemed overwhelming. Monroe stood there with a bloodied nose, big lip, and black eye. I wanted to believe that my mother would not take the word of this foul-mouthed woman. But when my mother flashed her trademark accusatory look, there was nothing I could say. As soon as they left and I entered the duplex, my mother was all over me with a leather strap, quicker than Monroe was with his fists. I learned two valuable lessons that day: remain silent in the face of controversy, whether I was guilty or not—and be prepared to strike first.

Later, Monroe and I would befriend one another. His family lived directly across the street from us. Whenever he showed up, I could tell that my mother disapproved of our friendship, but she never uttered a word. I preferred meeting at his family's house, because it was a poor child's Disneyland. The front yard was cluttered with all kinds of junk: broken toys, tires, hubcaps, refrigerators, television sets, car engines, radios, mattresses, bicycles, and other unwanted items. There were also dogs, huge white chickens, and roosters that Monroe and I used to chase around the yard.

Sometimes we positioned ourselves on the top of his family's house, armed with a BB rifle, to shoot at the old TV picture tubes that exploded with a satisfying BANG. Our affinity for mischief led us past other boundaries of curiosity and trouble. We had several brushes with the law for minor offenses. There was a time that Monroe and I were accused of stealing Oreo cookies out of a small sack in a liquor store. The older of two Asian-looking men claimed to have seen one of us do it, but he didn't know which one, since we looked alike. They threw both of us in the back of the store and then left. The back door was locked. I saw a window behind some stacked boxes. As I climbed on top of the boxes, I felt a sharp blow to my back, causing me to fall to the floor amidst tumbling boxes. I was then pinned to the floor on my back by the younger Asian with the butt of an ax handle across my throat. From the corner of my eye I could see Monroe creeping away like a thief in the night, only to reappear standing between two white cops. They were beaming with exaggerated pride, as if they had captured a vicious killer. The shorter, pudgy cop joked about how he should have fired a shot, just to scare the hell out of the little nigger. Immediately there was a chorus of laughter among the two cops and the Asians.

After the laughter died down, the younger Asian snatched me up by the collar like a rag doll and shoved me down on a box next to Monroe. For a moment the cops and Asians stood in a huddle, whispering. I was scared because I had heard that white cops were notorious for cracking black skulls in the neighborhood. When the huddle broke up, the cops tried to elicit a confession from us with the good-cop, bad-cop routine. It pissed me off that two complete strangers would try to get me to snitch. My own mother, who was deadlier than any cop to me, wasn't able to get a word out of me, yet these cops thought they could. Plus, every child in the neighborhood knew that cops were the enemy.

When the good-cop routine failed, the pudgy cop tried the "bad" routine on me. He threatened to bust me upside the head if I didn't tell him who ate the cookies. My silence infuriated him. He snatched me forward within inches of his face. His foul breath smelled like uncooked chitterlings, bad enough to curl my eyebrows. I held my breath for so long, I thought I would pass out. The other cop snatched Monroe by the collar, then held his nightstick in a threatening gesture above Monroe's head. I believe the cop would have cracked his skull wide open had Monroe not fallen to the floor and gone into convulsions.

Both cops and the Asians stood there dumbfounded, their smiles gone. I was shocked to see Monroe lying on the ground with his eyes rolling back into their sockets, saliva dribbling from the corner of his mouth. Though I didn't know what to do, I dropped to my knees and placed a hand underneath Monroe's head to prevent it from continuing to bang on the floor. After rolling Monroe over onto his back, I began to rub his chest in a child's attempt to comfort him. When his eyes closed, I thought he had died, and I began to cry. But seconds later, to my surprise and relief, Monroe regained consciousness. I struggled to help him back up onto the boxes. Meanwhile, both the cops and the Asians regained their composure, then they huddled. Afterward, they shook hands. They tried to save face by saying they were willing to let us go. The pudgy cop asked Monroe where he and I lived. In spite of his recent seizure, Monroe answered with clarity.

During the short ride home in the back of the squad car, I asked Monroe what had happened. He said he had experienced seizures since he was a baby. He was epileptic. I prayed that it would never ever happen again when I was around. As the patrol car pulled into the driveway where Monroe lived, the pudgy cop asked, "Is this where you really live, boy?" Monroe said yes, and the cop burst out in laughter at the bizarre, cluttered front yard. It was like *The Munsters* in Los Angeles.

From the patrol car I could see Mrs. Monroe staggering out of the house wearing a black ruffled dress, red stockings, a long red feathered boa, and a red flower in her hair. She looked like a 1920s harlot. The two cops nudged one another and again broke into hysterical laughter. The pudgy cop leaned his head out of the window and told Mrs. Monroe his distorted version of what had happened. He ended by pointing at me, then asking her if she could "take the mute boy home." He thought I was mute because, other than shaking my head no, I hadn't uttered a word. Though puzzled, she agreed to take me home. She muttered a few words of profanity and ordered her son into the house. She then whirled around and gave me a hard look that clearly said I was responsible for leading her son astray.

To me, Mrs. Monroe was a female version of Dr. Jekyll and Mr. Hyde. When sober, she was an amiable soul who liked me and didn't curse that much. But drunk, her facial expression became a scowl, her speech foul, and to her I was like a red cape to a bull. She actually enjoyed marching me home to tell my mother lies about my getting Monroe into trouble. As usual, I prepared myself for another biblical beating. But it was not a deterrent for me.

Don't get me wrong. I didn't enjoy getting into trouble. I just found the streets to be more interesting than being at home. We couldn't afford a television, so the streets became my TV set, where I played the leading role. It felt liberating to be able to face the street adventures and to make my own decisions about what I should do. Though I loved my mother, I wouldn't listen to her. There were many things I avoided telling her for my own safety, punishment-wise. There was nothing I had witnessed or experienced that I wished to reveal to my mother. Nothing!

She is not responsible for my actions. Any of them. My mother exhausted every possible effort to raise me properly, but she could not stand guard over me 24/7. She was in thrall to some handed-down black rendition of a Euro-American parenting philosophy that was in total conflict with the environment I saw around me and its stringent requirements for survival. Clearly, not even my mother's intentions and religious guidance could have compelled or prayed me into conforming to society's double standards. Her cordial instructions conflicted with the colony's exploitation of the underclass. I was a member of that class.

As a boy, I was incapable of articulating the contradictions I saw, or to dodge confrontations with the ominous influences outside my home. Each time I stepped out into this society—rife with poverty, filth, crime, drugs, illiteracy, and daily brutal miscarriages of justice— I inhaled its moral pollutants and so absorbed a distorted sense of self-preservation. As a child I was duped into believing that this toxic environment was "normal." I was unaware of the violence being done to my mind, but my behavior was revelatory. Lacking any real knowledge of African culture, there was a black hole in my existence.

As beneficiary of more than five hundred years of slavery, I was left only scattered remnants of a broken culture. Exposed to a multitude of ambiguous, mostly negative influences, I would pass through my young life with cultural neglect and a profound identity crisis. Though I knew I was black, I had no real perspective on being black. I had absorbed the common negative black stereotypes that eventually made me despise my blackness. But despite my envy of the privileges, wealth, and other comforts of life held by many white people, I never fantasized about being one of them. Without the cultural knowledge I needed to shape my identity, I was unable to give my mother the respect she deserved. Since I respected neither my mother nor myself, it was inevitable that I would grow up, as I did, to disrespect other black people.

Lacking an understanding of my culture, I blindly molded an identity that was a classic product of corrupt influences and my own vivid imagination. Though I was no angel, neither was I a child demon. Life deprived me of the blood of freedom and an equal opportunity to succeed. I was guilty by reason of color, convicted and sentenced at birth.

Like most of my peers, I stumbled through life "dys-educated," a very different quality than being merely *uneducated*. My options and opportunities were restricted. For me there were no Rotary Clubs, yacht clubs, Explorers Clubs, boys' academies, or any other privilege-bound associations. I was afforded equal opportunities on society's underbelly among street thugs, ex-cons, pimps, gamblers, con men, thieves, prostitutes, and other hustler types. Here, the prevailing motifs were violence and the daily battle to survive. Might was right, always.

Seen through my adolescent eyes, everything was at war: fathers battled their wives, neighbors were at each other's throats, and criminals fought criminals. Cruelty found its home in behavior unbecoming a human being. Sometimes at night I would see birds on fire soaring through the sky or crashing into a fence. I learned that gamblers were setting homing pigeons ablaze and then releasing them, wagering on which one would come closest to its destination. And we kids would imitate them. This was our culture, casually brutal and cruel in unspeakable ways.

The most popular blood sport for money was dogfighting. Men would show up with different breeds of dogs in hopes of winning the cash pot. A variety of breeds were represented: pit bulls, Great Danes, bull terriers, Labrador retrievers, chow chows, Doberman pinschers, Saint Bernards, bulldogs, German shepherds, huskies, bullmastiffs, and plenty of others. Back then the gamblers would use some of us to take care of their dogs. I was paid a couple of dollars to water, feed, or patch up a mauled dog. In most of the fights a dog would lose an eye, tail, nose, ear, and a plug of skin or part of a jaw. At first the sight of the blood, gore, and loss of body parts was sickening, and I felt pity for the injured dogs. But I became hardened to the gruesome scenes. Whenever a particular dog was beyond patching up or was no longer wanted, one of the men would pull out his pistol and shoot the dog, or simply beat it to death with a baseball bat. Since most of the dogfights took place in abandoned houses, garages, or in pits dug out in vacant lots, the dogs were buried there, or discarded elsewhere throughout the neighborhood.

These hustlers would bet on just about anything—even who could spit, urinate, or throw a rock the farthest. I have witnessed cockfights, cricket fights, fish fights, and pay-per-view street fights among individuals between six and fifty years of age. Older hustlers would bet on children to fight. To earn money I would put on smelly, ragged boxing gloves and swing wildly until the other boy fell to the ground, and then I wouldn't let him up. Some of the hustlers who wanted me to win would give me pointers on how to cheat. They would advise me to hit an opponent of equal height and weight while he was taking off his jacket, tying his shoe, putting on the boxing gloves, or when he wasn't looking. But win, lose, or draw, everybody received chump change—a small amount of money. Though I won my fights, I didn't always come away unscathed.

Often my mother would catch me trying to sneak into the house with a black eye, cut lip, swollen jaw, or just blood on my shirt. As far as she was concerned, fighting was a cardinal sin. Whether I initiated the fight or someone else did, a biblical beating was on my agenda. But for me, fighting was part of growing up in South Central. My mother, bless her soul, didn't have a clue about what was happening to me, nor what I was being exposed to.

Sibling Feud

I had no idea a storm was brewing, one that would turn into a raging rivalry with a sibling I didn't know I had. But in 1963 my mother told me Momma would be arriving, accompanied by . . . my sister, Cynthia! What sister? I couldn't remember my mother ever being pregnant, how could I have a sister? Then again, no one ever explained to me the fundamentals of childbirth, so I probably thought, at the time, that my mother's pregnancy was her normal shape.

Seeing Cynthia for the first time was for me a traumatic experience. I racked my brain trying to figure out what was really going on. Yes, Cynthia was supposed to be my sister, but were we truly related? She resembled absolutely no one I knew—not my mother, Momma, aunties, uncles, or me. Cynthia was a dainty and extremely light-skinned girl with shoulder-length hair and a quality of vulnerable shyness. But the moment we acknowledged one another's presence—it was pure hatred. I would come to call her "cow," which earned me plenty of biblical beatings.

During the few days Momma stayed with us, she cooked some of her famous sweet potato pies and delectable gumbo. To me she was the best cook in the world. Her corn bread melted like butter in my mouth, and her fried chicken, catfish, potato salad, collard greens, and sweet corn were good enough to eat for breakfast. The presence of

Momma had a tranquilizing effect on me. I tried to convince Momma to stay longer, but she had to get back to New Orleans. When it was time for her to leave, we hugged while she whispered in my ear, "Tookie, be nice, you hear? Be nice!" That was the first inkling I had that she knew of my antipathy for my sister.

It didn't take long for my mother and Cynthia to bond like two peas in a pod. My mother's preferential treatment of Cynthia allowed my sister to manipulate the situation to her advantage. It was obvious from jump street that our sister-brother relationship had deteriorated before it got started. For us it was blow by blow; pain for pain; and verbal abuse for verbal abuse. Our aversion for one another was defined by our actions, and in the usage of the word "mother." Cynthia or I would emphasize personal ownership by saying, "My mother said for you to . . ." We acted like our mother belonged to only one of us, but never both.

I knew the struggle for my mother's attention was a lost cause for me. It was out of spite that I fought for the sake of fighting. Many of my biblical beatings were due to my attempts to keep Cynthia out of my space and from getting on my nerves.

One day I was sitting on the couch trying to heal after a beating for going outside when I wasn't supposed to. From the couch I could see Cynthia in the single bedroom she shared with our mother, giggling, jumping around, and pointing at me. Angered, I wanted to throw something at her that wouldn't break. I reached underneath the couch pillow to retrieve my hidden yellow dart. I focused, aimed, and threw the dart with the accuracy of a sharpshooter, and hit her right between the eyes. She screamed so loud that I knew there would be hell to pay. But that beating wasn't too bad, knowing Cynthia was in pain too.

Neither Cynthia nor I could fathom the importance of a real brother-and-sister relationship. We fought like cats and dogs. She had everybody but me fooled with her sweet little girl act. The nursery rhyme about girls being "sugar and spice and everything nice" was not applicable to her. She was a crafty instigator, fabricator, and manipulator. Whatever Cynthia said I had done, my mother believed. She saw me, compared to Cynthia, as aggressive, vindictive, and devious.

As a member of the black male species living in a ghetto microcosm, circumstances dictated that I be either prey or predator. It didn't require deep reflection to determine which of the two I preferred. As predator, Cynthia was my prey. I was a quick study armed with contaminated knowledge, and Cynthia didn't stand a chance. She was more devious at buttering up our mother and therefore to cause trouble for me—but to avoid corporal punishment, I learned to finesse and outfox Cynthia.

At home Cynthia held a superior position; she served as our mother's third eye and ear. She would spy on me like the Central Intelligence Agency and then report back to our mother when she returned home from work. On rare occasions Cynthia could be bribed with nickels to keep her mouth shut. I led her to believe that a nickel was worth more than a dime because the nickel was bigger. I used to charm her with a few magic tricks, making black cough drops appear out of my ear, or with the matchbox trick, where a coin disappears into the matchbox. She enjoyed eating the cough drops, which helped to silence her. I guess magic appealed to Cynthia. She also believed in the tooth fairy, Santa Claus, and the Easter Bunny.

We never had any affectionate sibling moments. Perhaps neither of us had any to give. We were as unlike as night and day. Our differences were sealed forever when I saw her naked the first time. As a young boy, I had not yet grasped the biological distinctions between males and females. I was shocked to learn that Cynthia did not possess the male organ. I was tempted to question my mother about these issues, but such discussions were taboo for us. I just chalked it up as more of Cynthia's weirdness.

I noticed that sibling rivalries in the households of friends were a bit adversarial occasionally but tame in comparison to our feud. Though I hated her deeply, I discovered that there was a limit to my expressions of malice. Where we lived, on the other side of the fence there was a construction site and a huge dirt lot with deep trenches, a place where neighborhood children often played. On any given day children would have rock fights, play marbles, wrestle, or play war games with BB guns or wooden swords. Here and there lay piles of lumber, pipes, wires, nails, large buckets, and heavy machinery. Some of the trenches were too wide to cross. Over one such trench I constructed a makeshift bridge out of several long wooden planks and booby-trapped the bridge to collapse, so a person would fall into the six-foot-deep trench. Below I placed numerous heavy planks with long, thick, spiked nails pointed upward. This bridge of doom was a payback for whomever I despised.

Along came Cynthia. One day I spotted her skipping her merry way through the lot. Like a trapdoor spider I was hidden behind a high mound of dirt. The moment she stepped down onto the boards, I was ready to snatch the rope and send her tumbling down onto the bed of nails. Cynthia was halfway across, and I was about to yank the rope—but something stopped me. It was neither fear nor concern about a potential beating that stopped me. I just couldn't do it to her. Perhaps it was a moment of conscience—though later in my young life I would readily snatch that same rope to harm would-be enemies. But as much as I despised Cynthia, the booby trap was something I could not execute. Yet our feud continued well into our teenage years.

Hallelujah, Hallelujah

Long before I enrolled in school, I was familiar with the holy ambience of the Baptist church. It was a place where broken souls were mended, sins were forgiven, troubled minds were calmed, and incorrigible children were corrected. Back then, my mother may have thought I was a little Antichrist. She recognized my shortcomings and tried everything to rectify them. But nothing worked. I can still picture myself sitting in an old wooden church pew, most of the time unreceptive and steaming with anger at being forced to be there.

Occasionally, though, this house of worship was a place of wonder and excitement. I was mesmerized by the melodic voices of the choir and the rhythmic beat of the piano. When people were enraptured by the music, they would rock from side to side, clap and stomp their feet, scream, holler, or jump up and do a holy dance. The sweltering atmosphere was so charged with spiritual ecstasy that the ushers were kept busy trying to revive fainting women. There were no air conditioners, so people were sweating like melting ice cream. Most of them held paper fans with pictures of a white Jesus, and they pumped their fans like pistons to generate a little bit of cool air. Many of the women who fainted or were inspired to glossolalia—speaking in tongues—were seated next to us. Once a woman lightly patted my arm, said, "The Lord is with you," and then jumped up and down speaking in tongues. I was scared to death! I thought the woman was going crazy. I turned to my mother for support, but she was chanting hallelujah, hallelujah, hallelujah. I sat there rigid as a statue, hoping the woman wouldn't go off on me. It was always women who seemed to be spiritually touched by God. I prayed, crossed my fingers and toes, and hoped that neither my mother nor Cynthia would faint or speak in tongues. I would have run out of church in a flash.

The church barbecues, Easter egg hunts, and Christmas candies given to us made it worth my showing up. During the barbecue everyone took a paper plate overflowing with barbecued ribs, chicken, hot links, potato salad, and corn on the cob. These were the moments I really enjoyed. However, it seemed that all other activities were adult in nature and too serious. I wondered why I sat watching a preacher point his sanctimonious finger at everybody while spitting out his fiery sermon, looking down on his parishioners from his pulpit high above the congregation. Another time, we visited a different church for my baptism. I had to wear an ankle-length white gown, underwear, no shoes, and stand in a long line with other children and adults. My question to my mother was, "Why am I here?" Her menacing look—and her lightning-quick backhand that I couldn't dodge—convinced me to shut up.

Inside this gigantic church was a well-lit square structure for baptizing that seemed to me to be a large glass swimming pool with steps on both sides. Thus, the audience had a clear view of the baptism. In the pool were a preacher and several ushers, all dressed in white gowns, waiting for people to walk down single file into the pool. I watched as each person, one by one, was held underwater for a few seconds by two ushers. The preacher would mumble a few words, and then the person was raised out of the water, beaming. When I stepped down into the ice-cold pool, it came up to my chest. I stood there, frozen. The ushers had to guide me to the preacher. After he recited a prayer, the ushers dunked me backward into the water so quickly that I must have swallowed three pints of chlorinated water. I didn't even get a chance to hold my breath. I struggled desperately to free myself, but the ushers kept me under. I was waving my arms and kicking my legs like a drowning victim. When they let me up, I emerged gasping for air, choking, coughing, and spitting up water. Then and there I swore that my mother would have to straight-out kill me before I let someone baptize me again.

It wasn't all bad, traveling with my mother from church to church, singing gospel songs. In our family all three of us had the ability to sing with fine-tuned, high-pitched voices. People enjoyed hearing me or my mother sing a solo. When I sang "How Great Thou Art," the elderly folks clapped and shouted "Amen!" and "Hallelujah!" Mostly, I enjoyed singing because I believed it made my mother proud of me. I overheard her telling someone that I possessed a beautiful angelic voice. There was always debate about whether my vocal range was first or second soprano. It didn't matter because my mother loved it, and I enjoyed singing more than sitting around in the pew listening to the preacher.

It was in church where I first became interested in girls, after a couple of them showed an interest in my singing. Valerie and Shelia lived a few houses down from our house. Sometimes I would sit with them on their porch, crooning out a couple of songs, gospel or soul, that earned kisses afterward. Soon the word was out that I could sing, and other girls on the block began expressing interest in my singing. It didn't fare too well with the envious young males on the block, but the abundance of kisses were a highlight that made me feel tingly and warm all over.

Away from the adults, I managed to do a lot of kissing at church. I was surprised to learn that some of these girls knew hiding places where we could kiss and explore each other's bodies. In church I was always getting into something. Though I'm not proud of it, I would show up at church, stay for the offering, duck out, and then return before the service ended. When the usher passed around the offering basket, I'd drop a few coins into it and palm two or three dollars, sometimes with Cynthia or our mother sitting beside me. As a child of poverty I justified my theft as a need far greater than that of the other people in church. I knew the difference between the haves and have-nots. The preacher, his family and cohorts were living high on the hog. They had fine homes, fancy clothes, and jewelry, and the preacher sported a brand new Cadillac each year. Our family was broke, no car, no bicycle, no TV, and limited clothing. I figured the few dollars I pocketed wouldn't be missed. Hamburgers cost twenty-five cents, french fries twenty cents, sodas fifteen cents, and candy bars were five or ten cents. Each Sunday that I attended church, my stomach stayed full.

Clearly, my baptism was no more effective than being dunked in a local swimming pool by some homeboys. But my tenacious mother refused to give up on saving me. One sunny morning we rode a bus to a religious revival at, I believe, the Shrine Auditorium. The building was spacious, huge, with numerous seats and a balcony. There were hundreds, perhaps thousands of people from different ethnic backgrounds packed inside the auditorium. We managed to find seats in the upper balcony. Everybody was there to see Kathryn Kuhlman, the female preacher and revivalist heralded as a miracle worker. She was rumored to heal the sick, restore troubled lives, and perform other miracles. Her mantra—"I believe in miracles"—was well known. I dozed off and missed most of the service, and then was abruptly awakened. My mother stared at me and said, "Tookie, go down to the stage and get some help!" I begrudgingly got up and headed down toward the packed stage.

The line was long. Standing under the bright lights, Kathryn looked pale white and quite frail. There seemed nothing extraordinary about her, but when she touched a man, woman or child on the forehead, that person appeared to faint and fall backward into the arms of waiting ushers. I could feel my mother's eyes penetrating the back of my skull. Failure here was not an option. I could only hope that whatever happened to those people would happen to me.

My necktie felt like a hangman's noose. I was sweating profusely. When Kathryn placed her hands on my forehead, I felt absolutely nothing. I was tempted to fake a fainting spell, knowing my mother was eyeing me like a hawk. Kathryn removed her hand and mouthed the words, "Bless you, child." Nervously I searched her eyes for some plausible explanation to take back to my mother. But Kathryn had nothing more to say. There would be no miracles for me. Walking back to the balcony was like a death march. When I reached my mother and Cynthia, they were ready to leave. I could see my mother's expression of disappointment, shame, and God knows what else.

The Art of Dys-education

The time had come for me to enter a place of higher learning. But South Central's educational system was cloning and graduating students who could barely read, write, or reason. It really didn't matter which elementary school I was enrolled in, because I was destined to be dys-educated. (I've coined the term "dys-education" to depict the abnormal, impaired, and diseased knowledge I received in life and from the public school system.) The first school my mother enrolled me in was Menlo Avenue Elementary School, several blocks from where I lived. I braved the surroundings with a great deal of curiosity and eagerness to learn. My willingness to learn was somewhat hampered by Miss Atkins, the teacher assigned to the classroom. She and I would bump heads while I was there.

Miss Atkins was a rosy-cheeked, short, stout Caucasian woman, with her hair fashioned in a bun on the back of her head. She wore horn-rimmed glasses, with a shiny silver chain hanging slightly in front circling her head. She felt it was her duty to punish children in her classroom. The most popular method of punishment at that time was called "ferrule discipline"—a wooden ruler was used to repeatedly beat the inside of a child's hand. The child was told to stand before the entire class with palms up and endure the pain without moving. If the child moved, the discipline would start over. Just about every day I witnessed children squirming in pain as tears rolled down their cheeks. Just watching the ruler whacking a classmate's palm made me wince. Though I cannot remember a boy or girl crying out, not one of them refused to accept the punishment. When it was time to be punished, each one walked mechanically to the front of the class and assumed the position.

A biblical beating from my mother was one thing, but a school beating I refused to accept. I would run if I had to. It was inevitable I'd be called to stand before the class to be ferrule-disciplined. One day a classmate asked if he could borrow some paper, and I said yes. Miss Atkins saw me passing the paper and assumed I was playing around. Her voice resonated like a megaphone when she yelled, "Stanley Williams, report to the front of the class." The room fell silent. I could hear my classmates breathing. I refused with a single, firm "No!" Someone in the classroom gasped so loud I had to look around. Miss Atkins's face turned beet red in disbelief and anger.

Behind her desk, she used a more authoritative tone: "Stan, I want you up here in front of this class right now!" Again I refused. My refusal was a stinging blow to her frail ego; I had defied her system of voluntary discipline. Visibly shaking, she pointed a stubby finger and ordered me to report to the principal's office. I got up slowly and swaggered to the office. The principal, a tall, slender man, was pleasant enough, but his lecture was about one hour long. I sat there listening without saying a word. The principal decided not to call my mother and told me to return to class.

After that clash with Miss Atkins, my classmates seemed to warm up to me. I began to make friends and was no longer just a new arrival. I was the hero who had challenged the dragon lady. From that day forward, she never attempted to discipline me, but we did butt heads over other issues. In her class, reading and writing seemed to be prohibited, but we were provided with mounds of clay, papier-mâché, puzzles, and all kinds of noneducational items. Pencils and erasers were nowhere to be found. There were shelves of books that the students did not read. They seemed to be there just to decorate the classroom. I got on Miss Atkins's nerves, bothering her each day about letting me read a book. The more she refused, the more determined I was to read the literature on those shelves.

I was a darn good reader for my age. At home there was a box filled with books. Sometimes I would dump the books on the floor and sit in the middle of the pile trying to read everything. Often my mother would help me with the spelling and pronunciation of words. One of my favorite books was an encyclopedia on dogs, with numerous color photos. I could read for hours about different breeds of dogs. Reading was a pastime I truly enjoyed and a way of escaping from my often riotous thoughts. In my "reading world," there was no poverty, no discrimination, no violence, no racism, no pain—and no Cynthia.

Thievery became necessary to allow me to pilfer a book off the school library shelf and avoid being busted by Miss Atkins. My partner in crime was Shelia, a chubby black girl with a short, curly "natural," large brown eyes, dimples, and a contagious smile. Together, we pretended to be working on a project while taking turns reading from a book held in our laps. The first time Miss Atkins caught us reading, she thought there must be some hanky-panky going on. When we were made to stand up, the two books fell off our laps onto the floor. Miss Atkins had a fit, storming out of the classroom, shouting, "I'm calling your mother! I'm calling your mother!" This "phoning your mother" was a scenario that was played out with me three or four times a week, twice a day.

If Miss Atkins had her way, instead of calling my mother, I'd have been handcuffed by police and escorted to jail. Perhaps because she sensed my potential, she was driven to hinder or obliterate my intentions. To all who would listen to her outbursts, Miss Atkins would paint a false portrait of me, assassinating my character, behavior, mental state, and ability to learn. Perplexed, I watched in horror as she performed a masterful act of fake humility and concern for me in the presence of my mother. To parents, she was the epitome of what all teachers should be. But I had her number. I knew she was wicked.

All I wanted to do was become educated, not to battle with a deranged teacher over my Constitutional right to read schoolbooks. The odds were stacked against me. Miss Atkins's authority made her my nemesis. She had the principal, teachers, parents, my mother, and even the janitor in her corner. Who would believe me? Whom could I talk to? The more my mother came up to the school to chastise me, the more it strengthened Miss Atkins's assertion that I was a very disruptive child.

Whether Miss Atkins busted me, Shelia, or other classmates who joined us in a clandestine study program, she would call only *my* mother. For every minute my mother spent away from work addressing this conflict, money was deducted from her paycheck. Perhaps the teacher was aware of that. But she viewed me as just another little darkie whom she openly predicted would fail in life. In her warnings to other students about examples of bad behavior, she pointed a finger at me: "Look at Stanley—he is not what you want to be!" If ever a teacher needed psychological testing to be allowed to teach children, she was a prime candidate.

It was a surprise several months later when Miss Atkins implemented a reading and writing period in her class, but we were still largely on our own. As usual she sat behind her desk crocheting, head tilted down, looking over her glasses at us—mostly at me. She seemed to enjoy humming the hymn "Shall we gather at the river, the beautiful, the beautiful river. . . ." It was odd that such an oppressive person would enjoy singing a church song. Fortunately, before she was able to have me expelled, I was transferred to another school. Although there were no farewells, I knew I would miss Shelia.

Now I was able to breathe a breath of fresh air. Cynthia and I were enrolled in Normandie Avenue Elementary School and the adjacent day care center. Each school day after kissing our mother on the cheek, we headed toward the day care center, where Cynthia and I stayed before and after school, until 4:00 p.m. The breakfasts and lunches tasted much better than the school's cafeteria food. All in all, day care was a nice, clean place to be, with a lot of activities for children. There were two memorable figures who worked at the center:

Mrs. Blue and Miss Davis. Both of these black women were exceptionally kind to all the children. It was Miss Davis who comforted me when I had a run-in with the door and with the monkey bars. She accompanied me to a nearby clinic where I was patched up.

In her early twenties, Miss Davis was tall, slender, cinnamon-colored, with a curly, brownish-gold Afro. She would drive up in a small black convertible sports car, usually wearing brightly colored tennis attire and with a tennis bag over her shoulder. Her tennis dress was skimpier than a miniskirt, but I wasn't complaining. Watching her practice hitting tennis balls off the wall raised my interest in female anatomy to a new level. Whether retrieving balls or sitting on a milk crate, I admired her sleek movement as her skirt hiked up to unbelievable heights. She had a preachy saying: "We sisters are black queens, and we have to keep our bodies firm and beautiful." Amen to that!

In total contrast, Mrs. Blue was in her late forties, perhaps early fifties. She was short, with smooth brown skin and bluish, permed hair. Mrs. Blue was sweet as pie and loved reading stories to us. When I did get into trouble, she tried to rescue me from the school's impulse to expel me. Mrs. Blue would rather control me than threaten punishment. In a way, her religious quotes and sermons were similar to my grandmother's. But she always found something good to say about me. I remember sitting between Mrs. Blue and my mother as Mrs. Blue bragged about how smart I was. Her words were like sweet droplets of honey poured down my throat. Encouragement was an element I didn't receive enough of in my life.

In school I maintained between a B plus and an A average. My ability to read, write, and retain knowledge was evident with each passing year. So far my efforts and behavior were an A plus. I occasionally got into a few scrimmages, but what black man-child didn't rumble and tumble as a youngster? It was rare for me to fight a girl, but this girl named Janice was no ordinary female. I was about four feet six inches, and Janice stood about six feet tall. She was broad at the shoulders, with a hairstyle like Buckwheat on *The Little Rascals* and a mean expression.

I was told she liked me, but she had a strange way of showing it. In class, she would throw books at me when I wasn't looking, or place a thumbtack on my chair. One day I placed several thumbtacks on her chair; she sat down and jumped up screaming like a banshee. She stood there looking around at the entire class and screamed, "Who did that?" The frightened classroom didn't have to say my name—I was busted the moment they all turned to look at me. That's when Janice threatened to beat me up after school. She wasn't fooling around. I had seen her beat a guy to a bloody pulp in the school bathroom. Janice could fight like a dude. She was tough, probably too tough for me to handle. Seated several rows away, she stared at me while pounding her fist in the palm of her hand. Then, from left to right she slowly drew her finger across her throat, indicating my doom. She was dead serious about hurting me, and I didn't doubt it.

The general rule in the culture was never to strike a female under any circumstances. But Janice was no ordinary girl; she could fight. At that moment she frightened me so much that my mouth became dry and my heart jumped up in my throat. To further intimidate me, Janice started acting as if she was about to rush over and attack me. Since I wasn't packing my trusty butter knife or a set of brass knuckles, I was a nervous mess. When I looked up at the clock, it was 2:45 p.m. School was about to end, and Janice had dozed off. It was now or never. I eased out of my chair and circled around behind where she sat. Unmanly or not, I was on Janice like a wild man, knocking her and the chair to the floor. Fearful she would get back up, I was about to crown her with a chair when the teacher caught hold of it in midair.

To the amazement of the class (and me as well), Janice stayed on the floor, crying. For the first time I saw her as a girl, not as a bully or a beast. She was human after all. Though I felt a sense of remorse, I knew the fight was far from over. Janice had two brothers at the school—Vincent and an older brother, Arthur. I later learned that the two brothers agreed that Vincent would restore their sister's honor. Being bigger and taller, he bragged to classmates about what he was going to do.

It was on the day care's playground where I ran into Vincent and his stocky friend Frank. When he gestured for me to come where they were standing, it meant only one thing. I was taking a risk because no one was around to intercede if they both attacked me, or if I was on the losing end. As I approached, Vincent started taking off his sweater. When his face was completely covered, his arms held high in the air underneath the sweater, I attacked. As I rushed forward, Frank stepped aside as if he were a matador dealing with a charging bull. I threw a lot of haymakers that drove Vincent up against the fence. Out of nowhere Miss Davis appeared and held me in a bear hug from behind. Afterward, Vincent pulled down his sweater, picked up his glasses, and walked away, trailed by Frank. Miss Davis and I went inside where she wiped my face with a wet towel. She asked why I was fighting such a big boy; I told her we were just playing around. She smiled and said, "Maybe you were playing, but he sure wasn't!"

Escaping adult eyes was the backdrop of a training ground for fighting in (and away from) school. In street fights, fairness was an abstraction of moronic dimensions; it could get you killed. I learned from others to fight dirty, to cheat, and to look for angles, openings, mistakes. The prime rule of fighting was this: there were no rules, anything goes. In time, I found ways to cut an opponent down to size, and if I lost a fight, he'd better be prepared to fight me daily. Either that or suffer the consequences of being surprised.

Most opponents weren't willing to go the extra mile. To them it wasn't worth it, but to me it was. Fighting became my modus operandi for payback. Had I been aware of another reasonable and face-saving choice, I would have preferred not to engage in fisticuffs. Only a damn fool would do otherwise. For me fighting wasn't done for fun; it was a survival necessity. I wasn't a born fighter; I had to become one. Even if you tease a peaceful elephant, eventually it will charge at you. A man of ill repute once told me, "Little brother, sometimes a challenge to fight must be met. You don't have to be good at it, just know what, how, where, and when to do it, and the rest will take care of itself." It was a thug's maxim that gave me an edge.

The strangest things can happen, sometimes, after a fight—such as the friendship between Big Frank, Vincent, and me that blossomed after the fight. Frank and I grew to be the best of friends. He lived with his father, mother, and sister, Judy, just two blocks away from me. I noticed a sibling rivalry, but it was tame compared to mine with Cynthia. Despite Frank's size and tough appearance, he had a mild temperament. I never saw Frank in a fight or an argument in school or out. His height, stockiness, bubble eyes, and stern look probably intimidated others. But my presence was as nonthreatening as a butterfly's. Most everybody looked taller and bigger, so I was a sitting duck for any potential bully looking for easy prey. Although I didn't act, look, or talk like Urkel, the nerdy character on TV's *Family Matters,* I could have been mistaken for that type of person because I was small and mostly silent. But I wasn't a pushover.

Through my acquaintance with Frank, I was briefly introduced to the Cub Scouts, and then later to the Boy Scouts. The necessary funds for my membership dues, scout equipment, field trips, and other expenses were not available to me. I understood our financial situation; my mother didn't have a dime to spare. But I had hoped to explore the Scouts experience that was supposedly nonlethal. Who can refute that a change in my surroundings and activities might have been a life-altering experience? I admit being a little envious of Frank and other children whose parents were able to afford the Scouts and other similar opportunities. Though I felt deprived and sullen, I drew confidence by means of my ability to rebound from the many childhood disappointments.

When I wasn't at Frank's house, I was out hustling with James, who lived with his mother around the corner from 42nd Street. James was a short, light-skinned brother with freckles and a giant reddish-brown Afro. I met him during a serious rock fight in a vacant lot that was filled with tall mounds of dirt, trenches, and tunnels where Monroe and I had challenged everybody to a battle. Though James and his posse outnumbered us six to one, we held our own and never got hurt. Perhaps the combination of our giant homemade slingshots and chunking rocks gave us an edge.

Occasionally, I would bump into James here and there, so we ended up hanging out a lot. We had one common interest, a shared social activity: stealing. James was as slick as they come; he knew the ins and outs of many local business establishments. On weekends we would sneak on a bus to downtown Los Angeles with its smorgasbord of department stores, movie theaters, jewelry shops, and other places of business. James opened up a fascinating new world to me.

Together we roamed downtown Los Angeles, bootlegging clothing, food, jewelry, and shoes. Thoughts of my mother's wrath became a distant memory the moment I replaced the black brogan shoes she always bought me with my first pair of biscuits (a Stacy Adams–style shoe often called Southern Comforts). When we weren't stealing, our handmade wooden shoeshine boxes were put to work. As a street bootblack, spit shines ranged from fifty cents to a dollar, with hopefully a tip to come. Our entrepreneurial skills earned us a slow, slow ten to fifteen dollars. Eventually a tall youngster named Paul moved to the neighborhood and joined our crew. We became the Three Musca-Thieves!

As thugs and hustlers used to chant, "All money is good money"— but there are exceptions to any rule. One afternoon while shining shoes downtown, a substitute teacher from school, Mr. Len, showed up wanting a shine. Lined up side by side, our shoeshine rags were popping in rhythm like an orchestra of Rice Krispies, snap, crackle, pop! Mr. Len was a nice substitute teacher who often resembled the white guy with the thick mustache in the Village People, a popular singing group. Mr. Len offered to pay us to shine a closetful of shoes at his house, if we were willing.

Mr. Len drove us to his home near a Santa Monica beach. After he turned off an alarm, we walked through a festival of flowers to the back of the house where he lived. Mr. Len placed a gunnysack full of old dusty shoes on a chair and then left. We were shining shoes for about fifteen minutes. He returned wearing a gold silk kimono. He dumped several coin bags of quarters and silver dollars on the floor in a pile, then suggested we play a card game. The game was called "strip poker," an alien concept to me. Although he explained the rules, I had *no* intention of taking off any clothing. Mr. Len managed to lose the first hand—and disrobed until he was completely naked! The hairs stood up on my neck and arms, and my eyes became big as silver dollars. I wondered what in the world was going on here. With each trip Mr. Len made to retrieve another bag of coins, we stuffed our pockets with as many coins as possible. He knew we were stealing the money, of course. When all the coins had disappeared into our pockets, he stretched out on a nearby bed and said he'd give us twenty dollars to massage his back. His back was so hairy, he could have been part bear. It was a nasty sight, but we agreed. While Mr. Len was lying on his back, instinctively we each grabbed an item to substitute for our hands. I picked up a fly swatter, James a feather duster, and Paul had a fireplace poker.

Irritated, Mr. Len threatened not to pay us the twenty dollars if we didn't massage him with at least one hand. When he saw us putting socks on our hands, he said, "Forget it. You guys don't want to make any real money." During the ride home, he tried to convince one of us to meet with him tomorrow to earn a hundred dollars—but he had no takers. Several blocks from home I had him drop me off, and both James and Paul bailed out there too. I knew absolutely nothing about pedophiles at that time, but as I walked home, I knew I had shined my last pair of shoes.

Back at school my skills were growing, thanks to Miss Johnson, my sixth grade teacher. She was a master motivator. I'm reminded of how she looked each time I read *Ebony* magazine. Often there is a photo of a black woman to whom an *Ebony* literary contest is dedicated, a Mrs. Gertrude Johnson Williams. The resemblance to our Miss Johnson was uncanny. Our teacher was a husky black woman who seemed always to wear black clothing. She sported black-rimmed eyeglasses and her shoulder-length hair was curled underneath, all the way around. She had an imposing presence with a commanding voice, but exuded a maternal sensitivity that made the entire class feel special. Miss Johnson devoted ample time to each student and had no problem repeating herself until a message was driven home.

In spite of her classroom being void of a black curriculum, when we were alone, she talked about black greatness and the need for me to carry the torch. By then I needed more than Miss Johnson's occasional chats. My cultural awareness was zero. I needed a complete black history course and a thorough deprogramming. I had been duped into believing that all black people were inhuman and inferior, that we had made no contribution to the forward thrust of civilization. Negative black stereotypes were broadcast or implied by the news media, magazines, institutions, television, newspapers, books, and every other medium you can think of. Not to mention the countless delusional blacks I met who believed the myth of black inferiority. Their contempt for their own blackness was so dynamic, they had subconsciously stepped outside themselves to assimilate with any cultural group other than their own. Their dys-education was complete. The more I was indoctrinated by lies about my blackness, the more I grew to detest myself.

Miss Johnson did try but was unable to provide enough information to help me reassemble my mutilated outlook on life. She was restricted to the school's curriculum and subjected to rules that forbade any extramural teachings, in particular black history. She deserves credit for recognizing my potential and for trying to reveal it to me. Little did I realize how much I would miss Miss Johnson's style of teaching. However, I sensed that when I did enter junior high, it would be a turning point in my life—with a downward trajectory.

During the summer after my elementary school graduation in 1966, I underwent a radical circumcision. I was still twelve and the procedure was a shock to my psyche. The discomfort was inexpressible; and when aroused the pain was ten times worse than having one's member caught in a zipper. I couldn't help but wonder: Why

me? What did I do to deserve this? I knew nothing of traditions or rituals. The agony persisted throughout the entire summer vacation; I
was a model son during this period of hell. Nothing compared to the
pain, not even when my mother, Cynthia, and I were struck by a car
on the way to a movie theater. The impact knocked my mother back
onto the curb, and I was lying halfway on the curb and in the street.
Cynthia landed underneath the drunk driver's car. Though my entire
body was in pain, it did not compare to the soreness of circumcision.
I viewed the procedure as a form of punishment. It left a scar I drew
strength from.

When it was time to enroll in Forshay Junior High, the pain had
passed. At Forshay I mechanically went through the motions of showing up and performing each school task without an understanding of
its purpose or necessity. I never harbored dreams of becoming a president, astronaut, banker, millionaire, doctor, fireman, or lawyer. Such
reveries were as absurd to me as believing in Santa Claus. I was conditioned to anticipate a living hell. My vision of my future involved
no fortunes, no dreams, no miracles, no hope, and no peace.

Many of the teachers I faced at Forshay behaved like professional
babysitters, there only to monitor behavior and discipline or simply
expel students from school. The first day I was singled out as a student who needed watching. In all likelihood it was documented in
my school files that I was an incorrigible student.

Being under the school's microscope I believed I was expected to
behave outrageously—perhaps standing on top of the desk, fighting
in class, throwing books, or arguing with the teacher for no apparent
reason. Perhaps they thought that at any moment I would jump up
and start screaming like a mad child. These expectations never mani-
fested themselves. Had I truly been unstable, a teacher probably
could have pushed me over the edge. The teachers stood for authority and discipline. They were the school police.

There was no compulsion on my part to make friends in school.
The few youths I befriended were usually the so-called miscreants:
the aggressors, the loners, the defiant ones. All of us preferred being

around one another and had no desire to make new friends. There was nothing antisocial about me, but I was selective in my social choices. I couldn't be a friend to everybody, nor was everybody willing to be or interested in being a friend to me.

I might have fared better in school if my hustling buddy James had not transferred to Forshay. But it is unlikely. Though ditching never entered my mind, I did try to avoid school by pretending to be sick. But any time Cynthia or I became sick, our mother would break out a steaming hot batch of castor oil with squeezed lemon juice and a dash of salt. She used castor oil or cod liver oil for just about every ailment and stood guard to make sure we swallowed every drop. The smell was so vile it made me want to puke. When the choice was between school or castor oil, I chose school.

In truth, I really wasn't interested in going to Forshay. I felt that the teachers were insipid, and school was a bore. It was assumed I was a slow student, stupid, or had special needs. I received an F in all my subjects because I didn't do the work. In fact the school assignments weren't even a challenge, and when I did display my intelligence, I was accused of cheating. So for me, the eventual decision to ditch school wasn't difficult. Usually James and I would meet up at Forshay to catch a bus downtown to use our "poor-boy" routine, better known as panhandling. A sob story about having lost our bus fare to get back to school worked very well. We ended up splitting about ten dollars in a couple of hours. Then we'd buy junk food for lunch and sneak into one of the cheap movie theaters until school let out. Downtown Los Angeles had become our institution of higher learning; its curriculum of thievery, deceit, and robbery promised a diploma in criminality. The even darker side consisted of the weirdos, psychos, sickos, and other random twisted strangers to whom we were exposed. We braved these treacherous elements for mere pocket change. But to me, being downtown—or anywhere other than school—was worth the risk of getting caught or hurt.

At least once or twice a week, I stayed in school a full day for the sake of appearances. My attendance record was terrible, and my mother was always the last to know. The school principal finally revealed to her that I had been ditching for months. I know she felt like backhanding me right out of the chair. But when she turned to face me, I was a good six feet away. Though promising the principal that I'd never ditch again, I knew the promise would be broken the following day.

During the bus ride home, I dreaded the upcoming punishment with its leather strap or an electrical extension cord that left welts the size of a thick, braided rope. In silence I watched as my mother began talking to herself. She shook her head and asked, "Lord, what is wrong with this boy? Tell me what to do and I'll do it." Seconds later: POW! That swift backhand upside my head must have been God's response. Staring angrily out of the school bus window, I was convinced I could do better hustling in the streets than going to school.

This was the final straw for my mother. She decided to call in the big guns for help.

Voodoo Medicine

As a child I was content with my physical appearance. Within me there were no inner conflicts, no Dr. Jekyll and Mr. Hyde blurring the line where sanity resides. I had never seen, heard, or spoken to an imaginary friend, dead relative, ghost, devil, angel, or God. For me, bogeymen and monsters lurking underneath the bed, in the closet, or in dark corners were nonexistent. There was no fear of the dark; I needed no night-light, teddy bear, or security blanket for comfort. In spite of the cruelties I had witnessed as a child, of dogfights and pigeons set afire, I had an affinity for animals.

I was a normal child in an abnormal environment.

Although I was a quiet youngster who enjoyed playing with other children, I was also selective about whom I would befriend. My silence and my disruptive behavior were only a show of independence. The lines of communication between my mother and me were severed the moment I attempted to step into the male position vacated by my father. I believed I was grown, making it impossible for any male to substitute as a father figure. A child can adapt in even the most harsh of surroundings; and that is what I did.

Though my mother was the parent, I established early that no amount of biblical beatings could deflect my doing what I wanted to do. I was willing to suffer the consequences at my mother's hands. Through our lack of communication, my mother believed something was wrong with me mentally. I was then treated as being handicapped, impaired, or simply no good. She did not expect me to live past the age of seventeen, eighteen, or twenty-one. But she insisted that I receive some kind of outside help: a psychiatrist was found to treat me.

My mother had my best interests at heart, but her mistake was to seek assistance from a shrink, especially one who lacked the racial empathy or experience to effectively psychoanalyze me. The shrink's office was in a building on the east side of Los Angeles around 54th Street. I arrived there on Monroe's bike and pocketed the bus fare. Inside the office were shelves filled with medical books, and on the wall were several framed academic degrees. On the other side of the room was a long table with a buffet of assorted pastries, candy, chips, and beverages. The sweets were similar to a pedophile's use of candy as a lure, to break down a child's defenses, enter their world, and then corrupt it.

I can still visualize parking Monroe's bike inside the office and sitting in a large brown leather chair with my short legs dangling above the floor. There was a faint smell of cigar smoke in the air. Seated behind the cluttered desk was the shrink—a balding, yellowish-pink middle-aged man with thick bifocals reminiscent of Mr. Magoo, the nearsighted cartoon character. From the first meeting, it appeared we had a mutual understanding to avoid one another's space. He was quite content with my sitting there munching on pastries, as I was satisfied with his reading a book and leaving me alone. Sometimes I'd catch him peering at me like I was a lab animal, and then he'd scribble on a notepad. Our verbal exchanges were almost nonexistent with the exception of thank you, you're welcome, hello, and good-bye. On several occasions the shrink tried to inquire about two incidents when I was injured, but when I exhibited my mother's famous stare, he would back down.

The two incidents in question had taken place at the day care center where Cynthia and I were enrolled, adjacent to Normandie Avenue Elementary School at Vernon and Normandie. The first incident occurred when I slipped while chasing after a boy playing tag. I smashed my head against the side of a door. The impact resulted in a long, deep gash extending from the upper right side of my forehead down through my eyebrow and stopping just millimeters from my eye. I narrowly avoided serious damage. I was rushed to a neighborhood clinic where I was stitched up.

The second incident occurred less than a year later at the same day care center. While playing softball, I was showing off in front of a pretty black girl named Valerie, and I ran headlong into the monkey bars. Blood squirted like a geyser from a gash on the left side of my forehead. Again I was rushed to the same neighborhood clinic for stitches.

Both incidents were due to my clumsiness and to not paying attention. I can only assume that witnesses thought differently, perhaps that I was intentionally running into objects to get attention. I've never been a masochist. I don't enjoy pain, whether self-inflicted or otherwise. If I truly craved attention, I would have broken a large store window and stood listening to the alarm instead of running away. That would have gotten plenty of attention from the store owner, police, and my mother.

It was too simplistic to diagnose me merely as a clumsy child. But the decision was made to dissect my thoughts in order to get to the nitty-gritty of the problem. There was no way that a shrink could admit professional inadequacy or defeat; he could not simply say, "Mrs. Williams, I don't know what's wrong with your son." Or "Your son is clumsy as hell."

The color barrier between the white shrink and me wasn't the only problem. He could have been black, brown, yellow, or red and been equally unsuccessful. The problem, I now believe, was the absence of a valid psychoanalytic model designed to address black people, the black experience.

My mother was disenchanted with the failure of the shrink's voodoo to work its mojo on me. To illustrate his blatant disinterest, months earlier I had stopped going to his office, and he neglected to tell my mother. The long distance bike ride to and from the shrink's office had become too boring. It was cutting into my playtime, and it wasted everybody's time, especially mine.

My mother might have fared better standing me before some of the street-corner winos. It was rumored that a few of them graduated summa cum laude. Some of their alcoholic rants and prophetic warnings were more learned than the lectures of many academics. At least their analyses of racism, slavery, poverty, police brutality, politics, child psychology, and other topics were gained based on grassroots experience. It's a shame they weren't able to climb out of those wine bottles.

Stepfamily

I was blindsided by finding out that my mother had met a stranger at the laundromat. He was an ex-boxer, an amateur, five feet eleven inches, brown-skinned, with a muscular build and close-cropped Afro. His name was Fred Holiwell, and he was my future stepfather. He lived in an apartment on the corner of 41st and Kansas, down the street from the Laundromat where he met my mother. Usually on Saturdays I accompanied my mother to the Laundromat, but this day I was at home cleaning the stove, piece by piece. I expected this tedious chore to take several hours, which it did. But had I been with her that day, chances are that Fred and my mother might not have met. To stop any potential male acquaintances, I would have foolishly brandished my knife in a display of protective love for my mother.

The first time Fred showed up at our house, I recoiled into a defiant stance and refused to communicate. His cordial efforts to put me at ease fed my indifference. My mind raced with dreadful thoughts of being replaced by a dominant male. It was a devastating blow to my boyhood seeking manhood, and my world came crumbling down. Fred was the first man ever to enter our home as my mother's love interest and my potential rival. As it stood, I was being dethroned by a stranger. I was furious.

It is possible that Cynthia cozied right up to him in a need for fatherly attention, or that she foresaw the benefits of a new stepfather.

But Fred's arrival was too late for me; I had already established a warped sense of male selfhood. When he had moved to a more distant house on 69th between Denker and Halldale, I thought it was the last I'd see of him. Then one day Fred pulled up in his olive-green 1962 Oldsmobile to take us to his home for a visit. Living there were his son, Wayne, and his three daughters: Vicky, Demetri, and Bridget. It was an awkward moment, this meeting, with no greetings or exchanging of names. In a strange stare-down competition, we looked hard at each other for long periods of time without blinking. The hatred circulating around the living room suffocated any possible truce. We had invaded their home, and my mother was trying to replace their absent mother. They saw "us" as the enemy, and I reflected their sentiments precisely. As expected, Cynthia clung to my mother for safety while I engaged in a stare-down to the death against four sets of indignant eyes.

Almost from the start there were toe-to-toe scrimmages between Fred's daughter Demetri and me. Our hostility toward each other was adolescent foreplay. We actually liked one another, and Demetri was cute, but we still kept our distance. Her older sister, Vicky, was built like Josephine Baker, the singer, and could have passed for being a grown woman. At seventeen she could fight like a dude and knew exactly how to throw jabs, hooks, uppercuts, and combinations. None of her boyfriends dared to physically abuse her; they knew better. Vicky was cool, except when she tried to talk back to my mother, who would have none of that. Vicky treated us fairly and never punched any of us. We stayed out of her space, and she did likewise.

Our holidays and weekends were spent mostly at Fred's home, because our divided families had merged. We were spending a lot of time there; even the neighbors thought we lived at Fred's. The three-bedroom house was pretty much open to us, but the socializing factor was missing. At every turn we kids viciously degraded one another in an attempt to draw tears for blood. To them, our family was "proper," meaning that because our speech patterns were devoid of ghetto vernacular, we were acting "white." Being called proper was a euphemism for being an "Uncle Tom," a white man's black man. To me Fred's kids were country bumpkins, acting like "niggers." I had picked up the derogatory term from the streets, where calling a black man the "n" word resulted in a fight or death.

Throughout the house we youngsters launched verbal cruelties back and forth. Their stinging effects were camouflaged by outbursts of loud arguments that often required parental intervention. Perhaps things would have been different if they had known that Cynthia and I had no choice in our diction. It was either speak with fluent clarity or suffer the consequences, issued by my mother. We had to attend a speech etiquette class outside of school. Day and night our mother stayed on us for using incorrect language. The regimental practice to speak correctly was the only thing Cynthia and I shared equal footing for, when punishments were meted out. Our mother's tenacity in shaping and molding our speech was working, but we were certainly teased and tormented for our precision.

To stay out of each other's face, I spent much of the time in the backyard playing with their dog, Butch, a strapping jet-black Labrador retriever and German shepherd mix. He was a loyal guard dog and a fighter. Back then I felt more comfortable around dogs than humans. With no strings attached a dog would accept me for who I was. On a few occasions little Wayne had caught me letting Butch out to chase after the many cats next door. But despite our feuding families, the little guy never told on me, and for that I respected him. My taking the dog for long walks didn't seem to bother anyone—perhaps because I was the only one willing to clean up Butch's defecation in the backyard.

Taking Butch for a stroll was an opportunity to scout the neighborhood. I discovered that any unleashed dog was a potential target for Butch's aggression. He was willing to fight any dog, any time. Once I was walking him and stumbled into a dogfight in an alley across Florence Avenue. It took all my strength to hold Butch back as he snarled and barked at the two monstrous pit bulls locked in battle. The ambience was of men cursing and flashing currency, while the dogs were slinging blood and drool everywhere. The larger black pit, Crusher, won the fight hands down, but they had to use a wooden bar to pry his jaws loose from the other pit bull's throat. This gruesome sight was common among dogfights, but there was more to it than the spilling of blood and gambling.

A dog's chiseled muscles, its agility and the enormous jaw strength used to combat its foes appeals to the testosterone of males of all ages. Being no exception, I viewed a dogfight with fascination but was motivated mostly by the prospect of earning a couple of bucks. No doubt my mother would have been shocked to know that prior to the age of twelve, I had been present at more than fifty bloody dog maulings. She would have hauled me back to a shrink, pronto.

I'll admit that Fred's neighborhood was buzzing with activity that I looked forward to experiencing with each visit, but my future stepfather had other plans for the new expanded family. He introduced to us the foreign concept of a family outing. I wasn't alone in thinking that the idea of our warring families going out to have fun was absurd. Our pouting faces should have been reason enough to reconsider. Even Vicky was upset, preferring to stay at home with her boyfriend. During the ride, we pushed and shoved while complaining about the tight space. It was like being crammed in a foxhole with the enemy, unable to do anything else. My mother had to reach back and pop me a couple of times to get me to behave.

Each Sunday, like clockwork, we packed ourselves into the car and headed for the museum, for Griffith Park or Knott's Berry Farm, or to one of several public beaches. To us, the family trip was akin to walking to the gallows. After a while I didn't care where we ended up as long as it was far from home. The farther we traveled, the more home became a blur lost in forgetfulness. Almost instinctively, I tended to blend in with the surroundings and absorb the illusion of freedom from family damnation. As far as my eyes could see, I hoped that somewhere in the distance there was a utopian place to go and never return home.

Those family outings were the best form of rehabilitation for me. The therapeutic effect of escapism had made me a child of short-lived obedience. But back in the real world, the cycle of hostility between Demetri and me continued. Our fights had more to do with unfamiliar circumstances than personal grievances. No punches were ever thrown. We mostly wrestled, pushed, and tried to toss one another across the room. This was our way of touching without seeming interested or enjoying it. For about a week the house was blessed with peace and serenity. But the calm was shattered the day I returned from walking Butch to see a trail of blood leading up the sidewalk into the house. I found Cynthia stretched out on the couch with a blood-soaked towel on her forehead and a look of forlorn vulnerability on her face. But no one was willing to talk about what had happened, not even Cynthia. The incident was accepted by both parents to be an accident. I later learned that Bridget had somehow managed to hit Cynthia in the head with a piece of wood. Accident or not, had my sister chosen to seek an alliance with me, despite our sibling rivalry, I would have honored it. But she kept her silence.

Eventually, there was an unspoken truce among us, but with lingering spite between our families. Cynthia still remained the enemy of Fred's kids and I was pretty much despised by everybody until I stood up for Demetri years later by fighting a guy named Ollie who tried to molest her. That fight won the respect of all my step-siblings. But up to that day, the arguments, "accidents," and fighting like cats and dogs went on and on—there was nothing Brady about our bunch.

Adolescent Blues

My life continued to unravel with one controversy after another. Although I wanted to be left alone at Forshay Junior High, fate had placed a cloud of provocation above my head. It was inevitable that one of the several black male gangs would target me as prey. Whenever my friends Paul or James weren't around, I kept to myself and ate alone so that I could observe others. One day I was confronted by this curly-haired fellow named Lewis who hung with the Rough Riders gang, known for jacking other youths for lunch money. With the confidence of a bull elephant, Lewis approached and demanded that I empty my pockets. Without saying a word, I just looked at him as if he were crazy. When he reached to pat my pocket, I slapped his hand away and got up. We stood eye to eye, staring one another down to see who would look away first. Still eyeing me, Lewis backed away and then said, "Okay, I'll see you later on!"

Later, walking down the seemingly mile-long sidewalk in back of Manual Arts High School, Lewis appeared with five of his homeboys. Being outnumbered, I wasn't sure how placing my back against the wall would help, but I did it. Lewis stood directly in front of me, in my face, making a deliberate noise, sucking his teeth. The six to one odds made him feel invincible. He spat out, "How much money you holding?" To mask my fear, I bit down hard on the inside of my mouth to appear tough. My silence was interrupted when this guy,

Earl, hit my pocket and the jingle of coins prompted these predators to smile. While they demanded I empty out my pockets, Earl sucker-punched me from the blind side. I stumbled into Lewis and held on for dear life while the others pounded away at my head and body. Both Lewis and I fell to the ground on our sides. As they kicked and stomped me, I held on as long as I could, then released him. My body imploded with pain as I felt hands ripping my pockets. The ruthless beating would have continued had not an elderly black woman hollered out, "Y'all leave that boy alone or I'll call the police!" With the mention of the police, the boys scattered like roaches.

I lay there unable to get up right away. The elderly woman shouted, "Get up, boy, go home!" When I was able to raise myself up from the ground, I started limping toward home. Most of the way, I leaned my body against the wall for support as I walked. My entire body was a wall of pain. I was spitting up blood and my pants were torn to shreds. Fortunately, when I got home, my mother and Cynthia weren't there, so I discarded the pants and cleaned up the wounds as best I could with peroxide. Seeing myself in the mirror, with my fat lip, puffy eyes, and swollen jaw, was an embarrassing sight. The thought of having been beaten down frightened the hell out of me, and I felt emasculated. It sent chills through my body to visualize being circled, surrounded, cornered like a trapped animal. I lacked the pugilistic skills of Joe Louis, the heavyweight boxing champion, or the might of a military leader such as Hannibal Barca. But despite my inexperience and diminutive size, I believed that being able to instill fear in those who had hurt me was possible, with the right motivation. That night, though I had no course of action, I slept like a baby.

The next morning I woke up a bloody mess to a teary-eyed mother, who told me to get dressed so Fred could drive us to General Hospital. One of the doctors shook his head and asked, "My GOD, what happened to this child?" There was no way to hide it; I looked terrible. Afterward, Fred said he was going to teach me how to defend myself in a fight. Had it not been for the pain, I would have burst out laughing. Boxing was cool, but what I needed was a strategy to instill fear in that gang beyond their imagination. Slowly, a strategy began to take shape in my head, a strategy that would form the core of my life for the next few years.

Though armed with a twelve-inch pearl-white switchblade, the thought of returning to school paralyzed me with fear. Through the school grapevine I heard that Lewis, Earl, and some of their home-boys were in Juvenile Hall, or "Juvey," as it was called. The word was that they had gotten busted for trying to rob a liquor store. Whether true or not, I couldn't breathe a sigh of relief knowing that eventually, they would be back. It was unsettling, having to look over my shoulder continually, dreading being pounced upon again.

Months later, while emptying the trash, I heard a familiar voice on the other side of the fence. I peeped through a crack in the fence and saw Earl strolling by with several teenage girls. I decided to wait around with a stockpile of rocks the size of softballs and toss them over the fence if he returned. After a while Earl returned, singing, and when he was in range, I lobbed rock after rock over the fence. A few struck him on top of the head, and he let out a bone-chilling scream and ran away. There was no jubilation on my part in stoning Earl, the teenage giant, though it was a job well done.

Following the ambush, whenever I passed Earl on the street, he averted his eyes. Neither of us said a word, just begrudgingly nodded as we passed each other. I was certain he knew who had rained those rocks on his head. The rumors circulating had me beating down Earl with a brick and chasing him home. Most of the local youth thought I had to be crazy to attack him. Henceforth, I gained a reputation as a quiet, tough guy who was also crazy. I had become the slayer of Earl, the five-foot ten-inch muscular giant whose bullying days were buried under an onslaught of rocks thrown over a fence. More important, to my relief, Earl and his homeboys stayed away from me. That was all I wanted—to be left alone.

Meanwhile, my truancy at school had escalated, and my grades had slipped to an all-time low. To compound matters, somebody got the bright idea to assign me to the school "hash line" where they sold hamburgers, french fries, hot dogs, and other food items. Before long, I was pocketing money and passing James all the free food he could eat. The day the school security guard showed up in science class looking for me, I knew why. My front pockets were bulging with coins as I was escorted to the principal's office. After the security guard patted my pockets and discovered the coins, I dumped about twenty dollars' worth of coins on the principal's desk. When he asked where I got the money, I told him it was from selling newspapers. The principal suggested I have my mother and the newspaper owner show up to verify my story. For the time being, I was suspended.

As expected, I wasn't able to bring forth the newspaper owner, so I was expelled for theft and truancy. I was enrolled in Audubon Junior High, where I lasted a full week, until I was expelled for truancy and fighting. The next school my mother enrolled me in was John Muir Junior High, about ten blocks from home. The school's principal was aware of my poor attendance record and had a truant officer keep an eye on me. Unfortunately for me, this white dude took his job too seriously. For two weeks he was like a hound dog following me everywhere, as if I was about to shoplift something. When I went into the boys' bathroom, he'd come in and pretend to be washing his hands. Too bad he wasn't around to stop the fight I had in the cafeteria. I probably would not have been expelled.

To help me, my mother's mothering instinct was to send me straight across town to live with Fred and his children. For the moment, I'd share a bedroom with Wayne until my mother was able to locate an apartment somewhere in the area. Surprisingly, I was able to carve out a private niche in Fred's household while keeping to myself, minding my own business and avoiding everybody else's space. Meanwhile, I battled congested thoughts of meeting girls at school and the possible run-ins with thugs who underestimated me.

When I enrolled at Horace Mann Junior High, I was fifteen going on fifty. Wearing a black tam, a highboy shirt, heavily starched Levi's, biscuit shoes, and a black fake-leather coat—called "pleather"—I was cooler than ice. When I passed a crowd of girls who were smiling and checking me out, I thought I was looking good until Demetri told me the pleather coat had to go. It was a kind gesture, her way of saying, "Don't embarrass yourself and me." I immediately took the coat off and never put it back on again. For a while, the nuances of a new school and the girls were enough to keep me interested. In each class I took care of my educational duties, but the affable teachers lacked the expertise to motivate me. Though the school material was interesting, my motivation level was zero. It was during those moments that I recalled how Miss Johnson made learning so interesting that I didn't want to leave. Now, I would literally get up and leave the room if the subject matter was weak or the teacher was incapable of stimulating my mind.

Still, I managed not to get kicked out of school, and my mother found a place on 83rd between Denker and Harvard. It was an apartment complex with one unit on top of the other, and we lived upstairs. There were two bedrooms, and I had one all to myself, which provided me with privacy from my snooping sister. Once we settled in, I ventured outside to satisfy my curiosity and to assess the surroundings. Perhaps it was an omen when I noticed cop cars cruising the area far more frequently than other places I had lived. No matter where I lived, though, the cops were considered by many of the residents to be the number one enemy of black folks. The more contact I had with them, the more their actions proved to be a threat.

In spite of my being the most inconspicuous-looking youth around, the cops swooped down on me because I was a "black youth walking." Two white cops jumped out of the car with their hands poised on their guns and demanded I stand still. One cop asked, "Are you a Panther, boy?" At the time I didn't have a clue what he was talking about. I knew nothing about the revolutionary group called the Black Panthers. I thought the fool was trying to call me an animal, so I responded, "Of course not!" His rough pat-down search was a legendary law enforcement procedure known to virtually all black males living in South Central, involving undue intimate contact in the groin area. Preparing to leave me, smiling, the cop said, "I'll be watching you, nigger." This was his attempt to instill the fear of the law in me. I feared neither the law nor him—only his gun.

The following day at a local liquor store I met Donald, a large dark fellow my age who didn't mind indulging in mischievous—and criminal—activities. Later, at Saint Andrews Park, Donald introduced me to some of his cronies: Bub, Erskine, Cuz, Ronnie, Ricky, Keith, and two tall hulking fellows named Bob and Landry. They all eyed me with suspicion, not knowing what to make of such a little guy, except that Donald told them I was game to hang with them. For whatever reason, while we sat on park benches, Donald's homeboy Ronnie started cappin' on me (ridiculing). I didn't want to rock the boat so I bit my tongue and laughed along with everybody else. In any case, being the butt of his jokes wasn't my idea of having fun. For the sake of the homeboy 'hood, I hoped Ronnie had gotten the joking around about me out of his system.

A week later, while we were hanging out in the driveway of the apartments where Ronnie lived, he started cappin' on me some more. Then he tried to play the "dozens" by cappin' on my mother, which was something I didn't play. I can tolerate being talked about a bit, but to talk about my mother is to risk serious payback. Ronnie was able to spit out just two words, "Your mother . . ." before I was on him like a Tasmanian devil. Donald and Bub had to pull me off him. After calming down, I thought I had jeopardized being their homeboy and risked being jumped on. I watched Donald teasingly put his arm around Ronnie's neck and say, "Now see, I told you Tookie may not play the dozens." Unknown to me, this was a test to earn a place in their circle, but they hadn't anticipated the physical aggression. However, they agreed that I had *heart*. I didn't know what that meant, but I figured it had to be a good thing.

From that point on I never had any run-ins with Ronnie, and in time we blended like family. Often people outside our circle mistook us for being related, as cousins, perhaps, or even brothers. Though not a gang, we began to establish the missing link of camaraderie through common interests: partying, girls, fighting, kinship, and hustling. School wasn't part of the equation; it had been reduced to a pit stop where we met girls, fought, or hung around when nothing else was happening. Back then, ditching parties were the in thing for parties held at somebody's parents' home. The charge was usually twenty-five or fifty cents per person, but we crashed the party, paying nothing. There were wall-to-wall teenage girls who were eager to give themselves to whomever momentarily caught their lusty eyes. Sex was as plentiful as food, alcohol, weed, and other intoxicants. There wasn't a school in California that could compete with a ditching party hosting from fifty to more than one hundred youths trying to get in. There were four times as many people at a ditching party than in a classroom, where all of us needed to be.

When I did stay in school, I usually ended up arguing with a teacher or getting into a fight with someone vying to get a "reputation." Though I wasn't fond of fighting, it was an on-the-job training ground where I picked up many of the little tricks I added to my pugilistic repertoire. I remember fighting Ollie, a tall, thin youth, a bully who ran with a pack of his clones. He tried to talk to Demetri, but she ignored his advances. Ollie then made the mistake of patting her on the butt and she slapped him. If not for a teacher who intervened, they would have been fighting toe-to-toe. Ollie challenged Demetri to an after-school fight in an alley behind a café on Florence Boulevard.

As I arrived, there was a large crowd in the alley. I saw Vicky, Wayne, Bridget, and Demetri heading my way. Ollie was standing there with a huge grin on his face while his homeboys stood off to the side. When he called Demetri out to fight, she was ready to throw down, but I stepped out in front of her. A puzzled Ollie said, "Who in the hell are you?" Vicky shouted out, "Our brother!" I stood there in silence listening to Ollie build himself up by selling wolf tickets about what he planned to do to me. When he began to take his shirt off, my fists revved up like a lawn mower.

I used Monroe's rule of thumb and quickly took advantage of the situation. Behind me the crowd gasped in disbelief. Some of Ollie's homeboys had to be physically restrained. A couple of his homeboys yelled, "That punk cheated!" Then *I* had to be held back. Another of Ollie's homeboys, Lurch, stepped in between us. He was a tall, slender, dark-skinned youth wearing Eldridge Cleaver–style sunglasses. He calmed the crowd with a loud, "Shut up!" Lurch was the leader of the clique, and to appease them, he asked both of us if we were willing to fight again. I said yes, Ollie said yes—and then shook his head no. He was accustomed to having the upper hand in all his fights, except this time. Amazing how a bully's stance lapses into cowardice after getting a taste of his own medicine. Ollie respected me for flipping the script on him. Years later, both he and Lurch became my loyal homeboys. The fight also symbolized the ultimate show of kinfolk loyalty among my stepfamily. I was forever embraced as their brother.

In a short period of time Horace Mann Junior High had become popular among youths from other schools to ditch and hang out. I used to see individuals I knew from Forshay roaming around the school, trying to pick up girls. Often there were flocks of male and female youths waiting across the street for school to let out. One day my homeboys and I were hanging out across the street from school when a pack of youths showed up eyeing us down. I recognized Wolf, Swig, Caesar, and several others who were all from the Brims street gang. I grew up with most of them where I used to live. In fact, I knew Wolf's entire family, and I used to eat dinner at their apartment. So while he and I stepped off to the side to talk, our homeboys stood there eyeing one another. After a small chitchat, Wolf mentioned he had been hearing about us and wanted to know if we were interested in joining the Brims. In a polite gesture I told Wolf my homeboys and I were like family and we weren't into gangs. I left it at that. After a few more minutes of reminiscing, Wolf and the other Brims drove away. Though it was a bold move to speak as a mouthpiece for us, I felt comfortable doing it. Any one of my homeboys had ample opportunity to voice their objections, because I made sure they heard every word. The moment I stepped to the forefront, it was a position I would not relinquish.

My days of cavorting around Horace Mann were over. I had over-stayed my welcome, and the principal kicked me out for truancy and fighting with some of the Van Ness boys. Back in the day, some of them styled a reddish-brown streak on the side of their Afro and were known for jacking other youths for their money. Some of them had cornered Bub and taken his money, then beat him down. For payback we ambushed them at Horace Mann to send a clear message to all our opposition: *lex talionis,* an eye for an eye, for whoever dared hurt any one of us. It was my determination to retaliate and protect us from street gangs that rendered all other moral aspects insignificant. I had become the self-appointed warlord of our tight-knit circle and was the first to jump into the fray. I was the identifiable crazy one. Try as I may, I could not turn the other cheek to expose myself—or my friends—to further harm. So I fought and fought hard.

There were just two schools willing to accept my enrollment: Henry Clay and Brett Harte Junior High. I tried Henry Clay first, where both teachers and students complained about my threatening them. The principal's words to my mother were, "He prances around with an intimidating presence as if he owned the school." Neither my mother nor I could accept the intimidating part, especially given my boyish, innocent good looks.

Point of No Return

I felt trapped. My mother's attempts to rescue us from a disordered society caused us to jump out of one fire into a hotter one. This time we moved to an apartment located on 90th Street between Vermont and Budlong, an area alive with criminal potential. Society's underbelly was there to salute me the moment I set foot outside our home.

The only school in the city willing to accept my registration was Brett Harte. Having to rise each weekday morning to prepare for school had become a forced formality I despised and resisted. School had failed me and I had failed it. It would have broken my mother's heart to know the depth of anxiety I felt over an unpromising future. But no matter how much I yearned for help or how intensely sentimental I felt toward her, my world was closed to my mother.

At Brett Harte, I kept to myself and observed others from a distance. Though two of my cousins, Leroy and Roland, both of whom I cared about, attended this school, we didn't hang out together. The fact was that we were as different as night and day. Our interests differed; my cousins were bookish and dressed like so-called squares. On the other hand, I dressed to match the thug persona I had sculpted to mirror the territory. I wore Levi's so starched I could've stood them in a corner; a highboy shirt or green army shirt; black leather coat; black suspenders; a black tam or gangster brim; and a pair of black biscuits, spit-shined well enough to see your reflection in the toe. On occasion, I'd play football with my cousins and their friends, who also were the epitome of prey. Their mother, Delores, was my mother's sister, and she wanted them to stay far away from me, the black sheep of the family. But I was the iconoclast of bullies, whom they'd run to for protection from other bullies. I recall one day at school, Roland nervously told me about two characters, with some others, ordering him and Leroy to bring their lunch money tomorrow before school, or get beat down. If ever there was a portrait of being vulnerable prey, Roland and Leroy fit the picture. But they *were* my cousins, and I'd fight for them.

The next day we met on the corner of 90th and Budlong. I told them to walk ahead of me as though nothing was happening. While walking, I was distracted for just a minute by this girl—and when I turned around, two guys had my cousins trapped, their arms in the air and their pockets being rifled by the bullies. I ran toward them shouting, "Hold up, hold up, they're my cousins." Both of them stopped in their tracks looking in my direction. With an exaggerated cockiness, I demanded to know what was happening. The would-be jackers were members of a street gang called the Manchester Park Boys. Both of them were nonimposing and about my height, weight, and size. I felt the odds were even. I could tell they were sizing me up to determine whether or not to try me. But just in case, I had a concealed switchblade for an equalizer.

Maybe they recognized the fool in me, or saw themselves in me; I don't know. But I was able to thwart their jacking scheme. As we walked side by side toward school, one of them initiated the "Who's Who" name game, to draw out who I was. This was a thug inquisition with potential to get me gang-rushed if they discovered I was a loner with no backup. The guy running through a list of names was Lester; he had the biggest Afro I'd ever seen, about twelve inches in circumference. When I heard Terry's name, I said, "Sure, I know Terry, we're tight." It was an exaggeration of the truth. They both eyed me with suspicion, probably hoping they could catch me in a lie. It was a favorable moment that Terry turned out to be the mediator in this conflict, because he wanted a fair fight, not a mob beat-down.

During lunch period Terry waved me over to a crowd of hard-core gang members. One of them was Big Earl, a mammoth human being standing six feet six inches and more than three hundred pounds. I hoped I didn't have to fight that monster. While standing facing a rowdy crowd who stared at me like vultures surveying a meal, Terry convinced Big Earl to let me fight Lester or Harold head-up. He asked if I was willing to fight one of them. I boasted, "I'll fight them both at the same time!" My cavalier response brought a roar of laughter from everybody except Harold and Lester. Neither of them wanted to fight, so we shook hands and the crowd roared again.

Within a short period of time I was accepted, and respected, by two formidable circles of homeboys from different geographical areas but identical in behavior and survival mentality. It was an alliance unknown to either side. Both groups were willing, able, and ready to fight alongside me, if necessary. At times I traveled back and forth on foot to where my homeboy Donald lived, or he'd pick me up in a beige Plymouth borrowed from an elderly white lady whose lawn he cut. Together we crashed local ditching parties and got so toasted on ganja we had to kick back until our high came down. I was twelve when I first started sniffing glue and smoking weed with Wolf behind the 43rd Street apartments where he lived. Shortly after that, drugs in general developed into a weakness I employed to soar briefly into forgetfulness before crashing to reality.

Between getting high and ditching school, my grades slipped off the map. The principal warned, "If you don't buckle down soon, you won't graduate." I attended classes, did a little schoolwork here and there, and graduated by the skin of my teeth. Because of my low grades I wasn't allowed to walk across the stage; instead I was handed my diploma out of sight of the class—and good riddance! Graduation for me was just another insignificant formality that pushed me toward another phase of dys-education. Pathetic but true: I was better educated about getting loaded than I was on scholastic topics.

Long before high school, I was a user of street drugs. I had graduated from sniffing glue to smoking marijuana to dropping "red devils"—a barbiturate that is a depressant. I became acquainted with
downers by way of a five-foot three-inch pimp named Li'l Tony, a mean
little sucker who beat down his girls with a heated wire hanger, a baseball bat, or his fists. He lived with Billie, his number one prostitute, in
an apartment on 94th Street. Sometimes I'd be there nodding off on
red devils only to be awakened by the sounds of Li'l Tony beating one
of his girls, chasing her through the living room. While ditching
school, I ran small errands for him or one of his prostitutes, and was
compensated with drugs and money. Li'l Tony's apartment was heavily trafficked. His side job was as the local street pharmacist.

Sometimes the apartment looked like the set of a motion picture,
including a junkie's shooting-up gallery, a hard-core burlesque show,
and a favorite spot for local criminals. The most horrific sights were
of addicts overdosing and sometimes falling down, foaming at the
mouth. Overdoses were commonplace, but most addicts knew how
to revive a fellow addict who had passed out and was moribund. If an
addict was beyond reviving, he or she was dropped off in a secluded
area and an anonymous phone call was made to a hospital or
morgue. Though it was impossible for any of us to forever block out
reality with drugs, overdosing was always a possibility. I remember
getting high with Mary, a beautiful black teenager whom I foolishly
passed around like a marijuana joint to share. Somehow I ended up
stretched out on the steps of Saint Andrews Park gymnasium with my
head resting on Mary's lap as I slipped into an overdose. Mary contacted my mother, who showed up with Fred, and they drove me to
Morningside Hospital, where my stomach was pumped.

Still sick, the next day I was at the 77th Street police station being
interrogated about my drug use. That evening I was transferred to
Central Juvenile Hall. The facility festered with unwashed youth,
chaos, hostile attitudes, random fighting, and the nastiest food I'd
ever tasted. Each night I listened to the eerie sounds of other youth
whimpering and screaming, "I wanna go home, I wanna go home!" If

screaming was a sure way to get home, I would have outscreamed everybody daily. It was my first time in Juvenile Hall, and for a while I felt sick, terrified, trapped, and as though the walls were closing in on me. I was claustrophobic. For seven straight weeks I prayed and read the Bible on my knees, hoping I'd go home any minute.

Like some of the urban schools I had attended, Juvey was a warehouse for incorrigible youth where they would vegetate and sink into ignorance and confusion. It also served as conditioning and preparation for a youth's inevitable step toward prison—as though it was a boot camp, training recruits for the next level of armed services. At the facility I learned absolutely zip, but it was very professional in teaching me to be more indifferent and embittered. Some of the dispassionate turnkeys were more diabolical than gang members; they appeared to suffer from mental disorders while taking out their frustrations on us. The institutional setting aped a primitive version of a reformatory school where no parent could rush to your aid. As a ward of the court outside of parental jurisdiction, a youth could be subjected to involuntary psychotropic drugging and testing, prolonged isolation, bodily harm, degradation, sodomy, and even death at the hands of a turnkey or another youthful offender. Imagine me or any youth trying to explain to a parent about the facility's atrocities. We'd be seen as liars, plain and simple.

While in Juvenile Hall, I was often in lock-up for fighting with juvenile J-cats (distraught individuals with serious mental health issues), gang members, and some of the turnkeys. After each violent conflict, I welcomed the sight of a filthy bunk to rest and rejuvenate for the next encounter. It was during a brief stint outside of lockup that I ran into Bunchie, a homeboy I met at Horace Mann Junior High. At sixteen, about 240 pounds, Bunchie was barrel-chested with thick arms and looked wider than a door. Even though he was huge, Bunchie was a gentle giant and didn't fight unless roused.

One day I was being bum-rushed in the gym by some Sportsman Park Boys, and Bunchie emerged from his timid shell. He entered the fray, throwing bodies like human rag dolls all over the place. His size and strength were revered and feared, even by the ruthless turnkeys who sometimes had the difficult task of trying to restrain him. One day at breakfast a Caucasian J-cat, spaced out on medication, demanded that I pass him a pitcher of hot cocoa. When I told him to wait, he tackled me to the floor, but within seconds Bunchie picked him up and slammed him hard to the ground. While it took the entire squad of turnkeys to control Bunchie, I was able to accommodate the J-cat with the pitcher and the hot cocoa. They ended up pampering Bunchie, but I was thrown in lockup. After several weeks the courts released me into my mother's custody. Though relieved to get out of Juvey, I had a nagging suspicion I'd be back.

Returning to the neighborhood, I fell back into the predictable rut of street activities. I was now going to George Washington High School, home of several gangs, in particular the Sportsman Park Boys, Denker Boys, a few Denver Lanes, and the Figueroa Boys. At school or in the 'hood, the Sportsman Park Boys were our number one menace, known for bailing out of cars to attack any one of us. My road dog was Erskine, a stocky, bowlegged, quick-tempered youth with a flair for dramatic violence. His attitude was "I'll bring it to you!" Both Erskine and I gained a reputation at Washington High for our willingness to fight the street gangs head-up, or catch them off-guard in the school restroom or underneath the bleachers smoking ganja. In school, not too many places were off limits for us to initiate a blow against our so-called enemies, who suffered from the same misconception about who their true enemies were.

The classroom was a kind of sacred territory devoid of fighting. It served as a sanctuary where we could momentarily unwind until the school bell rang. Then it was time to tense up again for possible conflicts. Gradually, as a result of all the fighting on and off the school grounds, most of the known gang members transferred to other schools—Locke, Fremont, or Crenshaw High—to sidestep our mounting efforts to destroy them. We proclaimed Washington High to be *our* school. This was our stomping ground. My homeboys and I ruled. Yet we didn't financially own a centimeter of property.

During school days we'd meet and plan the day, foolishly sacrificing an education for the forbidden fruits of drugs, unprotected sex, fighting, strong-arming, and gambling. We could pretty much get away with anything, except murder. The staff knew who we were and what we were doing at and around school, but they were too scared to stop us—or didn't care. I believe the latter was the case.

The Institutional Shuffle

I n 1970 I was largely unconscious of the battle being fought on a higher level for black survival by civil rights organizations: Black Panthers, United Slaves, National Association for the Advancement of Colored People, Student Nonviolent Coordinating Committee, Nation of Islam, African National Congress, and other black organizations in the United States and abroad. I was brain-dead about the Soledad Brothers, Huey P. Newton, Angela Davis, Nelson and Winnie Mandela, Malcolm X, Bobby Rush, Bunchie Carter, Bobby Seales, Martin Luther King Jr., and other black leaders. Soon I was returned to Central Juvey, this time for suspicion of burglary and being under the influence of drugs. I had made the mistake of being intoxicated and running out of gas in a stolen car, and in a predominantly white area of Carson. While I was walking to the bus stop, the cops jacked me up for sticking out like a lone raisin in a bowl of rice. Before I knew it, I was back in Central Juvenile Hall for less than three weeks, and then transferred to another facility called Los Padrinos.

The staff at Central Juvey had mentioned that I was being moved because I lived in the geographical jurisdiction of Los Padrinos. But my mother said, "Boy, those people didn't want you there because you acted like a fool!" As it turned out, Los Padrinos was the Marriott Hotel of juvenile halls, with a swimming pool, clean rooms, and food that was gourmet compared to Central's food. There were numerous peacocks strutting around with their plumage displayed and making shrieking noises sounding like a call for help: "Hel . . . p, hel . . . p!" Rumors had it that there was a donkey that enjoyed chasing people, but I never saw it. The stoic judge had stated on the record, "In the interest of this court and for your welfare"—he was looking at me— "I order that you be sent to the Job Corps in Salt Lake City."

During the long bus trip to Utah, I didn't have the faintest idea what to expect. When the bus pulled up and I got off, there were twenty or more youths loitering inside the terminal. About half an hour later there was a broadcast message requesting that all Job Corps recruits report to the bus outside. As far as I was concerned, when the bus turned onto the grounds resembling an old army compound, I thought the judge had tricked me into enlisting in the armed forces. After being briefed on the rules and regulations, we new arrivals were assigned to living quarters in a quasi-army barracks. Like Juvey, there wasn't much privacy, only a wooden-style partition separating each bunk.

In front of the large school building was a huge cannon, and across the street was the cafeteria. On campus was a wide spectrum of black youths like me, the descendants, as far as I was concerned, of a slave diaspora throughout the North, Central and South Americas of the Western Hemisphere. Though all of us were of the same genotypical black ancestry, many of them were Puerto Ricans, spoke with a Spanish accent, and seemed standoffish toward us, their darker counterparts. The racial tension was evident, with contemptuous stares and a better-than snobbery despite our common poverty, fatherless home lives, and not owning a pot to piss in. It was a landmine of racial intolerance between blacks and Puerto Ricans that had been brewing for God knows how long.

Although I had no interest whatsoever in the Job Corps' educational system, the archery program was something different. I discovered that I enjoyed it. To stand and aim an arrow at a target attached to a haystack evoked some ancestral hunting desire. Out of the corner of my eye I caught the sight of a guy sitting on top of my leather coat. I asked him to put the coat on the back of the chair and continued to shoot at the target. When I turned back around, the guy was still sitting on my coat, so I walked over and asked him again. I thought perhaps he didn't understand English. Though he was Puerto Rican and may not have understood English that well, his diction was impeccable when he said, "Shut up, nigger!" That was the first time I've ever used my foot in a fight, and I didn't even know karate.

The gym coach broke up the one-sided fight and marched me in to the principal's office. The principal admonished me for my behavior and never asked what had happened. After some time he told me to go to lunch and return afterward to continue the discussion about my incorrigible behavior. Heading toward the cafeteria, I noticed two large groups squared off, blacks standing next to the cannon and Puerto Ricans standing across the street. As I cautiously walked toward them, an older black youth with an alarmed expression met me, stating that the Puerto Rican guy I sucker-punched and stomped wanted to fight me.

Standing in the middle of the street facing my opponent, I was confident until I caught sight of a shiny object flashing in his hand, slightly behind his back. Had not the sun been blazing that day, I would have missed the glint and walked right into a sharp blade. I was able to unloosen my belt and then wrap it around my hand with the thick buckle dangling by my side. In Spanish, his Puerto Rican *compadres* were egging him on to attack as their warlike chants of "Get that nigger!" resonated loudly. The sheepish silence on the part of the black group was a powerful signal, suggesting, "You're on your own, brother!" There's no telling what might have taken place had not the campus guards rushed in between us to end the drama. Oddly enough, that's when the Puerto Rican exploded and started yelling, "I'm gonna kill that nigger!" Several guards had to hold him while I was escorted to the campus jail, a place I didn't know existed until that moment. Being behind bars was a circumstance to which I never became accustomed. The walls were closing in on me when the principal showed up babbling excitedly about there being a possible racial riot and about my being dishonorably discharged, which I knew meant going home. According to the principal, before my arrival there was racial harmony on the campus, and everybody got along. Having to shoulder the blame for everything was commonplace for me. No doubt the other guy was allowed to stay and graduated with honors.

That evening the campus guard drove me to the bus depot, handed me a bus ticket and ten dollars, and said my leather coat would be mailed to me. When I arrived back in Los Angeles on my mother's doorstep, she simply shook her head, mumbling, "Oh, Lord." It was no surprise that the juvenile court judge didn't contact my mother and order me back to the courtroom. And since we weren't contacted, I went back to Washington High. Nothing had changed. The gangs were still seeking to make examples out of me and others for defying their fiefdom over the school and neighborhood. Personally, I was tired of seeing the labyrinth of gang members' territories where safe passage required sidewalk tariffs, else a passerby would feel the gang members' wrath.

By now, most of my homeboys were expert car thieves. We used the cars to impress young women and to track down Sportsman Park Boys who hung out at their park, what is now called Jesse Owens Park—and beat them down. One night we were out cruising in a stolen 1963 Chevy looking for Sportsman Park Boys. We stopped in Inglewood to get loaded, while Bub and Adam argued about who should be driving. Adam tricked Bub to get out and come around to the driver's side, then locked him outside. They continued to banter until the Inglewood police drove up, and we scattered in different directions. After jumping out through the car's back window, I climbed a tall wooden fence, fell onto some thorny bushes, and rolled into a mud puddle. I jumped up, ran past a Doberman pinscher, and hopped another fence. On the other side of the block, there was a crowd of teenagers in a driveway having a get-together, and I joined in. Trying to look inconspicuous, I stood there for more than twenty minutes thinking the coast was clear and that Bub and Adam had probably gotten themselves busted. When I reached the corner, several white Inglewood police cars crept up with their lights out. Guns drawn, the cops ordered me to hit the dirt. I dropped to my knees and lay flat on the ground while I was searched and handcuffed.

Back in Central Juvenile Hall, two detectives showed up to question me about the names of my two homeboys who eluded capture. One of the white detectives said, "Look, Stan, if you tell us who was with you in that stolen car, you can go home today!" I could not snitch under any circumstances, even if I were being accused of heinous crimes that others had committed. I was taught not to tell. As a little boy, I remember vividly how Big Rock used to be enraged when he talked about snitches being the lowest form of any animal. He said, "Better for a mother to cross her legs during the moment of conception to choke the life out of that child than to give birth to a snitch." When the cop asked again was I willing to give him the names of my homeboys, I said, "What homeboys? What stolen car?" Apparently I pissed the cops off, because they jumped up and stormed out of the room.

Later that week I was transferred to Los Padrinos, from which I would spend about three months going back and forth to court. While kicking back, minding my own thoughts, the Los Padrinos gym coach approached me and wanted to know if I was interested in lifting weights. I thought the muscular Caucasian coach was crazy and told him so. After about a week the coach asked again if I was willing to lift weights. I said, "Lift weights for what?" My response was a mistake, because the man launched into a lengthy monologue about health, muscle body parts, vitamins, protein supplements, bodybuilding shows, and weight-lifting routines. I was eager to try the weights just to shut him up. His persistence in showing me how to back-arm, curl, bench-press, and do pull-overs began to pay off big-time. Later that day, though sore, I felt good. The more I began to lift weights, the more I became addicted to the feeling of being bigger and stronger. I can still hear the coach's words: "You have the body and bone structure to be enormous if you continue to drive iron and eat properly." Of course I didn't believe a word he said, but he was able to motivate me to continue lifting weights. For me to find the raw power I never knew existed within me was a significant discovery. This was a discipline I could relate to and one in which I could see rapid results.

Meanwhile, the court judge had sentenced me to Camp Rocky, located in the mountains above San Dimas, California. Rocky was a fire-fighting facility with no barbed wire fences or guard towers, and there was nothing between me and distance but air. A few times I thought about escaping but figured doing time there would be a cakewalk. To me, Rocky was just another form of punishment I neither feared nor respected. With each incarceration, there were no life lessons learned. I simply entered into nothing, then was released, having been refined in bitterness and misdirection to slip further toward ruin. Camp Rocky would prove to be no different than Juvey and the Job Corps.

It didn't surprise me to see a peculiar alliance between the whites and Mexicans at Rocky, because I had noticed it first in Juvey. Whenever a fight broke out between a black youth and a white youth, the Mexicans, instead of being neutral, sided with the whites. It was odd because those same whites could not walk down the street in any barrio without being attacked. I had stumbled into another hotbed of unrest based on skin color. There was a lot of back-stabbing, not with knives but with racial epithets ping-ponging through the air: "You white devils," "You wetbacks," "You nigger." Most of the battles were verbal, but fistfights broke out here and there. I did manage to befriend some blacks from Los Angeles, including Tick, Anthony, Harper, Bobo, and others who would become part of my circle.

All of us slept in a huge dorm room with steel bunks lined up on both sides of a slightly elevated control center, where a counselor stood vigil over us. At night, everybody kept a watchful eye out for possible "rat-packing": blankets would be thrown over a sleeping victim's head and then he'd be beaten senseless. Though I'd only seen whites and Mexicans rat-pack the weaker ones among themselves, I still remained vigilant. I slept far in the back in a bunk next to the wall where I could see everything coming and going. The notion of "sleeping with one eye open" applied here—but it was next to impossible to perform effectively. I did become a light sleeper, however, and my ears were as sensitive to movement as a bat's built-in echolocation system.

Each morning the camp program began with our getting up at about 6 a.m. and washing up, then meeting outside around the flagpole. There a counselor would inspect our faces for any signs of facial hair. No youth was allowed to eat breakfast unless he was clean-shaven and washed up. After breakfast, we dressed in fire-fighting gear and went out in a truck that seemed to stop randomly anywhere on the side of a mountain for us to work. We were handed tools to firebreak certain sections, hard labor for a measly twenty-five cents per day, and fifty cents for working at an actual fire site. But I managed to get a position working in the kitchen, where I eventually became the head cook. Most of my time was spent cooking and driving iron. In a short period, I had buffed up my fourteen-inch arms to seventeen inches. I was walking around with my chest raised up, arms stuck out to the side, and I strolled with my feet turned outward. I didn't care how my stroll looked to others—I thought it made me look tough, and it felt right.

When I turned seventeen on December 29, 1970, there was no doubt I was bigger and stronger, but I lacked the necessary discipline to stay out of juvenile correctional facilities. Though I looked forward to returning to the streets, my thoughts focused on countermeasures to conquer neighboring gang menaces. No longer would my friends, relatives, or I be subjected to fear of bodily harm. No more waiting on the so-called enemy. It would be *seek and destroy* . . . attack, attack, and attack again. It was war!

Prior to my release date I was summoned for a reevaluation, a customary procedure for every youth. Seated inside the gymnasium before the staff's tribunal, I was subjected to a long list of questions.

The last question was fair enough: "Stan, what are your plans once you are released back into society?" With an indifferent expression, I replied, "I plan on being the leader of the biggest gang in the world." My unrehearsed response was as shocking to me as it was to them. It was as if a ventriloquist had unexpectedly spoken through me.

The very thought of joining a gang, or being a leader of one, was preposterous. I hated street gangs. I guess the counselors viewed my statement as being unrealistic, as I did. It was probably the first time the counselors had been left speechless. While they sat there befuddled, I waltzed out and slammed the chair behind me with the emphasis of a kick. One thing for sure: they were tired of my being there. For the first eight weeks I had given the staff hell. Two days later Fred and my mother picked me up and as we drove off, I didn't even look back.

Seeds of a Gang

hen I returned to the South Central colony, there were salutations all around from my homeboys. It was a customary gesture to pay homage to any one of us who had done time
without snitching. Bub was the first to shake my hand and comment
on how buffed up I had become. But mostly, he was showing gratitude for my knowing how to keep my mouth shut.

The streets hadn't changed much during the months I'd been
gone. The gang problem was still festering, and racial ferment was
everywhere. A riot occurred in Wilmington, North Carolina, where
the National Guard had to be called in. The Black Panthers' field
marshal, George Jackson, was shot and killed as a result of an alleged
escape attempt at San Quentin State Prison. The political activist Angela Davis was still in Marin County Jail, and a rebellion was in full
swing at Attica Correctional Facility in upper New York State. Not to
mention the usual problems: poor education, no employment opportunities for youth, lack of youth programs, broken family units—all
these negative realities fed the growing civil rights movement.

While black economic programs experienced a full downswing,
the gang factor and its circle of violence were experiencing a surge.
This was a growth industry! Throughout South Central there were
many factions of visible and latent street gangs with parasitical ap-
petites. Contrary to popular belief, black gangs were not a phenome-

non but rather a commonality that existed long before I was born. The older gangs—the notorious Slausons, Gladiators, and the Business Men—had become ethnicity-conscious and were absorbed into the Black Panther Party or other active political groups. A few remaining older black gangs were still hanging on: the Chain Gang, Low Riders, Avenues, Brims, Figueroa Boys, and the Van Ness Boys. These gangs gave rise to newer, more predatory gangs such as the Sportsman Park Boys, Denker Boys, Manchester Park Boys, Hustler Mob, New House Boys, and many other street cliques. But in spite of our lack of numerical strength, I had several trump cards over the other gangs. As I had moved from school to school, juvenile facility to another juvey, and 'hood to 'hood, I had established ties in each area with certain key youths who held influence over their circle of homeboys. Their homeboys became mine, and mine became theirs.

I was catapulted to the helm of our circle not by force or referendum, but by virtue of opportunity, conditions, and self-promotion. Simply, I stepped into a vacuum, an uncontested position tailor-made for me. My homeboys' acquiescence allowed me to follow through, to expand—although we were not a gang in the traditional sense. But as the bar was raised by a new level of aggressive attacks and strong-arming by our rivals, we morphed into a gang without a title. There was no turning back, not really, because the more we fought, the more deeply entrenched we became in vendettas. Though the black images we saw across the barricades were seen as the enemy, we had no notion that our true adversaries were the squalid living conditions, the vortex of powers confining us to those conditions, and our own unwitting perpetuation of those conditions. Like countless other black gang members and criminals, we were unconscious accomplices in our own subjugation—our own worst foes.

Gang battles raged, and we picked up the pace in drive-by beatings. Often we'd bail out of a stolen car to beat down unsuspecting rivals while I'd let them know it was me, Tookie, who was doing this to them. If they didn't remember anything else, they'd remember my name. As long as the local gangs were at each other's throats and didn't unite to smash us like ants, we could stand up against any of them, despite the fact that we were outnumbered. Though they despised us, the name they cursed most was mine. I had become the neighboring gangs' number one target, which I encouraged with my need to be feared and known by all of them. It was becoming a familiar sight for gangs to cruise the area leaving messages such as "Tell Tookie we're looking for him," or "Tell Tookie we're gonna kill him!"

One evening at a dance held at the Saint Andrews Park gymnasium, the Chain Gang caught a few of us off-guard. The guy who approached me was Daven, a twentysomething loudmouth who wouldn't bust a grape with cleats on. But surrounded by a mob of other grown men posing as his backup, Daven was bold enough to thrust a finger in my chest and ask, "Are you Tookie?" It was déjà vu for me, reminding me of the time when Louis and his cronies stomped me in the dirt behind Manual Arts. This time I flipped the script and lunged at Daven, causing both of us to fall to the ground. The darkness in the gym enabled me to crawl out of the scuffle while Daven's homeboys continued to punch and kick him, thinking that it was me they were beating. Meanwhile, Bub, in the gymnasium's kitchen, held other Chain Gang members at bay with a starter pistol, until they realized it was a fake. But like me, he managed to escape a serious beat-down.

Back then there were constant reminders of our mortality, especially when shots were being fired at us. Earning a reputation through fisticuffs was being replaced by gunslinging, by youths who lacked an ability to fight and needed an equalizer. It took nerve to fight with your hands—it's much easier to pick up a handgun and brandish it like a would-be tough guy. Even a child could do this, and with deadly effect. It is true that we had access to a cache of guns, but such weapons represented an imposing symbol of death that exceeded the limits of our intent to beat the rival gangs into submission. The horrors of gunplay disturbed me so much that for a long time, I had to distance myself from possessing one. Guns represented death, and I feared their potential.

Nevertheless, even while hot lead was flying in our direction, I still didn't give death a second thought. I had a false sense of invincibility. I wanted to live a full life, but I was presented with a meaningless future with no dreams, no tangible hopes. I lived each day with reckless abandon, not fearing tomorrow. "God looks out for babies and fools," as the expression goes. The fool in me was beginning to run amok: perhaps that's why death passed me by. Also, most of my rivals and enemies didn't even know what I looked like. I was said to be tall, with a scarred face and jet-black skin, a muscle-bound nut. I was pegged as a villain who harassed other gangs, didn't play fair, and needed to be taught a lesson.

My street reputation continued to grow, surpassing the leaders of all other local gangs, and although I wanted the notoriety, I didn't anticipate the headaches and other consequences. The police and school administration were receiving complaints about a student named Tookie who was causing trouble on and off the grounds. Both authorities wanted to identify this person. Even some parents of local gang members were up in arms about the mysterious troublemaker, but none of them could finger me. In school, gang members and everybody else knew me only as Stan, and I wanted to keep it that way as long as possible.

Our crew's fashion style was dissimilar to that of the other street gangs, but more and more we began to emulate them. My homeboys began to adopt gang names: Erskine became "Mad Dog," Terry was now "Bimbo," Big Bob chose "the Hawk," and Donald called himself "Sweetback" after the main character in a Melvin Van Peebles movie, *Sweet Sweetback's Baadasssss Song*. Other homeboys did likewise. Soon Terry and I got our left ears pierced, with the intent of enhancing our thug image. Other homeboys followed suit, styling the same kind of gold hook and cross, or a small gold hoop earring. We had gravitated toward the gang realm as if we belonged there.

The consistent attacks we initiated—assisted by street gangs destroying one another—were beginning to turn the tide in our favor. Several of the larger gangs showed an interest in switching sides—

extending an olive branch of compromise—while others reluctantly continued to fight. It was time to consolidate the friends and acquaintances I had cultivated for the past few years, to avoid making the divide-and-conquer mistakes made by other street gangs. It didn't take a mathematician to see that when a structure is divided into factions, each individual part loses its potency and thus is exposed to possible annihilation. I didn't want to make that mistake.

Crip Walk

The black community generally was blind to its defiant youth creating increasingly aggressive street gangs. Mislabeled by some as a "lost generation," we were instead forgotten prodigies who disappeared, children buried alive in a sandbox. We did what was necessary to exhume ourselves. Though we must share the blame, we were products of a culture that bastardized us.

In the spring of 1971 at Washington High, the gang challenge took on new energy. When the school bell rang for lunch one day, I started to go to meet Mad Dog in our usual spot but was abruptly distracted. There was no mistaking that the two strangers headed my way were looking for me, perhaps for vengeance of some sort. This scenario had become the prevailing motif of my life: I'd be confronted by the opposition and some sort of combat would begin.

Both strangers were extremely muscular. The taller of the two called out to me, "Hey Tookie," and stopped at arm's length from me. We stood facing one another while his homeboy stood to the side, watching us. "Are you Tookie?" asked the fellow. I said, "Yes, I'm Tookie. Why?" I figured if they were here to fight, there was no need to be sociable. The guy's face had a scar running upward from the corner of his mouth. He smiled and extended his right hand. "I'm Raymond Washington," then indicated his homeboy. "That's Bulldog." We nodded, acknowledging one another.

Raymond mentioned how his homeboy Clint, whom I had be-friended earlier, had told him about my willingness to challenge all the neighboring gangs despite my homeboys and me being outnumbered. He talked about how he was experiencing the same problem with gangs on the east side of Los Angeles, and asked if I was interested in uniting our homeboys. Though I had been approached with similar propositions on other occasions and turned them down, this time it was different. What caught my attention was the way that Raymond and Bulldog were dressed. Except for my wide-brim hat, the three of us were dressed identically, in black leather coats, black biscuits, and heavily starched Levi's. Had my enemies seen them, they would have been mistaken for being part of my circle.

With Raymond and Bulldog dressing like we did, I was confident that neither of them represented my rivals, nor did Raymond say he was part of a gang. Had he mentioned any gang connections, I would have declined his offer as I did with my childhood buddy Wolf, who was a Brim. During this conversation with Raymond, I made it absolutely clear how much I despised gangs. I told Raymond I'd give the alliance some thought and suggested we meet on Sunday at the Rio Theater on Western off Imperial Boulevard. We shook hands, and I stood there watching as they disappeared around the corner of the gymnasium. An alliance was possible, I felt, because it aligned with my agenda to consolidate the groups of homeboys I'd met over the years. I envisioned our being not a gang in the customary sense, but an unstoppable force that no gang in Los Angeles or the world could ever defeat. The thought appealed to my growing megalomania. I made up my mind right then that the alliance was on.

After apprising Mad Dog about the encounter with Raymond, I headed toward 113th Street, where Melvin lived in his mother's house, which was to become a regular hangout for us Crips. When I arrived, he was driving iron in the garage—huffing and puffing while curling a set of barbells. Though Melvin was thin, he had the heart of a lion and was equally dangerous. He was the newest among my circle of homeboys. I had met him earlier under precarious circumstances.

Melvin and about eight of his homeboys, armed with bumper jacks, crowbars, and baseball bats, had Mad Dog and me surrounded in a tight circle on the school grounds of Henry Clay Junior High. We were held hostage for about twenty minutes until it was determined that we weren't the ones who had jacked his brother and their homeboy. Mad Dog and I would have had to be Houdinis to escape unscathed. After an apology for delaying us, we walked away unharmed. Melvin and I began to see one another often at the Rio Theater and we established a connection. We later would fight alongside each other against numerous street gangs.

That Sunday at the Rio I was kicking back, watching the movie *Al Capone*, along with my homeboys Mad Dog, Bub, Herc, Cuz, Lurch, Bimbo, Sweetback, and the Hawk. Midway through the movie, the manager of the theater sent word that some people were outside, calling me. When I reached the lobby, I could see Raymond across the street with some of his homeboys. I waved them over. Standing in front of the theater, Raymond whispered, "Ah, Tookie, we don't have enough to pay for all of us." I told him, "No sweat, I've got it covered." Raymond looked puzzled, but they all got in free. The manager and I had an arrangement: as long as there was order inside the theater, myself and a few others didn't have to pay.

In the lobby, Raymond introduced me to Fernando, Douhane, Chilli, Ichy, and Little Sam. I shook hands with Clint, whom I already knew. We went inside. Raymond and his cronies sat in front of us, and I was seated directly behind Raymond. In order for us to talk, he had to sit sideways with his legs draped across the adjoining seats. Our homeboys were kicking back as if nothing was happening, except for Mad Dog, who was eyeing every move. I had a sense that something new was beginning here, a new alliance that would exceed our imaginations. Raymond and I had engaged in what I would read about, decades later, a street version of an ancient African war strategy to hype ourselves before a battle, to visualize domination over our enemies. For us the alliance would commence an urban cleansing of the gang element, or so we thought.

Back then, the chances of two strong-willed youth coming to-gether from opposite geographical sides of South Central to create an alliance—well, the odds were very long. For reasons I can't fathom, Raymond and his homeboys integrated with us as if we discovered we were long-lost cousins, kindred spirits. In fact, Raymond thought our circle consisted of relatives because we addressed one another as "cuz," short for cousin. Though none of us was related, we did have a homeboy nicknamed Cuz, so it really carried over from there. We avoided using "brother" as a salutation because it was no longer in-dicative of camaraderie. I knew at least when a person called me "cuz" that he wasn't my enemy. On the other hand, Raymond and his cronies had an affinity for the word "homeboy," which, like "cuz," eventually caught on with everybody.

Our meeting was not as newsworthy as the Appalachian meeting held in 1957 by more than one hundred Italian-American Mafia bosses. But in the cloak of darkness, the stage was set for a new "cousin-hood" under the banner of street gang warfare. After the Rio closed, we agreed to meet at Washington High on the upcoming Friday to seal the deal, to bring together as many homeboys as possible.

Fortunately, I needed only to contact specific individuals who passed the word to their homeboys to be up at Washington High on Friday during lunch period. That day when the school bell rang for lunch, it was a bell signaling a gathering of the west and east sides of Los Angeles's rebellious youths. By the time Bub and I reached the bleachers behind the gymnasium, I saw Raymond standing among twenty to thirty of his homeboys. With just two of us—Bub and me—showing up, it called into question whether my word had much weight. Raymond asked what was happening, and I told him they'll be here, but I was beginning to have doubts. Inside, I chastised my-self for being dubious about my own homeboys, regained my compo-sure, and looked confident.

I had been shaking lots of hands when Raymond's homeboy Craig shouted out, "Tookie, is that them?" I turned around to see the grand entrance: a smiling Bimbo strolling across the football field ahead of a battalion of his homeboys. I nodded to Craig, beaming, and assured him, "That's some of them!" Then, as if choreographed, rounding the corner from the 108th Street side of the bleachers, Lurch appeared, leading his homeboys in a quasi-militant-style march, while four separate groups headed by Big Curtis, Melvin, Fat Riley, and Big Tracy came from the opposite direction. I was filled with pride, knowing that my word meant a lot among my homeboys. They were dressed in a wide variety of styles: beige khaki suits, starched Levi's, black leather coats, silk suits, army boots, black biscuits, suit coat vests, and wooden canes carried for style but to be used mostly as weapons. There were certain styling differences between the west and east. For example, in the beginning most of us West Side Crips wore an earring in our left earlobe and styled a wide-brim hat. Not many East Side Crips wore earrings, but they often sported Ace Deuce stingy brims.

It would have been a police photographer's Kodak moment to have captured all of us on film that day. Standing and sitting around on the bleachers was the largest body of black pariahs ever assembled. I'm convinced that had the Black Panther party still been recruiting—uninterrupted by the duplicitous COINTELPRO (Counter Intelligence Program), a series of counterintelligence activities designed by the Federal Bureau of Investigation (FBI) to neutralize political dissidents, especially targeting the Black Panthers—Huey Newton and Bobby Seales would have salivated over the untapped youthful potential we represented. Throughout this state and country, we embodied only a small division within a multitude of reckless, energetic, fearless, and explosive young black warriors. Though we were often seen as social dynamite, I believe we were the perfect entity to be indoctrinated in cultural awareness and trained as disciplined soldiers for the black struggle. Nevertheless, this opportunity to mold us as a valuable resource was never seen in its true potential by society, schools, churches, community programs, civil rights movements, or other black organizations.

For me, the thin line between nihilism and being a warrior was blurred, so that I rushed headlong toward self-immolation. Little wonder I relished the deafening primal roar of our homeboys' approval when Raymond and I shook hands and then embraced. Finally, I belonged to something!

Later that evening after the meeting, both the west and the east sides met up at Sportsman's Park for the Tom Cross Record Hop. The dance was packed with young women, and my intent was to enjoy them and the scenery. However, in less than an hour, Raymond was prepared to go toe-to-toe with Stanley, an Andre the Giant–sized character who stood about six feet eight inches tall, a Sportsman Park Boy. Some of his homeboys were hanging around, not surprisingly, since this was supposed to be their turf. While standing there, Stanley got cute and boldly demanded, "What do you little fools want to do?" Without any signaling, Raymond and I hit him at the same time, and the giant stumbled to the side. I ran across a long row of chairs, continuing to hit Stanley as he staggered toward the door, while Raymond was running alongside him, unleashing body shots. But the giant wouldn't fall. When I reached the last chair and was about to jump down, someone blindsided me with a folding metal chair that knocked me and my hat in separate directions. Dazed, I crouched on all fours. Melvin and Warlock were beating down the Sportsman Park Boy who crowned me upside the head. I found my hat and headed outside, when my stepsister Demetri and some of her girlfriends noticed that I was bleeding. We went inside the girls' restroom; there I discovered that my right ear had been split and blood was flowing from the wound.

Outside the dance, more than one hundred of us headed down Western Avenue. In our path was a liquor store off the corner of 94th Street. We mobbed the store and stole about half the store's merchandise. Eventually, we ended up at Jack in the Box on Western and 83rd, staying until the wee small hours of the morning, when I finally went home. The next morning my mother discovered a blood-soaked pillow under my head and took me to the hospital, where my ear was stitched up. At these moments my mother questioned whether I was the same child who exited her womb, or was I switched at birth.

Life seemed to move at an accelerated pace after I met Raymond.

Now we were talking about a "title" to best describe our campaign. In the school lunch area at Washington High there was a great debate over the title, and most everybody involved was excited about it except me. It didn't matter what the title was because, for the west side, I planned to have "Tookie" in front of it. Thrown into the hat were names such as the Black Crusaders, the Terminators, the Mau-Maus, the Eliminators, the Rebels, the Annihilators, the Black Knights, the Warlords, the Black Gangsters, and many others. Raymond suggested the Cribs. The craziest title, the Snoopies, came from Melvin. In fact, he and some of his homeboys showed up wearing T-shirts with pictures of the *Peanuts* cartoon character Snoopy on the front. Melvin abandoned the idea after being ridiculed about it.

Not long after, my girlfriend Bonnie gave a party on 106th, in the garage at her mother's house. When we arrived that night, she told me about two neighborhood thugs, Buddha and Monkey-man ("Monk" for short), crashing her party and scaring some of her friends away. They had a reputation as a vicious tag team at Washington High, but we had never bumped heads before. That changed when Buddha's and Monkey-man's arrogance brought them back to the party, drunk and boisterous. After being thoroughly battered and thrown into the street, they regained consciousness and left.

The next time I encountered Buddha and Monkey-man was in the school hash line. They approached me and were quickly surrounded by Bimbo, Bub, Mad Dog, Cuz, Lurch, and others. With the looming potential of a violent repeat of the battering they suffered at the party, Buddha told me that they were looking to join our circle. No doubt we appealed to their militant spirit by challenging their thughood; they had to join us or be smashed by our power. When I embraced Buddha and Monk, I sensed their fire to fight, but I had no idea Buddha and I would become inseparable.

The following day we gathered in the cafeteria area. Our quest for a title was narrowed down to three names. Bub liked the Black Overlords, Big Curtis favored the Assassins, and Raymond had the unusual title the Cribs. In a unanimous vote, Cribs became our new name and epithet. When Buddha asked me whether I liked the name, I said, "Cool, Tookie and the Cribs, what do you think?" I'll never forget his expression of horror and disbelief and a genuine concern for my name being attached to the title. Buddha reminded me that the title meant the police would hold me responsible for everything that happened. I grudgingly listened because I knew what he was saying was true.

Though I dropped the idea of having my name before the Cribs title, the name itself was short-lived. Most of us, while intoxicated, mispronounced Cribs and started saying "Crips"—and it stuck. For a while on the east side the title Cribs was being written on walls. Throughout the west side the name Crip was being scribbled on walls. Surprisingly, the mix-up in the title didn't jeopardize anything. The alliance took precedence above all else. Eventually the word "Crip" replaced "Crib," but neither had any underlying political, organizational, cryptic, or acronymic meaning. Both titles depicted a fighting alliance against street gangs—nothing more, nothing less.

When Raymond and I became joint leaders of the Cribs, we functioned as a single federation. But during that period when our name, the "Cribs," mutated into the "Crips," tribalism began to develop. The two organizations were autonomous—and were allies with the same agenda: war against street gangs. Each side engaged in a competitive aggression to see which could conquer the most gangs, or take the most leather coats, cars, jewelry, or money from those gangs. In spite of all the inflated egos, there was no tribal Crip warfare between the west and the east, not even fistfights. The occasional verbal conflicts between homeboys were always settled in full-contact football games held on Saturdays at Saint Andrews Park. It was a magnificent scene, a collection of black talent on the field, although none of them would ever be offered an athletic scholarship, or even an education.

It was Raymond whom I first heard jokingly say, "The west side is cool but the east side rules!" My logical response was to simply reverse the phrase: "The east side is cool but the west side rules!" Our light banter was taken out of context by some of our homeboys who, years later, would take the braggadocio to heart. In the meantime,

Raymond and I held the alliance intact while I continued to solidify a connection among other proselytized and defeated gangs. Throughout the 'hoods we were becoming notorious as a powerful fighting machine with a numerical dominance over the gangs. Steadily multiplying and swarming like ants at a picnic, no gang wanted to go head-to-head with the vicious Crips who vastly outnumbered them. For any gang to match our strength was impossible; the West Side Crips' swift rise to infamy was a traumatic blow to the long-standing older gangs. Too often, when another gang issued a challenge to meet at a designated spot, we arrived and were ambushed in a hail of bullets. Even a coward strapped with a sidearm could readily chase fifty or more Crips down the street. Our marching orders became flight, not fight, because our fists were no match for bullets.

The reputation of a black gang was usually built on its use of pugilistic skills against its rivals. Toting a gun wasn't our style, but we were getting shot at too often. One day after we had left a Jackson Five concert at the Los Angeles Forum, we mobbed our opposition of more than forty leather coats, and then Crip-walked down Manchester Boulevard en masse, more than one hundred strong. Prowling in six cars, five in each car, were the Chain Gang, who did a drive-by on us. With an undercover police car passing by, they boldly continued to shoot at us while most of us ducked for cover inside Saint Andrews Park. As we waited for the bullets to stop flying, the air stank of potassium nitrate, and my heart was pounding. All of us were half-excited and scared, with the exception of Buddha and Mad Dog. The silence was broken from the other end of the park when the Chain Gang loudly taunted and challenged us to a fight. Knowing they were packing guns, we strolled toward them with the foolish audacity of men walking into a blazing fire wearing gasoline-soaked clothing.

As we approached, bullets began to zing past my head, and we turned and sprinted like Jesse Owens to the opposite end of the park, then darted across Manchester Avenue into a car dealer's shop. Hiding behind brand new cars, we watched as the Chain Gang passed by and shot up the car lot. Bullets ricocheted and smashed into cars and the wall. Some of us were trapped behind a row of cars and decided to make a run before they returned for another volley. But the exit route was blocked by big Bunchie, bawling like a baby, flatulent, refusing to budge. When the Chain Gang returned, the cars stopped and I heard a jeering voice cry, "We got your butt now, Tookie!" followed by rapid gunfire. In the midst of a hail of bullets, Buddha jumped up and ran toward them, cursing and shouting, "Over my dead body!" as he brandished a gun, returning fire. Then Mad Dog appeared, also blasting away at the Chain Gang, causing them to screech off down the street. It surprised me that both of our homeboys were packing guns. We knew they were coming back, so I hollered at Hawk to move Bunchie out of the way, and with one mighty kick, Hawk rolled Bunchie to the side and we escaped into the darkness.

That event provoked many Crips to discard their right-hand leather gloves, used for fighting, and pick up guns. We were enraged and strapping down for battle. Though I continued the old style of gang fighting and avoided toting a gun, I found security in knowing that those closest to me were carrying. Nevertheless, force and violence were a theme of our lives. The more we fought, the more we had to fight—a continuing escalation of violence.

Many of the Chain Gang members were grown men and had better access to weapons than we did. But they had to be taught a lesson, and it had to come swiftly. As the Chain Gang partied in their hangout late one afternoon, we surrounded the house. Big Curtis, Raymond, and Fat Riley kicked in the front door and rushed inside with other homeboys. The house exploded. Chain Gang members were thrown out of windows, and those escaping through the back door ran into more of our fists and canes. Throughout the entire battle gunshots were fired, but our only goal was to beat them into submission. Meeting up at Saint Andrews Park, I noticed blood trickling down Raymond's face. He had been hit in the head with a vase. But we knew the tables had turned. The Chain Gang had been trounced and eradicated on their own turf, although a few of them blended into a new and deadlier foe, calling themselves the Inglewood Family.

I remember Raymond pulling up at Saint Andrews Park in a small caravan of black trucks with some East Side Crips in the back. I recognized Head, supposedly a former Avenue Gang member turned Crip, driving one of the trucks. Raymond wanted to know if I'd accompany him to the Avalon Gardens (a public housing site) on the east side. He said, "There's this fool who lives there named Jimel who stole on me then ran. I want to address that." I told him no problem, then along with Buddha and others we piled into the black trucks and caravanned to the east side of Los Angeles.

The trucks parked on the outskirts of Avalon Garden Courts were arranged in a half circle. The area was small in comparison to Imperial Courts or Jordon Downs, yet it was exceptionally clean, with manicured lawns. As we walked down the street and turned the corner, I could see a small group of people standing on the grass in front of an apartment. Raymond said, "That's Jimel with the lumber jacket on." I saw a stocky, light-skinned guy with a large Afro standing off to the side looking guarded and uneasy. Raymond introduced Jimel to me. It was a tense moment when Raymond's homeboy Head had to be held back, and Jimel threw up his dukes in defense. That's when Raymond asked Jimel, "Is it going to be Crip or what?" Grudgingly, Jimel said, "Yes." They shook hands.

During the drama I was scanning the area for a possible ambush while Buddha fidgeted with the .38 in his waistband. At one point Buddha whispered in my ear, "Cuz, when are we going to blast these fools?" I told him to be cool, let's see what happens. While Buddha paced back and forth behind us, another homeboy named Herc nervously looked around with his hand on a gun inside his jacket pocket. When we left, Head was mumbling angrily, "I can't stand that dude, we don't need him anyway!" But Raymond had a mischievous grin on his face. "Well, Tookie, that's more added to the east side."

In the truck driving back to the park Head told me Jimel turned Crip because he didn't want to fight a war he couldn't win. Plus he was having too many problems with some of the neighboring opposition like the Wall Nuts and Bishops gangs. Jimel did have influence over a small cadre of youths in the Avalon Gardens. They too would become a part of the East Side Crips regime. While Raymond was around, Jimel and company were simply East Side Crips. But later, when Raymond went to prison for a murder-related charge, Jimel and company became the Avalon Garden Crips. Raymond was the unchallenged leader of the entire East Side Crips regime, as was I with the West Side Crips.

Both Raymond and I were out constantly mobilizing and expanding our horizons without encroaching on one another's area. Shortly after recruiting Jimel, Raymond introduced me to a gang that had turned Crip. The gang he proselytized was the Compton Pirus whose name became the Piru Crips. They were having a party in Compton to celebrate. I assumed Mac Thomas had sanctioned the alliance since he reigned over the Compton Crips, who were growing quickly. But unknown to me, Mac and Raymond were in conflict over the alliance with the Pirus, who Mac said were his eternal enemies. This entente that Raymond had inaugurated was about to take a turn for the worse.

As our convoy of trucks and cars arrived at the Pirus' party, I saw Mac sitting across the street on the hood of a car. After a lengthy conversation with Tam, Puddin, and other Pirus, I walked over to where Mac was brooding. He launched into a tirade about not trusting the Pirus. He complained about Raymond trying to compete with me for new recruits and said Raymond had no idea what was going on in Compton or with the Pirus. I listened as Mac talked about possible ambushes against his homeboys because Raymond had familiarized the Pirus with their hangouts. Mac gave his ultimatum: either the Piru and Crip alliance ended or he'd part ways, but remain allies with the West Side Crips, if I agreed. Mac predicted the Piru-Crip alliance would not last, even if he had to break it up himself.

The alliance was flawed from the start. First, the Compton alliance was an offense to Mac since Raymond didn't discuss it with him until after the fact. Second, the Pirus were Mac's nemesis—and third, the alliance could pit the Compton Crips against the Piru Crips and also against Raymond's East Side Crips. I would be placed in a position to choose sides or try to be nonpartisan, which was next to impossible. I knew if push came to shove, I'd choose whatever was best for the West Side Crips.

I liked Mac Thomas. He was a short, muscular, brown-skinned powder keg that didn't take much to ignite. Thus far, the bad history between him and the Pirus hadn't been revealed to me in detail, but I understood how some scars were too deep to allow certain alliances. I continued to listen to Mac while greeting numerous Crips showing up late. Buddha, Herc, Bub, Raymond, and others were inside the house party enjoying themselves. It was a gangsters' soiree, Crips and Pirus in thuggish attire and women galore.

The festive setting was interrupted with the sound of breaking glass, shouting, cussing, and Buddha's voice above it all: "Let's take it to the streets!" The house lit up, and people started hurriedly filing outside, getting into their cars and screeching off. When Buddha stormed through the door, Mac and I jumped off the car and crossed the street. I could see Raymond and several Pirus following Buddha and Herc outside. They were arguing about some brim hat Buddha took from a Piru. Guns were drawn in hopes of restoring a sense of order. Raymond complained that Buddha was trying to sabotage the alliance on purpose, which Buddha said was a lie. It didn't matter to me whether Buddha was at fault. In my eyes he could do no wrong. To a stunned audience, Mac boasted, "I'm glad the alliance is broken! If Buddha didn't break it up, I would have." Raymond spit back, "I don't want to hear that crap, fool!" For a moment Mac and Raymond stood eyeing each other, then Raymond shook his head in disgust and continued trying to salvage a broken alliance. Mac was all smiles because the alliance was ended.

The Piru Crips was the shortest pact in the history of black gangs. The Pirus became the Compton Crips' most deadly enemy. Mac was right—the Pirus were able to ambush Crips' hangouts with regularity. But the West Side Crips, the Compton Crips, and the East Side Crips remained faithful allies with no internal warfare. But Raymond would always despise Buddha and Mac for what happened that night. He indirectly blamed me for the break.

A short time later, Bonnie and I were sipping fruit punch at a Washington High School dance and listening to Buddha's tirade about the aftermath of the Forum concert and Compton party. He said he was tired of all the busters (cowards or squares) creeping up on us with guns, that we needed to fight fire with fire, wipe them all out. "I'm obligated to protect you, Tookie, and if I have to, I'll die trying!" Bonnie's eyes widened in surprise.

Before I was able to respond, Mad Dog came storming in, angry about our homeboy Cuz being jumped on by some Figueroa Boys whom we had mobbed for their leather coats at the Los Angeles Forum. I rushed outside to see Cuz standing in a huge crowd of Crips with a swollen jaw, busted lip, torn shirt, and knots on his forehead. Cuz was a lanky, six-foot homeboy with the heart of a warrior and now a casualty of retaliation. We moved out. When we reached the corner of 108th and Normandie, a caravan of ten low riders cruised by with Figueroa Boys hanging out the windows shouting vulgarities and challenging us to a gang fight. The Figueroa Boys parked their cars on 106th and walked toward us. We started walking from 108th and then picked up the pace to a slow trot, gaining momentum. As both sides neared the corner of 107th Street, gunfire rang out, causing everybody to scatter. Within minutes there were sirens blaring and police cars everywhere. It felt good to make it home safely and to have avoided the police dragnet around the area.

Later that week, in class, I was reading an essay entitled "What Would I Do If I Was Rich?" when school guards and several detectives entered the classroom looking for me and Mad Dog. We were led out of school, handcuffed, and driven in separate cars to Lennox Police Station. I was thrown in a different cell than Mad Dog. I steeled myself for the inevitable interrogation. I tried to figure out why we were dragged down to the hell-hole. I was escorted to another small room and seated under bright lights across from two plainclothes policemen. One of them asked if I had attended a dance at Washington High Friday night, and I shook my head no. That pissed him off, and he said, "Nigger, stop lying!" The other detective spoke in a milder tone and said that they had witnesses willing to testify that I was present at the dance and the murder. The word "murder" resounded in my head: Are these fools kidding? In silence I tried to read their stony faces, hoping this was a cruel joke.

The two detectives huddled in a corner within earshot, discussing whether they would place me in a cell with adult murderers who would kill me. One of the detectives eased behind me, then snatched the chair from underneath me. Hitting the floor hard, I gritted my teeth and tried to mask the pain. After being snatched up and shoved back in the chair, I heard one of them say, "He's just a juvenile." The other said, "There's no age limit on charges of murder. We have enough witnesses to charge him with first-degree murder. He'll get the death penalty." Their psychological gymnastics to scare me into spilling my guts failed. I was returned to my cell, still in handcuffs, and before long Mad Dog was thrown in the cell with me. Together we sat there cursing at the detectives, who occasionally peeped in at us. To ease our nerves, we laughed and joked around, but I said a silent prayer to be cut loose.

Mad Dog and I were released to our parents. I put the ordeal behind me. A couple of weeks later, my mother was contacted by the parents of Clint, an East Side Crip, and an attorney, asking that I testify on Clint's behalf at juvenile court. Taking the witness stand seemed harmless enough. I confirmed his statements that we were together and didn't see anything. Clint walked away from his charges, but later I heard Raymond and Bulldog had been connected to the murder and were doing time. While Raymond was incarcerated, several Crips from the East Side regime rose to positions of independent commanders but remained part of the East Side collective. Before Raymond's incarceration, at the Watts Festival at Will Rogers Park on the east side, Raymond introduced me to Mac Thomas, Mad Dog David, Little James, Eddie, Black Johnny, and a host of other Crips. (This was just prior to the short-lived Piru-Crip alliance.) There was an immediate rapport with me, and among all of them, that continued to grow through the years. Mac was beginning to build the infrastructure of the Compton Crips. Before long Little James and Mad Dog David established themselves as commanders of the east side. Black Johnny would become the commander of the 43rd Street Crips.

The Crips was a vehicle to provide us with illusionary empowerment, payback, camaraderie, protection, thuggery, and a host of other benefits. We wanted to be exempt from being disenfranchised, dys-educated, disempowered, and destitute, but opportunities for us were scarce. We were seventeen-year-olds with minds polluted by misconceptions, and we wanted to be emancipated from the struggle against the conditions seeking our extinction or emasculation. But regardless of the hostile opposition or lack of social privilege, my vested interest, like everyone else's, was simply to survive. The Crips became central to my self-destructive resolve.

This forgotten generation created a quasi-culture with its own mores, style of dress, hand symbols, vernacular, socioeconomic qualities, martyrs, rituals, blue color identification (for Crips), legends, myths, and codes of silence. There were coined words for our madness. Buddha called it "Cripping" or "Crippen." The newly found pride in the alliance gave birth to Crip mottoes such as "Crippen night and day is the only way," Craig's phrase. Melvin's favorite was "Can't stop, won't stop." Buddha's brainchild was "Crips don't die, we multiply." Raymond's favorite was "Chitty chitty bang bang, ain't nothin' but a Crip thang."

"Do or die" was a common expression among us, on both east side and west side. Crippen was our raison d'être, our reason for being. It grounded us in a way that nothing else had. It permitted us to lash out at gangs and at a world that despised our existence. This was an apocalyptic moment for countless black youths. Merely to survive each day was a personal victory. Our alliance was beginning to be noticed, and we were widely reviled.

Deprived by our color and class of access to the American dream, we began a Crip-walk toward self-destruction.

The Criplettes

I n 1971, during the same month of the Crips' origination, there
emerged a female version of ourselves, the Criplettes. They gained
notoriety for their indiscriminate attacks on both female and male
opponents, overwhelming them with numbers and jacking them for
their possessions. The founder of the Criplettes was my then-
girlfriend Bonnie Quarles. She resembled a younger Aretha Franklin.
Bonnie's close cousin Sheryl and I knew each other from school, and
Sheryl wanted me to meet her. Though Bonnie wasn't enrolled at
Washington High, I met her during a couple of my classes that she attended regularly, where she did whatever she pleased due to a doting
male teacher's approval.

Before Bonnie, Sheryl, and others were Criplettes, they were
groupies hanging around us. Eventually they became girlfriends to
some of us. They didn't fit the old profile of female gang members—
masculine, dirty, scarred, or nasty-looking. But in spite of their fresh,
innocent good looks, they were gaining a reputation for fighting both
in school and in the 'hood. Before long Bonnie's vanity and her need
to impress me gave birth to a girl gang trying passionately to emulate
us, and succeeding with deadly precision. I felt it was absurd for any
woman to adopt the dangerous lifestyle of ganghood like hardheads.
Some homeboys enjoyed watching women wrestling and fighting, but
I was neither interested nor excited. In fact I was revolted by the

Criplettes' similar misdeeds. I strenuously objected to Bonnie and her friends' fighting and trying to follow us to gang fights.

A handful of them—Bonnie, L'il Jackie, Black Connie, Bad Bessie, Goldie, Pretty Connie, Big Pam, Cookie, and others—etched their names in street infamy. Long life was no more promised to a Criplette than it was to any Crip. Drugs were destroying their lives, and bullets penetrated their beautiful black skin like anyone else's.

Bad Bessie had a face and body that made her the spitting image of the entertainer Lola Falana. She was a throwback to a 1920s gun moll but willing to do her own dirty work. Like a black widow spider, she would lure the opposition into her lair where Crips awaited. Motivated by lust and imagination, our unsuspecting foe followed Bad Bessie, the pied piper, to a beat-down, a financial loss, or to their demise. Bessie often dressed in a beige khaki suit, brown suede boots, and a brown Stetson hat. She was a trigger-happy gunslinger and a marksman. She practiced with pellet guns, .22 caliber or a .38 caliber muffled by compressed steel wool, twine, copper wire, and other items she bragged about. Her silencers seemed to work. Everybody wanted one.

As a rule I kept Criplettes away during gang warfare. Females were a distraction to an undisciplined homeboy. I have childhood scars on my forehead as a constant reminder. But Bad Bessie was different. She hung around Crips instead of Criplettes and was respected for keeping her mouth shut under the pressure of cops. She could stroll right up to a rival, blast him, and then calmly walk away. Bad Bessie's "gun rep" made her a wanted Criplette, and she was shot a couple of times. In a gang shoot-out with the Figueroa Boys, Bad Bessie was caught in crossfire and was shot about fifteen times. Buddha and other Crips who were present told me she died on the spot. Rumors later had her paralyzed from the waist down and living out of state. For a short while Bad Bessie was my best-kept secret, both from our opposition and from Bonnie.

Another one of Bonnie's homegirls, Pretty Robin, was also beautiful: cocoa-brown skin, a giant jet-black Afro, and a statuesque body.

She could've graced the cover of a popular magazine but aspired to be a Criplette. Although Pretty Robin did a lot of fighting and a little shooting, her favorite pastime was with reefer, bottle, or a glue bag. She was out to prove to any of us that she could outdrink, outsmoke, outsniff and outhigh any man. The new high for a while was a spot remover, ominously called Cryptonite, that fried brain cells like sausages. I tried it once and was zombified, scared straight—but to Pretty Robin, no high was too high. In her first experiment with Cryptonite, this seventeen-year-old died on the spot from cardiac arrest.

The Criplettes' legacy continues to serve as a deadly archetype for other young black women who have abandoned hope.

14

Tookie's Law

M urphy's Law—"If anything can go wrong, it will"—was hand-made for my life. My resolute struggle for order was unhinged by a conflicting need to indulge in the temptations of chaos and youthful indiscretion. I couldn't help myself in spite of myself— that was Tookie's Law.

Washington High was probably the safest school on the planet while I was enrolled there—it became the West Side Crip capital, and every local gang under the sun kept a safe distance. Crips went back and forth to Washington High so frequently that they appeared to have visas and diplomatic immunity. It was as if the school ceded its authority to us, resulting in a total breakdown of control and order, and of the teacher-student relationship.

As far as I was concerned Washington High was Crip High. We were in control. There was no gang bigger or stronger, no gang tough enough to dethrone us. For a short while Washington was a Crip paradise. We lounged around, got loaded, gambled, and pursued young women for sexual conquests. All was mellow until the day we entered the school cafeteria with shaved heads. This evoked snickers from a crowd of beefy football players and their women. Seconds later a few of the football players were stretched out on the floor, and the rest had fled.

After the cafeteria brawl the gloves were off. All guys were potential prey for us, in particular football players. It was a training ground for Crips, honing their thuggery at school and then venturing out to maraud others, block by block and then mile by mile throughout South Central. Like locusts we swarmed and stripped people of their valuables—and then melted quickly away. Leather coats and jewelry were the hot commodities, as precious to us as ivory and animal skins were to blacks in Africa. Our activity created schisms through-out the community, between parent and child, church and child, school and child, society and child. I'm certain that even the angels wanted no part of our forgotten generation. Everybody was caught off-guard by our rapid expansion. Even local black politicians who claimed to be in touch with the community didn't have a clue.

Crips were everywhere, visible day and night. There was even a song, "Crip Dog," played on Los Angeles area radio stations for a short time during the mid-1970s.

Bonded by our commonality—low economic status—the Crips became my family. I placed Crip above and beyond all else, even my life. Survival in this community meant slim pickings for a black youth such as myself, but as a Crip I could strive to be legendary. It was my intent to make "Crip" and "Tookie" synonymous, a matched set and a terrorizing force among every other black gang in South Central. My lack of anonymity and my obsession to be recognized enabled the school administration to identify me as the West Side Crips leader named Tookie, and expel me. It was a blow to my ego to be thrown out of a school I was supposed to reign over.

The following week when my mother and I entered Fremont High School for my registration, there were East Side Crips everywhere calling, "Tookie, Tookie!" My mother looked puzzled and asked, "Who in the world are all those hoodlums dressed like you?" When I said, "They're my cousins," she shook her head and shouted back, "Boy, I know all your cousins. They aren't any of my sister's kids!" I wasn't about to tell her that this school was the East Side Crip capi-tal, that those hoodlums were my relatives of a different kind. The very next day, in first period, a counselor escorted me out of class to the principal's office. It had been brought to his attention that I was Tookie, a known troublemaker to most local schools, and that I was a close friend of one Raymond Washington, another unruly youth who hung around the school. The principal said there were already too many problems at Fremont with Raymond and company to take on any more. So he politely apologized for the inconvenience—and then expelled me.

I was blackballed (no pun intended) by Crenshaw, Manual Arts, Inglewood, Gardena, Los Angeles High, and all the rest. The institute of learning supposedly tailor-made for me was California High, an all-boys' school formerly known as Reese School for Boys. California High was located near downtown Los Angeles. The school was a tall yellowish building with no windows, a steel mesh cage on top of the roof (a foreboding lookalike to the fenced exercise yards where I'd work out a decade later, on top of San Quentin's North Seg building), and thick chains and locks on the doors. The front door was patrolled and heavily guarded by rent-a-cops.

There was a large yellow school bus that started from Imperial Avenue and picked us up along Broadway Street. The bus was said to be carrying a bunch of society's degenerates and retards incapable of functioning normally in public schools. Actually the bus didn't faze me. It was the school I disliked. There weren't any female students. It reminded me of the Job Corps, Camp Rocky, or Central Juvenile Hall.

I managed to stay at California High for several months, though I did a lot of ditching. I didn't get kicked out for truancy but for a conflict with a guy whom I tried to choke out with a hoisting chain in auto shop. The teacher who intervened stammered with a Jamaican accent and jabbered about solidarity, unity, honor, and black power. I couldn't tell the teacher the other guy had pulled a knife on me at lunch, and this was my payback. After this incident, there were no more schools in the city willing to accept me.

I'm sure my mother missed the old days when biblical punishment was in effect, but that ended at fifteen when I was strong enough to catch her firm hand in midair. No more thick switches, leather straps, extension cords, or locking me outside the apartment. Now she ordered me to find a job—but where and doing what? Each morning when I left the house, it wasn't to hunt for employment. I was looking for gangs, leather coats, and women.

The Crip evolution had me spinning in fast forward. While mobilizing and expanding, I forgot that, back at home on 90th Street, I had befriended two brothers, Ronnie and Donnie, who had influence over thirty to forty other youths, mostly relatives and childhood buddies. They were jolted with excitement when I revealed that their buddy Stan was actually Tookie. Donnie whispered, "That's Tookie of the Crips, right?" I told them we were the West Side Crips and there were Crips on the east side and in Compton. When I said, "I want you both to be part of our Crip family," they looked at one another with huge grins. Then Donnie replied, "Of course, we've been waiting for this!" Ronnie, Donnie, and their homeboys would become known as the Budlong Street Crips.

Though my own recruiting efforts were beginning to taper off, my homeboys had the good judgment to enlist whomever they felt worthy of being a Crip. But hordes of other youths would track me down to enlist in our youthful army. I recall walking down 90th Street toward Budlong with a group of homeboys when two youths approached us, identifying themselves as Big Bamm and Buck. When Bamm asked which one of us was Tookie, Buddha, cradling his gun, said, "That's Tookie right there. What's the problem?" Big Bamm eyed Buddha for a split second, then like others before him, he expressed interest in being part of the Crips. En route to Saint Andrews Park I planned to take Bamm and Buck into our junta against other gangs. Recruiting was a natural process for me, a combination of observing a youth's street genetics, vibe, intuition, or evil connection. We just clicked. In lieu of the archaic gang tradition of "jumping in" a new member, I instituted an initiation by battle, requiring a new member to test his mettle against the opposition—not against his own homeboys. Everybody I embraced was a mirror image of myself. We swaggered with a defiant arrogance that screamed, "No one can whip me—no one!" That night, during several parties we crashed, Bamm and Buck initiated themselves into our Crip violence.

About a week later I met a youth named Alfred Coward, aka Whitey, a former Denver Lane gang member, at a Sportsman Park Boys' party where he and others were refused entry. After my homeboys and I demolished the Sportsman Park Boys, I introduced myself to Whitey: "By the way, my name is Stan but my friends call me Tookie. We are the Crips!" Even in the dark I could see his eyes widen to the size of silver dollars. That evening Whitey participated in a Crip stomping of the Sportsman Park Boys that earned him his way into our youth army. Later Whitey would ask me to give him a new nickname. I named him "Blackie" for no particular reason, and it stuck. Later, the person I called Blackie, whose life I saved on several occasions, would become a Judas and lie on me.

Like most of my homeboys in this volatile microcosm, I didn't dwell upon death. Blind ignorance made me indifferent to its possibility. Though my homeboys began to be killed off, my inner self remained untouched. I shed no tears. Growing up I had seen enough ruthlessness to desensitize me. By lashing out at gangs and the world, I felt no empathy, no penitence for what I touted as the ultimate display of manhood. At seventeen and a half I could not feel others' suffering or the loss of a loved one they felt. I stared at the corpse of each friend as if they were sleeping or in a drug-state coma. To me they were flashes of my future which I dared not face or feel.

There were Crips like Melvin's homeboy's fourteen-year-old brother Dee-Dee, murdered by the cops; Raymond's homeboy Craig, blown away by a vengeful adult; my homeboy Diver Dan, shot down because of his resemblance to me. I would have risked my life for them, but I lacked the humanity to mourn their deaths—even as I recognized that death would one day visit us all. I saw dying as the end of the losing equation in the scheme of survival. All of us Crips had witnessed death enough times to know of its inevitability. None of us wanted to die—but our haphazard style of existence was a form of hara-kiri.

If I wasn't undergoing near-death experiences in the gang area then I was clashing with the other maniacal foes, the 'hood cops, who could now identify me on sight. Like other blacks from my neighborhood, it was instinctive for me to run from the cops to avoid harassment, getting set up, brutalized, or killed. I knew that cops had carte blanche to violate my rights or blow me away, which made me nervous. Black people have known for many, many years that some white cops are racist, despite society's bland denials.

One evening while exiting a liquor store on Century and Budlong with Buddha, Herc, Monk, and Blackie, a lone cop car cruised by, then made a U-turn after catching sight of us "walking while youthful and black," a serious offense then and to the present moment. Two cops jumped out of the car, and one of them hollered out, "Halt, Tookie, halt!" I darted away, crossing the street under cover of darkness, and heard a volley of shots. Time slowed. I felt as if I was running in place on a treadmill. Bullets whistled by me as I ran through a vacant lot and cut into an alley. I stepped into a hole and flew out into the air, landed on my stomach, jumped up, and continued to run. Soon the entire area was alive with Lennox patrol cars and a helicopter. I was cornered in a backyard. The cops were doing door-to-door searches for a man who allegedly shot at a policeman. It was only a matter of time before I'd be discovered hiding in an old shed. I didn't expect to make it out alive. I heard the cops enter the backyard. I could see their flashlights shining through the tiny cracks in the shed. Seconds later the door swung open, revealing shotguns pointing inside, voices ordering me to not move. It was chaos. Some cops were telling me to lie down, stay still, while others hollered I should walk toward them with my hands in the air. Each command was punctuated with ". . . or I'll blow your black head off!"

An elderly black woman peeped her head through the screen door and turned on the light. I could hear her shaky voice asking, "Is that the dangerous killer, officers?"

One cop spat out, "Yes, that's him, madam, and he's going to jail!"

She gasped, "Oh my Lord! Thank you, officers!"

After being handcuffed I was dragged through a gauntlet of flash-lights, batons, fists, and kicks to the body. By the time I reached the Lennox Police Station I was hardly able to walk. They dragged me along and threw me in a cell. Buddha had contacted my mother. She and Fred drove around hoping to find me before the cops did. When they showed up at the station the desk officer said the charge was an assault with a deadly weapon on a peace officer. The cops spread the canard that I had shot several times at a cop. My mother was frantic.

The following day the cops stood outside the cell door threatening to pay me back for shooting at their partner. Since I wasn't hand-cuffed or incapacitated, their threats meant nothing to me. Later on I was told there were investigators in the field looking for the gun they thought I had used to shoot at an officer. I knew in order for them to avoid a lawsuit and to justify the shooting, they had to play the cha-rade to the end. Since the mysterious weapon was never found, I was released after seventy-two hours. On my way out the sneering desk cop said, "You are one lucky nigger, because my partner is an expert marksman." Before I exited, out of my mother's earshot, I told the cop, "Well, that devil buddy of yours couldn't be too much of an ex-pert . . . the cracker missed!"

I had become the cops' prime target. It was a perilous badge of distinction. My mother, aware of the cops' dangerous potential, feared that one day she'd receive a call that cops had murdered me. In South Central it was common for mothers to not only worry about street elements devouring their son, but also to worry about death-by-cop. Next thing I knew, my mother and I were on a Greyhound bus bound for Oakland, California, where my biological father was living with a new wife, son, and daughter. The plan was for me to live with them. They hoped this would change my life.

I recall sitting in the back of my father's 1971 Eldorado Cadillac in the parking lot of some park. I sat there making noises, sucking my teeth, disinterested in hearing anything he had to say. He blab-bered about how I looked crazy wearing a wide-brim hat and a long cross earring, and then laughingly said, "Hell, only girls wear earrings!" I had to press my hands together so as not to sucker-punch him upside the back of his head. I didn't know this man nor did I care to, and there was absolutely nothing he could tell me. When he decreed that I was going to school every day whether I liked it or not, I asked, "Are you man enough to make me?" My mother intervened with, "Shut up, boy, and listen! That's the problem with you!"

After this one-sided conversation, we headed back to the motel where my mother and I spent the night before. She gathered her suitcase, kissed and hugged me, and said good-bye on her way out the door. Before my father exited he dropped six twenty-dollar bills on the bed and then left. Meeting my father was a moment of disconnection: his face was blurred, his spoken words were academic, and his eye contact was nonexistent. His strategy to use the hard-core approach to reach me was as impractical as a cop's attempt to terrorize me into social reform. It was a weird father-and-son encounter—total absence of recognition and a reception cold as ice.

My father didn't return, so that afternoon I left the motel, returned to Los Angeles, and stayed with my homeboy A.C. and his mother near 112th and Budlong. Living at A.C.'s mother's house suited me just fine. It was the main Crip hangout for ditching school, getting high, and sexual pleasures. When A.C.'s mother was at work, the house was a revolving door for women. It was there I met Joanne, who came by looking for her seventeen-year-old-daughter. We struck up a conversation, and were soon in her Lincoln Continental headed for her home in Gardena off Vermont. Though Joanne was thirty-six years old and married with five children my age and older, she could easily have passed for twenty-one. She was attractive and voluptuous. After the first time having sex with her, Joanne tripped me out when she led me into another room that was red-padded and had three tables with two blender machines and a huge wooden bowl filled with fresh fruit. Standing in a corner in her panties and bra trying to look defenseless, she asked me to throw some grapes, cherries, and apricots at her. She told me not to use the larger fruits because they were for someone else who liked to get hit with them. I thought probably her husband. I obliged her, though I was edgy about Joanne's fetish. I couldn't fathom the connection between sex and being pelted with fruit. But I wasn't the weirdo—plus, the sex was excellent.

On the eighth or ninth occasion Joanne picked me up right after I had gotten loaded, sniffing glue and smoking weed. After sex we headed to Joanne's padded fruit room. She stood in a corner and while I was throwing grapes, Joanne cried, "No, stop, don't do that!" When I stopped, she said, "No matter what I say or do, don't stop!" As I continued to throw the grapes Joanne said, "Throw them a little harder!" which I did. But when she screamed out, "Harder, harder," I started firing those grapes and cherries with the velocity of a Major League pitcher. When the bowls of grapes and cherries were empty, I pitched plums, oranges, apples, and cantaloupes. Being loaded, I seemed to be throwing the fruit in slow motion but was actually moving at the speed of an animated cartoon character. When I ran out of fruit I even threw the wooden fruit bowls and the blenders. After regaining my composure, I saw that Joanne was crouched in the corner, cowering and crying. We rode back in silence to A.C.'s place. I realized our sexual tryst was over.

When I wasn't kicking it at A.C.'s house, there were other activities to keep me busy. Once a mob of us Crips from the west and east sides caught a bus downtown. After mobbing a couple of clothing stores, I spotted a leather coat shop near a corner down the street from the Greyhound bus station. I knew exactly how to seize the moment and elevate my reputation. There were no less than twenty of us prepared to try on brand-new leather jackets. I told everyone to find themselves a coat of choice, and then said, "Let's go!" When the saleswoman asked, "Sir, how do you intend to pay for all of this?" I told her, "Put it on the Crip bill!" I kicked open the little wooden swing gate, and we all walked out.

While we were at a hamburger stand, Eddie, Archie, and I took off ahead of everybody to get first crack at the merchandise. At the front door of May Company, several patrol cars pulled up. The cops jumped out with guns drawn and ordered us to raise our hands. We were handcuffed, put in the backseat of a car, and driven down the street to be identified for a robbery. As the car pulled up, six youths standing outside of Clifton's restaurant on Broadway mistakenly identified us. Apparently there were other Crips around because we got busted for something we didn't do at Clifton's. The three of us were taken to the police station and placed in separate cells.

Tookie's Law was firmly in place.

15

Boys Republic to Factor Brookins

From the police station, I was sent to Central Juvenile Hall, then to Los Padrinos. During my brief stay at Los Padrinos, I had a fight with some Mexicans and some white dudes. In one instance, while playing football I ran into a Mexican dude and knocked him down, then he jumped up cursing and called me a stupid nigger, which resulted in my thrashing him. As I fought, I was being hit on the head and back with metal belt buckles by a group of his white and Mexican buddies. Standing on the sideline in a frightened nonpartisan stance were about twenty blacks who refused to budge. Out of nowhere a tall, skinny, and blond-haired white guy stood back-to-back with me knocking them down like I was. Afterward while sitting in a classroom for a few minutes I thanked the guy for having the heart to assist me, but we forgot to exchange names. When counselors brought in the group of white and Mexican dudes, all of them looked pretty bruised up. Seeing them caused both the white guy and me to look at one another, then burst out laughing. Though a truce was made, I knew never to turn my back because those guys could become super-dangerous.

When it came time for the court judge to make a decision between Youth Authority and Boys Republic, I was shipped off to the latter. Boys Republic was located in Chino, California, down the road from Chino State Prison. The entire facility was huge, with about five cottages, each one two stories high with a lot of bedrooms. There was a large church, gymnasium, school building, workshops, football and track field, weight room, refreshment store, cattle, and other things I had never seen. I wasn't at Boys Republic a full week when I got into a fight in the wood-shop class with several Mexicans and whites. The blacks there had left me high and dry, but I got hold of a wooden table leg and chased my assailants out. No surprise: the only one ending up in the lockup was me. Despite my own bruises, I guess it looked pretty bad, me standing there with a bloody table leg in my hand.

After being in the Central and Los Padrinos lockup units, this was no different. I was isolated from other youths. There were no books, letters, or any kind of materials to occupy my time. When I wasn't sleeping, I was doing hundreds of push-ups or shadow-boxing, essential conditioning for gang battle. There were moments in my solitude when I reflected on my existence, wondering if this was all life had to offer. Such thoughts really didn't matter. Tomorrow seemed eons away. I lived only for today.

Isolation in the lockup unit was designed to overpower a prisoner's mind with diffidence and fear, to shock a person into rehabilitation, nihilism, or psychosis. In the event this didn't work, there were plenty of prisons, asylums, and graveyards to accommodate the failed prisoner. This was a reality too profound for me to articulate or to write home to "Moms" about. But I resisted its subtle coercions.

Once outside lockup I was greeted as a warrior by a group of blacks who proudly shook my hand. The telling and retelling of the wood-shop incident had been hyperbolized with biblical overtones, as though I had beaten down over twenty enemies with the jawbone of an ass. A stocky black teenager of my age named Barker revealed that the dudes I beat with the table leg hated blacks and pretty much called shots on everybody. He went on to say the majority of blacks here were busters and didn't want any problems, but if need be, he, George, Psycho, and others were ready to fight. Barker was from Los Angeles, on 90th Street, but had spent years in and out of state institutions since the age of twelve. When I introduced myself as Tookie, Barker's eyes lit up. He said, "Yes, I heard of you, the Crips, the Crips!" He shook my hand for so long I had to use force to retrieve it. I ended up welcoming Barker and five of his friends into the West Side Crips, and awhile later, following his release, he became one of the commanders of the Budlong Crips.

Christmastime brought the annual Boys Republic tradition of making Christmas ornaments. Any youth wanting to earn a furlough home had to reach a specific quota, making ornaments to attach to the wreaths. I reached my quota and earned the furlough. My mother and Fred came to drive me home—and the next day put Cynthia and me on a Greyhound bus to New Orleans. They intended to keep me out of trouble during my furlough by sending me to New Orleans where there were lots of relatives and no hoodlum friends. Cynthia stayed in the front house with Momma (my grandmother) and Aunt Dorothy. I stayed upstairs in the back with my cousins Sonny and Turo. Both of them were amazed at my garb and asked did all California teenagers dress like I did? I told them, "Of course not, only Crips dress this way." I explained a bit to them about the Crips then changed the subject.

When I wasn't with Momma enjoying her company and her home-cooked meals, I was working out with a sixty-pound dumbbell I tucked away in a travel bag. Once I ventured out to a seedy spot in New Orleans where the price of ganja was ridiculously inflated: ten dollars for an itty-bitty matchbox of weed, compared to South Central's three- or four-fingered dope bag for the same price. My cousins—who were not into drugs—convinced me not to jack the dealer for his dope because it would have brought heat down on them.

My stay in New Orleans was quite nice, especially after I met a young lady whose hospitality was downright accommodating. Though I enjoyed the visit, I couldn't wait to get back to California. Soon Cynthia and I were waving good-bye and boarding a plane to fly back home. The next afternoon I was back at Boys Republic driving iron in the weight room with Barker. I was briefly involved in the football program, which I enjoyed. I played wide receiver because of my speed. Playing against the public schools was interesting, although we lost every game, but a fight or two would break out afterward, allowing us to end the evening with a win.

Sometime later, I gave the dorm leader a black eye for turning off the TV while we were watching it. I warned him not to snitch, but he did. The next day I was expelled and driven home. I warned the counselor driving the van that he better not try to take me to Juvey because I'd cause him to wreck. He assured me that was not his intent.

I arrived at home. My mother stared at the counselor through the screen door and asked, "What did he do this time?" The counselor told her I had attacked a white guy for no reason and gave my mother a number to call to find out what the courts planned to do with me. When he left I told my mother, "Don't waste your time calling those people. I'm not going back to Juvey. They'll have to catch me first!" There was no doubt in my mind the court's next step would be to send me straight to Youth Authority. I wasn't going willingly. My mother looked at me bleakly but didn't say anything.

When I called Buddha, he told me about a place called Factor Brookins in Banning, California, a little over a hundred miles from Los Angeles. He gave me the number for Bob Simmons, the director, who told me he would contact the courts and have me assigned to his program. After my mother called Bob, he called back to tell her that I was enrolled in his program and to bring me on Sunday before 3:00 p.m. to the park on Willow Brook off Compton Avenue, where a bus would be waiting. When we arrived there were two buses, a crowd of people—and Buddha standing next to his mother, grinning. While our mothers talked, Buddha told me that Banning was cool, that we'd get furloughs, and that several of our homeboys—Little James, Warlock, Monk, Melvin, and other Crips—were there. With all my homeboys around, I figured how bad could the place be? I hugged and kissed my mother good-bye, and the bus took off for a long drive.

Banning itself was a barren pastoral town with a single police station, a bank, a theater, a club, a park, and a hardware store. It was the polar opposite of the chaotic madness in the Los Angeles jungle. Factor Brookins was sponsored by a man known as Jake the Barber, an associate of the notorious Al Capone. The facility consisted of four long rows of furnished two-bedroom duplex apartments and plenty of food. Buddha and I shared an apartment where we put our weights in the living room. If ever there was a youth's fantasy of freedom, Factor Brookins was it.

Shortly after settling in I noticed tension between my homeboys and the local youths, since young Banning females often invited my homeboys to their picnics, house parties, and other social functions. At one of these gatherings, jam-packed with my homeboys and plenty of local girls, an upset crowd of local dudes challenged us to fight. When we went outside, they scattered. At 10:00 p.m. when the gathering ended, some of my homeboys jumped into cars or into the back of a truck, but I decided to enjoy the night air and walk back to the boys' home. Though he knew I disliked guns, Buddha tried to slip me a chrome snub-nose .38 that I pushed aside. In typical Buddha fashion he stated, "Well, since you don't want my piece, I'll walk too!" I grudgingly accepted the gun, shoved it down my waistband, and walked away. As the truck passed by, Buddha and the others hollered, "Crip here," then stopped. Out jumped twelve-year-old Little Tee, saying, "Buddha suggested somebody walk back with you, so I volunteered!"

It was therapeutic to inhale the crisp cool air and stroll down the street without a care in the world. Nowhere in Los Angeles was I able to feel as close to being liberated as I did at that moment. It was 1972, I was eighteen, the Crips gang wasn't even a year old—but we were the baddest human beings on this planet. I started doing the Crip walk taught to me by Dancing Sugar Bear, who originated it. But thuds and sounds of glass breaking shattered my mood. There were bricks raining down on us, and two of them hit me square in the chest with enough force to stun and knock me back. Instinctively I whipped out the gun and fired blindly into the darkness to scare my attackers. Tee and I trotted some distance until I stopped, bent over in pain. I told Tee to run ahead to tell the others what had happened.

I walked down the middle of the street peering around houses, vacant lots, and cars, anticipating another ambush, possibly with a volley of bullets. From a distance I could hear Buddha cursing and hollering out, "Who were those cowards? Let's go smash them." As Buddha, Warlock, and Little James got closer I could see guns in their hands and rage in their faces. I told them it was too dark to see who it was, but I was sure it was the country bumpkins who challenged us earlier then ran off. Buddha swore up and down he would avenge the attack.

As I climbed into bed that night I noticed two nasty and painful bruises. All I wanted to do was sleep the pain away, then come back strong for whatever. The last thing I remembered before dozing off was Buddha telling me, "This won't take long, Cuz. I'll be right back." Around 7:00 a.m. the next morning I heard the sound of a police radio and jumped up to see what was going on. Buddha was in the backseat of a patrol car, beaming with a wicked smile. As I approached the car, Bob told me Buddha was accused of shooting up the movie theater last night and that he'd blasted at some of the locals, hitting one of them. After Buddha emptied his gun, he calmly reloaded then started shooting at them again. He often acted as if he cared more about me than he did about himself. The car pulled away with Buddha in the backseat. I wondered how long it'd be before I saw him again.

Factor Brookins soon became co-ed. Bonnie was in the program, along with a few other Criplettes from Los Angeles. Later, she became pregnant. Though I felt proud to be a father, I didn't know the first thing about raising a child. I had problems raising myself. But my elation and uncertainty came to a halt a month later when Bonnie had a miscarriage. The baby would have been a boy. That week Bob and the counselor, Kenny, suggested I become a junior counselor with a salary. I could be a counselor, get paid—and still be able to go out Crippen.

Bob then came up with an outrageous idea: we would attend Banning High and play football for Banning. What school in their right mind would accept a bunch of high school rejects with criminal records? But Bob pulled it off and began to train us like professional football players. Each morning before 5:00 a.m. we were up running wind sprints, obstacle courses, and laps around the track prior to breakfast. I trimmed down from 175 pounds to 160 pounds in a matter of weeks, and though I had a lot of definition I felt skinny. By then Sweetback was in the program too, and joined the football team. We were in tiptop shape—a fast, vicious, talented crew of athletic misfits, the best players on the team, exceeding Bob's expectations. Here we were: Crips, playing team football, attending classes, and actually doing schoolwork. None of us even thought about ditching class or school. I was attending school and enjoying playing on the football team, without pretext or profit. For the first time in my chaotic life there appeared a chance to uplift myself.

One day, preparing to run wind sprints, I caught site of Buddha in a football uniform, Crip-walking across the football field chanting, "Crips don't die, we multiply!" He had been released, was enrolled in school, and on the football team. Everybody extended their cousin salutations to Buddha and went through our welcoming routine: a split-second hug, handshake, and a Kool-Aid smile. In our practices we dominated so much that Bob told us opposing coaches from other schools accused Banning coaches of hiring ringers who played semiprofessional football. It was discovered that we had criminal records and that no school in Los Angeles would enroll us. Pressure was placed on Banning High, and they kicked us out of school. This was not a surprise since I had never experienced true accomplishments. I viewed everything through a negative lens, expecting only the worst.

Since we seemed destined to end up in prison, a rehab clinic, or a local graveyard, I felt the need to continue striking blows at anything in the name of Crip. In my mixed-up world everything was twisted: sin was my morality, an immature perspective served as my wisdom, and war represented peace.

In spite of my Crippen ways I was still receiving a paycheck of

$125 every two weeks as a junior counselor. I started saving money to buy a car so I wouldn't have to steal one all the time. Cars were vital to us. Sweetback had a stolen 1963 cocoa-brown Malibu. He was so possessive of it that he attacked our homeboy Cuz for spilling ketchup on it. Herc was so attached to his stolen 1964 Chevy that he bought new brakes and a new ignition for it. He kept that car for a year until he wrecked it during a shoot-out. The longest I held on to a stolen car was for two days, thinking that by then it would be on every cop's hot sheet.

I planned to give most of my paycheck to Bonnie to stash and attend a big dice game held in one of the apartments. Buddha enjoyed gambling and was darn good at losing all of his money. Every youth in the program received an allowance of fifty dollars twice a month and most of them gambled—but Bob or one of his buddies usually would win. Whenever the sole Los Angeles Brim, Little Dodi, won the jackpot, everybody wanted to rip him apart, and I had to prevent it. But once in a while a novice would win the jackpot—and this time it was me! I left with six hundred dollars! The next day I ran across a car outside the area of Banning where we lived. Catching my eye was an immaculate 1963 metallic gold Lincoln Continental with snow-white leather interior and suicide doors. After a smooth test ride I paid five hundred dollars for it, then drove it back to the boys' home. Buddha said, "Cuz, that's you, that car fits you to a tee." Everybody commented on how sharp, classy, and gangsteresque the car looked.

During our next furlough to Los Angeles, Buddha and I were scouring the area to appropriate a set of wheels with Cragar rims for my car. Spotting this guy Odel with a brand-new set of Cragar rims, I convinced him to follow me to a vacant house. Once there I coerced him to take the wheels off his car and then place them on mine. They were a perfect fit. Next, we had hydraulic lifts put in the front and thick whitewalls from the House of Chrome that gave my car a 1920s gangster look. The Lincoln was a real head-turner, a modern army tank creeping through enemy territory ready to do battle.

With a flamboyant air that surpassed Marcus Garvey's, I'd arrive on a scene, Buddha and I in the backseat and Herc driving. We'd step out in complete Crip attire with fancy wooden canes and a readiness to engage in combat. The arrival of the Lincoln struck terror that had my rivals fleeing on sight. The car also became a target for police harassment. I'd get pulled over several times within a radius of ten blocks. Under the watchful single eye of their revolver they'd hold me curbside hostage until a search of my car was complete. Throughout the day I'd be tag-teamed again by the Lennox sheriffs, the Los Angeles police, or the Firestone police harassing and searching for contraband. In front of Bonnie one cop scratched the serial numbers off my tape deck then arrested me for receiving stolen property. While I sat in jail, there was a seventy-two-hour investigation that culminated with the charges being dropped.

Plenty of times when the cops pulled me over and found nothing incriminating, they'd arrest Bonnie for truancy. She was seventeen and required by law to be in school. I thought marriage would resolve the problem. On our wedding day there were torrential rains, the window button on the driver's side was stuck, the window wouldn't close, and I got soaked. The wedding was simple and brief: no tuxedo, wedding gown, wedding ring, wedding cake, and no traditional honeymoon. Since Buddha wasn't on hand as best man, Bimbo substituted as witness and rice thrower. Being callow and unpolished, I didn't take the marriage seriously even though Bonnie was devoted and loving. I was loyal to Crippen and nothing else. Our wedding day was expedient and unsentimental. After the ceremony I dropped Bonnie off at her mother's house and went on my merry way.

The following day I was out caravanning with Buddha and other homeboys in a turquoise LeMans he had bought. We went to a self-service car wash on Western around 74th Street. While washing my rims I saw a couple of carloads of dudes drive up and park on the side street. As two people got out of the car and walked toward us, Buddha boldly confronted them and questioned their motives. Trigger-happy Herc stood off to the side. I stood up and walked toward Buddha. The larger of the two introduced himself as Big James and the slimmer fellow as Michael. As I got closer I heard Buddha say, "Well, there's Tookie. What's up?" After introducing himself to me, James stated he'd been hearing a lot about the Crips and that he wanted to join us. He mentioned a dance at the Young Men's Christian Association (YMCA) behind the Crenshaw Mall where we could meet later that night. Buddha kept tapping me on the arm, whispering, "Cuz, I don't trust this dude!" But I waved him off and told James we'd be there.

Buddha reminded me after they'd left that the YMCA was in the same area where we had raided several of the Rebel Rousers' parties a week before and seized a bunch of leather coats. But I didn't forget; I simply didn't care. I was no zip-zam fool. I did do some asinine things, but usually there was a method to my madness (except when I was loaded). I saw this as an opportunity to expand the West Side Crips and was going to take it.

That night we showed up at the YMCA after 10:00 p.m. and parked our cars across the street in the shopping mall lot. I left my keys with Bonnie in my car, while L'il Jackie stayed in Buddha's car. I opted for just a handful of us to be there: me, Buddha, Herc, Blackie, and Monk.

The YMCA looked completely deserted. There were no other cars nearby. I felt a little uneasy, wondering if this was a setup. When we entered, the YMCA was jam-packed. People were bumping with the James Brown song "Pass the Peas." Though Big James was nowhere around, I decided to wait awhile to see if he showed up. A short time later this guy showed up saying, "Big James is outside waiting for Tookie." Once outside I saw James standing on the corner next to his homeboy Michael and another guy, who had one hand in his coat pocket. As soon as we stepped out into the open, more of James's homeboys appeared, surrounding us in a semicircle.

Standing in creepy silence, the breeze chilled me. Is this a setup, was Buddha right? I sensed James was stalling—but for what, reinforcements? I tried to calm myself knowing that Herc and Buddha were packing, but was it enough to ward off the larger numbers? The silence was driving me crazy. I didn't like feeling trapped or vulnerable. As I looked eye-to-eye with James, anger began to swell up within me and my patience wore thin. I could wait no longer; I spat out, "So what's it going to be James, Crip or what?" If something was supposed to happen, then let's get the show on the road! Standing there at six feet two inches and more than two hundred pounds, Big James was larger than me, but I believed in the legend that I was a giant killer. I saw indecision in James's eyes. I repeated the question with some heat, "What's it going to be, Crip or what?" Big James then broke the silence: "Yes!" After a brief handshake the tension relaxed, but heightened when a squad of cop cars descended upon us from every direction. A helicopter's spotlight beamed overhead. They ordered us to get down on our knees and lock our fingers on top of our heads. Though the cops didn't find any weapons on us, several were found a few yards away. That was enough to take all of us to jail.

Bonnie had the presence of mind to follow the police car to the station. Inside, the cops interrogated us one by one. Since no one talked, we were charged only with possession of a deadly weapon. That's when James's homeboy Paul spoke up, "There's no need to do that. The guns are mine." Riding a beef was common among my homeboys, but to witness someone do it outside our circle was unusual. I was impressed.

Later on, Big James assured me they were ready to become part of my West Side Crips. Big James and his crew would become known as the Harlem Crips. During a brief stint in the Los Angeles County Jail, I ran into his homeboy Paul, who revealed that they were supposed to smoke me on that particular night. They also planned to smoke the madman Buddha because he was too dangerous to leave alive if I was dead. That was to be retaliation for our mobbing and Crip-stomping some of their relatives and homeboys at a party. Paul said, "Cuz, we literally mapped out a plan to smoke you, but Big James didn't follow through." They were now West Side Crips. That's all that mattered to me.

Driving back to Banning I relished the moment, knowing the West Side Crips were evolving into the dynamic force I had envisioned at

Camp Rocky. While buffing iron in the apartment at Factor Brookins with Little James and Buddha, I rehashed the latest addition to the West Side Crips and how we would continue to grow. I jokingly told them, "The world will know exactly who the Crips are!" When it was my turn to work out with the barbell doing back-arms, I stood before the full-length mirror and boasted, "One day my arms will be so yoked up, no one will believe it!" But Little James interjected and said, "That's cool, Cuz, but what about a powerful chest?" He was right. I needed a monstrous, powerful chest. Little James worked his arms but he also worked on his chest. He was the first Crip among us who bench-pressed more than three hundred pounds. He was the one who encouraged me to start benching, and soon I was out-benching Little James and any other Crip. When I wore a short-sleeved shirt, my appearance had a noticeable effect on women. It was odd how I always felt twice as muscular as I really was.

Bob was increasingly aware of the gang epidemic spreading throughout Los Angeles and Compton. In addition to establishing more boys' homes, he wanted to bring public focus onto the serious youth problem. Bob published a small Compton newspaper with an article called "The Baddest," with Buddha, Little James, Warlock, Melvin, Sweetback, Monk, and me on the front cover. It introduced the city to a gang called the Crips blowing up in Compton and South Central. Occasionally Bob would set up youth prevention workshops to expose this plague, but his warning fell on deaf ears. It wasn't long after his attempt to warn the masses that the Factor Brookins program was terminated. Our refuge was gone. We were kicked back into the gut of South Central, and into full-time Crippen.

Mr. Buddha! Mr. Buddha!

His name was Curtis Morrow, aka "Buddha." He had almond-shaped eyes (that became slits when he was intoxicated), crowned by the bald roundness of his cranium. Buddha was five feet eight inches, about 180 pounds, stocky, with a baked-brown complexion. As a Crip, the essence of his persona was atrocious. His nature was disguised by an angelic countenance; he could explode in a pico-second with rage capable of humiliating the devil. As a human being he was no better or worse than others, but as a Crip he defied imagination. Whatever anyone may have thought about him, good or blasphemous, for me he was Mr. Buddha . . . my friend, my brother.

The first time Buddha met my mother, he made a favorable impression on her, surpassing any friend of mine she had ever met. To her, he was a consummate gentleman who spoke with the benevolent diction of a choirboy. My mother had often expressed in earnest, "Son, why can't you be like Curtis?" Around her or any Crip's mother, Buddha was gooey-nice. He possessed a humanity within his soul, but for an enemy—beware. I'm grateful he was on my side. Our rivals—or Crips themselves who had a legitimate reason to—feared the hell out of him. He and I met under violent circumstances. He was beat down and thrown into the street along with Monk. I believe Buddha squashed any thoughts of retaliation against us because he respected the force that dared to enter his world, his domain, and smash him like a fly. Tough as Buddha was, he recognized a collective might bigger and stronger than he was, and he joined it.

I was the mediator between Buddha's wrath and the world. He knew only one way of doing things—with radical fervor. But if he had even an ounce of respect for you, then he'd listen.

The terror he unleashed in the name of Crip was widespread, but I cannot detail his ruthlessness lest some fool try to duplicate his misdeeds.

Shortly after the termination of Bob's program, there was a problem brewing with another west side gang, the Hoover Groovers, who dressed exactly like the West Side Crips. Things had gotten out of hand when Little Chocolate, a member of the Hoover Groovers, was murdered. The mysterious killing of Chocolate and the shootings of other Hoover Groovers were blamed on the West Side Crips, but mainly on one person, Buddha. West Side Crips were ambushing the Hoover Groovers regularly, but neither Buddha nor any West Side Crips killed Chocolate. Buddha did hate him. While in Factor Brookins, Buddha had held a lit cigarette to Chocolate's forehead and dared him to move for such a long time that I had to snatch his hand away. Chocolate was not an innocent bystander. He couldn't fight a lick but he fancied himself as a pistoleer and was a known shooter for the Hoover Groovers.

Through Bimbo, I befriended some of the leaders of the Hoover Groovers when I attended Brett Harte Junior High. My homeboy Fat Riley came bearing an olive branch from the Hoover Groovers for a sit-down at Saint Andrews Park on Manchester Boulevard, a park we had anointed as our own. When Boo, Diamond, Donnie Boy, and Big Chocolate of the Hoover Groovers showed up, they were surprised to see the large throng of Crips and Criplettes hanging out, some playing football. They had to walk past them to get to where Buddha and I were sitting on a park bench. Bonnie and a few Criplettes were watching, sitting in the children's swing set.

It was probably by design that Big Chocolate spoke for the group. Although he and I had known one another since Brett Harte, things were different now that his younger brother had been killed. He started off with, "Rumor has it that Buddha killed Little Chocolate." Buddha jumped up and said, "What, fool? If I had smoked Little Chocolate, I'd tell you right here, right now. If you truly believed I was the killer, you wouldn't be here! We'd still be at war."

I calmed Buddha down, then told Big Chocolate, "Buddha didn't kill Chocolate, none of us did. But time will reveal all."

Big Chocolate went on to say they wanted to establish an alliance but not until they learned who was responsible for the killing.

Buddha rudely interrupted, "Look here, dude. We're the Crips. We don't need anybody!"

I could sense Big Chocolate was trying to be patient so I eased the tension by appeasing them both. I said, "Buddha is right, we don't need anybody, but Big Chocolate, you're right too. An alliance will benefit all of us. We can seal the alliance when we smash whoever smoked Little Chocolate!" The mention of revenge brought a smile to Big Chocolate's scarred face and to everybody present, even Buddha.

Though no master strategist, I knew that a prolonged war with the Hoover Groovers would create chaos among many of my homeboys who had relatives in the Hoover Groovers. The last thing I needed was a division within our ranks, so I was willing to forge the alliance. As soon as I shook hands with Big Chocolate and his homeboys, they left. Buddha smiled and said, "Cuz, you are a shrewd character." I shot back, "And you, my cousin, are a crazy, crazy character!" I told him I needed him to calm down because his outbursts could mess up my plans. I understood his frustration. I too was tired of all the drama but more and more I was learning about the need for tact and diplomacy. This was a street war on a smaller level; however, there was no difference between our mindset and that of a nation seeking to eliminate its enemies through whatever method . . . life or death!

The Hoover Groovers held the Figueroa Boys responsible for smoking Little Chocolate. The Figueroa Boys were already our rivals, and attacking them fit in with my strategy. But not only were they difficult to find, they operated with the stick-and-move ambush tactics of guerrillas. The Figueroa Boys were notorious for popping up when least expected and spraying the area with bullets. Fighting hand-to-hand was an alien concept to them. A pistol or rifle was more their speed. They were quite deadly until more Crips began to arm themselves. Then things changed.

Wherever the Figueroa Boys were discovered, they were ambushed with a hail of hot lead, something they weren't used to. Then fate dropped our enemy into our lap. The leader of the Figueroa Boys, R.M., happened to be in a nightclub on Vermont where the West Side Crips and Hoover Groovers planned to meet up. When we entered the club, one of the Hoover Groovers recognized R.M. partying on the dance floor. For him to look up and see the room filled with enemies staring him down was a nightmare. I'm sure he wished he could turn back the hands of time. His scrawny body bounced from fist to fist like a Ping-Pong ball till he bounced into Buddha's knuckles, which knocked him smooth out. Even after R.M. had been Crip-stomped twice and riddled with bullets to his chest, the deadly sneak-up artist and gunslinger survived the vicious ordeal. Later, the Figueroa Boys seemed to fade away. Word had it that R.M. and some of his homeboys moved to Pasadena or Pomona. Either way, the terror of the Figueroa Boys was a thing of the past.

The alliance with the Hoover Groovers—now known as the Hoover Crips—had been cemented by violence. This was around the time Buddha rapidly rose to the top of the heap as a number one terror, playing shoot-'em-up, armed with two or three guns. If Buddha's gun wasn't present, either his fists or a baseball bat would suffice. At Saint Andrews Park during a dice game, when he and some of our homeboys lost some money to this street hustler, he hit the guy with a baseball bat, knocked him cold, and put him into a coma. Buddha took all his money—for cheating. Months later, as I lay in bed with a female jack artist named Kriss, she told me that that hustler was her brother and he was no longer in a coma.

Though our rivals feared me above all, they feared me more because of Buddha and his relentless pattern of vengeance. One evening after leaving Buddha at his mother's house, I was on my way to pick up Bonnie when Lennox policemen spotted my Lincoln and pulled me over to the curb. They claimed there was a warrant for my arrest for attempted robbery. I was handcuffed, taken to the station, and booked. The next day, I was booked in the Los Angeles County Jail, waiting for arraignment.

Several weeks had passed. I was transferred to the old Los Angeles County Jail, where I became a trustee. I was stuck for months with a bond over $100,000, and I had to rely upon a public defender to get it reduced each time I appeared at court. When I was able to contact Buddha, he said, "Tookie, when you get out, we have a lot to talk about, and you won't like it!" Sensing it was bad news, I brushed it off, and then told him about our West Side Crips homeboy, Black Dog, who was in the Old County Jail with me. One day as I walked by the module where Black Dog was housed, he was engaged in a dispute over money. He and another guy stood face-to-face arguing, then the guy slapped the taste out of Black Dog's mouth. The slap sounded like a firecracker. I expected him to unleash a flurry of punches to down his attacker but Black Dog just stood there sniffling, tears streaming down his face. All I could do was curse out the guy who slapped Black Dog. I told Buddha, after that, "I refuse to talk to him anymore!" Buddha said, "Cuz, I would've done the same thing. What is this world coming to when a Crip can't defend himself?" To me even if a Crip loses a fight, just return and fight again. But for any Crip to accept being slapped was an insult to the Crip god. Hell, it was an insult to me! I had met Black Dog through Victor, a West Side Crip who was a formidable bully. In my mind's eye, Black Dog was now a speck, a nonentity, expelled from my consciousness.

With my bail reduced and my car sold to make up the needed difference, I bailed out of the county jail. The first thing Buddha and I talked about was the divisions that had occurred during my absence and how he wanted to cremate those responsible. I surmised it was a natural process for someone to assume a position of leadership when their leader is out of commission. Because of this, prior to the Crip regime, I intentionally kept the commanders of different 'hoods incommunicado from one another to eliminate any possible subversion. But here, I was the only link to connect the chain of different 'hoods that I had established individually. As expected, when any Crip tried to assume my role, he was renounced, which caused the commander of each 'hood to recoil into autonomy. The first time I recognized this phenomenon was while I was away in Boys Republic. My homeboy Melvin tried to seize the helm of the entire West Side Crip regime but was quickly rebuffed. Disenchanted, he back-pedaled to his own 'hood, which he named the Block Crips.

Once at Factor Brookins, Buddha and I had Melvin hemmed up in the theater restroom. I watched as Buddha with his hand on his gun demanded of Melvin that he reveal where his allegiance was. He snarled, "Cuz, do you think you're Tookie? Do you think you can take his place? Is this 'block' crap a sign of your being a leader?" Melvin's responses were "No, no, no!" He proclaimed his fealty to me, and though I accepted it, I despised him for even considering that he or anyone could replace me. There are four conditions with which to test a friendship: money, loyalty, women, and a secret. To violate even one of them is a sign of an enemy.

While Buddha and I were working for Bob Simmons as junior camp counselors in the mountains of San Diego, the unified West Side Crip regime started crumbling into factions. Buddha fiercely reminded me that Raymond's East Side Crips broke into numerous splinter groups after his incarceration, as did Mac Thomas's Compton Crips when he was locked up. The explosion of the West Side Crips was matched by a kind of implosion, Crip cells splintering, reforming, splintering again. Factions began cropping up all over, and the West Side Crips became a cluster of autonomous sets: The Block; Underground; Harlem; Budlong Street; Sportsman Park Boys; Inglewood; Hoover; Manchester Park; 83rd Street Gangsters; Raymond Avenue; Magnificent 7; Payback; Rolling 60s; Sunshine; Gardena; Hollywood; and many other West Side sets. Some of these were vying for supremacy amongst themselves. Prior to this set-tripping, it was unthinkable for Crips to be warring against other Crips.

With no single gang capable of matching the Crips numerically or brute force–wise, the Crips imploded by pitting Crip against Crip. Inevitably, the Crips proved to be no different than any government that creates its own bogeyman and believes in its own invincibility. Such an entity—be it a gang, tribe, or nation—will unwittingly defeat itself.

The Crip factions muddied my masterpiece and stung my ego. Buddha remained fixated on a St. Valentine's Day sort of massacre. But if Mac Thomas and Raymond could adjust to the changing times, then by all means Buddha and I could adapt as well. I was still the arrogantly irreplaceable Tookie. Despite the new names, the Crip faction commanders I knew personally still held allegiance to me and were West Side Crips. I maintained a following and respect across the board, and I prided myself on never messing over another Crip.

The west side was always rocking with parties, picnics, dances, clubs, and especially concerts. There was a time when a crowd of us stood outside Sweetback's mother's house making plans to go to a concert at the Los Angeles Palladium. But the anticipation of going—for Buddha and me—was spoiled when Bob Simmons pulled up in his Ranchero and told us that we were needed back at the camp. We wanted our paychecks, so off we went with Bob. It was good that we didn't go to the Palladium that night. We would have met the same fate as some homeboys charged with murder. Bob told us it was in all the newspapers about a gang of Crips killing another youth over his leather coat. Of all the Crips accused of the crime, Bub was the most recognizable, an all-American high school track star (though it frustrated Bub when he tried to outrun Sweetback and me and wasn't able to, whether we were intoxicated or not). All those who were charged with that murder were homeboys I grew up with from the 'hood. Most of them ended up doing time. The zeitgeist was changing. Cops were getting a lot of help solving crimes from people with diarrhea of the mouth. The Palladium incident, where a black life was lost and other black lives ruined, had absolutely no effect on Buddha or me. Crippen night and day was the only way.

Our lives were spared for a moment. Being in the mountains only a stone's throw from an Indian reservation was a peaceful way to kick back from the urban madness. It was mellow at the youth camp but our hearts yearned to be in the thick of things to appease our restless souls.

Still, this boys' home located in the mountains outside San Diego left an impression on me. I wrote a short story for children a few years ago about my experience there, which is excerpted below.

This boys' home looked like a summer camp, the kind you see on television. There was even a small lake with fish. Buddha and I had never seen anything like it in our entire lives. It was beautiful. There was a corral in which Bob kept pigs and hogs. This was very different from what we were used to in Los Angeles. In fact, for a while we didn't even take any furloughs because we didn't want to leave the place.

Although some of our homeboys moved into this new facility with us, most of the youths housed there were around 12 or 13—much younger than our average age of 19 or 20. But as a junior counselor, I didn't have any trouble with them. They had heard of me and Buddha so they knew better than to test us. I used to sit around and watch Buddha play football with the youngsters. He enjoyed it as much as I did. While watching them, I would think about the difference between the life we were living there and our South Central existence. But I had no intention of quitting the South Central life for good. Neither did Buddha.

Buddha and I enjoyed harassing the pigs and hogs in the corral. There was this giant black hog that would chase people, though he mostly left me alone. He saw me often because about every day I had to shovel the dirt and mud as well as feed this hog and the other animals. One day, after feeding the animals, I was turning over the dirt with the shovel while talking to Buddha when he hollered, "Watch out!" As I turned, I saw the big hog running straight toward me. In a split-second decision, I had to defend myself. I swung my shovel as hard as I could, smashing it against his nose. The hog immediately dropped down on his forepaws with his back legs still erect. The hog and I stood there, eyes locked on one another, as blood trickled out his nose. I was wondering if he would try to make another charge at me, so I wouldn't turn my back on him. Buddha asked if the hog was dead. The hog's eyes were still open, and I could see that it was breathing hard.

Much later—I kept watching him—the hog fell over on its side and died. That night Bob held a meeting to try to find out which of us killed the hog. During his long, heated lecture about the incident, he mentioned me as being the best example as to how the rest of the youngsters should act. Bob was confident that I would never do such a thing. As he complimented me, Buddha was nudging me in the side, grinning. I didn't smile because I felt strange about it. I hadn't intentionally killed the hog. Bob never did find out how that hog died.

Bob soon calmed down and things returned to normal. Instead of harassing the hogs and pigs, we went fishing out in the lake using homemade poles. We would paddle a small canoe to the middle of the lake and sit there talking and getting high off of weed. We'd always end up catching some fish and bringing them back to the cook. Bob would fry them for us with a lot of seasoning, often with french fries. It was all delicious.

In the middle of that small lake sitting in a canoe, Buddha and I had cast our baited hooks into the water. It was an odd thing, two youths from our background, fishing. Buddha chose that moment to become sentimental but warned me not to get a big head. He said, "Tookie, you are an older brother to me, and I respect you. I admire you, and as long as I breathe there's nothing I wouldn't do for you." The words chilled me, like a last rite I tried quickly to dismiss from my mind. Not knowing how to respond, I told Buddha, "Ah, shut up, Buddha, you're my Cuz, and you always will be!" It was a strange moment for both of us, trying to articulate a foreign emotion of brotherly love with that machismo thing in the way. He was the essence of a best friend, a brother I never had, always there for me. Even when I frequented a clinic for radiation treatments to stabilize my vitiligo—a skin disease characterized by unpigmented areas of skin—Buddha would always accompany me on the bus. I regret never telling him how grateful I was.

It was difficult for Buddha to express his emotions. I had always seen beyond his toughness and identified with his hidden humanity. He was the most unique person I had ever known. We discovered while attending Banning High School that Buddha was a whiz with numbers, a potential mathematical genius. Buddha was also the first of us Crips to style a blue bandanna. Although there have been numerous false accounts written about the origin of the blue bandanna association with the Crips, it initially became a part of Buddha's color-coordinated ensemble of blue Levi's, blue shirt, and dark blue suspenders. Ofttimes Buddha's blue bandanna hung loosely outside of his left back pants pocket—or wrapped around his head, pirate-style, or used to wipe his brow. (Later, we would wear the blue bandanna in memoriam of Buddha's demise; that tribute to him eventually morphed into the allegoric color of blue for Crips.)

Under better circumstances Buddha's wit, fanaticism, and do-or-die spirit would have earned him an invaluable spot in any black movement.

On February 27, 1973, Bob Simmons called me into his office. We sat in silence for a moment. In the background, birds were chirping and I heard children's laughter outside. Bob was choked up when he said, "I hate to be the one to tell you this, Tookie, but Buddha has been shot and killed." The words ripped my heart out of my chest. Buddha was invincible! My world shifted, and during the ride back to Los Angeles I felt paralyzed. Kenny Thornton, the driver—a counselor and non-Crip mistakenly identified in the *Do or Die* book as being a Crip—asked if I was all right. I couldn't respond. How could such a thing happen to Buddha? He was always well armed with not one but two or more guns. My mind raced with all sorts of questions with no plausible answers.

The day before Buddha's murder, he and Blackie had gone down to Los Angeles to pick up some ganja and return to the youth camp. Blackie's version was that they, along with some women, stopped off at A.C.'s mother's house to sniff some glue with A.C.'s brother Paul. Later Paul accused Buddha of breaking his stereo player. Buddha slapped him. Paul left the room and returned with a gun, threatening to shoot as Buddha taunted him, "Kill me, fool, kill me! This is Crip!" Blackie said Paul shot Buddha and he fell to the ground. Then Paul stood over him and shot him again. Once assured that Buddha was dead, that he couldn't rise again to kill him and his entire family, he backed out of the house and ran away. That night we tried to locate Paul, but he had turned himself in to the cops. There was a vigilante outburst to blast Blackie, who was present, but he could not substitute for Paul.

At Buddha's funeral, while everybody else was seated, I stood in the back leaning up against the wall. What was happening to me was a total contradiction of my desensitized street conditioning. I wasn't supposed to feel anything, but Buddha's death devastated me. It scared the feeling of invincibility out of me. I realized the rhetoric of our catchphrase, "Crips don't die, we multiply," was a metaphor, not reality. I watched as a long line of family members, homeboys, and strangers did a slow march past Buddha's casket. There was no doubt in my mind that many who attended the funeral were there to make certain Buddha was dead. I watched as Buddha's girlfriend, L'il Jackie, sobbed uncontrollably. I thought the fetus in her belly was probably Bulldog's or someone else, but not Buddha's. Standing before Buddha's body, all eyes were on me, anticipating an emotional outburst of rage. I only felt numb. I stood there waiting for Buddha to leap up and prove to everybody he wasn't dead. Lying in the casket, with no expression, was my best friend, my partner in violence, my Crip enforcer, the deadliest of his kind—and there was nothing I could do about it. Our madness finally had a recognizable face, and it was the death of my closest homeboy.

While everybody seemed in a festive mood inside Buddha's mother's house, I sat on the porch wanting to be left alone. Later,

Buddha's mother brought me a plate of food and placed it next to me. I didn't touch it. She stood staring into space as we shared a moment of silence. She put her hand on my shoulder and whispered, "Curtis loved you like a brother, Tookie. I know he wanted me to tell you." She turned and stopped at the door, then said, "You know, Tookie, you don't have to always be tough and hold it in. You're human. There's nothing wrong with letting it out." She came back, kissed me on the forehead, and went inside. I got up and walked down the street. The night, cold and extremely dark, hid the tears streaming down my face.

Compton Ambassador

I t was shortly after losing Buddha that I found myself in a Los Angeles County courtroom, accused of the attempted robbery of a black and a Caucasian, both of whom were more broke than I was. Looking at these two characters, I wouldn't have needed a weapon or my fists to rob them. A simple "boo" would have sufficed. But being innocent made no difference. I was still charged with the crime. Luckily, my stepfather had a friend, a seasoned and skilled attorney, Johnnie Cochran. His brilliance in the courtroom had my two accusers tripping over themselves with so many obvious lies that the district attorney was shaking his head in disgust. Even though Johnnie told me not to worry and congratulated Bonnie for her splendid testimony, I was still worried about the unpredictable jury. The jurors reentered the courtroom in silence and the foreman read their verdict: not guilty.

If this trial was a warning, I failed miserably to pay attention to it and continued promoting the Crips and my reputation like a politician lobbying for office. I could see no further than my limited intellect allowed, and I relished the thug recognition even if it was for black-on-black genocide. My homeboys helped make me a street legend in their own griot recitals of my violent exploits. Often Mad Dog David, Madbull, Black Johnny, Peewee, and others boasted about my exploits to elevate me to thug royalty. Whenever Mad Dog David addressed his homeboys, he would cry, "My cousins, my cousins, let Mr. Tookie speak! He is the Crip King!" Black Johnny, an equal to Buddha in ruthlessness and flamboyant commander of the 43rd Street Crips, who ruled with brass knuckles, would lay out the blue carpet when I showed up. When I ventured into any of the commanders' strongholds, I was greeted as though I wore an imaginary crown. The respect I received inflated my head to the size of a watermelon. I earned it for oppressing other blacks. There is no bigger fool on earth than a man who destroys his own people.

Meanwhile, since the San Diego summer camp was terminated, the would-be king was castle-less and broke, and Bonnie was pregnant. So I went back to work with Bob Simmons in Compton. The boys' home where I lived and worked was a two-story reddish house with six bedrooms, two bathrooms, basement, dinette room, living room, and a garage with a half-moon circular driveway. The place was huge, located off Santa Fe on Pine Street next to a mini-mall that included a liquor store, barbershop, laundry, Italian takeout, record shop, soul food restaurant, and a gas station across the street that also sold dairy products. Bob called this house the Ponderosa, but to the outside world it would become known as the Red House, or the Crip house. Living there were mostly young misfits with Crip backgrounds, or an occasional Brim, Bounty Hunter, Van Ness Boy, Inglewood Family, or Piru. Also, Donald R. of the Van Ness Boys befriended me and even accompanied me on raids against the Pirus, who were not their allies. Thus, two violently opposed individuals fought side by side. The Red House was located in a clean, quiet residential area. Several neighbors contacted their councilman unsuccessfully to have the program moved.

I met Bob's wife, Ethel, and their children, and also his parents, who welcomed me with open arms. His mother, Edith, and I had brief conversations about my future plans—though I couldn't speak about that subject with any clarity or conviction. Sometimes we talked about Bob's efforts to help troubled youths and how I could help him with the gang problem. But I was in no position to address the gang problem—I was a willing participant. As I recall, Bob was the first to initiate a gang truce between several Compton gangs. He consistently tried to alert mainstream society to accelerating gang membership, but they assumed he was crying wolf. In one such attempt, Bob set up a gang truce held in the backyard of the Red House. I attended with Blackie, Monk, and D.N., the Oaks Park Boys leader. There were also some Bounty Hunters, and Pirus like Puddin, Tam, and others in attendance. No one appeared to be interested or was listening to Bob, but rather they were sizing one another up for future sightings. If stares could kill, all of the gang members present would have been dead. The meeting was a fiasco, producing not even as much as a handshake among us.

It didn't take long for me to familiarize myself with the different factions of Compton Crips. The Grandee Crips' hangout was around a block full of two-story apartments on a street shaped like a J ending in a cul-de-sac. Though some Crips lived in the Grandees, most lived on the outskirts in the immediate area. My first day in the Grandees I met Frosty, Bitter Dog Bruno, Mr. X., King Ning, Vamp, Salty, King Rat, Duck, Hoss, and Popcorn from the Park Village. Though Mac Thomas was incarcerated, he had established a Crip force here that was effective in its propensity for violence and destruction that mirrored the West Side Crips and the East Side Crips. When I wasn't kicking it with the Grandees, then I was in the garage at the Red House driving iron with the weights I had collected. When word was out that I lived in Compton, there were Crips showing up to meet me, drive iron, or both. The Red House was a quasi-Crip embassy, and I was the ambassador. Finding their way to the Red House from long distances were Mad Dog David, Big James, Jimel, Big Curtis, Lurch, Fat Riley, and plenty of others. A regular visitor here to drive iron was Little James, commander of the 118th Street Crips. In fact, Little James was my first training partner. We urged one another to drive hard to blow up our arms. If he and I weren't driving iron at the Red House, then we worked out in his mother's garage where there were weights, mirrors, and magazine cut-outs of professional bodybuilders on the wall for motivation. One in particular was Cuba's Mr. Olympia winner, Sergio Oliva, who was unbelievable in size. Tapping his picture with my finger, I told Little James, "Cuz, I am going to be bigger than this cat."

At the time, there were quite a few Crips and non-Crips who pumped iron and who were bigger than me: Seals, Pancho, Head, Bulldog, Raymond, Donnie Boy, Jimel, Big Bear, and the biggest of them all, Munson. The first time I saw Munson at Roosevelt Park, I couldn't believe my eyes. Buddha shrugged him off as a Goliath ready to fall on his sword. Head told me once that Raymond idolized Munson and wanted badly to join the Avenues but Munson objected. As a result, Raymond decided to create a junior version of the Avenues and call them the Cribs. Whether fact or fiction it was obvious Raymond respected Munson, because he spoke of him often.

One day a few of us drove over to where Munson, Bear, and Donny Boy were driving iron in a garage on a U-shaped street off Avalon. Munson acted aloof, and when he did speak, he spoke down to Raymond. I asked Eddie H. what was the problem here, and he said, "Cuz, that's the way they trip all the time!" Friend or no friend, I held no one in such high regard that I'd allow him or her to berate me without a comeback or payback.

After leaving that garage I was determined to become bigger and stronger than Munson—but without ever having to be in prison. A few of my homeboys used to brag about how they planned to get yoked up whenever they went to prison. I was convinced I could become yoked while on the streets. So I started driving iron obsessively, and with phenomenal results. Driving iron with Little James was what helped me pack on muscle and set the stage for more size. At the age of nineteen I had nineteen-inch arms that looked even larger due to my height of five feet ten inches. To be "yoked" was a new word in my vocabulary. I could stand in front of a mirror listening to any James Brown song while back-arming a 175-pound curl bar from afternoon till dawn. To say the least, having yokes was an intimidation factor backed up with strength, treachery, and opportunity that served me well in head-up fights and life.

My desire to fight was never for the sake of fighting, but rather to set an example for my homeboys and any opposition foolhardy enough to try me. When fisticuffs ruled in gang primacy, a Crip could boldly roam into forbidden territory relying upon his fists, win or lose, to back him up. Although I was a traditionalist in street gang fighting, I wasn't a fool. I bought a 12-gauge riot shotgun for safety.

It didn't take long for the Lynwood cops patrolling in their all-white cars to target me with their petty harassment tactics. Bob said the cops had mentioned having received word from the Lennox Sheriff's Department and the Los Angeles Police Department about me being the leader of a gang called the West Side Crips. According to Bob, one cop had said, "Tookie's kind can never change. He's anti-social, among other things." That statement was the general consensus of many other cops on the west side but their opinion never mattered to me. I was never antisocial. I was selectively social and refused to socialize with just anybody.

The cop's trite statement reminded me of the time when a county "voodoo" doctor had labeled me as antisocial and a fifteen-year-old revolutionary. Odd, because back then, I couldn't even define revolutionary, yet alone comprehend its concepts. His analysis of me was a typical racist stereotype used to describe every homeboy I knew. Instead of defining me as a defiant teenager, his amateur opinion tagged me as a revolutionary. But I was instead a model for a future Crip prototype.

Living in Compton, I needed a car bad, and Bob had an old buddy sell me his white two-door 1965 Chevy with a 396 engine and a four-banger stick in the floor. With my Compton Crip homeboy Lee, I drove to the west side and appropriated a low-rider Chevy car and boldly stripped it in the Grandees and left it there. A week later I had hydraulic lifts put in my car and I had a small black pirate's flag on the antenna to signify danger. The car itself was quickly becoming recognizable by rivals, and by both Lynwood and Compton cops.

With access to wheels, I entered the P.J.s (aka the Imperial Courts Projects), where I was introduced to A.B., Anthony Braylock, commander of the P.J. Crips, and his right-hand man, Poindexter. It was also where I met Beverly McGowan, the future mother of my son Stan. A.B. stayed in one of the many P.J. apartments along with a family practicing the religion of Islam. At five feet nine inches and with a medium build, A.B. was game for anything and was at war with the Bounty Hunters and the East Side Bishops. By Crip association, they were my rivals too. His low-rider 1957 gray-and-white Nomad station wagon was a magnet for his enemies to take potshots at him when he traveled near Nickerson Gardens, where the Bounty Hunters lived.

During several other trips over to the P.J.s, A.B. told me that all around the gymnasium were Crips. But on the other side they weren't interested either in Crips or in *becoming* Crips. Fistfights were still in vogue, and that's what took place despite the presence of guns. The scenario was a trip because on the opposite side there were youths our age partying with their older brothers, uncles, and fathers, but most of them were rowdy and willing to fight. They had no qualms about betting on themselves, relatives, or on any of us. Though most of the burly dudes I fought were unknowns, driving them into the dirt only increased the myths about me. I was known as a knockout artist with one punch and was dubbed the dirtiest fighter on the continent.

By no means was I comparable to Joe Louis, Muhammad Ali, or Mike Tyson. But back then, winning was required for me to set a standard in the name of Crip. High on arrogance, I'd drive to the opposite side of the P.J.s, then stop my car in the middle of the street, get out, and challenge whoever was present. If there were no takers, I'd stroll up to a crowd of dudes, then start sucker-punching them. They thought exactly what I wanted them to think: "Tookie is crazy." I was a spectacle, sporting a shiny bald head with sideburns and a goatee, dressed in blue overalls, army boots, no shirt, and with an oiled-up body too slippery for an opponent to grab. It was A.B., Poindexter, and their homeboys who applied consistent pressure that turned the other side into Crips. With the P.J.s under the control of A.B., they concentrated on the battles against their rivals.

Whenever there were rumors of a potential attack, the P.J.s morphed into an armed fortress that would be suicidal for any rival to attempt a drive-by. It was like trying to do a drive-by in the Nickerson Gardens, a death trap. During one of those false alarms, it was the first time I had ever seen nearly a hundred Crips en masse with guns and rifles out in the open. It was unbelievable. On other nights when we were hanging out getting high, an undercover cop car would do a drive-by and holler out "Bounty Hunter!" or "Bishop!" then peel rubber as a hail of bullets chased the culprit. Minutes later, the P.J.s would be surrounded by an armada of patrol cars and helicopters hovering above with spotlights. It was never a surprise seeing the same undercover car that initiated the drive-by earlier showing up alongside the many other cop cars. I recall A.B. telling me, "Those cops pull this crap off and on because they want us to ride down on the Bounty Hunters. It keeps them busy. Plus," he said, "the cops were shooting blanks." I looked at him like he lost his mind and said, "Blanks? Hell, blanks don't ricochet off walls and put holes in cars!"

Yes, America, as unbelievable as it may seem, 'hood cops, with impunity, commit drive-bys and other lawless acts. It was common practice for them to abduct a Crip or Bounty Hunter and drop him off in hostile territory, and then broadcast it over a loudspeaker. The predictable outcome was that the rival was either beaten or killed on the spot, which resulted in a cycle of payback. Cops would also inform opposing gangs where to find and attack a rival gang, and then say, "Go handle your business." Like slaves, the gang did exactly what their master commanded. Had they not been fueled by self-hatred, neither Crips, Bounty Hunters, nor any other black gang would have been duped.

The 'hood cops were pledged to protect and serve, but for us they were not there to help but to exploit us—and they were effective. With the cops' Machiavellian presence, the gang epidemic escalated. When gang warfare is fed and fueled by law enforcement, funds are generated for the so-called antigang units. Without gangs, these units would no longer exist. In the midst of the madness, my name was reverberating through much of Compton. Quite a few members of opposing gangs were offended. One night while I was in the P.J.s, a well-known Piru named J.B. and several of his homeboys paid the Red House a visit. They showed up threatening the youngsters there. J.B. boldly left a message: "Tell Tookie I'm looking for him."

I had to take J.B.'s threat seriously because he showed up on my doorstep, calling me out. He made it personal and offended my ego. I had to find him and make an example. While cruising with Norwood around Compton, I spotted J.B. and two females going into a liquor store. After parking, I approached J.B. and asked if he was looking for me. He responded, "Look here, brother, I don't even know you." But the moment I said, "I'm Tookie," his eyes became as big as golf balls. Moments later, he was stretched out on the cement as the two females ran back inside the liquor store screaming for help.

Later that night, Beverly and I were asleep in my recently obtained apartment across the street from the Red House when I was awakened by loud noises and people hollering, "Tookie!" Thinking it was J.B. and his Piru cronies retaliating, I jumped up and looked out the window. There were about six low-rider cars parked. Still groggy, I was able to make out Black Johnny, so I hollered down to him and his homeboys to hold down the racket.

Although it was nighttime, I could still see Black Johnny's teeth shining with a devious smile. He was a darker, taller version of Buddha, and to say he was crazy was an understatement. He was so mean it was said when he went to prison his own homeboys celebrated and prayed he'd never get released. "Locced out" (unpredictably crazy) or not, Black Johnny was the commander of the East Side 43rd Street Crips and would go to war at the drop of a hat. When I told him about what happened earlier, his first reaction was, "Well, I'll come back with an army so we can destroy them." Then he asked, "Is the man looney? Does he know who you are?" I told him, "It makes no difference. Whatever the problem is, I can handle it."

After a few hours of bantering, snacking, and reminiscing about the Watts festival, Black Johnny and his homeboys were ready to go.

While leaving, they chanted out loudly, "Crip here," and they all threw up the hand symbol for Crip that formed a "C." Black Johnny's persona reminded me of Buddha. His eyes had a tendency to turn blood-red when angered. He was hardheaded and combative and argued often with Raymond, Pitbull, and others. He used to intentionally annoy me until I began putting him in a headlock and applied pressure till he ceased the madness. Yet he was still one of the most reliable homeboys I knew. I recall thinking that Black Johnny would one day completely lose his mind because he was already beyond crazy. It was similar to my thought about Buddha not living long because of his extreme cruelty. But in both instances, I dismissed the thoughts as quickly as I did of the individuals who wanted to be Crips but didn't fit the profile. Either way, Black Johnny was a true-blue Crip, and other than Little James, he had a first-rate cache of weaponry.

The following night around midnight, Lee and I were sitting at the kitchen table smoking weed while Beverly prepared a meal. I heard a loud noise and someone repeatedly calling my name. I thought it was the madman Black Johnny and his homeboys again, outside, but I knew better when I heard glass breaking and a chorus of "Piru, Piru fool!" I opened up on them with an M-1 rifle that sounded like a firecracker going off with each shot. It jammed, and I had to feed the rifle one bullet at a time. After the crowd of Pirus dispersed in all directions, I saw J.B. slowly cruising by in his dark blue Chevy low-rider without a care in the world. I took aim, pulled the trigger, and the rifle jammed again.

When Lee and I ran downstairs and crossed the street to the Red House, we found out the youngsters were unhurt but my car window had been busted out. While cleaning up the broken glass, the Lynwood cops swooped down on the Red House and ordered me to hit the dirt, and everybody in the house to come out. They were responding to the dairy on the corner's having been burglarized earlier, not to mention the trail of spilt milk leading from the dairy to the Red House garage. The cops managed to get a confession from a thirteen-year-old runaway. Two days later, the Lynwood cops came back to the Red House to question me with Bob present, about the fire-bombing of J.B.'s mother's house. They thoroughly searched my car and the garage looking for incriminating evidence. The cops acted as if I was the only Crip in Compton when they assumed it was me who firebombed that house because someone had hollered out "Crip here!" I denied knowing anything about what happened or being anywhere near that house. Later there was a single-shot drive-by at the corner of Sante Fe and Pine directed at a young Crip named Shot-gun. The Red House was immune to any more violent disturbances, but Compton got hot for everybody.

Meanwhile, I was still making the rounds, like an ambassador on a public relations tour, meeting more and more Crips throughout Compton, on the east side, Centerview, and other places. During that period I met Peewee, commander of the J.D. (Jordan Down Projects) Crips on the east side. There were two sides to these projects, with a dilapidated factory separating the two sides. When I started hanging out in the J.D.s, Crips existed on both sides and their numbers were equal to the P.J.s if not slightly more. Peewee was dark brown, short, and thin with an aggressive heart. He wore the longest cross and chain earring of any other Crip; it extended from his earlobe to his waist. It was his way of being flamboyant and showing off, as all Crips were known to do.

Whenever I did show up at the J.D.s, Peewee rolled out the blue carpet and introduced me to all sorts of women. Sometimes he'd jok-ingly say, "Cuz, there's this woman such and such who's well built, but she's real ugly. Any problems with that?" Then he'd start smiling in anticipation of my response: "It's not the beauty, it's the booty!" Peewee would burst into laughter at that, especially when he was loaded. The J.D.s, P.J.s, and the Grandees were like second homes to me. I'd visit each one often, sometimes all three on the same day.

Three other Crip spots I frequented were Boothill, Park Village, and Centerview. Boothill was several sets of two-story apartments located on Alondra, next to a liquor store and directly across the street from the Park Village Crips. Less than three Crips actually lived in Boothill, yet thirty to forty of us Crips and Criplettes briefly commandeered the property. Most of the time, you could find Crips getting high or sitting up in second-story windows taking potshots at Piru cars—which triggered the Pirus' notorious sneak attacks.

A lot of Crips hanging out at Boothill were from the Grandees. They should have been called the Grandees' Boothill Crips. It became an active spot for Crips such as Big and Little Honcho, Mister X, Popcorn, Tick, Jonjon, and Bitter Dog Bruno, who was a character and a half. If Bruno wasn't warring against the Pirus, he'd be challenging any Crip foolish enough to think they could outdrink him. Bitter Dog Bruno would turn up a fifth of Mad Dog 20/20 with several giant gulps and finish it. The short-lived Boothill Crips lasted for a few months, which was how long it took the owners to get fed up with our presence and have the Compton cops make numerous arrests and then evacuate any remaining Crips from the premises. Things had gotten so petty around Boothill that the Compton cops arrested me for spitting on the ground.

The other spot where I made my rounds was a huge area with many fine homes called Centerview, on the outskirts of Compton. Mad Dog Wilson was one of the commanders of the Centerview Crips, though he often hung out at the Grandees and in Boothill. To get to where Mad Dog Wilson lived, I had to drive down an extremely long street with a wall on both sides extending about half a mile in distance. On the left-hand side is where the Centerview Crips lived, and on the right side resided the Pirus. As far as I knew, there was only one way in or out of Centerview on either side.

Sometimes when visiting Centerview, Mad Dog, his homeboys, and I would attend parties on the rival's side, looking for trouble and having no problems finding it. I never had any qualms about participating in any Crip feud. I felt it was my duty as King Crip not to kick back, but to be in the forefront of Crip wars. Plus, if I got hurt or

MWGB, (Murdered While Gangbanging) it would be in the name of Crip. Smash or be smashed! Mad Dog Wilson's aka reflected his actions perfectly. Back then, he was making a name for himself using mad-dog tactics. It was said that he was too bold for his own good, but then that was true of all of us.

Straddling the Fence

erhaps it was a strategy of Bob and his partner, Shaw, to try to steer me away from gang life by making me a full counselor and announcing I'd be operating my own boys' home within a week. My mindset clashed with the legitimate precepts of being a counselor. I was too dys-educated and self-absorbed to be concerned with adolescents confessing to the world they were baby Crips, Brims, Pirus, whatever. I wasn't ready for this—but surely I could fake it, having been a thespian in my personal drama, called "survival," most of my life. I was as ill prepared to be a full counselor as I was when I was thirteen and having sex with a forty-two-year-old woman.

I was set up in a plush area with a two-story house that had five bedrooms, a swimming pool, and a huge garage for all my weights. It didn't take the neighbors long to discover who we were and why we lived there. The second day in the house, two Crip youngsters, Tiny Man and Guy, got the bright idea of robbing one of the merchant booths up the street, at El Segundo off Avalon. After robbing the booth with a gun, they high-tailed it back to the boys' home and were followed by the same man they robbed. They were probably kicking back counting their loot when the cops banged on the front door and demanded over a loudspeaker that everybody in the house come out with hands up. Since I was in the garage driving iron, I slowly raised the garage door to see the familiar sight of a squad of snarling white faces with badges, guns, and the certain predilection to blow me smooth away.

In a crescendo of provocation, a cop barked out, "That's right, Tookie, walk slowly toward us with your hands in the air! No quick moves!" Exiting the garage, I probably looked like a huge black beast to them, with no shirt and still sweating profusely from my workout. As Tiny Man and Guy walked out of the house looking guilty as sin, a black man hollered out, "That's them, officers, those are the two boys who robbed me!" I shot an angry look at the two youngsters who bowed their heads as if in earnest prayer. Though they were placed in the back of a patrol car, I knew they'd be back in a week or two since they were minors. Meanwhile, this cop with his gun pointed at me said, "Of all people, what are you doing in such a fine, upstanding neighborhood? You don't belong here. We should just blow you away and get it over with!"

Though I remained silent and felt defenseless, I sought comfort in the fact that under any other weaponless circumstances, I could've snapped his neck like a twig, and he knew it. Another cop approached and told his buddy who was pointing his gun at me, "He doesn't have any warrants, so we have to cut him loose. It's a shame. We know the boys' home is a front for criminal activities. Tookie, you're free to go—but we'll be back!"

They kept their word and returned with what appeared to be FBI agents who never spoke a word but only observed. Neighbors gawked as I was handcuffed and taken downtown to the Glass House (a local Los Angeles jailhouse), where I underwent several lie detector tests. This time I was accused of having burglarized the Compton's military armory and stealing a large arsenal of AR-15s, rocket launchers, and ammo. In their minds either I did it, ordered some Crips to do it, or had knowledge of it. This was the beginning of the mythical "super-nigger" stigma that cops branded me with. In their minds I could perform the impossible, even steal their guns while they were looking at me. For the first time in that neighborhood, cops were patrolling, and surveillance was established to watch my movements. The following week we were out of there after a petition was filed against us to leave.

The next house we moved to was located off Compton and Avalon in the neighborhood of the Swamp Boys, allies of the Pirus. It didn't take long for the Swamp Boys to find out who I was, which prompted them to cruise by in snail fashion "red-eyeing" me and flashing their guns. Often as I washed my car, Lee stood guard with a visible weapon, and several times I had to restrain him from blasting the cars. I knew it wasn't kosher for a counselor to be openly involved in gunfights.

Shortly after, a homeboy of mine, L.C., from the east side Back Street Crips, started visiting me at the boys' home. Years earlier, before he became a Crip, he and his homeboys stumbled into the Rio Theater and were relieved of their leather coats, hats, money, and dignity after being stomped. Though he knew I was the one who took his white wide-brim and decked him, we became tight over the years. Around that time there were regular sneak assaults launched against the Swamp Boys, and the cops blamed me, L.C., and Lee. During the short period we lived in that area, the Swamp Boys converted into the Swamp Crips. In fact, some of them used to visit and drive iron in the garage with Lee. I don't know what he told them, but they used to darn near salute with excitement whenever they saw me out and about in the 'hood.

Meanwhile, Lee and some of the Swamp Crips went out to a party in another neighborhood and turned it out. The next thing I knew, the cops were looking for all of them, and the community had posted fliers throughout Compton with photos and descriptions of Lee, accusing him of rape. By then, some of the Swamp Crips had been busted. I saw Lee a few times before he was arrested. He didn't seem the least bit worried about being the subject of a growing manhunt. He finally succumbed to his mother's pleas to turn himself in.

Not long after Lee was locked away, Bob suggested that I enroll in Compton Junior College. What motivated me to enroll was that I'd be getting paid for going. While in class I had mixed emotions, boredom with some interest. I used to look around and wonder what in God's name was I doing in here amongst all these busters. Many of them were struggling to get an education to obtain a vocation, but here I was already employed without an academic degree. Plus, the extracurricular ambience of the school was about fashion, gossip, and sex. I was trying to balance an educational impossibility, an alliance between stupidity and wisdom, and trying to straddle the fence between Crippen and counseling. The school odyssey lasted for only several months—then it was sayonara.

A couple of weeks later, an English teacher from Compton College called and tried to convince me to come back. He said, "You're quite intelligent, Stan. You should rethink coming back to school!" I believe he heard the loud "Hell, no!" before the click. With school out of the way, I was beginning to settle in where we lived until Bob told me we had been petitioned to move once again. We were relocated in another fine-looking house on Slater and Stockwell. It was beautiful inside, with thick cocoa-brown carpet and matching shades of wood paneling. There were ceiling-to-floor mirrors that covered an entire living room wall, with the same kind of mirrors on the closet doors. The place had two baths, three bedrooms, a large breakfast nook, a large patio with artificial turf, flower beds, floodlights, a huge pool table, and security bars around the entire house. There were also two backyards separated by a brick fence and a large garage. It was a place tailor-made for me.

I had two full-grown Doberman pinschers for each yard and a pit bull puppy named Cuz. Under my guardianship the house was kept immaculate. The youths were well fed, clothed, clean, and attending school. Odd that I could play father to them but was too trifling to take care of my own sons, Travon and Stanley, whose mother was my then-girlfriend, Beverly. Being irresponsible and low-minded, I convinced both Bonnie and Beverly to not list me as the father, to say they weren't sure who the father was so I could avoid paying child support. I had stooped low and didn't feel the slightest discomfort about my lack of ethics. But I was at the same time the paternal figure for a houseful of youngsters: Cross, Guy, Tiny Man, Dennis, Leroy, and others. Though it was hypocritical of me to try to convince them not to live foul when I was living fouler than foul, I tried anyway. It didn't matter that I was unreachable, unsalvageable, and unethical, there was still something inside me that wanted better for them than I had for myself.

I was expecting these youths confronted by damned conditions and caught in the cycle of ganghood to accomplish the elusive goal of getting an education, uplifting other blacks, and living a productive and peaceful life. My hypocritical theme—do as I say, not as I do— was a garbled message. They totally ignored my words and held the worst in me as being the paradigm of what they aspired to be. It was difficult to disguise the Crip aura that exuded from me like liquid fire. These boys heard my name resonating throughout the streets, associated with ganghood above and beyond anyone else's—and they loved it. And unfortunately, so did I.

Outside the door of the boys' home I was involved in a casus belli (acts used to justify war), which produced nothing but Pyrrhic victories. I fought for three years alongside the Compton Crips and was so recognizable that I was often mislabeled as their leader. Though I was in the forefront of a lot of madness occurring in Compton and other places, I was merely doing my duty to represent Crip and myself to the fullest. It made no never-mind where I represented Crip. It was West Side Crips today, tomorrow, and forever!

I still managed to travel to the west side, where the Los Angeles Police Department and Lennox cops quickly learned I now drove a 1965 white Chevy. It was during my crisscrossing from Compton to the west side that I had the suspicion I was being followed. There were occasions, looking through the rearview mirror, that I'd detect a car that was following me but then would veer off. The cops were fanatical in their harassment of me. They acted as if I was some kind of notorious drug dealer, maniacal racist, mad bomber, corrupt politician, spy, or revolutionary. My being black provided a cop's justification for harassment; and being a Crip only exacerbated an already volatile matter. There were times when I was stopped, frisked, and held at gunpoint. Other cars showed up with some official types looking on while other characters took pictures of me. My homeboys dubbed me "super-hot," meaning I was the central focus for the cops' harassment. This also meant this level of focus would bring unwanted attention to those around me.

Back then, a thirtyish black woman named Bessie who was like a mother figure to the Avalon Garden Crips warned me about the cops' plan to set me up or to murder me. She had relatives working for the Los Angeles Police Department who told her that my name and Raymond's were on a roster called the "Alpha List." From what she gathered, the list consisted of blacks who were a menace and merited extermination. Her worried suggestion was for me to immediately leave town, and although I believed her, I was too foolish to listen. Before long the American Civil Liberties Union (ACLU) had gotten wind of the Alpha List. *The Los Angeles Times*, on December 13, 1974, ran an article, "ACLU Sues to Kill Police List of Allegedly Dangerous Blacks!"

A black man in his twenties had first told us about the Alpha List. He used to show up at the gym in the P.J.s to teach us karate. He claimed to be a member of the Black Stone Rangers in Chicago. The Alpha List, he told us, was a well-kept official secret, a police list of black male youths and adults who were systematically bumped off by the cops and then had incriminating guns planted on them. The cops, he said, were mostly setting up black Chicago gangs like the Black Stone Rangers, the Disciples, and others. I listened but dismissed him as being a nut. I thought that whatever happened in Chicago couldn't possibly happen to me here in South Central. Short of killing me, they had pretty much covered all the bases in violating my civil rights.

It was better for me to stay in Compton than to cruise on the west side where I caught all the hell. At least in Compton I was living a poor man's life of Reilly: access to a palatial place to rest, an easy job, paycheck, women, and several choice spots to get free gas and dairy products. During the gasoline shortage, I met several gas station attendants who assisted me with free gasoline. One such gas station and dairy combined was owned by this guy Gerald's father. He wasn't a Crip but he knew who I was and what I stood for, so I could go there and load up on anything I wanted. On a couple of occasions, I took Cute's brother Mouse from the Magnificent 7 Crips to the gas station to fill up his car. Then one day while high as a kite Mouse showed up trying to get gas from Gerald's father and destroyed that particular connection. You can believe my other spot remained a secret.

Still, with one foot in the Crip life and the other in the counselor realm, I decided to upgrade my image. I had to meet and talk with parents, particularly mothers, so I had to appear presentable. When I located a clean two-door 1967 powder-blue Cadillac, I started styling slacks, dress shirts, suit vest, biscuit shoes, and a bald head without the thick sideburns. I still wore an earring, but I bought a Gruen watch with four diamonds inside, and a diamond ring. The only things thuggish about me were Crippen thoughts and behavior.

Though I was in a position of mundane opportunities and felt comfortable operating the boys' home, my mindset prevented total commitment. I had been inculcated into the streets where neither employment nor millions of dollars could have altered my behavior. I bought into the rhetoric about survival being based on the principles of accumulated wealth, force, and violence. This was the American way! Neither the Crips nor our rivals invented greed or violence, the basic capitalistic theme for man-eat-man. No surprise that my foremost concern was self. Although I would have defended any diehard Crip to the death, my own survival was paramount. I bear witness to my own mindlessness.

After Buddha's demise, I really didn't care much about anything except Crippen. The most lavish aspects of that life were funerals for our dead homeboys. These mini-extravaganzas for mourning featured colorful wreaths, plush caskets, stylish clothing, and limousines so royal they made death seem appealing. A dead, martyred Crip appeared to receive more kudos than he did alive. In Islam it's paradise, in Christianity it's heaven, but for Crips it was the expectancy of an elaborate wake. Such was the case with a young Block Crip named Odie, murdered at Sportsman's Park. The funeral setting for Odie's mourning was the prototype for others. A Crip's death was the last hurrah, like a falling star kissing the universe before it fades into nothingness. When Odie was laid to rest, people paraded by his casket dropping in jewelry, pictures, drugs, Crip bandannas, money, and other memorabilia. Had Odie still been alive, many of those same people would not have given him change for a phone, yet alone a meal.

After viewing Odie—who didn't look remotely like himself—I expressed my condolences to his surviving family and prepared to leave. The spectacle had turned my stomach so much I opted not to go to the gravesite with the long caravan that was being followed by a convoy of detectives and cameramen. Instead, I headed back to Compton to confront the cycle of violence, debauchery, treachery, death, and other injustices received or that we dished out. I never expected nor cared if anyone else understood me, because the only ones who could were those involved in ganghood, and like me they had no solution.

My path was a path of ignorance. I learned nothing, gained nothing, and had nothing of worth to offer anyone. I was trying to counsel teenagers not much younger than I was, in age, mentality, or behavior. I was no more prepared to be a counselor than I was to be president of the United States. Being a counselor was self-serving. It provided me with a steady paycheck so I wouldn't have to be in the streets hustling or strong-arming people.

The fence I sat on could no longer hold the weight of irresponsibility. The chickens were coming home to roost.

Invincibility Shot Down

I continued to go through the motions of play-acting the role of counselor, which made me look good. Because the Slater home was running smoothly, Shaw found a bigger place. It was a spacious double duplex converted into a single unit with four bedrooms, two kitchens, two baths, two living rooms, and two yards. I immediately set up a mini gym in one of the kitchens. An East Side Crips homeboy of mine, Jackie, called it "the sweatbox." The house was located on Palm Street off Compton Boulevard behind Zorber's hamburger stand. Several blocks away was Compton High School, and hanging out down the street were some Compton Crips—Movie Star, Ron Dog, Boo, Crusher, and others.

At one time or another, I worked out with some of the serious iron drivers such as Little James, Big Vertice, Marcellis, Bunchie, King Rat, Mouse, Big Jackie, Jimel, and Pretty Mike, who became a professional bodybuilder. My best training partner was Jackie. He was willing to drive iron anytime and anywhere. Jackie became like a biological brother to me; his family became mine, and vice versa. If we weren't driving iron at the Palm House or in the backyard where his mother, sister Gloria, and brother Joey lived, then we'd drive out to different gyms like Babe's Gym, Bill Pearl's, or Gold's Gym in Santa Monica. At Gold's Gym I met Mr. Olympia, Arnold Schwarzenegger. One day Jackie and I strolled past Arnold and a female on the boardwalk at

Venice Beach. Indicating me, Arnold said to his companion, "See that guy there? Those aren't arms—they're legs."

Jackie was like Buddha to me, a true friend. He was my closest homeboy, a loyal sidekick who would defend me to the end. His favorite saying was, "Tookie, you are the first, the last and the only one. After you there will be none!" Jackie was six feet tall, brown-complected, and big-chested, with eighteen-and-a-half-inch arms with a lot of definition, skinny legs, and long braids. He got a kick out of my taking off my shirt to flex and make my chest jump up and down for women or a crowd of children. We coined the phrase "breaking out" for taking off our shirts to flex for people. Like break-dancers competing against one another, Crips would break out and compete to see who was the biggest and the best built, especially for female attention.

When Jackie and I weren't hanging out, I was over at the apartments on Central off Imperial where a homeboy of mine, Godfather, was the manager. The place was a modern-day Sodom and Gomorrah where fornication, gambling, drugs, and other debauchery were rampant. It was also where I was introduced to a variety of drugs, including paper acid, called blotter acid back then. I tried orange sunshine and microdot acid, but I preferred windowpane because it kept me hyped up without tripping out or seeing bizarre things. Admittedly, I did see traces, after-images, like when I spit or waved my hand, but that was tame in comparison to seeing monsters and other horrors. It was odd that acid didn't seem to affect my energy or my strength while driving iron, very unlike the lethargic feeling when I smoked weed, a rare event.

I hid my drug problem from everybody, even Jackie. There I was, King Crip, seeking comfort in drugs like a drunkard seeking salvation in a bottle. I needed desperately to escape the madness around me, so I used acid and other deadly stimulants to block out the living nightmares, even though the blockage was temporary. My sharpness of wit was leaving me like water seeping through hundreds of tiny holes in a bucket. Though my chameleon role as a counselor was working—I believed I had most everybody fooled—I was destroying my mind in the process. My life was a contradiction. I didn't really expect to die, but I didn't care if I lived or died. In the back of my mind was the delusion of invincibility. With my soul unrepentant, I continued to engage in secret night raids on my rivals who knew darn well it was me though I left no calling card. To avoid the cops, we'd dress up as if going to church or a social gathering and creep around in an inconspicuous car, then park down the street. It was in the name of Buddha and other slain Crips that I had no compunctions whatsoever about retaliation, nor did the rivals who opposed my existence. Strange how we Crips, Bloods, other black gangs, and the black street drug dealers were so gung-ho to obliterate one another— but would shy away when it came to confronting poverty, unemployment, politics, cop brutality, and other social inequities.

Throughout most of my life, I was psychologically scarred. I carried an inner loathing of self and my own culture. Since I wasn't psychotic—Bobby Wright's book *Psychopathic Racial Personality* confirms my analysis—self-hatred motivated me to seek a kind of accomplishment by hurting other blacks. That's why I could stroll through Will Rogers Park during the Watts Festival, eager to impress my fellow Crips by knocking unconscious any target they pinpointed. The Watts Festival was a knockout day for Crips. Most any rival who stumbled into the park was spotted, then pounced upon. For me, the defensive measure for fighting had been overshadowed by the need to show off. I relished the moments to unleash my raw, repressed power in a single punch that drew oohs and ahs from bystanders.

After such a display, cops made a clean sweep of the park to round up suspects, so Godfather and I ditched the crowd and headed in the opposite direction. A gang of cops met us at the far end of the park, and when I backtracked, I was met by yet another squad of cops coming up from behind us. Sensing a showdown between me and the Los Angeles Police Department, I took out my long earring in preparation. One tall cop nicknamed Red barked, "So, Tookie, you're a big and bad Crip, do you think you can fight all of us?" I looked at this cop who seemed to be growing horns and spewing hatred. I smiled and then said, "I can whip all of you idiots if you put your guns in the trunk of the car!" I heard guns and shotguns being cocked, then Red said, "Raise your hands, Tookie, you're under arrest for assault on a peace officer." I actually had to bail out, hiring Johnnie Cochran once again to defend me.

When I arrived at the Palm House, Godfather told me that Tam, one of the most respected Pirus, had been murdered (may he rest in peace). It was time to be on extra guard because Puddin—one of the more lethal Pirus—and his crew would now be on the warpath. In an unsurprising attack, the apartments Godfather managed were being firebombed in the front, along with constant drive-bys. But the Carver Park Crips—R. Tucker, U.T., Terrible Tee, Trouble Man, Willie Herb, Big Chuck, Felton, and plenty of others who frequented the apartments—were eager to assist. In systematic fashion, the Pirus were hitting Compton Crip hangouts like they had a license to do so. This was the dawn of a Compton war between the Crips and Pirus. Drive-bys took somewhat of a nosedive, and Buddha-like walk-up ambush shootings escalated on both sides.

Living and working in Compton, the most devastating year for me was 1976. My grandmother, Momma, was on her deathbed, and from what I gathered, she was a little delirious. But when I spoke to her, she articulated herself with clarity. My mother told me that the day before Momma died, she had a premonition. Momma said, "You have to get Tookie out of California. Something terrible is going to happen to him. Please get him out of there!" I brushed off the revelation as paranoia. I was Tookie, and I was invincible.

Ever since I'd known Momma, she was elderly. It seemed as if a grandmother would live forever, so her death devastated me. I was supposed to have a stony heart wrapped in machismo, so Momma's death (may she rest in peace) was like a powerful electric jolt. To divert the pain, I immersed myself even deeper into the abyss of Crippen. I was never known for packing a gun, even though I kept my pump shotgun in the trunk. I started toting a chrome two-shot .38

Derringer for protection. I sought solace in night raids against my rivals to release my frustration, pain, and rage. I was still arrogant and foolish, with a drug addiction that rendered me lax and vulnerable to my opposition.

Often I attended social gatherings packing heat like I did at an adult night school graduation held at Crenshaw High. My stepsister Vicky was scheduled to receive her diploma. When I arrived, the graduation was under way, and the auditorium was filled to capacity. Always the performer, I grabbed a folding chair, sat it down in the middle of the aisle, then took off my coat. Dressed in all black with my Derringer's white pearl handle exposed in my vest pocket, people couldn't believe their eyes. Security guards watched me from the other side of the auditorium. Sitting with my head shining and muscles bulging through my long-sleeved shirt, I was a monstrous size and more hostile than I ever had been.

Not long afterward, Lee got out of jail. We were in my car headed toward Shaw's home when he nudged me and said, "Look out for those fools, Cuz!" When I turned my head to the left, another car had pulled up parallel with us. I was staring into the barrel of a gun. Pointing the gun was Little Vince, one of the Pirus' most deadly gunslingers. He had a demonic smile, knowing he had caught me dead bang. I was furious for being in that position. Instead of shooting, he chuckled, then the car sped off. Lee said, "I hate it when they do that!" I said, "Let's give them something to smile about!" After picking up a fancy new 9-millimeter that converted into a pistol, I had Lee drive while I rode in the backseat with it on my lap.

Driving down Alondra several blocks before reaching Atlantic Drive, I spotted Little Vince and the other Piru parked on a side street. We motored up behind their car before they realized it. Suddenly they were looking down the barrel of my 9-millimeter. Little Vince's face twisted with fury, probably regretting not blowing my head off, or from fear of meeting his maker. Staring at him with hatred, I envisioned bullets slamming into his forehead. Then he oddly asked, "Did you get that 'nine' from the Western Surplus?" I was about to get out when Lee whispered, "Let's go, Cuz, here come the pigs!" I nodded and we drove off. Being eternal enemies, Little Vince and I regretted the missed opportunity.

That wasn't the first time I was caught under the sights of an enemy gun. That deadly dance occurred occasionally between me and other Pirus: you pull up alongside an enemy, point or flash your gun, and then spare his life as if you are God. Had they known for certain I was involved in numerous night raids against them, the Pirus would've focused harder on offing me. Catching each other off-guard during daylight without blasting away had more to do with the timing and too many witnesses around than with a generosity of spirit. Piru Puddin was known for playing that cat-and-mouse game. He was a slinky character whom no one would take seriously in fisticuffs, but he possessed superior night-creeping ability. He was hard to catch. There was only one person crazy enough to hunt Puddin down no matter where he was, even on Piru Street or at Lueders Park—but Buddha was dead.

At the Palm House, I was giving barbecues, and some Crips—like Bitterdog Bruno and Pretty Skip—had a knack for showing up exactly when it was time to eat. This was an era when Crips, Criplettes, and others would show up with moneymaking schemes, mostly absurd, though some of their schemes had potential. But there were three things in life that I stayed away from because they unnerved me: rape, drugs, and burglary. Odd that I would use drugs all day but refuse to deal them. Though I was lacking in ethics, I drew the line when it came to rape. Burglary I avoided too, because I pictured myself entering a window in a home and getting blasted back out with a shotgun.

There was a Criplette named Shirley who used to show up often with moneymaking schemes. One in particular that got Godfather's interest was the street trade, pandering female flesh. I never envisioned myself as a pimp, though I grew up around quite a few. When I was a youngster, I noticed that tough thugs used to rob pimps, beat them down, and treat them like punks. A thug named Big Rock used to say that any man who makes a living off pimping women was the lowest of scum. He said pimps weren't respected on the streets or in prison. That's the main reason I shied away from pimping no matter how often I was approached with tempting propositions. I did know some homeboys who had turned pimp, like Crazy Crip, Undertaker, and Que. But it didn't interest me.

I recall sitting in the living room at the Palm House with Godfather, a roomful of Criplettes, and a number of other females interested in selling flesh. Both Shirley and Godfather had high hopes of schooling me on the fundamentals of pimping, but I wasn't motivated—and I stayed too high to really focus on their schemes. Godfather's pretext was simple. He was greedy. But Shirley's objective was to have me sexually. Though she was a fine woman, she looked like a thinner version of Bonnie, so I treated her like a sister, which she hated. Her get-back strategy was to make me jealous. Whenever I visited her at her grandmother's house on the east side, she would break out letters from Raymond. Her attempts to make me jealous weren't working, but after reading Raymond's letters, it was obvious he felt something for Shirley—or told her what she wanted to hear. It appeared Shirley had exaggerated our relationship in a letter to him, and Raymond blew a gasket! Then someone, probably somebody close to Raymond, whispered lies to him about me trying to encroach on his territory, similar to what he did to Mac Thomas in Compton. The fabrication was preposterous, so I paid it no mind. I had done all that was humanly possible to expand the West Side Crips so that it could multiply on its own. In a bastardized version of Shaka Zulu's brilliance in absorbing other tribes to make them Zulus, I did the same with the West Side Crips, though I didn't know that my strategy paralleled Shaka Zulu's until many years later. I had no desire for more territory. I had pushed the West Side Crips so far west that only the Pacific Ocean could thwart further expansion.

As for the pimping scheme, well, there were close to thirty females willing to hook up with me, and promises of many more to come. It was a pimp's fantasy to be handed a flock of women without having to catch them or turn them out, but for me Crippen meant more than pimping, money, or the women themselves. Had I not been intoxicated most of the time, I probably would've designated Godfather as Mack Daddy and received my cut off the top, like Black Johnny, who always kept his palms fed. But any Machiavellian skills I may have possessed were waning with every tab of acid and every puff of angel dust.

What really prevented me from being involved in the criminal rat race was my counselor's paycheck, and not having to buy food or pay the bills out of my pocket. Since I was able to splurge, I bought two cars, a 1963 lime-green Chevy in mint condition and a 1953 cocoa-brown two-door Oldsmobile that needed engine work but was gangster down. I decided to give the Chevy to Godfather to assure myself that in case of any emergency he and Mad Bull could get to wherever I was quickly. There were numerous rumors floating on the air about the Pirus' plan to ambush me. A Criplette named Sally warned me about this but I was too hardheaded to listen. The thought of the Pirus bringing it to me was absurd. I was Tookie, King Crip! They wouldn't dare try something like that. Didn't they know the repercussions? It angered me so much that I initiated a couple more night raids for good measure.

Sally was another gorgeous femme fatale, able to maneuver among the Piru circle and among other rival gangs. She was gifted with the looks, the shape, and the ears to listen to the braggadocio of certain Pirus. But the more Sally told me about what she heard, the less I took it seriously. But just in case, for back-to-back nights, Godfather and others were holding down security from the rooftop. I never changed my itinerary; it was business as usual for me. One night while in bed with Sally watching TV, I decided to take my pit bull puppy for a walk around the block while puffing on some Thai stick. In my long tweed coat was my .38 Derringer and a pocketful of loose bullets. When I rounded the corner, a car slowly drove by with a bunch of hardheads inside staring at me. I continued to walk with my hand in the coat pocket. Then they drove off. Whoever they were,

I had been recognized, so I headed back to the house where I had several weapons more powerful than my Derringer.

When I reached the house, I made sure everything was all right, then placed my pump shotgun on the floor and closed the door. Earlier I told Godfather, Madbull, and Terrible Tee that I could handle it, but before they reluctantly left, Godfather asked several more times did I think it was cool? I simply patted the pump shotgun and said, "Yes, it's cool!" Later that night, sitting on the porch watching my dog run around the front yard, it seemed darker than usual and there was an unnatural peacefulness. As I puffed on the Thai stick I thought about my homeboy Pretty Skip, a Long Beach Crip killed a couple of nights before on the west side, deep in the Brims' territory. He was caught in bed by this woman's boyfriend, and he beat the guy down. That same night Pretty Skip returned to the scene and was shot to death by the boyfriend and his homeboys. It puzzled me as to how someone could catch Pretty Skip off-guard when he was always packing. I wondered if he was high.

I snapped to alert when I heard my dog barking and growling. I turned my head in the direction where he was standing but it was too dark to see anything. When I looked the other way, the darkness lit up with reddish-gold flashes and the crackling sounds of fireworks. The Thai stick had me toasted, and I thought for a moment I was hallucinating—then realized I was being shot at. I dove off the porch and crawled to the side of the house. By the time I pulled out my Derringer and took aim, the shooters had vanished.

In the sudden silence, the stench of gunpowder dominated the night air. A couple of times I tried to stand up but my legs wobbled and I fell back down to the ground. Gritting my teeth, I used the water hose to cool down my legs and feet that were in fiery pain. I wondered what in the world was wrong with me. A faint light enabled me to see blood streaming onto the grass and into the earth. In agony, I had never felt so alone or vulnerable in my life.

I had been knocked off my imaginary throne. I wasn't scared. I was horrified.

The Big Comeback

Word travels at mach speed when you're doing bad. I wasn't at Martin Luther King Hospital—or "MLK," as we sometimes called it—for ten minutes before people I knew started showing up in droves. MLK had never before received so much attention for a patient. There were countless calls tying up the lines, and numerous visitors, mainly Crips and Criplettes packing visible weapons and demanding tight security. Drifting in and out of consciousness, I saw Bessie standing beside the gurney with tears in her eyes. Sally, between sniffles, kept saying, "Tookie, I asked you to be careful. Why didn't you listen?" I remember being annoyed and telling her to shut up before I passed out.

The following day, I awakened with a serious headache, excruciating pain, and a cast on each leg. Seated in a chair across from the bed was Godfather, grinning and eating from the hospital food tray, while Criplette Debra stood with her hands on her hips, dressed in supertight khaki pants nearly too tight to hold her shapely basketball-sized derriere. When Godfather launched into a strategic dialogue about retaliation, I waved him off and told him to save that for later on. He said, "All right, just kick back, Cuz, here's your Derringer and box of shells." Then, indicating Debra, he said, "Oh, by the way, I also brought you some stank!" Debra fired a few expletives ending with ". . . and your mammy too!" Godfather mentioned something about going to go quiet the crowd before the cops showed up. He suggested that Debra and I could use some privacy, and quipped, "If *she* can't soothe the pain, nothing will!" Debra rolled her eyes, gave him the finger, then wantonly smiled at me. I had no intentions of doing anything. My mind may have been strong—but the flesh was extremely weak. I couldn't resist the primal urge.

Later that afternoon when the nurse reentered the room, she was shocked to see Debra lying beside me partly nude. She politely scolded me: "Mr. Williams, you're not allowed to have a woman in bed with you. This is a hospital, not a motel!" It didn't matter what the nurse said. My concern was the painkiller medication. I looked forward to the next shot like a junkie in need of a fix. My discomfort could not be alleviated by sex, banter, or getting loaded. I needed the powerful sedative to knock me smooth out.

Early the next morning, I felt someone rubbing my bald head and heard people laughing. Jackie was peering down at me. "He's alive, folks!" he said. Raymond was there, and interrupted, "I see the man, but what are we going to *do* about this?" Both of them wanted to know who shot me, but I didn't know. Godfather speculated, "It was probably the Pirus trying to make a name for themselves." Raymond said, "Well, it doesn't matter who the idiots were, they have to pay!" At the moment, my least concern was payback, but it sure felt good to see the camaraderie and hear them fussing over the next course of action.

Being in a debilitated state didn't tarnish who I was. The supreme sacrifice for representing Cripism was martyrdom, retaliation, or shedding one's blood. Even from the gutter level of existence, and detested as the scum of the earth, I sought approval and respect from my peers—no different than anyone else. But being bedridden and aching, there wasn't too much I sought other than relief. Jackie tried to cheer me up, but I wasn't in the mood. Raymond started going down memory lane, reminding me about the time he tried to shoot a double-barreled shotgun with one hand and it almost knocked his shoulder out of the socket. Though it was a hilarious moment, I hurt too much to laugh, so I just nodded. He asked did I remember the time when a gang of us were strolling down the street and he kicked Melvin in the butt so hard he jumped in the air? The kick was so loud that our homeboys, Warlock and Steven G., wheeled around to see what the sound was. Raymond went on to explain that he didn't like Melvin because he reminded him of the other so-called commanders of Crip factions—which wasn't supposed to happen. He chuckled and said, "Melvin's the same guy who wanted our alliance to be the Snoopies!" (What surprised me was that trigger-happy Melvin didn't shoot Raymond.) He then launched into a tirade about Crip factions springing up with self-appointed leaders who were giving Crip a bad name. I agreed with him, but it was too late to change the course of history.

Raymond and I were more alike than we cared to admit. Both of us were defiant, aggressive, tactful, quick-tempered, and egotistic. To hear him rail against the attack on me and advocate payback really felt good, especially since we were at odds on the touchy subject of shared rule. The slight discord was based on my self-promotion and the assumption that I had a motive to be numero uno over the West Side Crips, the East Side Crips, and the Compton Crips. This was absurd. It didn't matter what the incompatibility was, the Crip agenda outweighed our trivial differences. Though there were rumors about Raymond plotting to smoke me, abandon Crip, and start a rival gang, I didn't believe it. Our behavior in the hospital room showed our willingness to rise above such foolishness, and above Shirley's attempt to manipulate a rift.

Being cooped up in the hospital, I couldn't escape its sanitized odor that failed to camouflage the presence of sickness, disease, bloody wounds, and death. While there, I didn't reflect upon my own mortality but I thought about Buddha, Robin, Craig, Dee Dee, Odie, Diver Dan, Pretty Skip, Bebo, Big Boo, Kane, and the other Crips who had been killed. I remembered Mr. X telling me about Salty, a Compton Crip I knew who was ambushed and killed. His last words were, "Don't let them forget me, Salty, a do-or-die Compton Crip." I pondered whether Crippen was worth all the deaths, suffering, or the tears.

The trauma of the shooting was not a defining moment for me, more like an acknowledgment of being able to take a bullet and keep on stepping. But the problem was that I wasn't up and walking. When a group of doctors entered the room with medical charts, they exchanged ideas and opinions about my situation as if I wasn't present. I gathered from their medical jargon that the bones in both feet and ankles were shattered, and a calf was fractured by .45-caliber bullets. Their consensus was that I would never walk again. The thought of never being able to walk was terrifying, equal to being dead. I pleaded with God not to let this be my cross to bear. I didn't want to be like Koolaid or Toosweet, trying to Crip from a wheelchair.

I snapped out of my self-pity when I saw my mother enter the room with a mingled expression of grief and horror. There is nothing like a mother's comforting presence in a time of need. While she sat there in a dignified fashion, I felt awkward trying to explain what had happened. As she prayed over me, I dozed off—that way I didn't have to explain myself. When I awoke, my mother was gone and there was a new nurse in the room cleaning up. After cleaning the table stand she opened the drawer and spotted the gun and a box of bullets. She closed the drawer, played it off as if nothing had happened, continued to clean the room, and then left.

Not taking any chances, I placed the tiny arsenal under the pillow. I was about to enter la-la land when security guards burst into the room demanding to know where the gun was. Two of them started searching the room while one guard looked inside the table drawer, then underneath the pillow. With the discovery of the gun they stood around the bed giving me the third degree: "What did you need the gun for? Who are you? Are you a Black Panther or something? Why are there so many people concerned about you?" Then the cops entered the room with some questions of their own: "Who shot you, Tookie? How many shooters were there?" Even if I knew their names, height, weight, and phone numbers, I would not have uttered a word. That was the ganghood code.

Later, I was told by a nurse that for the safety of the hospital and other patients, I had to be moved from the premises in the morning. The nurse told me this was the first time a patient had ever been kicked out of this hospital. She asked, "Mr. Williams, are you some kind of gangster?" I told her I was too broke to be a gangster. The next day, Fred Shaw's son and another counselor, Kenny, picked me up in a van. While being wheeled out, I tried to retrieve my gun, but a sheriff informed me if I wanted the gun I'd have to come down to the station—if I wanted it bad enough. I cursed as I was wheeled past a crowd of Crips and Criplettes and into a waiting van. The cop yelled, "We got your gun, Tookie, come and get it!"

The van pulled up in front of Shaw's office across the street from the Red House, and I was carried in and placed on the couch. While I was resting, Bonnie appeared, staring down at me with tears in her eyes. She asked what had happened and where was Shaw planning to take me? I was too tired to answer any questions, so I waved her off. It was Shaw's intent to find me a Shangri-La-type setting where I could fade into anonymity. The house turned out to be located in Pasadena where two women, sisters, planned to look after me. I was placed in a bedroom with a well-lit bathroom. Next to the bed was a walker and a small table with a bowl of fruit, cups, and a pitcher of orange juice. Without any communication between me and the two females, it became evident that if I wanted to use the bathroom I'd have to travel back and forth on my own. There were no bedpans and no one around strong enough to assist me.

Somehow I'd have to call forth whatever strength wasn't drained from my body to make the bathroom trip. It was less than ten feet away, but it was like walking a mile. The question wasn't just whether or not I had the strength but could I bear the pain. Due to soreness, I had lain in bed for days unable to get up and relieve myself. Finally when I couldn't take it any longer, I managed to maneuver my legs to the side of the bed. It was physically impossible for me to stand up, so the only option was to crawl, and crawl I did. The entire process took from thirty minutes to an hour, depending upon how many rest periods I needed. With each grueling step I cursed the maggots who put me in this condition. It burned me up knowing that I'd probably never get my hands on the perpetrators, especially since no one was eager to lay claim. If I was serious about a comeback, I'd have to do it on my own.

After several weeks I was able to use the walker, though it felt like hundreds of daggers were poking my legs and feet. To go back and forth to the bathroom left me weak and drenched with sweat. During my hospital stay, I didn't eat but I did drink a concoction of high protein, ice cream, baby Similac, cherries, and condensed milk mixed in a blender. Drinking two to three glasses of this each day, I could feel my strength slowly returning.

When the two sisters got wind of who I was, they were scared to death and wanted me to leave. I was booted back to the Slater Boys' Home in Compton. From what the elder Shaw, the director of all the boys' homes, told me, a young Crip from the Red House had shot at Jimel. Jimel got into scrapes with other Crips, most often over a female. Either they took potshots at him, or they wanted to go one-on-one. Jimel was all right. He was becoming a close homeboy of mine, but he was misunderstood by most Crips. There were times when I had to step in to prevent a serious casualty, like when Godfather, Madbull, and Terrible Tee were plotting to smoke Jimel. Ambushing was their specialty, and they were more than eager to follow through.

But I wasn't interested in any madness. All I wanted was rest, and the Slater Boys' Home provided a peaceful habitat where I could convalesce. My physical rehabilitation had me returning to Martin Luther King Hospital—provided I agreed to enter from the side-back door with just one person, Shaw Jr., no guns, and leave immediately after each session. The doctors had said I'd never walk again, but I was already walking in casts, without the walker. I figured if I was unable to walk with the casts removed, then I'd need a set of customized leg supports made. Eventually the casts came off. My legs were skinny as toothpicks and very weak, but they were able to hold up my weight. I used the walker for a while, then graduated to a wooden cane like the ones we used to crack people over the head with. Talk about karma.

The doctor made the decision to leave the bullets in my feet. To remove them would cause more damage. He told me that, over the years, each bullet would make its way back to the surface, to the entry point. On the final day of rehabilitation, the doctor warned me that I'd have a permanent limp. I refused to believe him. Doctors have been wrong before. In the midst of all the prognostications, no one bothered to address the lingering trauma of being shot. The realization that I was not invincible, knowing I was vulnerable, was a rude awakening. Paranoia gripped me. I didn't feel comfortable unless Godfather, Jackie, L.C., or others were around for security.

For the time being, my flamboyance and boldness had been shattered like glass. I was leery about strange noises and tentative about my movements outside the house. Everywhere I went, either Godfather or Jackie was there to drive me. We were armed as if we were going to war. Godfather's constant bragging about the retaliations that had taken place in my absence and future paybacks didn't restore my confidence the least bit. My nerves were so rattled that just hearing the sound of a gunshot, I'd almost jump out of my skin. There was a moment at Bonnie's mother's house while I was visiting my son Travon that I heard a volley of gunshots. Though in casts, I managed to dive to the floor with a quickness that stunned even Bonnie. Somehow I had to regroup and learn again how to cope with the madness out in the ganghood.

There was no time for self-pity. My rivals would have no problems trying to finish their bungled job, especially since I was immobilized. I needed my size, strength, and ability to walk if I wanted to aggressively confront the opposition. With the discipline of a celebrated African distance runner, I underwent a strict regimen of workouts that forced me to grow into a massive rage. Never before had I possessed such one-pointedness. I was motivated, dedicated, and more than enthused to retaliate.

During my recovery phase, there were Criplettes like Crip Connie, Tasha, Tina, Goldie, Shelly from Long Beach, and the east side's Li'l Pamm who were in and out of the Slater House. The most consistent was Li'l Pamm. She was one of many very attractive Criplettes: Crips chased after her like hounds in heat. Pamm had no qualms about packing a gun or using it. She reminded me of Bad Bessie. I knew my back was covered with her around. She was more than a pretty face. We would stay in one another's life for a while, drift apart—and then from time to time hook back up for a day or two. It felt good to have Pamm and the other Criplettes around to extend their time, attention, and assistance. But in spite of their feminine tenderness and attempts to be Florence Nightingale, they were just as calculating and cold-blooded as we were. Had they been born male, they would have gained street reps equal to or greater than those of some Crips. I respected the Criplettes to the best of my limited male Crip nature, but they were still an enigma to me, as were all other women.

As the months passed, my legs became stronger but I still limped badly and wasn't able to run or even to walk fast. What I lacked in foot speed and agility, I made up for in physical strength. From time to time I would drive iron with a close homeboy, Marcellis, one of the spearheads of the Lantana Crips. We found common ground on the weight pile and in knocking our opponents senseless at parties with every opportunity. Other than Crippen, driving iron was the pinnacle of Cripdom. It was rare to find a Crip who wasn't into driving iron or didn't try to become yoked. Being able to work out seemed to get my life back on track, but I felt that time was running out for me.

Bob Simmons knew several people who tried in vain to convince me to participate in their youth programs. A black man named Fred Horn had an idea about creating a program for individuals in gangs to promote peace. This eventually became known as the "Round Table." I didn't participate because I wasn't interested, not to mention that Bob felt the guy was questionable. Another black man whose name escapes me was the director of the Uhuru Center on the west side. He had an idea for a program, but I waved it off too. Then Bessie, who warned me about the Alpha List, wanted to introduce me to another man interested in establishing a youth program. Godfather and I arrived at Bessie's apartment in the Avalon Gardens where I shook hands with a tall, burly figure I didn't recognize. His name was Rosie Grier, an ex-football player. I'd never heard of him. I sat in silence listening to his plans to make the community better and safer, but it just didn't jibe with me. I wondered what this fat guy's angle was. He appeared from nowhere with this grand idea in his mind that missed my interest by a thousand miles.

Whether Rosie's intent was legitimate or not, his agenda clashed with my ideas of revolting against other street gangs and against the status quo—of which he obviously was a member. My rejection of outside help was indicative of the juices of rage flowing through my veins. There was nothing Rosie could have said to incite me to alter the only lifestyle I knew. Crip defined who I was. I didn't need a cane, blue rag, or tattoo to confirm it. My name spoke for itself, and everybody knew what I represented. I was the Crips' figurehead and politician rolled into one. And I was recuperating in record time.

The Old Stomping Ground

Since my rivals failed to lay me to rest in Crip martyrdom, I knew I'd be back in commission sooner or later. For a while I traveled throughout Compton, feeding my ego with night raids that felt ridiculous as I limped away after each dirty deed. Terrible Tee and Godfather enjoyed the action, but for me the thrill was gone. I was the walking wounded, unable to perform the simplest of movements with my crippled legs. I was tormented by thoughts of never being able to smash the so-called death squad, haunted by feelings of inadequacy. Returning the favor, *lex talionis* style, was something I needed and wanted.

This was 1977. I was comfortable enough to be out driving alone though I was packing heat for potential trouble. I drove a souped-up 440, a green Charger with thick racing tires and phenomenal speed. I wasn't the speed racer type, but to compensate for limited movement, a muscle car wasn't bad. I could often be seen flying down the block with some undercover cop car trailing in the distance. I'm sure they followed us when Jimel and I tried our hand at becoming professional bodybuilders with the Joe Weider establishment. A photographer arranged to take some photos of us at Santa Monica Beach. My employer's son Fred was also at the photo shoot, and he thought everything was turning out well. I don't know about Jimel but I was embarrassed to be posing in a pair of tiny trunks I called bikini panties. I wore my robe for dear life up until the very second it was time for me to pose. After the photographer finished, he assured me that I was a shoo-in for becoming an upcoming bodybuilder and that I resembled the former Mr. Olympia Sergio Oliva. But who's to say he didn't tell Jimel that *he* resembled Dave Draper or somebody?

A few days later the photographer said they were impressed with my physique, but I couldn't be accepted because of the rumor that I was the leader of the biggest gang in Los Angeles and would bring bad press. Jimel didn't fare any better. Though I couldn't prove it, I suspected it was the cops' trailing me that foiled my plans. I was disappointed but accustomed to calamity . . . next!

Back at the Slater House I was confronted by a problem involving a fourteen-year-old named Creeper, from the boys' home, who claimed he was a bounty hunter. He had been arrested for armed robbery. At the police station, he allegedly told the detectives he had been pulling robberies, then bringing half the loot to me. Later I was told the cops had coerced Creeper into fabricating the robbery story. The lie stunned me, but the cold part was that Shaw believed it. The years of outstanding service meant absolutely nothing, and I was fired. But being fired felt more like a relief. I was freed from having to live a double life. Crippen night and day could now be the only way.

I packed my weights and other belongings, left Compton, and headed for the west side, my old stomping ground. I went straight to my stepfather's house on 69th. Across the street in a duplex lived my stepsister Vicky and her children, Baebae and Kameshi. They were planning to move to San Pedro. Although I had no idea as to what I would do to maintain a steady flow of cash, I agreed to take over the rent after they moved. But instead of looking for a job, I was out in the street reestablishing old ties with homeboys I hadn't seen in years. Much had changed on the west side. Quite a few Crips had been killed and imprisoned, and there was a new breed of young Crips anxious to make names for themselves. They were also dying fast.

The ultimate platform then for attention was Centinela, the park of all parks. It used to be the favorite hangout for the Inglewood Family gang, but the mass migration of Crips from all over the city changed the tenor of that park without a single battle. For Crips, local families, and children, Centinela was probably the safest park in America. Other than me or some other Crip knocking out an unfriendly guest here and there, the park was peaceful. Both Jimel and I used to stroll throughout the spacious park in overalls, shirtless, wearing power-lifting belts. Under the sun, our muscles sparkled with baby oil. Fascinated women and wide-eyed children would ask for our autographs on paper or paper plates: local people and street celebrities mingling on the same playing field.

The stage was set no matter where Jimel or I took off our shirts. Prior to "breaking out," Jimel would perform his usual round of push-ups to feel pumped. One evening we were planning to attend a concert at the Forum. Jimel and I drove iron for two hours at the Slater boys' home, so I offered him the shower in the back bedroom. To my surprise, he declined, stating that "the water will take away my tight!" As a substitute, Jimel loaded up heavily on my Old Spice cologne, slipped into his white tailored suit, and was raring to go. Then at the concert inside the men's rest room he still did close to two hundred push-ups.

Though the Forum was a highlight performance where we would flex for the entire audience and receive a standing ovation, nothing could beat being at Centinela Park on a bright Sunday afternoon: family picnics, children playing, women galore, and the sweet aromas of barbecue chicken and ribs. On Sundays, the park was swarming with Crips strolling with their pit bulls, playing football, gambling, getting loaded, hawking females, breaking out, or just kicking back and snacking on barbecue.

On one particular Sunday, I was listening to Godfather's not too subtle comments about Jimel being a joke, that nobody could stand him: "Let's just blow him away and get it over with!" Before I could respond, somebody hollered, "Fight," and a crowd ran up the hill toward the parking lot. At the top of the knoll, Godfather, smirking, blurted out, "It's your doofus buddy Jimel about to get beat up!" I

headed toward the giant circle of fifty or more Crips with two com-
batants in the middle—Crazy Ed from Hoover and Jimel, with Raymond acting as referee. Bare-knuckled street fighting had its own
mystique about it. Being trained in boxing, karate, or jujitsu was
sometimes a liability, especially if you were expected to win. I've seen
plenty of cocky boxers and karate enthusiasts get mopped up quickly.
There were no limited rounds, no cut man, no water, or no ringing of
a bell for a hiatus. When you fought, you fought for however long it
took. Inside the gladiator circle of testosterone anything goes: punching, kicking, biting, cheating, spitting, kneeing, eye gouging, arm or
leg breaking, cursing, and any other weaponless tactic. Though I
didn't approve of Crips fighting one another, it was by far better than
their killing each other.

In this brief fight, Crazy Ed was looking stylish, throwing jabs and
combinations, but he made the mistake of getting too close and Jimel
grabbed him. The tables quickly turned. Crazy Ed was sitting on the
ground with his legs stretched out and Jimel kneeling behind him,
holding him in a choke hold. Everybody stood there in a trance while
an infuriated Jimel tried to choke Crazy Ed out, but Raymond and I
stepped in to stop it. Though the fight had ended, a feud was brewing. Some Hoover Crips flashed their weapons, ready to blast Jimel
on the spot. Raymond and I talked them out of it.

Later, East Side Crip Bulldog, one of the spearheads of the Hoover
Crips, told me that Jimel was very lucky. Violence was the primary
Crip negotiation technique as well as an attention-getting device. My
own need for attention now had become an effort to blot out the un-
healed scar of being shot down like a mangy animal in the street. In
truth, being blasted had me trying to piece together a shattered ego.
Flamboyance, rage, self-hate, drug stimuli, and Crip aggression had
become my pillars of support. I didn't have to peruse Frantz Fanon's
literary works to perceive violence as a means to an end. Urban street
violence had long since mutated into a common ganghood practice
introduced in particular situations. I was so permeated with self-hate,
Caucasians were safe from my wrath unless they foolishly stumbled

into my path. But black humanity beware! I was death in a tinderbox ready to explode. I was conditioned to loathe myself and all aspects of black reality.

The same enemies I had repelled for years were now watching me and Jimel strolling in their territory with our shirts off. It was lunacy to be out there flexing our muscles in the midst of gang warfare but that was the insolence of Crippen, do or die, can't stop won't stop, or this is Crip, fool! I still managed to hurl my body into the fray for any Crip. No Crip who knew me could deny that in a pinch, the words "go get Tookie" would call me forth to redress their problem. In the 'hood where East Side Crips Commander Little James lived on 118th Street, he and his homeboys clashed with a big, stocky, armed lunatic. When James called I didn't hesitate to show up and confront the figure, who looked every bit a lunatic. I pulled the guy to the side, and he quickly started nodding his head in agreement to everything I said, like those dolls attached to a car dash whose head bounces up and down. In his mental turmoil he understood it was in his best interests to leave Little James alone. Perhaps he had recognized a slight madness in me. Little James didn't have any more problems with that guy, nor did I ever question why they didn't smash him. I knew they could.

It was this sort of incident that made me appear bigger than life. Whether it was acting as a negotiator or as an aggressor, I always managed to quell the storm or carry the day. Crips like my stepbrother Wayne, Godfather, Sweetback, Blackie, Big Marcus, Mansion, Samuel "Capone" Coleman, and a long list of others would routinely seek my assistance. Though Godfather had warned me about Jimel bringing trouble to my doorstep, I didn't mind because I never discriminated against a Crip homeboy. Once Jackie and I had finished driving iron when Jimel met up with us on the corner. He was huffing and puffing after running from his mother's apartment on Century Boulevard at about 100th Street, all the way to where we lived on 69th. Jimel complained about some youngster with several friends who had crowned him with a baseball bat, busted out his back car window, and appropriated his tape deck. The feud involved this high school guy's girlfriend whom Jimel tried to hit on and who rejected his advances.

When I arrived, Jimel's car, parked in back of the apartments, had been vandalized. I talked with the youngster's father, who had his son return the tape player and agreed to pay for the damages. Whether or not he followed through with the payment I don't know, but the conflict was squashed. I relished doing the dirty work because it added to the legend of who I was. I seized every angle in life to define myself as being *somebody*. It didn't matter how ruthless or despicable I had to become in the realm of ganghood as long as I was the best. Gradually, I was morphing into a combination of Buddha and Black Johnny, becoming one highly unstable character. I was back home on the west side—this time bigger and worse.

Float On, Float On, Float On

The years 1977 to 1979 were the lowest point of my life. I allowed drugs to rule my consciousness and render me an addict. Much of my existence in one fashion or another was connected to drugs. Having used marijuana, angel dust, LSD, barbiturates, cocaine, Thai stick, and glue, none of these were more chronic than sherm, a cigarette soaked in Phencyclidine, better known as PCP.

The first time I was introduced to this powerful drug it rocked me to the core. While walking toward the liquor store for some orange juice, Calhoun, an Avalon Garden Crip, and I detoured through an alley and puffed on a sherm. It was an immediate high that scared the hell out of me, and I told Calhoun never again to offer it to me. But a month or two later at the Festival in Black held at MacArthur Park, I smoked a sherm with Lynn after she cornrowed my hair. This time I felt wonderful, euphoric. Later, what really caught my attention was that it didn't seem to hinder my ability to drive iron—but appeared to enhance it.

For a while, I smoked sherm "only on the weekends and for recreational purposes" . . . and so from Friday to Sunday it was on! Whatever excuse I could find for frying my brain cells, I used. The illusion was that my troubled world magically disappeared. Poof, gone, just like that. Reality and delusions intermingled in a deadly cocktail of phantasmagoria. It was a personal hell where the longer I remained in such a state, the further I was alienated from society. I failed to notice the increase in my aggression and outlandish behavior.

Needless to say, jacking the local dope dealers for their supply of drugs or money was an act of need, greed, or for the hell of it. My homeboys and I viewed dealers as just another street gang with limited options for dealing with us Crips. Since they couldn't complain to the cops, they either had to fight us or pretend it never happened. They weren't chumps, but they were less ruthless, they were outgunned, and we had a numerical advantage. In spite of my roguish lifestyle and drug use, I still managed to drive iron five to six days a week.

The 69th Street duplex that Jackie and I shared was the West Side Crips' embassy, where youngsters flocked around, starry-eyed, wanting mostly to watch me driving iron while James Brown's "The Payback" was playing. The song had become the Crips' theme melody for retaliation. On just about any occasion they would see Big Vertice, Bogard, Jackie, Raymond, Big Bamm, Cutes, Mouse, Big Lunatic, Rusty, Godfather, and a host of others. Young Kody, who would grow up to become known as Monster (and to author a book of the same name), lived down the block. He used to show up bright and early to help stack weights, run errands, or help me wash my car. He and I would stroll to Centinela Park or long distances to some woman's house. I preferred walking because it was the best way to be seen flashing my muscles. Sometimes Kody would sit for hours on a milk crate watching us drive iron, amazed at our size and strength. I regretted our smoking sherm around Kody because we made it appear to be cool. Sometimes Kody joined right in and ended up zombielike, as most of us did.

Smoking sherm, a person's behavior can range from a zombie state to streaking naked, to moving in slow motion, being hyped up or immune to pain, amnesiac, or becoming violent and with enormous physical strength. When my stepbrother Wayne was floating on sherm, he sometimes moved in slow motion as if he was in another dimension. Once while I was getting my hair braided by my stepsister

Demetri, Wayne was high on sherm and got up in super-slow motion to creep over to where Demetri's friend's purse was. He took out the wallet and placed it under his jacket, then returned to his seat as if nothing had ever happened. I shook him out of his trance, and he wasn't even aware of what he had done. Though we all laughed, it was one of the most bizarre things I had ever seen. In time I would do stranger things.

Sherm was cheap, and if it was from a strong batch, a few puffs could keep you high for hours. It enhanced my mood swings, making me far less tolerable of petty things I'd normally let slide by. At the height of my aggression I developed a terrible habit of "jap-slapping," spitting in somebody's face to provoke a fight. I'd even launch into a debasing monologue about a guy's mother, and if that failed, I'd simply knock him out. As for women, I was never hostile toward them. They were always on the agenda. No matter how high I flew on sherm, I didn't let it interfere with my womanizing. I was fascinated with a black woman's rear end, resembling as it does two volleyballs tucked under tight skin. Most Crips I knew felt the same. It's not the beauty—it's the booty!

It wasn't long before I accepted employment along with Godfather, Madbull, Big Curtis, and about twenty other Crips working for Wayne's mother, whose company was the C-and-C Dog Academy. She had no idea that her son and her new employees were Crips.

The job was simple enough. All I had to do was keep an eye on a German shepherd or Doberman pinscher guard dog while it patrolled a particular work site. I reported to work at a beer distribution plant in Compton not far from Compton College. When I arrived, the dog handler was nowhere in sight, but outside the building stood a large crowd of angry strikers who were vandalizing cars and beer delivery trucks and threatening employees. Prior to my coming, the same rowdy crowd of strikers had chased off several other people standing guard.

I didn't realize that the plant's boss was viewing the entire scene from a car in a nearby parking lot. For at least thirty minutes underneath the sun I sat in the chair with my arms crossed while observing the crowd that was whispering, pointing in my direction. A small group of ten Caucasians, Mexicans, and blacks finally swaggered toward the left side of the lot. I got up and matched them stride for stride as I slid completely out of my shirt ready for a fight. We met in the middle of the parking lot where they stopped and stood staring at me. A short pudgy black fellow and a tall and husky white guy took turns running off at the mouth about what they planned to do to the building and me if I tried to stop them. The black guy asked what I was going to do when all of them rushed straight at me. I responded, "I'll knock you and your hillbilly friend out first, if you're stupid enough to try me!" It's true they had the golden opportunity to rush me, but none of them was willing to be the first. I gladly would have fought them all. I knew that had I been defeated, a Crip force would have retaliated. My confidence was higher than the moon, heightened by intoxication.

The following morning, the plant boss greeted me at the gate with high kudos for doing what I often did, "standing up against the odds." He shook my hand in a pumping fashion for about two minutes while stating he had watched the entire thing from the next-door parking lot. He thanked me fifty times, then vowed to always be there for me if need be, but I knew he was just caught up in the moment and didn't really mean it. One night I heard several gunshots in the back of the building. Being drug-inspired I no longer feared gunshots as I scanned the back area and discovered nothing. I knew right then I'd arm myself for work. The next evening after parking my car, I had my pump shotgun resting on my shoulder when I told the crowd that last night somebody shot several times and almost hit me. I warned them if it happened again, I'd be forced to hunt them down like dogs. I ended with a parting remark, "Remember this, fools, I'm not alone. There's more of me around!" My words may have been ignored, but the shotgun was respected.

The following night, the strikers watched as a ten-car caravan of my homeboys and some homegirls pulled into the driveway flashing their rifles and guns out the car windows. The music blasting from car speakers was "The Payback." Big Curtis and Godfather stepped out Crip-walking, and immediately after, a group of Crips and Criplettes Crip-walked with their weapons gleaming from the car lights, hollering, "Crip here! Crip here!" The strikers seemed to have disappeared. Meanwhile, the party was on. Some of the empty beer trucks served as mini motels, the parking lot became the dance floor, and there was a buffet table inside the building replete with cookies, doughnuts, cake, candy, chips, coffee, tea, and sodas. Coming to work each evening was nothing but a party, or a workout session, since Jackie would show up with his car trunk filled with weights, and we'd work out in the parking lot. Literally, my job consisted of getting loaded, lounging, partying, working out, and using the trucks as motel rooms.

There were times when I was supposed to be at work that Jackie and I were in Marina del Rey socializing at two of the most popular clubs, the Bahama Mama's or the Juke Box Jury. Neither of us was there to dance, but only to catch a different female to take home or at least get her phone number for a future sexual conquest. The area was really squaresville. Fortunately for them, most Crips felt it was too far to drive to a club. I entered these clubs with an unmistakable air of malice. If I wasn't mellow on sherm, I was sky-high loaded, but either way it didn't take much to piss me off. Crip rage was my response to just about everything, so it was no surprise that I collared a few people there, especially for accidentally stepping on my biscuit shoes, a cardinal sin. After leaving the club, I'd return to the workplace, where I kicked back until my shift was over.

Though I worked twelve-hour shifts, there was no way I'd stay there the entire time. When I wasn't partying on the company lot, I'd simply unmuzzle the dog and let him run loose, then vacate the premises and return a few hours before I clocked out. There was nobody there to hassle me or to report to, so I had free reign. Once while on my way to work, I saw a bunch of cop cars parked around the building, so I made a U-turn to drop my rifle off at my friend

Janice's house and then returned to work. The strikers had discovered who I was and snitched to the cops about us packing weapons. Earlier that day, the cops mistakenly arrested this guy Bear (years later he would end up on San Quentin's death row), who didn't remotely resemble me. But after that episode there were no more run-ins with the strikers. They never crossed their side of the picket line. It was reminiscent of the 1920s when big companies hired the Mafia or other thugs to guard their property against strikers—who seemed quite tame to us. Crips were hired to work because no one else wanted to deal with the hostile strikers. For us it was easy money.

Within a matter of weeks I purchased a clean gold 1970 Cadillac with spoke rims. Cruising around Compton with a nice-size Afro, I was unrecognizable, but I still traveled with a weapon for security. Ever since I was a counselor, I purchased all of my weapons legally and kept the ownership documents in my wallet to avoid going to jail, I hoped. The law states that a legal gun owner can carry a gun in the vehicle as long as it's not loaded and the gun and bullets are carried separately—the gun or the bullets had to be in the trunk or somewhere inside the car but never together. To some cops the documents didn't make any difference. They'd take me to jail on general principles just to have the papers authenticated. In South Central the simplest of civil rights are lost at the moment of birth for blacks, even when you are confronted by an authority figure of the lowest status.

Working at the beer distribution plant was easier than being a counselor. I didn't expect to hold the job for long. Somehow I would deny myself prosperity, or fate would do the same. There was an incident where one of Wayne's mother's female friends had argued with me over the smaller paycheck I received from her. I was told later that the dispute had more to do with her affinity for me (which I didn't reciprocate), rather than the payroll check. While I was kicking back at work, the woman showed up with her husband and several cop cars and escorted me off the premises. So I packed up the few scattered weights and drove away, not knowing that I'd never again return to Compton.

Back at the duplex, my morning routine began with puffing on a sherm, then I'd prepare for whatever the day would bring. I lived in three worlds. There was the real world that I didn't fathom, the violent gang world, and the illusory world of intoxication where past vulnerabilities were suppressed, where I was the man of steel living in a fool's paradise. I spent all that time indulging in the frivolity of drugs and becoming a sherm addict. During my mind-altering experiences, I slapped longtime friends Bimbo and Mansion, broke a broom handle over Eddy's head, and was said to have attacked many others for no apparent reason. Not too many people wanted to be around me because I had become too unpredictable. There were episodes when I waddled in dirt, got down on all fours, and challenged a vicious dog bark for bark and growl for growl through a fence. I was on the brink of insanity.

When I wasn't tripping out, I was chasing after women like a dog in heat. Calhoun used to show up bright and early all excited about us going out to scour the west side for available women. One sunny morning he showed up talking about how we had to go to Southwest College where the campus was full of beautiful black women. After we puffed on some sherm, I was raring to go. I went through my usual ritual of oiling up my yokes just in case I needed to "break out" in front of women. When we arrived the college looked deserted, and I asked Calhoun what was up with this madness? He assured me everybody was in class, but at lunch I'd get an eyeful. In the meantime we strolled down the hill toward one of the tiniest gyms I had ever seen. For kicks I worked out alongside some of the football players, who asked if I was planning to go out for football practice. I responded, "And what, mess up this beautiful body?" Calhoun almost fell to the floor laughing.

Before I left the gym, I gave a few of them some pointers on how to build up their arms, then we were out of there. As we were walking up the hill I saw a small crowd of women walk by and all of them were thick and shapely. A black man sometimes chooses a woman in the image of his mother in hue and stature. Perhaps that's why the beauty of this female caught my eye, not to mention her tiny waist. As we passed, I turned and smiled, then complimented all of them on how well they looked that afternoon. They smiled and giggled.

When we reached the grassy area in front of the college, it was packed. A music box was blaring out Marvin Gaye's song, "Got to Give It Up." I didn't have to scan the crowd because I already chose the voluptuous beauty I wanted. Calhoun, knowing the catch action was good, urged me to "break out," but I told him it was all about timing, to be patient. Minutes later, with the sun beaming, I sauntered over to an area where I couldn't be missed. I slid out of my shirt and started flexing my muscles. The moment I started making my chest jump to the beat of Marvin Gaye's song, women started ululating and clapping like they were at a Teddy Pendergrass concert. After flexing, I made a beeline to my female of choice, who had been ogling me.

I introduced myself to the woman. "Hello, my name is Stanley Williams, but my mother, relatives, and close friends call me Tookie." Her eyes widened. "You're Tookie?" I answered, "I sure am." Her name was Michelle. She told me her brother was Michael, who was known as a hustler and was in a wheelchair, paralyzed, having been shot for gambling with loaded dice, according to the story. It was awkward when she talked about all the horrid stories she'd heard about me, especially when she asked if I remembered when some of my crazy Crip homeboys and I trashed her mother's apartment during a late-night party across the street from the golf course on Western. I remembered that party all too well. I told her things had gotten out of hand that night and I apologized. She talked about how different dudes she knew described me as being bald-headed and muscle-bound, with scars all over my face. They told her I was mean, ugly, and always jumping on people. She said, "You don't look anything like they said, and you don't appear to be mean!" After a lengthy, pleasant dialogue, we exchanged phone numbers and I promised to call her later that day. Calhoun and I then left.

When I called Michelle that evening, she sounded downhearted. Her mother disapproved of her having anything to do with me and didn't want me calling the house, because she knew exactly who I was. Michelle told me she cried for hours pleading with her mother to allow me to call the house, and she claimed her brother Michael cried alongside her in an attempt to change their mother's mind. Her mother finally approved of my calling.

Floating on sherm, Calhoun and I arrived at Michelle's mother's home in Gardena. It looked like a family tribunal. Michelle's mother was beautiful and gracious, and not once did she bring up the madness of my past. I met Michelle's stepfather, her sister, Nunu, and one of her four brothers, Michael. I had met another one of her brothers, Lewis, at Washington High School. I'd been surrounded by him and some of his homeboys. At that time, he stood there with a blackjack in his hand trying to question me about a run-in his brother had with my homeboy Bimbo. Whatever Lewis and his cronies' intent may have been, it was foiled with the realization that Buddha and twenty of my homeboys were observing. The misunderstanding immediately disappeared. Lewis eventually began hanging out with Melvin and his crew. A decade later, Lewis's younger brother Michael would claim untruthfully to be a founder of the Crips. Odd that Michael would make such a bogus claim. His brother Lewis became a Crip before he did.

The checkered history between me and her family members didn't stop Michelle and me from hooking up. Though I was able to hide my addiction from her for many months, she heard vivid accounts from others of my drug escapades. Like the time Blackie and I visited the "Coolie Cools," the notorious Inglewood apartments, nicknamed "Sherm Alley," with its two giant stone statues of African heads in front. Blackie's car was parked in the middle of the street with the motor running as I jumped out, mobbed a drug dealer, and pummeled him to a bloody pulp. Then before a cheering crowd, I held a shopping cart overhead and slammed it down on the guy several times. The cops had a warrant for my arrest, but the guy regained consciousness after his coma and refused to press charges. To Michelle, the story was untrue—but for me it was real life concealed in amnesia.

My troubled life was a maze of contradictions that rendered me a hypocrite of the highest order. Absurdly, I believed that I could maintain a job and smoke sherm simultaneously. I began working again as a counselor for a boys' home near West Hollywood on Normandie Avenue. The two-story home was an ideal place for youngsters to try to get their lives on track, far removed from the urban tapestry of gang propaganda. Though there was racial diversity in the home, there were only minor conflicts that made my job less hectic.

Serving as a live-in youth counselor had its challenges. Sometimes, when I was too high to drive home, Michelle would stay, keep me company, and then leave early in the morning. Other times, Calhoun showed up and we'd drive iron, then puff away on some "love leaf" (marijuana dipped in PCP). Love leaf caused more blackouts—amnesiac incidents—than sherm. One evening, prior to taking a shower, I entered the living room where counselors and youths were watching TV. Wearing a pair of boxer shorts, stoned out of my mind, I demanded that they "look at me, I'm beautiful!" I then pounded my fist on the big wooden dining room table, splitting it in half, causing everyone to run out of the house. Then I went out in the middle of the street and tried to pull people out of their cars, ranting and raving like a madman. I remember none of this.

When I snapped back into reality, I found myself standing in the shower. After I dried off, I heard cops calling my name on a bullhorn. When I opened the door, there were cops everywhere pointing guns and ordering me to walk toward them. I was then handcuffed and placed in the backseat of the patrol car. On the freeway, I asked the cops what was the problem, and one of them told me, "Just relax, Tookie, the doctors are going to take good care of you." Drifting in and out, the next thing I knew I was in Metropolitan Hospital strapped to a gurney and being intravenously given some kind of drug. The next day when I came to, I was sitting in a day room chair wearing a quasi-straitjacket. Then, to make matters worse, I was sandwiched between a white guy in a hospital gown who rapidly recited, "Do you remember me, do you remember me?" and, on my left, a Latina woman who gently stroked my face, saying, "Pretty, pretty, pretty!" I figured I was still high on love leaf and that this nightmare would end in a minute.

Nearby, a female was singing a country-western song, and some guy was swatting at imaginary objects. A black fellow was tap-dancing, and other people were walking around like zombies. It still didn't register that I was in a loony bin. It was a scene right out of *One Flew Over the Cuckoo's Nest*. Then a black guy hollered out, "Tookie!" This stranger launched into a dialogue about knowing who I was and said that he knew Raymond too. He said, "Tookie, you've been living a wicked life. It's time for you to stop and repent. Bow your head and pray with me, my brother!" He babbled on for several minutes about revelations, fire and brimstone, then digressed into pleading that I allow him to join the Crips so he could help purge the world of the Brims. This had to be hell. I was unable to silence these characters whose unified front was to antagonize what little bit of sanity I had left.

I believe it was two days later when I sat in the day room waiting to see the resident psychiatrist. Then reappearing like incubi were the same three figures I thought were part of the earlier hallucination. No longer in a straitjacket, I still felt disoriented. As I headed toward the restroom, moving with great difficulty, I was escorted by the three irritants. While standing and relieving myself, the self-professed black preacher stood off to the side preaching. The white guy kept restating the phrase, "Do you remember me?" The long-haired female stroked my face saying in repetition, "Pretty!" I was escorted into a psychiatrist's office where he asked questions about my drug use. I denied ever using drugs and stated that someone must have spiked my protein drink with LSD or something. I told him I was a bodybuilder and that getting high would destroy my chances of becoming a professional. When he started asking me weird questions about whether I'd ever had sexual relations with my mother, sister, and aunts, I almost exploded. Instead, I countered, "Have you ever gotten a blow job from your mother?" Fortunately for him I was physically incapable of reaching across the table and slapping the taste out of his mouth. I noticed whenever I was seated before a white voodoo doctor, his analysis of me would center on either a personal demon or an occupational trend, based on his psychosexual standpoint.

Perhaps my expression of scorn and silence convinced the doctor to change the subject. He asked if I was released, was there anyone who could pick me up? He didn't see why I should be kept there any longer. When I responded with a yes, he gave me the phone and exited the office. I contacted Michelle and Jackie and later they picked me up. Having floated into the Metropolitan Hospital, I just as easily floated out, untransformed, with no reconciliation of my divided life.

Schemes and Things

S omehow I continued to avoid the traps of the law. In a Los Angeles courtroom, Johnnie Cochran, my attorney, persuaded me to accept a $100 fine and six months' probation for the charge of "assaulting a peace officer." As long as I wasn't doing time, I didn't trip. After shaking my attorney's hand, we parted ways. With the court case behind me, other troubles found me. There was a bookie called Chunky who knew a white guy in debt to him for five grand from gambling. Chunky gave me the guy's address along with his description and said, "My brother, if you can collect the money, half is yours." Now, though his offer was gracious, I planned to pocket everything. Nothing personal, just a Crip thing.

When I knocked on the white guy's door in Gardena, Wayne stood off to the side. In these kinds of situations I felt I had the upper hand. The guy was living foul, and for him to call the cops would be a joke, because he was considered white scum. The moment the guy opened the door I grabbed him by the collar and demanded Chunky's money. He said, "I only have two hundred dollars in my wallet." When he handed it over, I asked what else he had that was worth the debt. The guy blurted out, "Take my car, it's a 1975 Monte Carlo that should settle the debt, and I can sign over the pink slip right now." I smiled and said, "OK, but we'll go to the DMV and have it put in my name."

At the Inglewood Department of Motor Vehicles I paid for the registration, then we left to get a smog device. The car was legally mine. Throughout the day I spread the word that I won a car in a big dice game. However, the next morning some cops showed up to inform me that the owner of the Monte Carlo claimed I took his car and forced him at gunpoint to sign over the pink slip. Therefore, if I wanted to keep the car I'd have to submit to a lie detector test to prove I didn't coerce that guy into giving me the car. Once again, I found myself at the Glass House police station. I failed the test. But when they completed testing me and the white guy, I heard a detective say the test showed that we were both lying. That's when I also heard a female officer whispering to other officers, "I was told the white guy was lying. There were no weapons involved because Tookie had been under surveillance."

Before I was released, a detective said if either of us wanted to own that car, we'd have to go to small claims court. For days I toyed with different schemes to get the car back, but decided the hassle wasn't worth it. If nothing else, the ordeal confirmed my suspicion that I was being followed, that it wasn't paranoia or my imagination. Here I was painted as the villain, and this was the type of cop harassment that inevitably leads to a frame-up or extermination. Being harassed was business as usual. This became evident one early morning around 3:00 a.m. when Michelle and I were asleep, and there was a loud knock at the front door. Moments later, an excited Jackie banged on the bedroom door alerting me that a battalion of cops were outside, for me to be careful when I came out. In a gallant gesture I told her I'll go out first just in case they started shooting.

It was pitch dark as I eased down the narrow hallway into the living room where I had to weave past a maze of weights and benches. Through the opened front door, I could see Jackie spread-eagled on the wet grass surrounded by cops and a helicopter overhead. The door opened and an armed cop barked out, "That's right, Tookie, just keep walking with your hands up and don't try any Crip heroics."

Outside, I was ordered to lie down next to Jackie. Moments later,

Michelle was lying beside me. While we were on the ground, an elderly lady named Opa, who lived two houses down from me, stood
several yards away. I had known Opa ever since my family started living on 69th. She was mother to five sons and a daughter. Her two
youngest sons, Frank and Aaron, would as teenagers become Crips.
Opa stood there demanding to know what the problem was. A cop
told her there was information received that gunshots had come from
inside my apartment. Opa shot back, "Gunshots? That's odd, because I've been awake all this morning, and I haven't heard anything
until you guys and the helicopters arrived!"

Although she continued to protest their harassment, it was to no
avail. Meanwhile, a cop came out with a huge grin holding up my
AR-15 and a pump shotgun. He asked if I had ownership papers for
the weapons. When I produced the documents, it seemed to piss
him off. As soon as the cops finished searching the apartment, one of
them warned me, "Make sure you watch your back!" When the cops
had gone, Opa asked, "Tookie, why are they always harassing you,
and what in the world have you been doing?" I smiled and said,
"Miss Opa, your guess is as good as mine!"

It was Jonjon who approached me with a harebrained scheme to
rob a particular church of its monetary offerings. I looked at Jonjon as
if he were Mephistopheles himself, then said, "Hell, no, are you
crazy?" Even after he told me it was an inside job, that his cousin had
helped him and that there was nothing there to stop us, I couldn't do
it. I may have been immoral to the bone, but I was never crazy or sick
enough to desecrate, vandalize, or stick up a church. But mobbing
other criminals wasn't a crime. In fact, it was open season on them.
Whenever my homeboys and I heard about a dope dealer, street
jacker, bookie, hustler, thief, or any non-Crip who had come across
some money, he was in trouble. Like myself, most of my homeboys
didn't put much stock in their lives.

Case in point: East Side Crip Syles was daring enough to rob an
east side gambling shack. He knew there was a strong possibility of
losing his life, but the potential for financial gain outweighed the con-

sequences. Syles probably would have escaped with the loot, but the back door and windows were nailed shut. Syles was shot dead. Another youngster's death for a worthless cause. May he rest in peace.

Then there was Mac Thomas, a Compton Crip leader turned full-time hustler. It was said that his adopted running buddies were the shadiest of characters, but he insisted on being with them. I remember when Mac was released from Youth Authority, he told me that he was no longer interested in Crippen, and his conversation only revolved around hustling. He tried in vain to convince me to hook up with his crew, but I declined. Later on, from what I gathered, Mac's life was snuffed out by some of his hustler cronies who wanted his share of the heist. I didn't know too much about Mac's last days, but he was another Crip companion who was around during the early days of the Crip legacy and became another black statistic, dying from a thug lifestyle.

I personally have known hundreds of Crips exterminated while traveling down the path of drugs, gangbanging, pursuing money, whatever. But I wasn't intimidated by the possibility of death, and continued to sift through the schemes coming at me from all directions. On one occasion Sweetback approached me with sketchy details about a score that involved mobsters needing some outside help to pull a big heist. There were tens of thousands of dollars to be made by each of us. Though Sweetback didn't know the mobsters personally, his friend James Garrett knew them. I thought, why not? If we were being hoodwinked, hell, mobsters could bleed just as quick as any Crip or Blood could.

The plan was for us to meet the following day at the Marriott Hotel not far from the Fox Hills Mall to discuss the heist. When we arrived at James's home at 104th Street at Western, in the living room were Juice and Hillbilly, two 83rd Street Gangster Crips I had known since their childhood. After a brief chitchat, we caravanned and parked down the street from the hotel. I noticed I wasn't the only one packing. A few other weapons were flashed in a show of confidence and readiness. Inside the hotel we waited in the bar until a short, stocky Italian guy wearing a suit and tie appeared. He briefly talked with James and his hefty wife Esther, then picked up the big duffel bag James had been carrying. Before they left, the Italian told us that someone would be down to get us, but until then the drinks were on the house. Meanwhile, as I sat around looking uneasy about the entire setup, two other mobster-looking guys in suits appeared and motioned for us to follow them. Once upstairs, one of the mobsters turned around and said with an Italian drawl, "Okay, the boss doesn't want anyone in there packing heat, it's for security. So if you're holding something, leave your gun with my partner here and you'll get it back on the way out." I failed to comply.

When we entered the room, two scantily clothed white women were holding silver trays of hors d'oeuvres. On the table were more refreshments and an opened black duffel bag on the floor exposing numerous handguns. I sat in a chair next to the slightly opened window in case there was a need to jump down several stories. Minutes later, two figures, one black and the other Italian, both in suits, entered the room. It was the tall black guy who began talking about jacking a train that supposedly carried a shipment of high-tech weaponry and hundreds of thousands of dollars in UPS bags. While he continued to talk, another Italian guy entered the room with a huge suitcase and pulled out a replica of the type of rifle that would be on the train. The weapon was impressive, twice the size of my AR-15 rifle. It resembled a James Bond rifle with a long clip and silencer. But I was still suspicious of the setup, and the black dude just didn't fit in with the Italians.

Maybe this was how the Italian mobsters did business, but before I left, I wanted to hear more. To my surprise, the black guy broached the subject of each of us having to be questioned prior to the heist to determine if we had what it took to pull it off. Being the last one to enter the separate room, I was asked, "So, Tookie, how many people have you killed?" The query caught me off-guard. I almost stammered when I told the guy, "Hey, dude, I never killed anybody before!" The guy said, "Look, Tookie, everybody in town knows you're a dangerous dude and that you have a reputation for killing people." I stared that dummy in the eyes and said, "Whoever told you that is a liar." He tried to laugh it off to ease the tension and said, "We need someone like you who has the guts to kill." Infuriated, I told him, "I'm not a killer. I'm a fighter."

Back inside the living room I told Sweetback I didn't like the setup and was ready to leave. Seconds later the door burst open with plainclothes cops rushing in, hollering, "Lennox Police, FBI!" A quick glance outside the window revealed cops down there, pointing their guns up at the window. For me there was no escape.

We all were handcuffed and driven to the Lennox Police Station, then transferred later to the Los Angeles County Jail. At the court arraignment, James, Esther, and Sweetback were released, but I had to reappear in court the following day. Both Juice and Hillbilly had pending charges of allegedly robbing a Big 5 Sporting Goods store for its guns, and I was charged with possession of a loaded weapon, which I had stashed earlier under a couch pillow. Unknown to any of us, James and Esther had conspired with law enforcement to set up a sting operation. For many years, James had been an agent provocateur working undercover for the FBI, the Bureau of Alcohol, Tobacco and Firearms—better known as the ATF—and other law enforcement agencies. He was a paid snitch, ready to lie, frame, fabricate, and commit whatever duplicitous act his law enforcement masters commanded of him. Needless to say, James was playing a deadly game. In Africa a snitch would undergo an African-style "necktie"—a car tire would be placed around his neck, doused with gasoline, and set afire while a jubilant crowd watched.

Back in the Los Angeles courtroom, the judge dismissed the charges against me for lack of evidence, but years later I'd be charged again for the same offense and much more. I was used to it. Happiness was something I'd never experienced.

Living the Funk

L iving in South Central, an environment that made it difficult to be a dreamer with idyllic views, I didn't have the cerebral stability usually found in hope. I lived in a mental funk, craving salvation, but the Crip god denied me reprieve from my hell. I was dying a slow death with no purpose or legitimate cause worthy of such a sacrifice. Though I'd boldly challenge any gang rival, I shied away from revolting against the conditions I allowed to dominate my past, present, and future. I was a total mess.

My life's sound track was P-Funk, music that was notable for the funkadelic phase of musical madness, drugs, sex, and urban violence. Popular funk artists like Bootsy Collins, the Ohio Players, Rick James, The Bar-Kays, and the greatest of all funksters, Parliament, reigned supreme in South Central Los Angeles. Parliament was going to appear at the Inglewood Forum, and most Crips I knew were pumped up for the concert. Prior to their performance Parliament drove through South Central in a green limousine, amazing the residents. Though everybody else was looking forward to being entertained, I was preparing to be seen.

The evening concert was so packed that Jackie and I had to park several blocks away from the Forum. Myself and others had devised ways of gaining free admission into concerts. If we were unable to rip a door off its hinges, then somebody would jimmy a door, or in this case, one person paid to get in and then opened a side door. Inside the building there were wall-to-wall women, while speakers blasted Marvin Gaye's "Got to Give It Up." When the time was right Jimel and I started strolling around the Forum with our shirts off before crowds of people shouting, "Tookie, Jimel!" During our posing routine the crowd began to chant, "Go to the stage, go to the stage!" We descended parallel stairways toward the center stage. Abruptly, the lights were cut off, the music stopped, and the Parliament's mothership—a replication of a spaceship—was lowered onto the stage. Though our unscheduled performance rocked the house, we were upstaged as Parliament tore the roof off the sucker.

From musical funk to a funked-up situation: Jackie and I were evicted from the duplex for refusing to pay rent because of a serious roof problem. Jackie moved in with his sister Gloria and brother Joey, and I drifted like a nomad. Other than a razor, toiletries, and a few clothes in the trunk of my car, I left the bulk of my clothing at my mother's and Fred's apartment off La Cienega, or at some female's house. As for the weights Sweetback suggested I talk to James and Esther Garrett about storing my weights in their garage. They agreed, and I unloaded more than three thousand pounds of weights, dumbbells, squat racks, and five different heavy-duty weight benches.

The Garretts told me I had access to their garage anytime, or if need be their home was open to me. They were seemingly friendly people willing to help. None of us suspected that they were agent provocateurs, snitches. Plus, I didn't know the Garretts had informed on Juice and Hillbilly. Being smoked out, I had long since lost my edge to detect a snitch when no one else could. The Garretts managed to snake their way around without exposure while plotting nefarious schemes with anyone seeking to make a buck—then later they would turn the unsuspecting "friend" in to the cops.

Loaded or not, I managed to drive iron with consistency. Between workouts I Crip-walked around with my chest stuck out, playing a man of indomitable posture along with my trusted stepbrother and sidekick Wayne, sometimes known as Li'l Tookie. Wayne was shorter than Napoleon Bonaparte but his madcap exploits elevated his stature. When we were there, we made the Coolie Cools apartments a terrible place to be. Only women, children, and other Crips were exempt from our hostile greed. With sick insolence we caught a lone dealer before he could hide his drugs, which were several jars of wet sherms. Wayne was supposed to search the dude for a weapon but being loaded he did a sloppy job. When we turned to walk away with the loot, the guy whipped out a gun and I heard it click several times. It had misfired, unfortunately for him, which caused *him* to become a human punching bag at our hands.

That was the incautious me, always tempting death's embrace. I lived my life looking through the lens of a movie camera, seeing a caricature of myself going through the motions with an impersonal existence. I can't recall why, but one day Jonjon—former Compton Crip turned West Side Crip—broached the subject. He asked, "If you had to pick between death row or life in prison, which one would you choose?" Without thinking, I nonchalantly said, "Death row." Looking bemused he asked, "Why death row, big homie?" I told him we were already living on death row, biding our time, so to me there was no difference. Oddly, I forgot to mention having already envisioned myself being in a death row cell sitting in Rodin's thinking man position. Jonjon's eyes lit up as he smiled then said, "That's deep, Cuz, but this"—he pulled out a wet sherm wrapped in aluminum foil—"is deeper!"

Although there were other dreams and omens warning me about a ruined future, what other than death could possibly be worse? I was already living the funk. By no stretch of the imagination could I conceive any Crip or acquaintance conspiring with the cops against me. Such Shakespearean intrigue only happened in the movies. I was susceptible to being blindsided. Trusting people would be my undoing.

In 1979 I met Samuel at the Workshop Club on Western. Jimel and I were semi-bouncers at the club and were given free passes inside, provided my homeboys maintained their composure. On a particular evening Samuel and a handful of his cronies tried to bully their way through the side door of the club—which I stopped immediately. His expression told me he was shocked. Under the streetlight I could see Samuel for the first time. If looks could kill, he could have murdered an entire army. Dressed in all black with hand gloves and dark shades to match, his ensemble mimicked the movie character Shaft. Samuel was about five feet ten inches, dark-skinned and muscular, with a manicured Afro. He had unique features, resembling a swarthy monitor lizard with a fierce grimace that alone probably won many battles. He had an unforgettable mug.

When I stepped from the club onto the sidewalk, Samuel's posture was begging for a right jab, and I was positioning myself to do just that. Stepping into full view under the light I heard a few of his homeboys acknowledge loudly, "Hey, wait a minute, Cuz, that's Big Took!" Immediately there were smiles and "C" handshakes (thumb and forefinger made to form a *C*, then connecting with someone else's forefinger), and even Samuel had a toothy grin. While introducing themselves as Harlem's Crips, somebody from behind us hollered out, "What's the problem, Cuz?" A small crowd of West Side Crips approached Jonjon out front doing the Crip walk. Being a showman he said, "I hope I don't have to get physical here." It was hilarious because Jonjon weighed no more than a buck-fifty. After introductions, a few of us caravanned to other parties in the jungle, then to an after-hours club off Crenshaw on Adams. When we arrived, there were cars and people all over the place. I bumped into my stepfather, Fred, a professional photographer who worked concerts, fashion shows, professional fights, weddings, clubs, and premieres, among other events. I was trying my best to stay out of his view because my homeboys and I were acting like complete fools.

Back then the after-hours club on Adams was a predator's paradise for us Crips, with an abundance of women, drug users, and suppliers. Samuel and I started hanging out there, getting high like there was no tomorrow. We clicked like junkies sharing a needle, but in our case it was sherms. Sometimes, sitting in Samuel's black Chrysler car blowing our minds off of sherm, he'd complain about not getting the respect he deserved while crocodile tears flowed down his face. I thought the most ugly thing was a man bawling like a baby. I'd humor Samuel—also known as Capone—by telling him, "Cuz, you have to start acting mean and crazy like the real Al Capone." Other times I'd say, "Look at me, I'm Tookie! I attack first and ask questions later. You're Capone, so be Capone, and stop all this boo-hooing!" Using sherm seemed to affect each person differently, but for me aggression was always up front.

One sunny afternoon while driving down Adams and getting high, Samuel spotted two dudes he had had a run-in with a few days before. I told him to pull over, and then I bailed out of the car. One of them ran off, but the chubbier of the two was a bit too slow. He received the brunt of my physical rage. With a beaming grin and no remorse, I Crip-walked away and got back into the car. Samuel sped off shaking his head, stammering, "Man, I didn't expect that, Tookie . . . you are crazy." That was music to my ears. Being viewed as maniacal or whacked out fed my ego. With my brainwashed mindset I felt unstoppable, unbeatable, lawless, fearless of God, and irresistible to women.

For over a decade, I had been driven by self-hate, eating me up like streptococcus consuming an inch of human flesh a minute. Had I run into someone who acted like me, I would have peeled his cap without hesitation. My blue rage was now mimicking Buddha's. I believed my quest for money and drugs was the only way but failed to realize my poverty transcended the physical. It was a state of mind that shackled me, rendering me incapable of emancipating myself. Darn near everybody I knew was a psychological captive to poverty.

Further, I was unable to evacuate these ugly premises—where could I go? During the worst moments I'd drive to Santa Monica beach to sit with my bare feet under the sand and stare out into the distance. Under a starry sky with the comfort of a cool breeze, the demon of anxiety was held at bay. There were no deep thoughts during those moments. It was a high of a different kind, inhaling the pure oxygen of relief before I had to return to the toxic world called home.

I sensed a finale of some kind coming. Like a madman I was on the move, crisscrossing throughout the west to the east side 'hood of the Q-102 Street Crips. I hung out there with Frog and company or with D-Dog in the J.Ds. Other times I'd show up at the P.J.s in the wee hours of the morning to visit Beverly and our son, Stan. Though she welcomed me with open arms, I wouldn't blame her or Bonnie if they resented me for being absent, for drifting in and out of their lives. Watching my son Stan playing on the carpet, I knew that any effort to reconcile would be too late. It felt the same way when I was with my other son, Travon, whom I drove to school occasionally in a pitiful attempt to play father. In a moronic haze of drugs I was seeking redemption for abandoning my children.

The world was closing in on me.

Cruising in a recently purchased gold two-door 1974 Fiat, I was game for anything. Driving down Hoover Street I spotted Bulldog with a voluptuous female. He was limping badly, having been shot in the leg, and was using a walking cane. Bulldog introduced the female Glenda as a Criplette who was a relative, and they were headed to a Crip house to get high. Inside my car I whipped out aluminum foil with a sherm inside, and Glenda's face lit up as she made a wink-wink gesture. I had high expectations about what was going to happen between Glenda and me that afternoon.

In front of the shabby house off Broadway, a lot of Hoover Crips were outside driving iron or standing around getting high. We entered the house, and I sat at the kitchen table kicking it with Devil. I heard Glenda call me, then motion for me to follow her. Inside the bedroom we sat on the end of the bed and talked for a few minutes, then started kissing. After I pulled out a sherm and took a few puffs, I handed it to Glenda, who had already slipped out of her khaki suit to reveal a leopard ensemble. Maybe it was because I was loaded, but she looked like the poster on the wall, an African warriorette kneeling beside her man. I watched as Glenda took long drags on the sherm, then asked if I was going to undress. As I took off my khaki shirt Glenda's eyes looked as if they were about to pop out of their sockets. She started screaming, "Ah! Ah! Ah!" I almost panicked, thinking that my yokes had melted or something, but when I looked in the mirror I saw nothing amiss. This chick had to be crazy!

Seconds later Bulldog burst into the room asking Glenda what was wrong. Cowering under a bedspread, she continued trembling and screaming as if she had seen a ghost or monster. Furious, I left the room and went outside to sit on the porch. Minutes later Bulldog came out and sat beside me. He mentioned how Glenda had a tendency to trip out when she smoked sherm. I said, "That's an understatement." Bulldog went on to say, "You won't believe it, Tookie. She hallucinated that your veins had turned into snakes, and your yokes were about to explode." Every Crip standing outside burst into laughter except me. Several hours later when Glenda asked if I could drive her home and spend time with her, I angrily declined.

I left the house and returned that evening with Kriss and Opa's young son, Frank, who kept pestering me to let him ride with us. At the Crip house I kicked it for a while with Hoover Crip commander T.S. and drove a little iron. I came back to jack a drug dealer in the area along with a couple other Hoovers. But the guy's stash turned out to be quite low. Disappointed, I returned to the house, snatched up the dude who gave us the bunk info, and dragged him outside by the collar to the back of my car. I popped the trunk, pulled out my pump, jammed it in his mouth, and told him not to move. I launched into a holier-than-thou lecture about the perils of lying to us, and especially to me. I was flying high as a rocket, but my intent was to put the fear of the Crip god in him.

A large crowd of Crips had gathered outside to observe the bizarre spectacle. A smiling T.S. advanced to the front and appealed to me to spare the guy further humiliation or worse. Removing my weapon, I kicked him to the ground. Nodding to T.S. and the other Crips, I got in my car, threw up the Crip sign, and sped off.

It would be over a decade before I'd see T.S. again.

My role as protector continued to be called upon. My stepsister and her man, Allen, were having problems with some fools who mistook their apartment for a dope house. Although they were told differently, the troublemakers continued to harass them and threaten bodily harm. For two evenings straight I camped outside from dusk till dawn waiting to ambush the culprits, who wisely didn't come. James's son, Li'l James, contacted me about bullets flying through their windows. I rushed over to protect them and their visiting nieces and nephews, and I hung around watching over them. The drive-bys ended as quickly as they started. When I told James that I had to leave, he begged me to give him my 12-gauge shotgun for safekeeping. I agreed and told him I'd check in periodically. I didn't know that the drive-bys were a retaliation for James's having set up Juice and Hillbilly.

The Longest Day

March 15, 1979, was chaos. Around 8:00 a.m. Jackie and I were driving iron over at the Garretts while Jonjon huffed and puffed with a set of dumbbells too heavy for him. I went to my car to retrieve my "Paycheck" tape. Returning, I saw James pointing a .38 caliber pistol at Jackie's head, warning him to leave or he'd shoot. I hollered at James to put the gun down, that he better not shoot Jackie. Whether James knew it or not, he had severed the ties between him and us. As I drove away I assured Jackie that tomorrow I'd be moving all the weights over to his sister Gloria's house and that payback was imminent.

That afternoon at McDonald's on Century and Avalon, I ran into an irate Calhoun. He accused Wayne of ripping off a large container of PCP. Though Calhoun was a good homeboy of mine, I warned him not to retaliate against Wayne or I'd come looking for him.

Shortly after the encounter with Calhoun I visited my stepsister Bridget, who told me about several dudes barging into her apartment looking to kill her boyfriend JoeJoe. With Godfather, Bear, Creeper, Diamond, and Crusher, we scoured their hangouts but were unsuccessful. I assured Bridget I'd be back to resolve the madness.

En route to see Lynn I stopped off at the apartments where some of the Q-102 Crips lived and hung out. As we were sitting around smoking some sherm, a guy showed up wanting to purchase a sherm stick and started haggling loudly over the price. I had him kissing the cement quickly, compliments of my wrath.

Finally I arrived at Lynn's apartment, exhausted, hungry, and in need of washing off the day's filth. Lynn was lying on the couch crying when I arrived. Someone had broken in and stolen her brand new entertainment center. She said, "Baby, I know who and where they live, too!" Though my slate was full, I told her I'd handle it later. But first I wanted something to eat, to bathe, then to sleep. On the stove was a huge pot of seafood gumbo, rice, corn bread, and for dessert, German chocolate cake and vanilla ice cream. After eating I stretched out in the bathtub trying unsuccessfully to free my mind of the necessary tasks at hand. Kneeling beside the bathtub Lynn washed my back while whispering sweet nothings in my ear. Soon both of us were in the tub, where we appeased our libidos. When I finally did lie down to rest, it was lights out.

Hours later I awakened with Lynn lying next to me, grinning and rubbing olive oil on my chest and arms. I perceived her oiling me down as a ritualistic anointment prior to my going out to face the unpredictable night. What would be the toll, would I return unscathed? There was the pungent smell of a recently lit sherm drifting with a beckoning aroma. I reached over, pulled the sherm from her lips, and inhaled it like my life depended upon it. The septic smoke shot up to my brain, where it exploded with the force of a grenade, charging my mind and body up like an energized Frankenstein. I was ready to roll.

A strange thing happened after I embraced Lynn and kissed her before leaving. It felt like farewell. Needing more clothes, I headed toward Fred and my mother's apartment where I stayed off and on. I felt I was going away—but where? I put more clothes in the trunk and planned to return later to get my car. Samuel then picked me up, and we drove out to Jackie's pool hall on Avalon off 107th Street. He was still vexed about this morning's conflict with James. We shot some pool, then I told Jackie I was headed out to Peewee's spot. He said Peewee was at the car shop several blocks away. We jumped into Samuel's car, and Jackie gave him directions to the place.

We parked down the street and walked through a short alley to the entrance of the repair shop. The garage was well lit inside with people working on cars. I heard Peewee in the back of his low-rider car arguing with his woman. I had known Pewee for about six years and we had become tight. He too enjoyed driving iron and was yoked up. As I approached he smiled and said, "Big Cuz!" then went back to arguing. I stuck my head through the window and said, "When you finish, Cuz, I need to holler at you!" Our plan that night was to jack a known dope dealer. The last jack was a fiasco because the several bottles of PCP had exploded in Crip Coco's car trunk. No one had seen Coco since.

I could tell Peewee was whacked out on sherm when he jumped out of his car screaming, "Tookie, I love you like a brother, but don't you tell me how to treat my woman!" He became incoherent, saying that if I didn't stop interfering he would have to fight me.

"I know who you are, Tookie, but I'll still fight you."

I asked him, "Are you sure, Cuz?"

"Hell, yes," he said, "let's fight right now."

As we walked outside I planned to grab Peewee and put him in a headlock until he lost consciousness. But the moment I turned around, Peewee whipped out a .45 caliber pistol bigger than his hand, pointed at me. Tears were streaming down his face and his expression was maniacal. Jackie walked over, stood beside me and then told Peewee, "Don't shoot my homeboy! You'll have to shoot me too!" Peewee shouted back, "No problem, my cousin, that can be arranged too!" Samuel had vanished. I stood there with my arms folded defiantly, and Peewee was still crying when a truck pulled up, people jumped out with rifles, and ran toward us. When they got closer, someone said, "Peewee, are you crazy, that's Tookie!" When his brother tried to take the gun away, Peewee told him to stay back. Pissed off and growling, I said, "Look here, I'm tired of this madness, I don't have time for this. So if you guys are going to shoot me, then shoot, I'm out of here." That's when I stormed away with Jackie trailing me. I didn't care if they shot or not.

At the end of the alley Jackie caught up with me. We were confronted by DeeDee, whose hustler brother I had slapped several nights ago outside Jackie's pool hall. But I brushed past him and said, "Buster, if you're going to shoot, shoot!" While walking down Avalon, Jackie tried to reason with me, but I wasn't hearing it. Back at his pool hall I decided to hang out and went outside to get toasted. I vowed to return and make examples of everybody. While I puffed on a sherm, Samuel drove up, jumped out of the car with his double-barreled shotgun, and said, "Where are they, Cuz, I'm ready!" I continued to hit the sherm and ignored Samuel's comedy act. I shook hands with Jackie, told him I'd be back later, then motioned to Samuel, "Let's go!"

I went to the Garretts' house to retrieve my shotgun. The ambience felt weird. There were several suspicious white vans parked out front. When Samuel and I reached the front door, it was ajar. I could hear the TV playing. I rang the doorbell a few times, but there was no response. I chose not to enter though the door was slightly ajar. It was a good thing too. I found out later that cops were inside waiting to arrest me and that they had been told to shoot if I resisted—which I would have.

We returned to the pool hall, where Jackie and I had a brief chitchat. I agreed to meet with Peewee's brother the next day to iron things out and to follow through with jacking that dope dealer. But there was no hope for DeeDee when I caught up with him. We drove on down Central Boulevard on our way to see Bob Simmons, but we never made it. We were pulled over by two sheriff cars from Firestone. Their bullhorn blared, warning us to exit the car with arms raised above our heads. Four sheriffs, guns drawn, approached us cautiously. After they searched us, we were handcuffed and ordered to sit on the curb. Two sheriffs guarded us while the other two started tearing apart Samuel's car. Within minutes, at least five more Firestone patrol cars appeared. There were so many white sheriffs around, it looked like a Ku Klux Klan meeting. The air stank of racial slurs and hate.

During the race-based insults by the sheriffs, Samuel fell out in the street on his back, behaving as if he were having a heart attack, asking the sheriff to contact his wife to bring him his medication. Samuel's health problem was news to me. "Nigger, get up," one of the sheriffs said. But Samuel persisted in his plea for medication until the sheriff pointed his gun at him, fingered the trigger, and threatened to blow his head off. That's when Samuel, with the agility of a gymnast, jumped and landed upright on the curb. His antics caused the sheriffs to laugh for several minutes. "You believe that coon could move so fast?" asked one sheriff between gales of laughter.

The merriment of the sheriffs quickly vanished with the announcement that a double-barreled shotgun had been found in the trunk of Samuel's car. Samuel produced a license for the weapon, but the sheriffs refused to accept it as valid. As we were being pushed into the backseat of the patrol car, I heard a voice say, "I know who that big dude is, that's Tookie."

As if on cue, every sheriff said, "Who?"

"You know, Tookie!" responded the first sheriff. "The big Crip leader everybody talks about."

I then became a specimen for all of them to gawk at. "Are you really Tookie?" "How big are your arms?" "Can you really bench-press over five hundred pounds?" "Are you still leading the West Side Crips?" The queries continued as if I were being mobbed by reporters, but I refused to answer. Samuel made an absurd statement, which I ignored, about preparing to jump through the closed window of the police car to escape. Arriving at the Firestone Sheriff's station, Samuel became more eccentric. He paced back and forth in the holding tank with tears streaming down his face, mumbling over and over that his wife needed him.

After our one phone call, I was escorted from the holding tank into a cell with a steel door. Several minutes later Samuel was brought to the door. Bracing himself in the doorway, he refused to come in. He yelled out, "I don't want to be locked up, I want to go home." Two sheriffs tried to push him inside the cell, but he wouldn't budge.

Finally, one sheriff snatched Samuel by the collar and pulled him backward from the doorway. The other sheriff slammed the door shut. I could hear Samuel screaming like a woman in labor and the sheriffs hollering, "Stupid nigger!" I could also hear the sickening sounds of a stick hitting flesh.

After a few hours had passed, Samuel began to cry and scream, "Let me out of here, please let me out of here!" I called out to him numerous times but he never responded. After a while Samuel quieted down but still refused to answer when I called his name. This was the first time I had ever seen a black man react so strangely in jail. I didn't know then that Samuel had never before been arrested. I had never known a black man about my age who had not spent time in jail, whether he was guilty or not.

Before the night ended, I heard someone yelling at Samuel, "Didn't that nigger do it? Didn't he murder those people? Or was it you, nigger?" Samuel again started to cry. His wails were punctuated by denials, that he knew nothing and had nothing to do with a murder case. After being beaten again, though, his story dramatically changed. "Yes, yes, yes, he did it," I heard Samuel scream. "He did it, I'll say whatever you want. Please, just don't beat me anymore." I had no idea who "he" was.

Later, legal documents would show that Samuel's ribs were fractured that March night over two decades ago, that he was beaten unconscious by the sheriffs and left lying on a cell floor in a pool of his own blood. I did not see Samuel again for two years, until the day he took the witness stand to testify under oath—untruthfully—that I had killed three people, though I was ultimately charged with four counts of first-degree murder and two counts of robbery using a firearm.

Rage of Another Kind

This was the beginning of phase two of my life. I was twenty-five years old.

Up to this point, my life had been possessed by a Crip rage, a lethal momentum hurling me into perilous situations where the odds of living were long. Playing my own version of Russian roulette, I got an adrenaline high from roaming the streets and terrorizing entire communities, as if daring someone, anyone, to fire the bullet that would stop me forever. My Crip rage was a distorted expression of my virility. I felt invincible. Indifferent to societal or mundane affairs, I lumbered through life fueled by brute strength and bent on intimidation. I held no allegiance to anything other than Crippen, and I beckoned violence like a bullfighter beckons a bull with his red cape. My rage was nourished by the hate I saw and felt from mainstream society and white people, a hate based on my black skin and my historical place at the nadir of America's social caste. I was filled with hate for injustice. Yet my reaction to the hate was violence directed only toward blacks.

Unlike those ashamed to admit their motivation or too blind to recognize it, I forged through much of my life locked into a hostile intimacy with America's wrongness. Conditioned and brainwashed to hate myself, and my own race, other black people became my prey and the Crips my sword. Though I cannot condone it, much of the

violence I inflicted on my gang rivals and other blacks was an unconscious display of my frustration with poverty, racism, police brutality,
and other systematic injustices routinely visited upon residents of
urban black colonies such as South Central Los Angeles. I was frustrated because I felt trapped. I internalized the defeatist rhetoric
propagated as street wisdom in my 'hood, that there were only three
ways out of South Central: migration, death, or incarceration. I located a fourth option . . . incarcerated death.

The day after Samuel's beating I was moved from the Firestone
station, entombed within the Los Angeles County Jail, and assigned
to the High Power unit. A mix-up occurred, and I was thrown in with
the general population. I ended up in a cell with six other black men.
They were engaged in a great debate over the black market rate of a
pack of cigarettes. The parasitic merchant was a black trustee standing six feet five inches and weighing over three hundred pounds. He
stood in front of the cell with a smirk and berated these men like they
were children.

I interrupted the guy in mid-sentence and asked, "How much do
you want for those filthy cigarettes?" Annoyed, he spat out, "For you,
twelve dollars!" After evil-eyeing one another I said, "OK, it sounds
fair to me." When he handed me the pack, I told him, "You're paid."
Fuming, he threatened to beat me down and take all my money when
the gates were racked open. When he left, there was complete silence
among these dudes. They were so terrified that when I offered them
cigarettes, not one of them would accept. Tearing up an old T-shirt on
the floor, I used the strips to wrap my knuckles because I planned to
put on a vicious display. Dressed in an oversized shirt and pants, I
guess to them I looked incapable of challenging this mammoth bully.

When the gates racked, I stepped out to a completely empty tier,
and the guy was standing at the end of the landing. There was nothing between him and me but funky air. As I approached him, some
deputies rushed out to intervene. I was handcuffed in front of the
heckling giant. One deputy reached into my front shirt pocket and
snatched out the pack of cigarettes. Behind me someone said, "Don't

you know you can't just go around taking other people's property?" It was obvious that this big oaf posing in the corner had snitched on me. Later I'd come to know him as Dan, aka "Too-Sweet," a bounty hunter of notorious ranking from the Nickerson Garden projects.

Sitting in a small room with a large computer, a deputy was telling the others that with my attitude I should have been in High Power. When the deputy punched in my name, he said, "Whoa, wait a minute, this guy shouldn't be anywhere near the main line. This fellow here is who they call Tookie, the leader of the West Side Crips, and he's charged with four capital murders." There was a chorus of wows! I was quickly escorted to the unit called High Power. At the time I wasn't aware that High Power was a security section of the county jail designed to house individuals with high-profile cases; detainees displaying defiant behavior; celebrities who need to be kept apart from the main jail population; and snitches and dirty cops who require protective custody for their own safety.

High Power was also used by sheriffs and other law enforcement agencies to plant an informer in a cell near a particular prisoner, hoping that the informer could extract a damaging statement or confession that could then be used against the target prisoner in court. Informers are notorious for faking results, pretending a confession has been secured to use as leverage to reduce the criminal charges that they themselves may face.

I was confined to High Power for several reasons. I was fighting four capital offenses, my reputation as a Crip leader had preceded me, and I was labeled as too powerful a negative force in my 'hood. My enormous size from pumping iron also frightened hell out of the authorities. At that time I sported a pair of twenty-two-inch arms and a chest over fifty-five inches. Back then, High Power had a certain reputation: black men knew that inside this unit, Klansmen found it unnecessary to wear their trademark white linen hoods to conceal their identities. The sheriff's uniform itself symbolized racism and ruthlessness. Certainly, not all white sheriffs in High Power hated black men, but those exceptions were few. The majority needed no excuse to exhibit sadistic aggression, especially with a handcuffed black detainee. That's when sheriffs were most dangerous. Moreover, there was always a brainwashed black or nonwhite bootlicking sheriff around who would ingratiate himself with his fellow officers by brutally pounding on a handcuffed black or minority prisoner, smiling all the while. Even now, more than two decades later, my experience in Los Angeles County Jail still affects me. Whenever I am handcuffed, I immediately begin to sweat profusely.

The atmosphere within High Power was no doubt established to isolate, humiliate, dominate, violate and, when convenient, to eradicate. My size and seemingly antiestablishment posture quickly drew the attention of sheriffs of a Gestapo mentality. For a voyeur's pleasure, in front of the tier of cells was an enclosed walkway with walls that featured tinted glass windows, each window positioned directly across from a nine- by seven-foot cell. The darkened windows permitted deputies to observe prisoners, ostensibly without the prisoner's knowledge. But the sheriffs' silhouettes were quite visible; we could always tell when they were watching us. As far as they were concerned, just watching me was rarely enough. During my two-year stay in High Power, it became customary for the officers to try to provoke me by yelling racial epithets through the glass. At other times they would watch me in silence. But their observations lasted much longer than normal. They would often stare for two or three hours, no matter what I was doing.

To those racist voyeurs I no doubt seemed a gargantuan black beast whose presence evoked feelings of inadequacy and apprehension. In an effort to camouflage their fears, they sought to emasculate me and to destroy my sanity. They went to the extreme. On occasions I would find objects in my food: staples, thumb tacks, paper clips, clumps of hair, and broken glass. I leave it to your imagination what other items were mixed in my meals, items that I overlooked and ate. They were terrorists by any definition of the word.

My response to attacks like these were limited to verbal warfare or to throwing objects. Sometimes I lowered myself to primitive levels of retaliation by spitting on the officers. I was not yet familiar with the jailhouse art of weapon making, so my tormentors were exempt from the true violence they had earned and probably would have respected. They had become manipulators of my reactions by knowing how and when to aggravate me, to draw out my rage. I afforded them a monopoly over my responses to their abuse.

My attempts to protest the injustices committed fell on apathetic ears. It was my word against the supposedly respected, infallible sheriffs. Help was nowhere to be found. Treated worse than an animal, I was expected to tolerate the abuse as many captives before me had done. But even the most debased human being has limits.

On one particular day, after being the only one harassed by two cell searches a couple of hours apart and being bombarded with racial slurs and taunts, I was directed over the loudspeaker to prepare for a dental appointment. One sheriff was sent down the tier to handcuff me; the other sheriff waited outside the all-steel-bar door at the front of the tier. Once I was handcuffed, the sheriff found it amusing to use undue force by twisting my wrist, which resulted in an exchange of verbal threats to smash one another. I was serious. I can't speak for the other guy. Afterward he waddled away toward the front of the tier. A minute later when the electronic door opened, I exploded and broke the handcuffs in two, then dashed toward the burly sheriff, snatching only a piece of his shirt before he escaped through the open door, which immediately closed behind him.

I could smell the stench of his relief that he had evaded my grasp. It didn't take long for a mob of sheriffs to respond to the alarm bell. I steeled myself for the inevitable onslaught, but instead over the loudspeaker I was repeatedly ordered to return to the cell. Once I calmed down and was back in the locked cell, I was puzzled that the sheriffs did not rush in on me. As a common scenario, this was an opportunity to brutalize or kill me—and then justify it under the law. Around dinnertime an officer appeared to serve the meal. While handing me the food tray, he offered to take off the broken handcuffs, which I refused, believing it was a ruse. Once the officer exited, I went through the ritual inspection of my food, probing for foreign materials visible to the eye. I ate the meal while continuing my vigil for an attack against me, which never came—at least not visibly.

That meal had been spiked with a tranquilizer that knocked me out cold.

When I regained consciousness, I found myself in the jail's medical unit. I was in excruciating pain from the neck down, harnessed to a steel bunk in "five points." Five points refers to five leather straps attached to a bunk. Each strap is positioned at one of the four corners, or points of the bed, to secure both wrists and both ankles. The longer, thicker, wider fifth strap extending from the middle point of the bunk is wrapped around the upper torso. Since I was neither apoplectic (a stroke victim) nor narcoleptic, it was apparent the food I had eaten was spiked with a powerful sedative. Later I found out why I was in such pain when I awoke.

They really didn't know what to make of me, especially given my ability to rip off the handcuffs from behind. The authorities intentionally labeled me as a powerful madman who needed psychiatric sedation. From the start it was clear they were trying to make me loony . . . but why? Whenever the sheriffs wanted to move me from High Power to the medical unit to be placed in five points, I was drugged. My defiance encompassed a wide variety of offenses in their eyes. If I refused to respond to their insults, paced the cell too much, didn't eat, displayed a facial expression of disdain, did not follow their ridiculous commands—such as stand on one leg in a corner with one hand on top of my head—I was labeled as defiant, and then drugged.

My only defense was to avoid eating the jail food, so I tried to subsist on store-bought candy to avoid the druggings. I remember devouring so many candy bars, sometimes for weeks on end, they caused serious acne problems and made me constantly nauseated. I didn't want to wake up in five points—and I couldn't survive indefinitely on a diet of sweets. Eventually, I had to take my chances and eat what was placed before me by the sheriffs. Though I discussed these matters with each of the three successive attorneys who represented me during the two-year period, nothing was ever done to stop the periodic druggings.

On several occasions, despite being drugged, through force of will I remained semiconscious enough to witness the sheriffs' ritual. Once I appeared to have passed out, they would come into the cell and handcuff me, wrists behind my back, then drag me to the medical unit. Before I was put in five points, I was thrown to the floor, then stomped and kicked in the groin and other parts of my body (though strategically they avoided head injuries). The sedatives were a fortunate anesthetic that dulled the physical abuse. I felt nothing while all of this was going on. It was no longer a mystery why when I regained consciousness, the majority of the time I felt pain. I now understood why it often hurt in the groin area and why I sometimes urinated blood.

The violence being done to my mind was far worse. I'm convinced there was a deliberate attempt to render me certifiably insane. Sometimes the tranquilizer was administered intravenously by medical staff while I was in five points. Its effect would be to suspend me in oblivion for days. Even when I awakened, there was no way to banish the experience from my mind because of the lingering after-effects: drowsiness, poor coordination, slurred speech, and general mental confusion. Other times the mind-altering drugs would be handed to me by a nurse disguised as part of my hypertension (high blood pressure) medication. She would stand and watch to make sure that I put all the medication in my mouth, then swallow it. Like any person who's suffering from a physical aliment and wants to get better, I felt obligated to take the medications. And since I wasn't able to recover my drug-blown senses in between these regular druggings, it was easy to dupe me into believing that all the medication I was given was improving my health.

The most frightening reality of being forcibly drugged is that no one was trying to revive me from my coma-like state. My mind had to be strong enough to override the power of the sedative and burst through the horror of total darkness. I do not remember dreaming during that period. Not even a nightmare pierced my consciousness. Nothingness was all that embraced me during sleep. It was a living death. Waking up, I always felt bewilderment, then despair. I would think, "Where is my do-or-die passion?" At those moments the crazed passion that once fortified my boldness, the stimulus familiar to every Crip who defied bullets and fought foes, was completely absent. I felt defeated and engulfed by desolation. If there was a psychological value in their (the powers that be) intent to demoralize me, then they succeeded a thousandfold.

Prior to my abduction from South Central I had spent purposeless years under the influence of drugs such as PCP and LSD. I will never forget the weird trips I experienced nor the violent aggression I initiated because of my personal drug use. Nevertheless, the psychopharmacology employed against me in High Power proved far more devastating. It was like being buried alive. I felt my brain was suffocating, felt as if I was falling through space deep into nothingness. This was nothing like getting high off of street drugs. The Medical Unit's medication was a mind killer.

In May of 1979 I was taken to a Torrance, California, court for a pretrial hearing. I sat in the courtroom fully shackled, with bright lights beaming down on me. Physically I appeared to be in perfect health but my mind was in a psychotropic uproar. The presiding judge noticed something was wrong; something about me was not what it should be. He asked if I understood what was going on, but my disjointed mind would not permit me to respond. Instead of words coming out, giggles or laughter overwhelmed me. Other times I was just completely out of it. At times I understood what the judge was asking and wanted to answer properly, yet I could not. My disjointed mind and body kept betraying me.

The judge turned to my stepfather, Fred, and asked, "Does he get in these moods frequently, Mr. Holiwell, where he won't speak?" My stepfather responded without having the knowledge of my being unlawfully drugged. "Well, he's been on PCP, and ever since then . . . he just hasn't been alert. He goes into strange moods." Court transcripts indicate that the judge said, "All right. Well, I'm aware that at least he's alert and looking at me and he's not choosing to respond to my words. But I can't say he's understanding what I say." Common sense would have picked up that something was wrong right then and there. Had I been nonblack and exhibited such quaint behavior in a courtroom, I'd have been analyzed by the best psychologist the county had to offer.

During the preliminary hearing in April of 1979 the drugging affected me differently. I couldn't laugh, but instead groggily gazed at the inside perimeter of the courtroom and saw that it was overrun with armed bailiffs and undercover detectives. Scanning the room I noticed that most of the spectators were white, were unknown to me, and wore unmistakably angry expressions. In sharp contrast stood my mother and stepfather, their African features marked by worry rather than fury. Apart from my parents the crowd radiated a lynch mob's enthusiasm while it waited for the proceedings to start. As in all my courtroom appearances, I was shackled around the waist, wrists, and ankles. I felt like a wild animal. I'm sure to all the strangers I looked like one too.

When the judge read aloud from his record of my presumed sins, a gasp went up from the spectators as he detailed the allegations: multiple robberies and the shotgun murders of four people, three Asians and one Caucasian. Vaguely I recall the judge's grimace, which caused me to reciprocate whenever we locked eyes, neither of us hiding our mutual disdain. I wanted desperately to holler out disparaging insults at this white figure who sat high on a pedestal as if he was better than me. But the nexus between my mind and voice had been severed. I possessed no defensive or offensive capabilities. All I could do was sit there and listen.

During my prime I had felt as powerful and invincible as a bull elephant in its primal rutting stage. But in the courtroom I felt as weak as a lamb, physically defenseless, in chains and with no control over what was being done to me. My reasons for feeling mentally defenseless were twofold; my mind was unstable due to the "therapeutic" druggings I was enduring; and, though I would never have admitted it, the courtroom's legal language and maneuvering were beyond my comprehension. What limited skills I possessed were of no value in this setting. Neither street savvy nor intimidation produced results within this world. I was reduced to marionette status, nodding my head if and when an attorney suggested it, though I comprehended absolutely nothing.

Instinctively I knew to expect the worse from the judicial system, since it reflected society as a whole. I never allowed the self-indulgence of false hope. During that stage of my captivity, facing America's killing apparatus meant no more to me than being given a speeding ticket. The truth was, I didn't care what happened to me or to anyone else. My indifference to life or death was exacerbated by my imprisonment, the coerced tranquilizers, and the officers' brutality in High Power. But long before this most recent arrest, I had retreated into the psychological death chamber of my blue rage. I had become a castaway within my own mind. I felt no hope, saw no dreams, expected no bright future.

Death was the only reality I anticipated. I was even convinced that love was unattainable and incapable of penetrating my stone-encased heart. I possessed the death look of the wretched. I devalued life since I saw no worth in my own. No matter how many people visited me while I was in the county jail, I still felt alone and abandoned. My smile served as a theatrical means to influence a given circumstance, or as a tight, cold gesture of formality. Not even my beloved mother could reach me on my mental island of drugged alienation, an island where I was neither safe nor secure.

Under these psychotropic assaults I probably lent credence to the racist notion that I was subhuman. I believed I was supposed to accept the tribulations inflicted on me while in captivity. So I gritted my teeth and absorbed the injustices just as many of my slave ancestors had accepted their plight for centuries. There were fleeting moments when I railed against the sheriff's madness, but most of the time I was either too drugged to resist or too acclimated to my outcast status to know that I should challenge what was unjust. Even I, a person who lived as foul as could be, deserved justice. Yet I experienced only a great separation between the system of law and the ethics of justice. Since life for me had always been a callous existence, what was the difference now? If the system wanted to exterminate me, I thought, so what, feel free to do so. Perhaps I'd fare better in death than in life.

Part 2

BLACK REDEMPTION

The Missing Years

In my life, truth, justice, and liberty were absent.

The druggings inflicted on me during my incarceration in High Power were compliments of the district attorney's acquisition of a court order to have me placed in the medical unit. This tactic was an attempt to monitor my visits and telephone calls and therefore, they hoped, to obtain self-incriminating statements. Perhaps the district attorney thought I was able to use the phone and entertain visitors while comatose. This was the type of irrational thinking and duplicity, in concert with the questionable justice system, that I was up against.

This is not a conspiracy theory, phobic anxiety, nor my imagination that America has not allowed justice to embrace the likes of me. I was expected to acquiesce, to accept a one-sided version of justice. I wasn't able to perceive then what I know now—that *anything less than justice is an absolute injustice*. Still, the pathetic reality was that although I had no concept of justice, I knew the vulgar variations of *injustice* intimately. This literary platform allows me to voice a legitimate grievance that most Americans cannot understand, even begin to approach.

My stint in High Power from 1979 to 1981 was an amnesiac episode that flew by with the speed of light. I sleepwalked numbly through the majority of the ordeal. I can recall no specific details about the trial proceedings, nor do I remember engaging in strategic dialogues with any of my several briefly glimpsed attorneys (two different public defenders and two different private lawyers). Lynn hired the first of my private attorneys, Harry Weiss, who handled the preliminary phase and then vanished. After that my mother and stepfather tried to hire two black attorneys, Carl Jones and Charles Lloyd, who both declined on the basis that the case was too hot. Then my family hired an attorney whose name deserves no mention. This attorney would later deliver testimony during a federal deposition that assisted the state attorney general *against me.*

The list of parasites anxious to violate my life were mostly imprisoned snitches out to liberate themselves from the consequences of their crimes by sacrificing me to the court of law. Virtually all of the people who testified against me struck deals for lesser charges or immunity. Samuel Coleman was physically beaten by the police so that he would implicate me in crimes that I *did not* commit. Literally selling their souls, none of these career criminals had any compunction about ruining my life to save their own scrawny necks.

In the midst of this madness, Michelle came to visit me along with Wayne, but he was arrested for possessing a loaded weapon in the visiting room. As expected, the investigative detectives turned the incident into a conspiracy depicting my having Wayne attempt to break me out of jail all by himself. To compound matters I was accused of another escape plot, prefabricated by George Oglesby, who many years later was revealed to be a jailhouse snitch working in tandem with the sheriffs and district attorney. This new fantasy plan involved me and other Crips, of course, high-powered weaponry, and of all things, dynamite. The mention of dynamite and black folks in the same breath should have automatically been dismissed as highly unlikely. How many blacks in America have access to dynamite, and what company would ever sell explosives to a black man or woman without immediately notifying the cops? It was a ridiculous as well as an untrue accusation. But Oglesby's lies were believed by the jury.

While in High Power I was unable to exercise to relieve all of the pent-up tension, to get the blood circulating throughout my body and brain. The problem was that I was incapable of exercising, and most people around who knew me had expressed concern. Doc Holiday, alleged leader of the Black Guerrilla Family, was housed in the cell next to mine. Often he would tell me about his son, also a Crip. There were occasions when Doc and I initiated a push-up routine five to six times a week, but I couldn't maintain it because I was always too tired, drowsy, or asleep. There were times Doc would holler over and ask, "Say, Took, how come you don't work out anymore? Are those people drugging you?" I'm sure I mumbled something incoherent. When I was on other rows, other individuals I knew such as McFarlane and Dale were puzzled by my condition and assumed I was still whacked out on PCP. When I spoke, no one could decipher my words, not even me.

Throughout the two years of being disoriented I completely forgot that Raymond Washington had been murdered in August of 1979, five months after my incarceration. I believe it was Criplette Jackie who visited me and broke the unbelievable news. Her version of what had taken place was sketchy, and I can't remember too much about what we talked about. As with Buddha, I couldn't picture Raymond dead. How could that have possibly happened?

Raymond's death remains a mystery, but when the Crips became a media magnet, it seemed like everybody was Raymond's closest homeboy, his comrade, his loved one, his buddy, and cofounder of the Crips. Preposterous! How many of those same individuals were turning over every rock in society to locate his assassin? How many are in pursuit today, or how many truly care? It reminds me of young Odie's funeral, where individuals were tossing all kinds of memorabilia into his casket. Had he been alive, he would have been hard-pressed to borrow change for a telephone call from most of them.

Raymond and I were brought together for a purpose beyond our limited understanding, and somewhere along the way we veered off the righteous course. It was a youthful mistake that chased us into adulthood, where we left a legacy of pain and tears among grieving black mothers and other loved ones. We had no legitimate dreams or attainable visions, only a cruel future, one capable of poisoning our souls. I never knew Raymond's ambitions, but in our small world, ambitions were rare, and mostly fantasy.

Raymond was a black man with potential overlooked by the old guard black leadership who could have used his street savvy, organizational dexterity, and his popularity. He and I co-founded the Crips, a legacy of blood, rage, and death; but if his true worth and potential contribution to the political struggle had been tapped into, his life might have been different. We'll never know. May Raymond, Buddha, and the countless others who senselessly lost their lives to violence rest in peace.

Several months prior to my court trial, I was uprooted and housed alone, incommunicado, on G-row in High Power. This was a place designed for disciplinary actions, and though I had violated no rules, I would reside on G-row until the jury rendered its decision. I knew the verdict beforehand. I knew the outcome the moment I was abducted from society on these trumped-up charges. Oh yes, I knew.

The all-white jury marched single file into the courtroom like a firing squad and blasted me into cinders. They found me guilty of all charges. On April 15, 1981, I stood before the Torrance Court judge bound in the usual chains and handcuffs as the verdict of the penalty phase was read aloud with unprecedented malice: four death sentences—as if executing me once wasn't enough.

Once again I was dealt a dead man's hand in life and was shuttled back to the county jail awaiting transfer to San Quentin. I sat on a bunk in the last cell on the tier by myself, punch-drunk from psychotropic drugs that were supposed to have murdered my mind but failed. Though it has been said I received numerous visits, only a handful come to mind. Besides my mother appearing to offer stability in that chaotic setting, others came mostly bearing tidings of deceit or gloom. Once when Michelle came to visit, she told me that she ran into Jimel in the visiting room claiming to be waiting to visit me. It was news to me. During my entire captivity, not once did he ever visit. Michelle went on to say that Jimel had asked, "Why did you pick Tookie over me when I met you first? You turned me down." He answered his own question. I wasn't shocked. I recall Jimel asking his own woman, years before, "Who looks the best, Tookie or me?" All she did was laugh nervously and refuse to answer. My homeboy Jackie stood there shaking his head in disbelief.

After Michelle's revelation, I shrugged it off and said, "Well, I guess Godfather and others' opinion about him were right!" That's when she lowered the boom. "Ah, by the way, baby, I've found somebody else because you're not out here for me." She was right: I wasn't out there in society for her. There was a pang of regret for losing her, but I sucked it in and blew it out, knowing I had to move on.

Though I never fashioned myself as a lothario, I made myself available to other females to soften the impact of a "Dear John" drama. During the same time I was hooked up with Michelle, I was fornicating with Monica and other black beauties. But it was a surprise when Monica and Jackie hooked up, although it pissed me off at first. At least he had the decency to break the news to me face-to-face.

There was a void I'll never be able to recapture from those missing years. Although through most of my life I was a willing sinner of the highest magnitude, in my voice to God's ear I prayed earnestly for the strength to survive my social drug use and the involuntary druggings by law enforcement. I vowed never again to get intoxicated.

My decision to repudiate drugs was the beginning of my redemption that would bear fruit, for children, nearly a decade later.

"Momma," Tookie's grandmother, in Shreveport, Louisiana, in the 1950s

Tookie at four years old in Shreveport

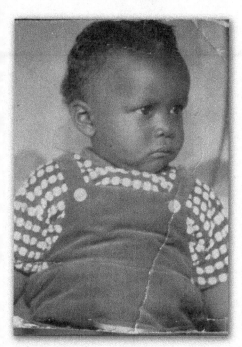

Baby Tookie at home in Louisiana

Tookie at twelve in Los Angeles

Tookie at twelve with his dog, Rex

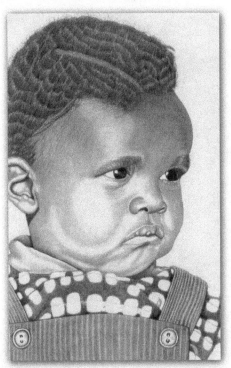

Sketch of Tookie as a two-year-old, drawn by Tookie (with only a tiny pencil stub) in the early 1990s, while in solitary confinement

A fifteen-year-old Tookie with a "gangster lean," though he was not yet a gang member

Tookie at fourteen with his stepfather, Fred Holiwell

Posing by a car in South Central Los Angeles at thirteen years old

Tookie at eleven years old wearing his first suit

A self-assured Tookie at sixteen, posing for a picture in Los Angeles

At twenty-three years old, having spent years building his body to legendary proportions, his nickname became "Big Took"

Tookie at nineteen in a muscle pose, demonstrating the size of his biceps

At twenty-four, Tookie's arms stretched the sleeves of his suit.

Funeral program for Crips cofounder, Raymond Lee Washington, shot and killed in 1979

On San Quentin's exercise yard, Tookie in his late twenties

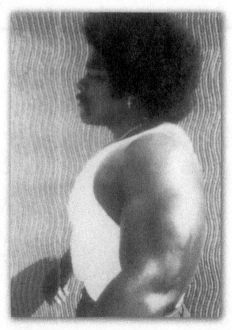

At San Quentin in his early thirties

At San Quentin, posing with his blue Crip rag on his head

At San Quentin in the mid-1980s

Tookie, thirty-nine, made a habit of closing his eyes when being photographed to "block out the madness" of prison life.

Steve Champion, formerly known as Treach, now Adisa, a death-row friend

Craig Ross, once nicknamed Evil, now called Ajani, another death-row friend

Tookie's friend Ghetto was on death row until he won his removal from "the Row" in 2002.

Dennis Brewer, known as Herc, one of
Tookie's friends on death row

Tookie and Grandpa on the death-row prison yard

Young Kerm, another of Tookie's friends on
death row

Cane, one of Tookie's
friends on death row

State of California   Department of Corrections   San Quentin State Prison

M e m o r a n d u m

Date: July 7, 2000

To: Inmate Stanley Williams
        C-29300   4 EB 70

Subject: **YOUR LETTER OF JUNE 27, 2000**

I am in receipt of your letter, dated June 27, 2000. I also note that you have raised the same issue in a CDC 602 Inmate Appeal, Log # SQ 00-1828. Your appeal was granted at the informal level by Captain Fuller in that a CDC 128-B identifying you as a member of the Crip street gang was ordered removed from your file.

In referring your CDC 602 to the next level of review, you argued that you are being singled out and you fear that a pattern of harassment, labeling, staff reprisals, planting contraband, set-ups, etc. is developing. You offered no evidence of this in your documentation, however, during interview, you noted the recent confidential disclosure form which was delivered to you stating that a confidential informant has provided information that you are attempting to organize other inmates into assaulting staff.

You were advised that if the information from the confidential informant had been determined to be valid, action would have already been taken to segregate you from other inmates.

Your appeal response advised you that you can rest assured that you will not be singled out for harassment in any form. If information regarding your activities is received, it will be appropriately disclosed to you and then it will be evaluated for validity. No action will be taken without consideration of the validity of the source and the information in accordance with Departmental policies and procedures.

J. S. Woodford
Warden
San Quentin State Prison

Department of Corrections memorandum, July 7, 2000, in which then-warden J. S. Woodford of San Quentin State Prison ordered that the document identifying Tookie "as a member of the Crips street gang" should be removed from his file. It further acknowledged that Tookie was not "organizing inmates to assault staff" as was alleged by a confidential anonymous note they had received.

Tookie at age forty-one, having renounced his gang past

Tookie's younger son, Stan, also called "Li'l Tookie"

In 1999 Winnie Mandela visited California and the Neighborhood House of North Richmond's youth program—the Internet Project for Street Peace—which was conceived by Tookie.

Barbara Becnel (left), executive director of the Neighborhood House of North Richmond and co-author with Tookie of nine children's books, with Winnie Mandela (center), and Tookie, in the San Quentin condemned prisoners' visiting room in October 1999

Shirley Neal (right), president of Park Hill Entertainment, which produced Tookie's antigang public service radio messages, visits Tookie with Barbara Becnel.

Former California state senator and 1960s activist Tom Hayden, with Tookie

Tookie in 2003 with actor Jamie Foxx, who played the role of Tookie in Redemption: The Stan Tookie Williams Story; *Marcus King, Jamie Foxx's manager; and Barbara Becnel*

I, Samuel Coleman declare as follows:

1. I was a friend of Stanley Williams at the time he was arrested. We met over our common interest in weightlifting and dogs and occasionally worked out or exercised our dogs together.

2. I was with Stanley when he was arrested for the crimes that put him on death row. We were riding together in my car when the police stopped us. They immediately ordered us both out of the car, threw us spread-eagle against the car and handcuffed us. They then searched the car. They found my gun, which was properly registered and licensed to me and removed it from the trunk. They removed some shotgun shells which were in the glove compartment and loaded my gun with the shells.

3. We were then taken to the city jail and booked and fingerprinted. I still had no idea what was going on or why they had arrested us. It was the first time I had ever been arrested. I was forcibly shoved into a cell. I was followed in by about seven or eight white police officers, who without saying a word began to attack me. They beat me like I've never been beaten before in my life. It seemed as if they would never stop punching me and kicking me. They cursed at me, calling me a stupid no good nigger. I finally lost consciousness. When I came to, they were gone, and I was laying in a pool of blood. I was hurt, scared and crying out in pain. I heard Stanley yelling to me from his cell, asking me if I was alright and trying to

A three-page declaration signed by Samuel "Capone" Coleman, who was beaten by the police shortly after he was arrested with Tookie for crimes that ultimately sent Tookie to San Quentin's death row. In this declaration, Samuel Coleman states that after having his ribs fractured by law enforcement, he "told the police just what they wanted to hear about Stanley."

make me feel better by telling me that it would be okay. I was
crying too hard to answer him, and too scared that the police
would come in and beat me again. The police came in a while
later, picked me up, slapped some cuffs on me and removed me from
the cell. I was then taken to the infirmary at the central
county jail for medical treatment.

4. A while later I was taken into an interrogation room.
They told me I was there because I did a murder. At no time did
anyone read me my rights or inform me that I did not have to talk
to them and could even have a lawyer. The beating put so much
fear into me -- I was so terrorized and in so much pain
physically -- that I told the police just what they wanted to
hear about Stanley. I was visited by someone from the District
Attorney's office who informed me that I would be given immunity
from prosecution if I testified against Stanley. Still believing
that I could be charged with murder and afraid of further
beatings, I agreed.

5. I bailed out of jail the next day and was given a court
date to answer the fabricated charge of carrying a loaded weapon.
Before that date arrived however, I received notice that the
District Attorney had rejected the charges against me.

6. Still suffering intense pain upon my release from jail,
I saw my own doctor who informed me that several of ribs were
fractured.

7. I was arrested again in 1980 on an unrelated drug
charge. The cops knew who I was, knew that I was to testify
against Stanley, and I was not beaten this time. I was however,

threatened with jail time on this charge if I even thought about deciding not to testify. Eventually, I received a diversion sentence. This incident in 1980 furthered my belief that I didn't testify the way the cops wanted me to, I would be facing nothing but a lifetime of beatings, detentions on the street and harassment by the police.

I declare under penalty of perjury under the laws of the United States and the State of California that the foregoing is true and correct. Executed this 23rd day of March, 1994.

Samuel Coleman

ACLU and Civil Rights Groups Urge Court to Consider Racial Bias in Death Penalty Case of Nobel Peace Prize Nominee
Stanley Williams v. Woodford

SAN FRANCISCO, November 7, 2002 – The ACLU of Northern California and a number of prominent civil rights organizations representing diverse communities throughout California filed an amicus brief in the Ninth Circuit Court of Appeals in support of San Quentin death row inmate Stanley Williams's claim of racial bias. The brief is in support of a petition for rehearing en banc, after a panel decision ruled against Williams. It was filed late Wednesday, November 6, 2002. A copy of the brief is available online at http://www.aclunc.org.

The civil rights groups argue that the prosecutor's past racial bias in selecting juries and his racist closing argument in Williams's trial should be relevant in determining whether he used racial bias in selecting the jury and in disqualifying all of the African American jurors. Williams was sentenced to death in 1981 for four robbery-related murders by an all-white jury in Torrance, California.

"Courts must be vigilant to prevent racial bias and stereotyping from determining the selection of juries, particularly in a capital case where it is a matter of life and death," said Alan Schlosser, Legal Director for the ACLU of Northern California. "Exclusion from a jury on racial grounds undermines an individual's – and a community's – participation in the democratic process. Rehearing should be granted because the three-judge panel's decision in this case would exclude the best evidence of a prosecutor's racial bias."

During jury selection, the prosecutor removed the only African-American citizens called into the jury box and during the trial engaged in a racially-coded closing argument that compared Williams in trial to a Bengal tiger in the zoo and Williams "in his environment" to a Bengal Tiger in its "habitat." This same prosecutor was censured judicially twice for the same jury practice.

The list of amici also includes the National Association for the Advancement of Colored People (NAACP), Arab American Attorneys Association, Mexican American Legal Defense & Educational Fund (MALDEF), Southern Christian Leadership Conference of Greater Los Angeles, Lawyers' Committee for Civil Rights of the San Francisco Bay Area, San Francisco La Raza Lawyers Association, Chinese for Affirmative Action, Asian Law Caucus, and the Ella Baker Center for Human Rights.

A press release issued by the American Civil Liberties Union

Forty-eight-year-old Tookie

Tookie at fifty, in San Quentin's visiting cage

IN LIVING MEMORY

STANLEY
TOOKIE
WILLIAMS

TUESDAY, DECEMBER 20, 2005

SUNRISE
DECEMBER 29, 1953

SUNSET
DECEMBER 13, 2005

BETHEL A.M.E. CHURCH | 7900 SOUTH WESTERN AVENUE | LOS ANGELES, CA 90047

On December 20, 2005, Tookie's memorial service was held at a South Central Los Angeles church. More than three thousand people attended to honor him and his work as a street peacemaker.

Stanley Tookie Williams did finally make it to the Motherland—Africa. On June 25, 2006, his ashes were scattered at his request by Barbara Becnel and Shirley Neal at this spot in a Thokoza Park lake in Soweto.

Inside the Beast

t was early in the morning when I was again shackled around the waist, wrists, and ankles and hustled to a black-and-white county bus. En route to the infamous San Quentin prison I made it a point to sit in the back of the bus to guard against potential enemy attacks. No doubt defending myself would've been next to impossible. I was the only person fully shackled while the other thirty or more men wore a regular pair of handcuffs with hands in front. I felt nervous, angry, and hyped. Though my mind was swirling there was nothing wrong with my vision; I was hawking everybody's movements. The majority of those on the bus were blacks and Mexicans, with a few Caucasians and several flamboyant homosexuals.

There was a lot of focus on the female impersonators who giggled and laughed like teenage schoolgirls. The conversations drifted from criminal cases, drugs, women, weapons, jokes, and gory prison tales to talk about Folsom, Soledad, and San Quentin. Each story was bloodier and more violent than the last. As I sat listening I remembered my stepfather, Fred, warning me to be careful: "Prison is no joke. Make sure when you use the toilet, always take your underwear and pants completely off. Better to fight with no pants and drawers, than to be hindered with them around your ankles!" It made sense to me, so I incorporated this habit into my defense. I vowed to beat down anyone challenging me, even though I didn't know the first thing about prison life except through word of mouth. I actually believed convicts fought toe-to-toe, gladiator style, with shanks and knives, a naïve notion capable of getting me killed. Hell, there were more knifing drive-bys in prison than on the streets. As I listened to the stories I braced myself for whatever was going to happen.

It was obvious the bus was nearing San Quentin, because the boisterous crowd began to talk less and less. I guess the full impact of having to face the beast was enough to temper their chitchat. The bus pulled inside the medieval-looking stone fortress. The ambiance was eerie and gloomy. From the department called Receiving and Release I was marched in shackles and leg irons to the hospital for a physical examination. I sat in a caged-off area alone until the nurses were ready for me. After an hour had passed, guards wearing oxygen masks started filing in dragging a prisoner between them. Each guy was drenched with sweat or water and appeared half-dead. When they passed by me there was an unfamiliar foul scent that first irritated my nose, then caused my eyes to sting and water. I learned later there was a riot in the Hole (the Adjustment Center, sometimes abbreviated as A.C.), and the guards used tear gas. While I was there the guards continued to drag in convict after convict. Each one smelled as though he had been swimming in tear gas.

This was my first day in San Quentin, christened with the noxious scent of tear gas. Once the examination was complete, I was escorted to North Seg, where I'd be housed on death row. To reach the top floor we had to use an elevator. The lighting upstairs was so dim it made the place look haunted. After the usual humiliation of being strip-searched by complete strangers, I was handcuffed and escorted to a cell. There were two sides to death row, north and south, with thirty-four cells each. I was to be housed on the north side in Cell 32, way in the back. I was the forty-fifth person on death row, and though it was my first time in prison, it definitely wasn't my first time being confronted with death. Here in prison there wasn't too much of a psychological adjustment to be made for me. Any setting where treachery and violence dominate was nothing new to me—all I had to do was carve out a niche.

Being on death row was the proverbial end of the line, unlike prisons in general where prisoners fight for freedom, civil liberties, and the dignity to be treated like a man. Here we fight with limited time, opposing the death chamber to stay alive. I wasn't sentenced to death row to be rehabilitated. Whether it was my preference or not, I had to battle with the Court of Appeals to prove my innocence. Though nobody believed me, I proclaimed my innocence from the beginning, and I'll never stop doing so. But many years would slip by as I languished in the utter darkness of apathy and dys-education. To sit in a death row cell was not a moment to reflect on my life; it was more an insult to my fervor to survive, another roadblock, a hindrance. The combination of ignorance and the hazy lingering effects of the druggings prevented me from attacking the law books. Instead I readily gravitated to the perils of disorder and the posture of a hardened convict, which required only minor adjustment on my part.

In the cell next to me was a native Indian from the Mono tribe called Chief. A young Crip, Little L, on death row, had told Chief about me. He reached out with some stationery and personal care items. This Indian, it turned out, was down for anything.

The first time I saw Chief, he was being escorted on his tiptoes, with officers pulling his handcuffed wrists up high. As they passed by Chief's long black hair was draped all over his face, and he was smiling like a madman. I figured it was only a matter of time before I too ended up in the same uncomfortable position. Though I didn't know what to expect on death row, I was hyped up. Bring on the madness!

The program for the condemned was simple enough. There was a two-grade system of status. Grade A meant that one was afforded privileges—phone calls, contact visits, and a few other amenities. Grade B offered no privileges and less yard time to exercise. On the first day I received Grade A, I got into a brief dispute with a Mexican guy over phone time. Unfortunately, the death row counselor happened to be walking on the gunrail side and witnessed the entire conflict. The counselor seemed to take it personally. After expressing his displeasure with my refusal to stop beating the guy, he vowed to keep me on B grade until he retired or was transferred.

Regarding the counselor's threat about keeping me in the Hole—he proved to be a man of his word. The Hole is a place for men involved in revolutionary movements, gangs, escape attempts, protective custody, or other circumstances, such as prisoners with serious mental health problems. It is also a place where some men have been killed, or entered with a backbone but left with it bent or broken. Naturally there were examples of men who were defiant exceptions to the rule. Exactly ten years earlier a charismatic black man, George Jackson, had a vision to elevate his spirit. His consciousness of self and others defied the status quo. He was murdered by a prison sniper's bullet but his spirit was emancipated. He had often stated he'd never leave prison alive.

When I stepped into this penal colony, I was faced with that grim possibility of never leaving alive. The notion of liberation was poised between doubt, apathy, and the slender and naïve possibility of "maybe." I took a deep breath, then plunged into this segregated unit of isolation, the Hole. This detached San Quentin building has three tiers on two sides, and back then one side of the third tier was for the condemned. My first day on the yard I met a black from the Long Beach Crips, Big Bub, his brother GeeGee from the Jordon Down Crips, Big Chief, Hootie, and an Asian guy, Choosoo. We were a cast of characters that probably would not have met under any other circumstances. But inside prison, on death row, we shared a common denominator.

After a scan of the three exercise yards, I discovered that there were no weights. When Choosoo introduced me to the 602 Inmate Appeal Form, I submitted an appeal for weights. To my surprise, one month later weights were placed on the condemned yard, then later on the other yards. I was ready to regain the size and the weight I lost while in the county jail. At twenty-seven I was still brawny enough to bench 370 pounds for ten repetitions. In a short period of driving iron with Big Bub and Chief, I was back on double swoll (very "swollen," meaning extremely muscle-bound). Though I was bigger than Bub, he was no joke, standing five feet ten inches, 240 pounds, with over twenty-inch arms. Proud of his shiny bald head, Bub was a dedicated Crip with a consistent mindset for bullyism that kept him in trouble. But then again, that's what all Crips were—sheer trouble.

While I was in the Hole, individuals were coming in and out like it was a train station. I had a chance to briefly kick it with another homeboy, Hoover Joe. He was a muscular Crip with a curly handlebar mustache who reminded me of a book cover portrait of W.E.B. Dubois. Huddled on opposite sides of the fenced exercise yards, we briefly discussed progressive possibilities. The conversations were interesting though our ideological approach differed, mine being apolitical and on the ganghood level: Take no prisoners! Seek, seize, suppress! The conversations would have been even more interesting had Hoover Joe not been transferred. There were plenty of other Crips passing through A.C. like Bad Habit Rabbit, a former Crip from the Imperial Court projects. Although he mentioned many Crip episodes that occurred in the projects, for the life of me I couldn't remember him. Every time I saw Rabbit we went through a ritual of trying to get me to remember him. No doubt the county jail druggings had a lot to do with my memory loss, but I regret that Rabbit and the many other Crips slipped through my mental net into oblivion.

Every now and then, triumphant moments occurred on death row. Two individuals, Choosoo and Hootie, got a full reversal of their cases and went home. Both of them were fortunate to have had the aid of their family, efficient attorneys, and their ethnic community to back them up. I would have been hard-pressed to expect the black community to embrace the likes of me. I symbolized all that had gone bad, and, like a multitude of other imprisoned blacks, I was written off as worthless. The way I behaved back then, I can't blame them.

My only concern dwelt on what I was intimately familiar with . . . Crippen. I found a comfort zone in idiocy that required no laborious effort or intellectual rigor. To Crip or not to Crip was not the question, it was the answer. To me life after Crippen could only mean one thing. I was dead.

Most of my time in the Hole was spent driving iron, reminiscing, and watching the hypnotic tube, television. Over the prison airwaves, whether interested or not, I got an earful of uncut versions of revolutionary theories, religious doctrines, Communist dogmas, and Afrocentric philosophy. Though I could read, people were sending me literary material beyond my comprehension. It was akin to feeding a newborn baby solid foods. The attempt by some of them to wake me up was doomed to fail from the start. Intellectually I was bankrupt, and as quickly as they passed books down to me, the faster I sent them back.

No dogma was powerful enough to permeate my thick cranium nor threaten my allegiance to Cripdom. I knew many hardcore Crips who played their role to the hilt, but I took it beyond the limit. Crip was my religion. I was its cocreator and star-crossed prophet, and I critiqued all other Crips by my own standards. With a weary eye I scrutinized individuals professing to be a Crip because I knew some were perpetrating fraud.

Life as I remembered it would never be the same, nor would the revered Crip connection. Despite my lack of discipline and my underfed intellect, I recognized the imbalance in the institution's racial favoritism that boldly excluded all blacks except those who were informants on other blacks. The Hole was a center of communal dysfunction: quick and violent dramas contrasted sharply with the gladiator tales told to me by Big Rock when I was a child. This was survival of the fittest. I was familiar with the requirements of that game.

At that time there were no mesh fences on the outer cell bars to hinder the use of a prison-made blow-dart gun, a fashioned spear, a match bomb, a zip gun, or a simple but deadly dousing of scolding hot liquid consisting of syrup, battery acid, or whatever else was available. Usually when an incident occurred on the tier, I found myself blamed. In one instance a death row snitch was being escorted down the tier by a female guard when a boiling hot concoction was thrown from one of the cells. The solution burned the inmate, and some of it landed on the guard, resulting in severe burns and a sick leave. A guard went on record, stating, "I saw Williams' arm stretched outside the cell bars, then he threw some kind of liquid on the inmate." The accusation was false, absurd, and impossible, considering that my arms were too large to squeeze through the narrow bars. I filed a 602 appeal form. I was innocent, and I lost the appeal.

Strange things happen behind these lurid walls. Once I smelled smoke while writing a letter. Peering through the slits of the cell bars I saw grayish-white smoke belching from the cell of an inmate who was out to court. The smoke began to hug the ceiling, then crept down the tier toward the front where I was housed. Within minutes the entire tier was engulfed in smoke and all the windows that were usually open were now shut. Along with Bub, Black, and GeeGee, I hollered for the guard to open the windows, but for fifteen minutes my shouts were in vain. By the time the guards arrived the entire tier had turned grayish-black with thick soot floating in the air covering the walls and everything else in the cell.

The thick smoke had me blowing my nose and coughing up jet-black mucous. Nauseated, I dropped to my knees with my head inside the toilet and threw up. Emanating with each flush was a welcoming surge of air for my smoke-filled lungs. It was ironic: the breeze carrying the oxygen of life to my lungs was the same inimical gust of cold air beneath me whenever I used the toilet.

When the guards finally opened all the windows, they placed a giant fan on the tier to blow out all the smoke. In the back of each cell the guards systematically used an oxygen tank with a mask held up against the square-shaped window and bars, for whoever needed it. As I stood there inhaling fresh oxygen, I couldn't help wondering if this experience of moribund asphyxiation was a vile precursor to being gassed in the chamber. That evening I actually thought all of us were going to die. It was a horrific reality I hoped never to undergo again, under any circumstances.

Despite these melancholy moments in the Hole, I was able to hone my knowledge of prison interactions. I was becoming a student of sociology and psychology, owing to my keen observation of others. People can be creatures of habit, and in significant ways it was necessary for me to be aware of such behavior. The parasitical environment was contagious, and I was infected. But occasionally conflict arose between Crippen and an intrusive question, "Where do I go from here?" In retrospect it was a moment of skepticism that challenged the Crip reality I held to more than anything. But at that time I was opposed to self-change or to anything I felt would diminish my Crip image.

I was always willing to aid a Crip in distress—that was a given. But for some reason other than impulsive stupidity I opted to assist another black man who was under siege by guards. I didn't know this death row prisoner. But it offended me to see one of the guards outside his cell preparing to shoot him with Big Bertha, a sawed-off shotgun that shoots a thick plastic wad that is painful to be struck with. If the guards used it, they would then rush in to seize the guy. I hollered loudly, "Why don't you cowards come down here and try to shoot me with that gun?" A sergeant shot back, "Who's that talking with the big mouth?" I said, "Stanley Williams, C29300, I'm in cell 58!" Within seconds there was a crowd of guards standing in front of the cell gawking at me.

As the sergeant walked up, I heard him say, "Let me see who this big mouth is." I stood there with my shirt off and prepared for an attack.

When the sergeant peered in at me, he said, "Well, well, well, look who we have here, it's Tookie. What's the problem?"

I spat out, "If you plan to shoot that black man down there, then prepare to shoot me right now."

While the sergeant and I eyed one another, a guard in the crowd said, "Sarge, let's shoot him too!"

Looking at me, the sergeant told the guard, "Shut up, you don't know what's going on here!" He then said, "All right, Tookie, we don't want a riot, but if we have to come back to deal with Coleman, and you interfere, then you're going down too!"

"Fair enough," I responded.

The next day while I was on the yard, a black man, Mahfahali, hollered out from another one of the alleged Black Guerrilla Family exercise yards, "Brother Tookie, that was a courageous gesture to stand up for that brother. Black man, you should be proud!" Mahfahali was a thin six-foot-three-inch spiritual revolutionary who was notorious for stabbing guards. I smiled and said, "Mahfahali, it's nothing but a Crip thing!" He smiled and shook his head, knowing that all of the revolutionary chats we engaged in had had no effect on me. Every conversation we had was unilateral. He talked while I watched TV. Sometime later, the counselor who had threatened to keep me on Grade B was transferred to another prison. With him out of the way the Classification Committee restored my Grade-A status, and I was sent back to North Seg. Arriving there was like starting all over again as far as the weights were concerned. There were just two lightweight barbells and one set of forty-pound dumbbells. Once again I filed a 602 appeal form. As a result a stockpile of heavy barbells, dumbbells, and weight benches were brought up to death row. Within months I was tying dumbbells on a 370-pound bar, more than 560 pounds total, for doing reps.

Occasionally guards would show up on the opposite side of the gun rail fence and watch in amazement as I lifted the monstrous weight with relative ease. A few of them tried unsuccessfully to get approval for me to enter the San Quentin weight-lifting contest. They had no doubt I'd win. Though I was driving iron on a regular basis, I was still bored. I took up drawing, which became a pleasant pastime. I began drawing animals and birds, then people. With no assistance I developed a style enabling me to do pencil-drawn portraits of my mother, Martin Luther King Jr., Sojourner Truth, Malcolm X, Coretta Scott King, Frederick Douglass, Dorothy Height, and others. Drawing in itself had a halcyon affect on me, like music, calming the beast within. It was a form of escapism. Hours flew by as I lost myself in the godlike power to create life on paper. It amazed me that a person like me could pick up drawing and actually succeed. In addition to lifting weights, it was a personal dexterity I relished.

Another skill I discovered by serendipity was memorizing large numbers of words and their definitions. It frustrated me to be unable to comprehend legal terms and other words I came across while reading newspapers, magazines, and books. I was tired of skipping over certain words, or having to stop and jot down a word to look up later on. In time I started browsing the dictionary and became fascinated with the different words, definitions, and foreign phrases.

In a short period I developed a style of mnemonics for memorizing long lists of words written on one side of a sheet of paper, then folding it with the definitions on the opposite side. It became clear that the more words I retained, the better I was able to understand what I read. Months earlier I had been given an old pocket-sized dictionary with most of the pages scotch-taped together or missing. I tried to hustle the prison chaplain out of a dictionary, but a few weeks later he surprised me with a large *Webster's Collegiate Dictionary*. After I expressed my gratitude, the chaplain said, "I know you'll put that book to good use—but use the Lord's book too!" Shortly afterward I asked a prison imam for a thesaurus, which he provided. I tried Malcolm X's alphabetical technique for remembering words, which I found to be tedious. Instead I randomly selected words from the dictionary, thesaurus, and other books. In spite of my former schoolteachers' assertion that I was ineducable, my intent was to memorize the entire dictionary.

This was the early 1980s. The Crip population was increasing, becoming a force to be reckoned with throughout the prison departments. Whenever I was escorted to the dentist's office in San Quentin or to the walk-in clinic, I'd pass a large crowd of Crips hanging out on the mainline. It felt good being recognized by other Crips, whether they personally knew me or not. In spite of being handcuffed behind my back, I exhibited a posture of dignity and Crip defiance. I was still only barely bursting through a violent drug haze but remained a street folk hero of the wrong path, a purveyor of foolishness.

San Quentin was hundreds of miles from where I used to stroll through South Central Los Angeles, buoyed up by the illusion of freedom. Years earlier there was a Watts Stax concert held at the Los Angeles Coliseum. Hundreds of Crips attended from west and east, and some from Compton, prancing around, numerically strong, cocky, and seemingly invincible. I felt the illusion of being free that day—although there was a brief disruption. Big Country from the Brims gang was stomped and beaten down the escalator for giving East Side Crips Syles a black eye. While some Crips were jacking other people for their drugs and money, someone hollered over the microphone, "Will the Crips please come down and clear the field of these troublemakers?" When I looked up at Raymond, Bimbo, and Caesar, we burst into laughter. It was our homeboys down there who were creating the madness. Times such as that made me feel more invincible, more free, more in control of my destiny. A foolhardy illusion.

Here I was now, at San Quentin, freedomless, confined to death row, wondering if I looked as strange to some of these characters as they did to me. There was a Caucasian guy who thought he was a modern-day vampire and avoided bright lights by wearing a blanket or sheet over his head. He was rumored to eat raw meat and drink blood, which was highly unlikely unless he was self-anthropophagus (a cannibal). The would-be vampire was later found dead in his cell supposedly by his own hands. The concept of suicide had never registered in my life as an option even during the worst of times. I never knew anyone who attempted or committed suicide.

While in North Seg, I became acquainted with a few blacks—Blue, Peanut, Ed, Ex-lax, Bedbug, Gangster, Milton, J.P., Snow, Zoom, Little L, Maddog, P.R., and Grandpa. Having given Maddog and Gangster their akas, I also gave Grandpa his moniker. He was an older black man, six feet two inches, muscular and agile enough to play basketball with any of us. Sometimes after driving iron, I'd kick back in a small group and listen while they engaged in a session of "bullology" (braggadocio gossip on women, sex, money, drugs, and war stories). Being a private person and cautious, my conversation was limited. It was amusing to hear Grandpa launch into a political diatribe about death row being a racist slaughterhouse for society's blacks and other poverty-stricken people. He'd go on and on about governmental collusions, assassinations, tainted history, COINTELPRO, and the black struggle. Usually there was nothing comforting about what Grandpa talked about, nor was it meant to be. Most of the conversations I heard went in one ear and out the other. My true interests lay in being vigilant and restricting my trust to a very few cohorts.

At least once or twice a week I started experiencing bouts of claustrophobia—a relapse, I feared, into the abyss of psychotropic insanity. I felt I was losing my mind when the walls appeared to be closing in on me. Panic-stricken and drenched with sweat, I'd grab hold of the bars with a viselike grip and try to rip them apart to free myself. But regardless of my lifting massive weights and breaking handcuffs in the county jail, the bars refused to budge.

For years it was a silent battle to maintain my sanity. I found solace in driving iron, drawing portraits, reminiscing, and doing whatever gobbled up the hours. Big Bub and GeeGee had gotten their Grade A, and were placed on the tier side with me. To my dismay Bub had lost a lot of weight after having a major operation. The doctor had to cut into his chest cavity to retrieve a malignant cancer, leaving a long scar. Bub was a shell of himself but managed to keep his predatory instinct intact. Though he could barely walk and limped with a cane, he instilled fear in others and was active in chaos.

Rumors began to circulate that Crip intimidation and petty jacking were going on in North Seg. Bub and his brother GeeGee were the first to become suspects: they were charged with strong-arming a guy for his tape player and tapes. Both of them were sent back to the Hole.

While sitting in my cell, drawing and minding my own business, Ed showed up with his face and lips turned ashy gray as if he had seen a ghost. There were visible streaks of blood on his T-shirt and he nervously said, "Cuz, those racist Aryan devils cut me with a razor!" Gangster looked stunned. When the bars were racked open and I stepped out, Ed pointed at the culprits standing bunched together at the end of the tier. Looking in their direction I bragged, "Oh yes, I can whip all of them, and I don't want any help."

Standing off to the side was a crowd of blacks, mostly Ed's home-boys. Gangster asked Ed, "Why didn't they help?" He said, "Those niggers were too scared to move." I Crip-strolled down the tier toward the large group of whites. I bumped into an inebriated white guy, rumored to be their leader. With slurred speech the guy said, "Watch where you're going, nigger," and when I turned around he threw a jab that I avoided, then countered. While he was uncon-scious on the floor I stooped down and used my fist as a hammer to bash his face in. A guard stood behind a fence, pointing a gun at my head. With each punch I growled viciously and asked, "Is he out?" The guard hollered, "Yes, Tookie, he's out, please stop, I don't want to shoot you!" Though I intended to continue, another guard from the back of the tier started shooting and that caught my attention.

Once back in the cell I discovered my hand had a fractured bone protruding upward beneath the skin, and was swollen. After having my hand x-rayed the doctor put a cast on my hand and forearm that I later took off. The next day in the counselor's office there was no mention of taking me to the Hole. In fact, all he wanted to know was whether I was willing to squash the conflict. I responded, "No problemo!" I assumed the counselor expected the incident to escalate into a bloody racial war. After the unit lockdown, the white guy openly apologized. Privately he thanked me, knowing I could have killed him in the name of self-defense. In prison it's known as a "freebie killing," justifiable homicide.

The conflict was resolved. For a while the unit operated as smoothly as a prison setting could run. But of course we black folks tend to argue and fight amongst ourselves. As I recall, Grandpa and this fellow TJ (Troy Jones) started arguing over the weights, and TJ called him a homosexual. A fight quickly broke out, and TJ tried to flee the scene but got trapped between the weight benches. His blood splattered on the wall and floor. It was reported that a knife was in-volved so both of them were transferred to the Hole. Though in his late forties Grandpa handled himself quite well. Maybe all the years he had spent in other California prisons had something to do with it. The penal system has a knack for eliciting the beast in man.

Things Happen

I n 1985 I was back in the Los Angeles County Jail for an evidentiary hearing relevant to my automatic appeal. It wasn't until I was again sitting in the jail cell on G-row that memories of the medical unit's druggings and other dastardly plots resurfaced. I was uncomfortable being back in a predicament beyond my control. At the Torrance court, where I was held in a glass booth, the guards put the lying snitch Oglesby in an adjacent booth. Even though I had never known what Oglesby looked like, I remembered his name from reading my trial transcripts. When I overheard a guard say, "George Oglesby is here for the Williams case," fury grew within me. I envisioned myself picking up the nonfunctional water fountain next to me and hurling it through the big glass window at him. Oglesby must have sensed something, because when I stood up, he immediately started banging on the glass and hollering for the guards to take him out of the booth. That court date was the last time I saw Oglesby.

Though I was in the county jail for two weeks, it seemed like several months. Periodically sheriffs would stroll by and gawk at me. The more inquisitive ones stopped and asked, "Are you Big Tookie from death row?" All I could do was ignore them and turn my head. I despised being viewed as a monkey in a menagerie. It infuriated me to be treated as a mindless, lowly animal held captive for the amusement of others. I was more than satisfied when the court hearing was over and

I left the county jail. When I arrived back at San Quentin, awaiting me were allegations of extortion, intimidation, and conspiring to commit violence. Of course it was easy for staff to find some fool who was willing to sell his soul for peanuts. They found an ideal stool pigeon in TJ, the same black inmate Grandpa had properly touched up.

As a result of TJ's fears and untruths, I was soon transferred to C-section, where the larger overflow of death row's condemned men were housed. Once I settled in, the first person to reach out to me with a care package (books, food, personal care items, and stationery) was Evil, a spearhead of the Raymond Avenue Crips. When I was finally cleared for the Grade-A yard, I spent time driving iron with Evil while digesting his analysis of the prison politics in C-section. Firsthand knowledge of your surroundings can prevent your being triple-crossed, hurt, or killed.

From the moment Evil and I introduced ourselves, we clicked like biological siblings. He reminded me of my stepbrother Wayne. At five feet six inches, dark-complected, with long tresses, his short stature belied his body strength. We shared a common interest in vocabulary development, so we exchanged lists and quizzed each other on enunciation, orthography, semantics, and correct use of each word in a sentence. Evil introduced me to black history with a book entitled *Destruction of Black Civilization* by Chancellor Williams. The study of black history, law, psychology, math, religion, Swahili, spirituality, and other subjects became a staple of our daily discipline in the scheme of survival.

I had been in C-section for about three weeks when a sergeant was murdered, prompting an immediate lockdown. For more than a month everybody was subject to disruptive cell searches and occasional harassment by antagonistic guards. Rumor had it that there were so many inmates willing to snitch about the sergeant's murder that staff started to turn snitches away. It's pathetic how some grown men deem themselves to be adults, yet break down like little boys and lie on others. The prison mystique was being stripped naked before my eyes.

During the lockdown there was still a lot of interaction. Every morning large segments in the unit exercised as one physical machine that resonated loudly in numerical cadence. Being an iron driver, I disliked the burpy exercises, military-style calisthenics with an innovative prison twist consisting of push-ups and kick-ins. But the atmosphere was so energetic, I got caught up in the exercises.

There were Crips all over the place and in the same vicinity. Above me on the third and fourth tiers were Treach from Raymond Avenue Crips, Bub, and other Crips on Grade B. Being on that status I knew they were limited on food, so when I received my food package I sent them a pillowcase swollen with food. No guard's assistance was necessary because we used a line to pass the pillowcase up to where they were housed. I'd learn later that they were as freehearted as I was.

Once the investigations had subsided and the suspects rounded up, San Quentin was off lockdown. In C-section were two yards, one for death row and the other one for the AD Seg prisoners, mostly parolees and others doing hard time. On occasion I was able to "Crip-reminisce" through the fence with young Hawkeye, Clarence Hoover, Spud, Tomcat, Rebo, Woodrat, Turtle, and plenty of others from Los Angeles. Seeing so many Crip homeboys brought back memories. It was a reassuring reality to know that if it came to an all-out war against any enemies, the strength and numbers were there. Then again, misery loves company, and I had plenty of it. It was pathetic how many of us Crips were languishing behind bars with no prospects of a future.

Back in those days, when death row prisoners were escorted to the yard, the shower, or anywhere inside the unit, they were not handcuffed. One day while heading toward the shower I stopped off to talk with my homeboy Ghetto. I caught sight of TJ strolling down the tier, with a guard several yards behind him. If a camera had been available the lens would have captured the fury in my stare. The first thing Ghetto said was, "Cuz, it might be a setup!" I thought the same thing seeing TJ walking toward me with one hand thrust inside his prison coat pocket. There were no gunmen in sight, and the escort had disappeared. Whether TJ's intent was harmless or not, I beat him to the punch. He fell like a sack of potatoes and ended up with half his body dangling over the tier between the bottom rail. I tried to get at him until I found myself staring into a rifle barrel the diameter of a grapefruit. The black guard frantically yelled out, "Stop hitting him, Tookie, or I'll shoot!" As crazy as the guard looked, I knew he would shoot, so I slowly raised up, then backed away. Several guards approached, I was handcuffed, and then escorted to D-section, another disciplinary lockup unit for Grade B condemned and others.

In D-section I was housed next door to Grandpa. He was there for having another run-in with TJ just weeks before I did. On a line, he sent over the violation report that quoted TJ stating I was the Godfather of the Crips and Grandpa was a member. He went on to say that we wanted him to pay rent and when he refused, I ordered Grandpa to move on him. The accusations were indicative of the prevaricating snitches and their masters who hounded me.

My life, though insignificant to the world, continued to be plagued by plots and conspiracy theories. I wasn't in D-section a week when I received a document (dated May 24, 1985) accusing me of a possible escape attempt. The prison handlers and their snitches had concocted yet another implausible story in which I plotted an escape with a man who had been dead years prior. But I'm Tookie, a man who could use a dead man and still be successful. Later these bogus charges were dropped.

There were other bizarre things occurring. This black guy, Sticks, presented himself as an affable fellow, eager to engage in political conversations. On occasions he'd ask for a book, and I'd send him one to read. Sticks often talked about being proud to be a vegetarian, but he took every meat product served on the food cart.

One day I stopped by Stick's cell to drop off a book, and he was in the back of the cell, naked, using a slice of bologna and cheese to wipe between his butt cheeks. I quickly turned my head and walked away as he hollered out, "Brother Tookie, let me explain!" I shouted back, "To each his own, I'm not tripping." I had ended the conversation, but Sticks continued defending his kinky behavior. He pleaded, "Tookie, I'm not a pervert or a homo, and I wasn't flashing my buns at you. I wipe my butt with the meat, then give it to my neighbor, who I hate with a passion. Since I can't get my hands on that scumbag's throat, I do the next best thing to retaliate." Sticks carried on his one-sided talk about all of the despicable things he did to the food he passed to his greedy neighbor.

About a week later Sticks had the audacity to call over and ask if I wanted some cookies out of his food package. No matter how hungry I was, I remained silent. Minutes later he asked, "Bro, do you want one of these Gallo dry salamis?" Fed up, I said, "Hell, no, and don't ask me again." Sticks's voice quivered, "If that's the way you want it." I was harsh—but better to offend him than eat food sautéed in his feces.

Grandpa, my neighbor, was transferred back to C-section, and Evil's close homeboy Treach moved in next door. Immediately he and I clicked as Evil and I had done. This was the beginning of an inseparable triad of minds. I discovered Treach also possessed an affinity for study. Our first dialectical exchange—one of many to come—centered on who most deserved a national holiday in his honor, Martin Luther King Jr. or Malcolm X. Treach defended his position on Malcolm X and I on King. I didn't know much about either of these black men, but I was less familiar with Malcolm's history. However, the hours spent defending our philosophical positions were memorable, and we gained new insight and respect for both slain black activists. I also gained respect for this young Crip who articulated himself with aplomb. Though Treach's skin hue of burnt sienna was darker than Malcolm X's, he resembled him in disciplined composure, height, goatee, and ferocious intellect.

Treach asked if I was doing any writing. I said, "Sure, I write missives from time to time." He let out a hearty, deep laugh and said, "Not that kind of writing, Cuz. I'm talking about literary writings, compositions, essays." I told him it never dawned on me to capture my thoughts on paper. Treach responded, "You know, Cuz, a man with your vocabulary should have a collection of essays. One day your work may prove to be a valuable asset." I didn't envision the possibilities then, but he inspired me to write my first essay, "Black Unrest," and plenty of others.

I started off with a style of writing intended to impress people with my flair for words. But in time I toned it down, breaking the stereotype of a prisoner being grandiose in his use of language and vocabulary for the sake of appearing intelligent. Studying was becoming a noble reality for me. The prison cage was transformed into a study laboratory; a secluded place of challenge to mold an educated mind; a quasi-university where I could increase my familiarity with my culture as well as politics, religion, criminal law, and the world—and get in touch with myself.

Seeking to reeducate myself was the first step toward reasoning. Without a conscience I'd remain an educated fool doomed to repeat his mistakes. I didn't know why I was driven to study. It was beyond anything I could fathom. Was I destined for something outside of Crippen?

When I wasn't studying or debating with Treach, we were on the exercise yard three days a week driving iron with a huge segment of Crips representing many sets from South Central. The yard was replete with other diehards: Cool Breeze, Crazy Crip, Turtle, Bobcat, Timebomb, Crusher, Tee Dee, and others I can't remember. Being in D-section afforded me the opportunity to hear about what was going on with other Crips in San Quentin and throughout the penal system. There were plenty of war stories about Crips. I was told my homeboy Black Johnny had lost his mind. Hearing this news I couldn't help think about the omen I had about him and Buddha.

There was also mention of the ambushing of several homeboys, which infuriated me. Usually with the assistance of a rogue guard, a nonblack prisoner would be allowed to hide in a black prisoner's cell underneath the bunk. Once the handcuffed black man entered the cell and the door was locked, the ambusher would quickly crawl out and stab him thirty or forty times. This deadly warfare—a dishonest guard aiding a nonblack prison group—is a reality every black man is aware of. Although there were individuals who survived these attacks, most of them died. I always checked under the bunk before entering my cell to thwart any unwanted guest lying in wait. To hear about these kinds of setups where a Crip, Blood, or another black man was carried out on a gurney paralyzed, moribund, or dead, was enough to enrage rage. How can a man defend himself while handcuffed and locked in a cell, with a hands-free enemy on a mission to stop his heart from beating?

There was a time, after yard, that I returned to the cell and all was clear under the bunk. But while leaning on the bars, talking to Treach, the cell door swung open. Hurriedly I closed it and whispered over to Treach that the door was unlocked. Treach's immediate response, "Cuz, it's probably a setup, don't come out!" When a guard came to the cell, there were two gun-rail guards slightly off to the side watching. When I told the guard the door was unlocked, he simply smiled, then locked the door. Before leaving the guard said, "Tookie, you are fortunate you didn't step outside, because they were waiting for you!" It didn't surprise me.

There are subtle moments of humor squeezed in between the prison madness. I knew quite a few Crips who were jokesters, but none as hilarious as Tee Dee from the Harlem Crips. He was a maestro of jokes, playing the dozens and always cappin' on somebody. Tee Dee had a comical and animated flair that either made you want to kill him or laugh. He could look a guy straight in the eye and compliment his intellect, while secretly tapping someone else to indicate he's jiving. Or Tee Dee would call a homeboy "handsome homie," knowing darn well he meant the opposite. I was never the joking and laughing type, but Tee Dee had Treach and me rolling with laughter. Unlike Black Johnny, a pressure-hold headlock didn't work on Tee Dee; he'd just come back for more. He was also good at engaging in private bull sessions. During one such chat he said, "Tookie, I need several photos of you as soon as possible." I asked him for what? "Cuz, you're the only celebrity I know," was his insane response. He said, "I can have pictures of you blown up to poster size, then sell them at the Inglewood Forum." I told him that was ridiculous. But he said, "You're the most famous person in prison since George Jackson. I'm going to make some money!" I figured Tee Dee was joking. But after paroling, that nut actually did sell posters of me.

Change Will Come

P lenty of people have claimed they had an epiphany that radically altered their lives. I wasn't fortunate enough to encounter a dazzling light, visions, or a voice of infinite wisdom to shake my world to its foundation. Being brick-headed, it would've taken the sky falling on me to notice the need for a change in my life.

I failed continually to see the bigger picture. I trudged through life with no purpose or direction. All I saw were steel bars, thick walls, armed guards, and madness. Fighting the good fight was my motto, so in lieu of sitting around in D-section on Grade-B, I decided to challenge a violation report against me with a 602 appeal. Months later I won the appeal, and my Grade-A status was restored. It was bittersweet leaving Treach in D-section, thinking he'd arrive later. I had no idea years would pass before I'd see him again. I relished our Crip reminiscences, dialectics, and other philosophical exchanges.

Back in C-section I was able to regain enough strength to bench a 500-pound bar that had Chief's name soldered on it in bold letters, though he couldn't bench the weight. The day I benched the weight with ease for reps, Crip Slim threw his beanie up in the air and started jumping up and down as if he won the lottery. Slim told me that he was proud and happy that a Crip—and nobody else—was able to lift the weight. There was also dust gathering on a set of 130-pound dumbbells I started using for standing or sitting shoulder presses, curls, and back-arms for ten to fifteen reps. My true feat of strength was being able to perform seated behind-the-neck shoulder presses for reps with a 375-pound bar. Some guards were still trying for permission for me to compete in the San Quentin weight-lifting contests, but the higher echelon vetoed it.

While we were driving iron, watchful eyes were always scanning the area. In the background was an unassuming-looking Crip, Maddog, one of the most loyal and most deadly. He was a wily army veteran who looked like a tall and burly black mountain man. Like sentries, he and the stocky faithful Crip Ghetto stood around ready for any intruders, prepared to smash anyone was foolish enough to violate our territory.

At San Quentin, the population of death row for minorities was disproportionately increasing, mostly for black men and Mexicans from South Central Los Angeles, including Bloods from different sets (gang factions). But the interactions between Crips and Bloods on death row (what prisoners call "the Row") were in sharp contrast to the violent exchanges back in society. Though we drove iron side by side, I can't say we trusted one another. Nevertheless, we did share a commonality in backgrounds, and we were pitted against the same alien penal setting of death. With rare exceptions, there was no squabbling between Crips and Bloods. We were never at war. We did our thing and they did theirs.

During a renovation, C-section's death row population was moved to D-section, which was evacuated for our arrival. There was no difference between the units; I was locked up and forced to battle my inner demons. Most of the time I spent concentrating on drawing, which shielded me mentally from the chaos of prison life. When I was drawing, time was irrelevant; not much else mattered. I had no idea drawing was a defensive mechanism for me to combat the negative elements of an idle mind and hands. My life was adopting an alien concept: productivity.

On the condemned yard was a huge weight pile and a small universal-type bench press machine attached to the back wall. Right next to us was the Max-A yard, consisting of Crips, Bloods, the Black Guerrilla Family, the Aryan Brotherhood, and other gang factions. The Max-A yard was a potpourri of unstable lunacy that could erupt at any time. Back then a politicized version of the Crips, the Consolidated Crips Organization, gained considerable notoriety. Perhaps in the beginning its intentions were honorable, but later allegations of coercive recruiting, cronyism, intimidation, manipulation by the Black Guerrilla Family, and improprieties against other Crips cast a long negative shadow on the Consolidated Crips Organization. One of its biggest canards was that I sat on its board. This was a ploy to attract more Crips. Evil pointed out that if I was at the top of the Consolidated Crips Organization, other forces could not have subverted it as they did. If it had transformed itself into a political prison entity and cast out the gangster mentality, it would have been the most powerful black group in the prison system.

But the Consolidated Crips Organization's rapid deterioration was hastened by internal conflicts and external antagonists from numerous Crip factions. Crip scrimmages were played out on the Max-A yard and throughout other California prisons with deadly force. Many of the organization's leadership jumped to the formidable opposing side. In San Quentin it was pathetic to hear or catch sight of Crips engaged in a blow-for-blow campaign for dominance. In the final analysis there were no winners, only disunity.

Aggressive interactions between prisoners—or between a guard and a prisoner—were all isolated in these close quarters. While working out on the bench press machine, I caught sight of Freaky Pete, another death row prisoner, a few feet away, backing up quickly from the fence. I knew something was amiss. On the Max-A yard I saw a black prisoner and a Southern Mexican guy engaged in battle, with the black man having the upper hand. The tower gunman fired a couple of live rounds, and the black man crumbled to the ground, killed instantly. The Mexican guy died later at the hospital.

This violent scenario was as graphic as striking a wooden match and watching it explode into flame. It was a moment of cold-blooded brutality that captured the attention of every prisoner present. After the guards ordered everyone on the Max-A yard to hit the dirt, blacks and Mexicans made halfhearted attempts to wage war, but more shots ended such notions. On the condemned yard we too were ordered to get down on the ground. A nervous black guard who seemed to have lost his mind screamed, "Tookie, you better hit the ground right now if you want to live!" I stood looking up at the guard as if daring him to shoot, before Ghetto and Maddog pulled me to the ground.

Later I wondered how it was possible for such an attack to occur in the midst of other black men. It was irrelevant whether the black prisoner was a Crip, Blood, or a member of the Black Guerrilla Family. Where were his friends and comrades? I remember asking Ghetto, "Cuz, what was wrong with that picture?" He replied, "No *usalama* [which means "security" in Swahili] whatsoever. If that man had homeboys, they all froze. Cuz, you never have to worry about that. I'll be there for you." I voiced the same sentiment to him. Having witnessed two men get smoked, I knew my life wasn't worth a wooden nickel in here.

Around this time it came as no surprise that the state-level court denied my appeal, ruling against me. Once the prison staff found out, they took the unprecedented step of sending me to the Hole. Other than for harassment, it's difficult to understand the staff's reasoning. Since then, no one else has undergone such treatment. After numerous requests to phone the state-appointed attorney, I was able to make contact and convince him to call the warden to rectify the situation. So I was returned to D-section, where the entire death row unit was preparing to move back to C-section.

Then, in June 1987, I was uprooted and placed in the Hole under suspicion of another escape plot. This time the so-called conspiracy had me teamed up with a cast of unknown Crips. The next day I was provided with a document that revealed a phone conversation between a person identifying himself as a Crip talking to a San Quentin operator. Not able to speak to me directly, he told the operator, "The

Los Angeles Crips have a job to get Tookie out of there!" The person left his full name, address, and three phone numbers. Every lying syllable uttered about me was likely considered gospel by the staff. They were eager to believe the worst about me.

At the unit classification hearing it was clear that I'd remain in the Hole pending an investigation. Assigned to the same yard as my homeboy Evil, I met Owl, Double Life, Tee, Little Owl, G, and about twenty other Crips. I just missed Treach. He had been called down to the Los Angeles County Jail by Crip Kato's attorney. Each designated yard was then split in half with different yard schedules. As a result Evil and I ended up on separate yards, with our homeboys split up. The same was done to the southern and white yard, and the Black Guerrilla Family and the northern yard.

This allowed me to become better acquainted with the homeboys. Double Life, G, and I engaged in a quasi-study group to expand our political dialectics and vocabulary. To better understand politics and other topics, it was necessary to learn thousands of new words. Following our workouts on the yard, Double Life didn't hesitate to pull out a long list of words to test me. There was never a moment that I missed the orthography or definition of a word. Studying had opened a new world for me.

One day out of curiosity I asked my homeboy what the initial G stood for and he said, "God." Other than being born in God's image, he didn't have a leg to stand on. I'm sure it annoyed G when I asked why he wasn't able to liberate himself or me, since he was God. But who was I to challenge another man's belief, regardless of its oddity?

After a few weeks all the separated yards were restored. In several lengthy discussions with Evil, we concluded that Crippen wasn't what it used to be. There was nothing worse than Crips giving "Crip" a bad name. It was a stunning realization to witness Raymond's and my brainchild becoming a caricature of what it once was.

In the Hole there were no weights on the yard, so I improvised with push-ups, chin-ups, and basketball. Since I didn't want to lose my yokes, I avoided the burpy exercises, which would have trimmed me down like a greyhound. Prison burpies are the hardest exercise known to man, and I disliked them so much I refused to do any until years later. For many of us basketball is a frustration releaser. But it is a pity to see so much raw talent deflected from greater possibilities.

In the prison grapevine, news traveled fast, especially when someone turns informer. We received word that Crime Dog McGruff from the Rolling 60s was a snitch and headed to death row. According to Buthalezi, his crimie (crime partner) McGruff snitched on him, and it was his intent to snuff him. The day McGruff was placed on the Crip yard, Buthalezi had a decision to make. At his disposal were enough knives for a small Ninja army. Nervously he blurted out an obscure excuse: "Cuz, I'm going to bust on him, but I need some steel to do the job right!" Perhaps he was still rattled after witnessing his CCO homeboy getting a hit on the basketball court days before. Buthalezi had ample time to handle McGruff himself, which he vowed on his life. If Buthalezi violated his Crip word, it would render his voice forever unworthy.

Later that week the counselor announced that the investigation of my so-called escape plot revealed that it was a teenage prank. With a brief warning to stay out of trouble, my Grade A was immediately restored. I was transferred to C-section. But it was like playing musical chairs: I wasn't there more than a month when C-section was moved to East Block. Outside the unit there were six fenced yards with weight piles to accommodate death row prisoners. Gone were the days when friends or warring foes either exercised on the same Grade-A yard or stayed locked up in their cells.

The atmosphere in East Block was laid-back. I found myself reading less, although occasionally I worked on expanding my vocabulary. The central focus in my life was to develop bigger muscles than I had when I was in society. But because I was shuffled back and forth to the Hole, my goal eluded me. With Bub out of commission, Ghetto's newly arrived cousin, Herc, became my workout partner. Standing over six feet, he was a yoked-up cocoa-brown lothario thug with a cooler-than-cool stroll. The county jail had sapped his size and strength, but persistent workouts got him back on track. Each day we eagerly looked forward to the gates being racked open to do battle with the weight pile.

Around this time a buzz circulated that McGruff had received Grade A and was on his way to East Block. His crimie Buthalezi had been talking long smack about what he planned to do. Now it was time to put up or shut up. Once again Buthalezi had a decision to make, but he did nothing. Buthalezi's failure to follow through enraged another Crip sufficiently to fulfill the task. Quickly McGruff was stretched out on the cement suffering from multiple knife wounds. Buthalezi ran off to the other side of the yard.

The following day I received a copy of a Confidential Information Disclosure Form (CIDF), a bureaucratic euphemism for an unnamed person snitching—typically lying—on someone. I was accused of being the leader of the Blue Note Crips, actively recruiting others, and having inmates assaulted. In the next preposterous CIDF I received, a Crip power struggle was allegedly brewing between Buthalezi and me. The administration's attempt to characterize Buthalezi as a controlled pawn against me was a fiasco from the start. Any aspiration on his or "their" part was stagnated by Buthalezi's delusions of grandeur, his inability to honor his word, and fear that rendered him incompetent and foolish.

Though not all of Buthalezi's violations have been mentioned here, I believe his misdeeds continue to eat away at his soul.

Trials, Tribulations

I t was foolish of me to believe that my grandmother would live forever, but I felt the same about my stepfather, Fred Holiwell, who died in 1988. I remember listening to this once strong, proud black man, who was now dying of cancer. He whispered in quivering tones that tore at my heart: "Tookie, call the police, somebody's breaking into the house." Hearing him made me cringe in despair. I could do absolutely nothing for this man who had so often helped me.

Though Fred wasn't my biological father, he was the paternal fixture in my life, a man I could always call upon in times of trouble or need. After hearing of his death, I stretched out on the mattress on the floor of the cell and visualized my own personal eulogy about him. I wasn't his real son, but Fred did for me what he'd do for any of his four children. He tried desperately to protect me from mistakes growing up and from the racist system of the law, an impossible aspiration for any black man.

The best thing I can say about Fred is that he loved my mother and was always there for her, and for that I give him high praise. His impact on my life is forever etched in my mind. Rest in peace, my father.

On occasions the inevitable question, "Why me?" came to me. I wondered how this crooked cycle of misfortune could be reversed. For years I obliged this system designed to destroy me. Clearly, as long as I continued functioning out of criminal intent and robotic stupidity, I'd be assisting the system with its destructive intent. Later I'd learn that to buck the awful conditions with any positive agenda would only trigger efforts to discourage me. As a guard once told me, "You're here [only] to die!"

There's enough intrigue here in prison to put the Central Intelligence Agency to shame. I was not shocked when the classification committee lowered my status to Grade B, along with Ghetto, who was fingered as one of my bodyguards. Just weeks earlier the staff had converted part of East Block's second tier to serve as a lockup for Grade-B condemned prisoners. When Ghetto and I arrived, Evil, Treach, and a few others were already housed on the tier. Though we weren't allowed any weights on the exercise yard, it felt good being around Crip allies.

I was housed in a cell adjacent to Evil, which enabled our continued conversations. I recall him talking about this black actor, Philip Michael Thomas, who had mentioned during a radio interview a book entitled *Perennial Psychology of the Bhagavad-Gita.* Evil, Treach, and I obtained a copy of the book. Though it didn't alter my life as I thought it might, it did cause me to challenge my own stance on personal thoughts, behavior, and the conditions around me. But I was still torn between my fealty to Crippen and becoming a new being. Did Buddha, Raymond, Mac Thomas, Ode, and all the rest die in vain?

I was embarking upon a task that had broken other men when they altered the course of their lives. A stumbling block was the shallow concern of how other Crips would view my change. To say I wasn't interested in what my peers thought of me would be a lie. I wasn't about to lower my convictions. Though I was no longer an impulsive reactionary, I was neither a pacifist nor would I turn the other cheek if physically threatened. The natural do-or-die instinct of self-defense is a reality I'll forever adhere to. Still, the scariest thing to me was life after Crippen—and the idea of developing a conscience to counter the injustices of my own ignorance.

In 1989 I received a court order for a Los Angeles County child custody hearing for my son Stan. When I arrived at High Power I was placed on B-row. Around the corner on A-row was Evil, who had been called down by Kato's attorney months earlier. The following day Evil reached out to me with a huge plastic bag filled with food, personal care items, and books. Although I was unable to see him or Kato, we communicated through the wall vent, an improvised telephone. Over the years of traveling back and forth to the Los Angeles County Jail, I ran into Crazy Dee, Timmy Tucker, Animal, Big Bamm, and Little Kill-Kill. Other than strolling down Crip memory lane with them, I found solace in having Animal test me on numerous words, and I returned the favor.

Shackled and seated in the Los Angeles County courtroom, I saw my stepsister Demetri there. I hadn't seen her in nearly a decade. I had hoped to see my son, whom I hadn't seen since 1979. Finally the judge entered the room, sat shuffling papers for a few minutes, and then rescheduled my hearing for an unspecified date since neither my son nor his mother, Beverly, was present.

I was still shell-shocked from being in the Los Angeles County Jail in 1979–81. Before my departure Evil hollered through the vent to ask if I wanted to stay down there a little longer. I shot back, "No way, Cuz, I'm ready to split!" Even though I was in good company with Evil and other Crips, I wanted out of there, and soon wasn't quick enough.

Arriving back at San Quentin, though no delight, was better than being in the county jail. In East Block I was housed a couple of cells from Treach. Soon he started sending me books by authors such as Chancellor Williams, Runoko Rashidi, Danita R. Redd, Cheikh Anta Diop, Frances Cress Welsing, Dr. Yosef ben-Jochannan, A. J. Rogers, Ivan van Sertima, John H. Clarke, and many others. These writers helped reveal the truth about the history of our culture. The more I read, the more I discovered the contradictions in myself and in the world I thought I knew.

Somewhere I read, "Nothing remains the same, and everything changes." My change would be invisible to the vindictive and myopic staff and others who preferred I remain fossilized in the amber of the

Crip legacy. It was slow and difficult for me to shake loose the Machiavellian mentality that served for years as my apologia for manhood. I had always scraped and struggled for the tiniest of morsels, even self-change. The mental and behavioral evolution that Treach, Evil, and I were seeking transcended ourselves; it was larger than any one of us as individuals. We wanted to set a standard others could follow, create a natural transition from criminal to black man of learning. We wanted most to understand why we Crips chose this path to take in life. We wanted to kick the door wide open so any imprisoned black man could enter and begin to initiate a productive change within himself.

Sometime in 1990 those of us on Grade B in East Block were moved to the Hole, with our property on carts trailing behind. Though everybody else had been scattered on different tiers, Treach and I were on the same tier with an open cell between us. Not long after our arrival, a man from India calling himself Mahindi was placed in that empty cell. For the moment Mahindi was quietly memorizing names of prisoners for future cell soldiering. ("Cell soldiers" are prisoners who will challenge others to fight, or will throw things on prisoners passing their cells, knowing that they can't get beaten up because they *never* leave their cells.)

It was obvious to us that Mahindi was a J-Cat when he started ear-hustling, intruding into everybody's conversation. Treach and I knew it was futile to argue with a man who wasn't wrapped too tight. Clearly he was intentionally placed next to Treach and me. For weeks Mahindi angered everybody on the tier with his abrupt intrusions, using his makeshift fish line—a long string with a hook used to slide items down the tier from one prisoner to another—to snatch up others. He stole fish lines so regularly some of the Aryan Brotherhood members tried to buy him off with cigarettes and candy, which didn't last long. Though we shined Mahindi on, he would bang on the steel toilet and the wall during all hours of the day and night. The guards tried to calm him down, but as soon as they left, he'd bang in rhythm to some imaginary tune in his head. When Mahindi wasn't banging, he held one-sided conversations with Treach or me. Other times he'd wait until we started talking, then lash out, calling us niggers and other expletives. In his whiny, nasal voice he'd sometimes say, "Hey, Tookie, how come you look like Black Hercules, but you speak with a soft voice like a woman. Hell, you should switch voices with Treach! But maybe you two are playing games with my mind by throwing your voices like a ventriloquist. I'm not crazy, you know. Tookie . . . Treach . . . is that what you're trying to do, make me lose my mind? Answer me, *answer me!!*"

Treach and I sometimes wished for the opportunity to snatch Mahindi by the collar and beat some sanity into him. Darn near everybody on the tier was waiting to catch him during cell search, when each person stands handcuffed outside the cell. With no hands available, feet would have worked just as well. But he was no fool. Mahindi never came out of his cell for searches, yard, or to shower. Since no one was willing to bite when Mahindi sold wolf tickets, it started driving him batty. At first he began to mumble to himself, then he'd loudly speak out in detail about his uncle molesting him as a child, or give accounts of other bizarre sex stories. This man needed treatment, to be housed in a medical ward, not in the Hole. I returned from the yard one day to see a guard cleaning out Mahindi's cell. From what I heard, he tried to commit suicide and almost succeeded. As cold as it may sound, his departure was a relief for everybody.

In the midst of these distractions I still possessed the enthusiasm to reinvent myself. It was difficult to transform my criminal mentality into a mindset with a conscience. Everything was working against me: I was an imprisoned black man; condemned to die; cofounder of the infamous and hated Crips; and no one believed I'd ever change. Even I had doubts.

I now had knowledge of what *not* to do. I had studied the lives of numerous imprisoned men who professed to be revolutionists— Christian, Muslim, Buddhist, Rastafarian, ex-drug addict, or former gang member—while still acting out their gangster fantasies. I had read about George Jackson and his comrades, about their courageous attempts to convert the black criminal into the ultimate revolutionary. They were stifled by individuals straddling the fence between revolutionary duties and criminal gain. It would be a harder challenge for me to transfigure my Machiavellian mode to an educated and redemptive mindset. You cannot serve two gods.

The recording of human errors must be a vivid reminder of what to avoid repeating. Often during yard time, in my discussions with Treach and Evil, we harped upon the foreseeable pitfalls and our determination to sidestep them. But despite the books we read, we knew that our life-altering transition had to be based on our own personal initiative or a relapse would be imminent. Only after undergoing personal transformations could we individually meet at the crossroads to compare notes. Until then, everything we pondered was pure speculation.

In the meantime, Bad News—from the Rolling 60s Crips—moved into the cell on the other side of me. He had accidentally cut off his fingers with a saw while working in the prison industry. Luckily, Marin General Hospital—outside the prison—was able to reattach his fingers with reconstructive surgery. It was also around this time that I began to exchange letters and photos with a Puerto Rican female name Rosa. She was an attractive, generous, and intelligent woman who was an expert computer troubleshooter for a large corporation. We slowly developed a cordial relationship although, judging from her few photos, Rosa appeared to be tipsy, no, a sloppy drunk. But I felt self-conscious and hypocritical about questioning her behavior because of my own past, so I tried to be indifferent.

I received a missive from Leon Bing, a woman writer working on a book entitled *Do or Die*. Monster Kody from the Eight Tray Gangster Crips had told her about me, and she wanted to learn more about the history of the Crips. I decided to call Leon when Kato's attorney summoned Treach, Heron, and me to the Los Angeles County Jail. The first time I met Ms. Bing, it struck me as odd that a white woman would be interested in writing a book about street thugs like us. I was skeptical of her motives and was unwilling to divulge the information

I planned to use for my memoirs. Though Leon was congenial enough I truly believed it impossible for anyone—white, black, Mexican or other—to chronicle this specific black tragedy when he or she had not lived it. She would inevitably lack understanding of the essence and subtle contradictions of the Crips experience. There is already too much misinformation being propagated. I politely suggested at the end of our first and only visit that she talk to Treach, who might be willing to help her.

Perhaps had I not been expecting a food package already en route to San Quentin I would have stayed a little longer with Treach, Kato, and Heron in the county jail. The package I expected was sent by Rosa, who was quite reliable in taking care of my needs. She was impressed with my eagerness to read and provided me with all the books I wanted. From the outside, the relationship appeared to be running smoothly. Evil was curious as to whether I'd marry her. He looked perplexed when I said marriage was out of the equation, period. Dealing with Rosa was a handful. She had issues and wasn't too keen on accepting advice. I knew she had a drinking problem, but I was caught off-guard when she admitted that she was a kleptomaniac and had contemplated suicide. Then she mentioned that a psychologist was charging her $250 an hour to discuss her problems. I quipped, "Two hundred and fifty dollars? Hell, you'd do better paying me to resolve your problems instead of some quack."

Each visit was a trying moment for me. I had to determine whether I'd wear the hat of a psychologist, friend, physician, father, counselor, brother, lover, or objective listener. In Rosa's mind all of her problems far outweighed the seriousness of my execution. Though Rosa was affable and sweet, she was spoiled, expecting everything to go her way. One day Rosa said, "Since I'm looking out for you, Tookie, you can't complain or criticize me!" That was our final visit. The materialistic items she rained down upon me were a blessing, but I wasn't hard up enough to kiss anybody's butt for them. No matter how many women slipped in and out of my life, my mother was always the superior constant.

To relieve my pent-up frustration I started doing burpies with Evil out on the yard. Within months burpies became an enjoyable challenge to test my endurance and strength. Pushing the envelope, I created other higher burpy counts, along with double, triple, and quad-count Jashiri burpies with a pause, and crunch burpies. Though the burpy routine started off with just Evil and me, others began to join in. Before long the entire yard was, in prison parlance, "busting down." Even Mario, a Blood, participated in our routines and didn't miss a workout. His presence on the yard was no oddity, because Crips and Bloods had been coexisting under the same roof for years—on death row—with no serious conflict.

But of course with a bunch of men playing basketball, there are bound to be disagreements. On the basketball court one day, I saw out of the corner of my eye a flashing silhouette, a hand going upside Little Man's head. He and Mario squared off to fight. I stood between them demanding to know the problem. Mario spat out, "Tookie, this dude Little Man has been dogging me ever since I've been on the court. I told him I'm no chump and to stop dogging me, but he kept doing it, so I popped him." Pulling Mario to the side, I asked was he willing to fight Little Man head-up, and he quickly responded, "Yes!" However, when I asked the bigger and more muscular Crip, Little Man, about fighting Mario, he responded, "Can you have somebody make a knife for me?" Disgusted, I said, "Hell, no! This is a simple fight with no knives, so either you fight him toe-to-toe, or not at all." Little Man opted not to fight Mario, stating he'd take care of it in East Block, whatever that meant.

Only later did I realize that, at that moment, I initiated the beginning stage of fair play fighting. It made no difference to me that Mario and Little Man were gang rivals. Each deserved equal footing in a fight. Imagine me, developing a conscience—and with a Blood, a sworn enemy of what I stood for. Years previously, things would have turned out entirely differently, with a free-for-all. But my decision for judicious evenhandedness was a response that earned Mario's and Little Man's respect.

This was a bad time for the disenfranchised. California's criminal judiciary was handing out the death penalty like government food stamps in a depression. A youngster from the Lynwood Crips, Kerm, had just been driven up from the county jail and was immediately placed in the Hole with us. His first day on the yard, I watched as he cautiously surveyed the territory and us. Kerm was a slender Crip with barely suppressed rage. I was impressed with his gung-ho attitude toward exercising and studying. Soon Chico, from the Eight Tray Gangster Crips, arrived. He too was thrown in the Hole for evaluation. Both he and Kerm had to remain in the Hole until the committee determined whether or not they would receive Grade-A status.

During a chat with Chico I discovered he lived just several blocks from where I had lived on 69th Street. He was one of the many youngsters, along with Monster Kody, who sat around gawking at my homeboys and me driving iron. Chico was now taller than me and quite muscular. I could sense his fiery spunk—but more important, Chico had a penchant for study and exercise.

Occasionally I'd cross paths with a Crip with something to hide. Such was the case with Otabenga from the Long Beach Crips, who had been on death row for a few years. He seemed to have a huge chip on his shoulder ever since Gangster attacked him for calling him a punk. As he and I strolled on the yard, Otabenga voiced his disagreement with a rule for exercising. I assured him that there was no obligation to exercise.

Apparently Otabenga mistook my humility for weakness. He blurted, "I hope I don't have to hurt anybody over this exercising thing, because I *will!*" Ordinarily I would have clipped his chin without a second thought, but I only stopped and warned him about his hostility—somebody might take that as a threat. His response was, "I don't care!" His hand flinched upward, perhaps as a nervous tic or an attempt to strike. I defended myself with a slap across his face that sounded with a sharp crack. He stood there, shocked. One of the gunmen heard the slap and ordered us to stand still. He told Otabenga to walk toward the caged entrance. As he passed he made a halfhearted attempt to swing in slow motion from eight feet away. Standing nearby, Evil took this gesture as aggression against me. He rushed the much larger Otabenga inside the caged area. It was natural for Evil to retaliate on my behalf, as it was for Treach and me to run from opposite sides of the yard to assist him. The other gunman fired a shot landing inches from my foot. I met Treach shoulder to shoulder at the entrance of the cage. It was impossible for all of us to fit inside the tight space. Evil continued his attack as Otabenga pleaded with him to stop.

At that time, none of us was aware that Otabenga had snitched on his crimie. The incident triggered a ten-day lockdown at San Quentin.

By then I started corresponding with another female, Benita, a fitness instructor from Los Angeles. Ever since I've been on death row, I envisioned one day meeting a beautiful sister with a huge Afro and her fist raised high in a symbolic gesture of black power, or at least meet a woman who looked black. Benita was a Caucasian with fiery red hair, the antithesis of my ideal woman. But she was responsive to me, more than willing to help.

I've often questioned why there are so many black men in the visiting room hooked up with white women. I have come to understand that there is a paucity of sisters willing to come visit black men behind bars. But white women—and especially those from foreign countries—visit black men in large numbers. And behind these walls, when compassionate assistance comes knocking—as it rarely does—you simply open the door.

Let There Be Light

I t was 1992. I was preparing to leave for another evidentiary hearing in the Los Angeles County Court Building downtown. Prior to my departure Treach, Evil, and I collaborated on a book of poems entitled *Unchained Voices* with hopes of getting it published. Benita had contacted a noted black historian and author, Runoko Rashidi, who agreed to edit our work and try to find a publisher. The possibility of having our literary work in print and bearing fruits of wisdom for our homeboys and society had all three of us hyped up.

Early in the morning when the black and white Sheriff's County bus drove away from San Quentin, I reflected upon the prospects of our literary project. I was also trying to digest the latest news about a riot in South Central, a reaction to white Los Angeles cops being acquitted for beating black motorist Rodney King. It was a *felix culpa* (fortunate fault) that a citizen with a video camera captured the public flogging. Mainstream society would not have believed the brutal police injustice that black people know all too well. The Los Angeles Police Department described the brutal beating as an "isolated incident."

The unshocking fact that a predominantly Caucasian jury acquitted the four cops had South Central inhabitants bracing for a volatile response. Though the county bus was miles away from Los Angeles, the air had a caustic charred smell. Public frustration and despair had ignited a riot. In the far distance a thick, black cloud of smoke hovered over South Central like a suffocating blanket.

I arrived at the Los Angeles County Jail and was placed in a one-man holding tank, where I saw the words "Crips and Bloods United Forever" scrawled on the wall in big black letters. A détente is something for all Crips and Bloods to consider. Regardless of how much we might celebrate each vindictive strike against one another, in the long run, we all lose.

My evidentiary hearing was turning out to be a lopsided version of justice. For a defendant it's a legal crapshoot, especially when the state-appointed defense attorney's preparation and case management are perfunctory. But during the few weeks of court proceedings I did manage to contact the black author Runoko Rashidi. It was an awkward moment when Runoko brought up an incident during which my homeboys and I jacked him up for money. This was probably true, but I could neither deny nor confirm it. I did express my gratitude for his offer to help us.

Although I went to court each weekday, it didn't hinder my visits or phone calls. Benita visited on a regular basis and made sure I had more than enough money for canteen. She turned out to be a dedicated woman who even looked out for Evil and Treach. Even after Benita got married, she still came to the Los Angeles County Jail to visit me. During one of her visits we were interrupted by Baboon, a West Side Crip from way back. He acted a complete fool, hollering, "Hey, Tookie, long time no see, cousin!" Armed with an expression resembling a baboon, he wanted the world to know he was a g-h-e-t-t-o thug through and through. After Baboon calmed down for all but ten seconds, he said boisterously, "Wait a minute, Cuz, I got a surprise for you, be right back!" He returned in a moment with Li'l Pamm, who was beaming from ear to ear. During our chat Pamm revealed that she was now a legal investigator and would be visiting me in the attorney room. Both Pamm and Baboon gave me their phone numbers, suggesting I call often.

Days later I was told Baboon had been gunned down in retaliation for another murder. There was a heated war going on between some

Crips and local Mexicans. When blacks weren't killing one another, then trigger-happy cops or other people were trying to wipe us out. This "ghetto martyrdom" had gotten out of hand, with Bloods, other blacks, and my homeboys disappearing fast. Hundreds of homeboys I knew personally had been murdered for an illegitimate legacy of embedded cultural racism. From Buddha on down to each dead Crip, we acted invincible—but knew in our gut that we wouldn't live long.

When Pamm came to visit me again, her investigator's license had expired and she was arrested on the spot for trying to visit with an invalid license. Talking to her later that night her voice quivered as she talked about how they had interrogated her about me. This wasn't the same brash Pamm I knew more than a decade ago; she was literally scared to death. She asked, "What in the world have you been doing, Tookie, that caused those crazy people to question me about you?" I told her I hadn't been doing anything but that my past would forever be used against me. I could tell she had to distance herself from me, and I understood. We never spoke again.

While in High Power at the Los Angeles County Jail, I began to revisit the devils of my past. This critical reflection exposed a litany of fiascos, scandals, mayhem, nihilism, and deaths of my homeboys, ending with the Crips entity fading into obscurity. At that moment I knew that my life as a Crip had come to an end. In a cold sweat I shook myself out of this awful reverie, consumed by sadness—not for Crippen, but for the lives of all the Crips who had died, for the innocent black lives hurt in the crossfire, for the decades of young lives ruined for a causeless cause.

Wide awake I lay there thinking about how, most of my life, I lived it for Crip, but the Crip god had abandoned me. I had poked so many holes in the thin fabric of my thug experience that I could no longer sustain a conscious apologia for Crippen.

During the bus ride back to San Quentin, I realized I was wading into uncharted territory that would bring unwanted attention on me from prison authorities. They would try at every turn to discredit me . . . but I was game. In this setting—authority versus prisoner—

the chances of my succeeding in atoning and changing were very slim. But I didn't have to stand alone. Treach and Evil were undergoing the same transition, from thug to thinking black man with a purpose. This is a concept—redemption—that criminologists, prison authorities, psychologists, and law enforcement officers refuse to believe unless the transformation is accomplished under their "spirit breaking" guidelines.

Back at San Quentin and in the Hole, I was placed in the first cell, 52, on the second tier, one cell away from Ghetto. I began studying more black history. I attribute the restoration of my self-confidence and self-worth to reading about my ancestors in America and Africa. I began to see that all I had learned from some Caucasians and Uncle Toms about black reflections of myself were lies.

Recapturing a more accurate picture of black history inspired all of us on the yard to teach ourselves to speak Swahili. We had to become autodidactic—self-taught—and continue learning from one another as well. Outside on the yard after each exhaustive workout of burpies and "Kenya laps" (very fast laps), we'd walk around in small groups and practice speaking Swahili. When Young Kerm moved into the cell between Ghetto and me, our study regimen included him in an hour each weekday practicing Swahili.

Studying was easy compared to controlling my temper. Since childhood my temper or rage was an explosive defense mechanism, whether triggered by threat or irritant. Controlling my temper would be a matter of resolution and discipline. I resolved to transition my rage into something more beneficial.

For decades I had participated in my own dehumanization. The word "menticide"—brainwashing—coined by black psychologist Bobby Wright, perfectly depicts my state of mind. I had been menticided about my culture, my ethnicity, and my purpose. There was much work that had to be done to reverse the damage. I'd have to rehumanize myself. I had no road map. Though I really didn't know how to accomplish the task, I knew not to indulge in hours of gazing into the hypnotic box (TV), dulling my senses with drugs, gambling in any form, intentionally drawing attention, or losing myself in the fantasy world of pornographic sex with two-dimensional females.

It was impossible for our peers to see by our mere appearance a change. But one result of the conversion was our ability to introduce the concept of autodidactics to the younger generation of Crips entering death row, lest they too be corrupted by the duplicitous surrounding or by other duped or scandalous Crips. The premise was that any Crip armed with correct knowledge about himself, culture, spirituality, and the world would see the light and begin to change. There would always be exceptions to the rule but at least we were offering an option. Once when I was kicking back on the yard, Kerm thanked me for introducing him to scholastics. He explained how fortunate he was to have been assigned to our yard because we (Treach, Evil, and I) helped him tremendously. Had he been sent to any other yard, he admitted, he would be gangbanging.

This was a refreshing moment: to see a man open up with no reservation, no fear of humiliation or ridicule. This illustrates how a young do-or-die Crip not of my generation was intelligent enough to acknowledge our scholastic teachings as a sign of strength. Moreover, it was a validation of the value of the transition from being a Crip to an adult Afrocentric male. None of us could relate to other racial groups until we established a firm footing for our own—and then began to reach out.

Any form of positive awakening behind these walls of chaos can be considered a miracle. Especially since the age-old mechanisms that engender racism, violence, collusion, deprivation, frame-ups, and other injustices continue to exist here. Though I was finding internal peace, I was not exempt from the external chaos. That was made perfectly clear the day I returned from the yard and learned that all my property had been confiscated. There was a note on the bunk informing me that due to a criminal investigation, my property had to be searched.

A week later when my property was returned, many pictures were missing from my photo albums. An attached note stated that after the photos had been copied, they'd be returned. There was another confidential disclosure form placed on the bars alleging that I had issued orders for certain staff and inmates in East Block to be hit. This was one of many examples of the authorities' stool pigeons "dropping ice" that melts into lies.

Human Angel

During my darkest moments, when the burdens seemed too heavy to bear, a human angel came into my life to help lighten the load.

In the latter part of December 1992, as I was exercising, a guard placed a letter on the cell bars. I stopped and read the letter from a black journalist and author, Ms. Barbara Becnel, then tossed it on the bunk and continued my workout. Usually after reading missives from journalists, authors, and the news media, I'd tear them up and flush them down the toilet. Throughout the years I sensed many of them were parasitical opportunists seeking to exploit the Crip legacy and line their pockets. But something urged me to reread this letter.

Once I finished my workout and took a birdbath, I sat down and perused Barbara's letter again. It was both fate and good timing that induced me to even consider responding. Barbara assured me that her intentions were honorable. She was writing a book about the history of California's black gangs. Because of Raymond Washington's demise, she wrote, I was the sole surviving person who could provide an accurate account of the Crips' growth to become the most notorious black gang in California and to expand its reach across the U.S.A., into South Africa and elsewhere. Though I didn't detect duplicity on Barbara's part, I still viewed her with suspicion.

The following month, January 1993, the first visit with Barbara was scheduled in San Quentin's brown-paneled room where all media interviews were held. I was in chains with handcuffs and sitting in a chair, waiting for Barbara's arrival. Two guards were stationed behind me. Seated in the back of the room was the prison's black mouthpiece. A smiling Barbara entered the room—tall, svelte, elegantly dressed, and a beautiful brown-complexioned sister. She spoke with polite eloquence, neither cloying nor condescending. I had assumed she would be an uppity black bourgeois whom I'd browbeat or intellectually spar with to bring her back down to earth. I was a bit nervous and started to sweat profusely, as if I was about to be interrogated, but Barbara's manner set the tone for a pleasant dialogue. Her objective was to spend a single day gathering data about the Crips and me for the book. But this first interview encouraged her to schedule another meeting two days later.

During that second interview I revealed to Barbara my interest in writing children's books to warn them about drugs, gangs, prison, and crime. Judging by her expression, my literary offer blew her away. The more I explained my intent to deliver a positive message through books, the more the idea made sense to her—though I sensed a slight hesitation on her part to fully commit. Little did she know that my enthusiasm for writing children's books was greater than my zeal had been for Crippen.

With each exchange in letters on the subject of my writing children's books, the more Barbara got caught up in my literary vision. Still, she had reservations. I wished people could read me better instead of suspecting that I had an angle. Months earlier, while strolling the yard with Hollaway, a friend not affiliated with gangs, I told him I wanted to do something positive with my life, to help children to stay out of this filthy hellhole and out of gangs. He said, "You know, Tookie, I believe you." Besides Evil and Treach, Hollaway was the only other person who was able to feel the truth of my words.

Barbara and I began working on the first manuscript. She explained that I had to use the simplest language so that children could comprehend and enjoy reading the book. I discovered that writing the book had a sublime effect on me. It seemed to melt away the years of being desensitized and callous. I felt a sense of genuine purpose: to create a book that might tap into the social pathology affecting black children. Though I held no academic degree, I had created my own college curriculum through years of study, extrospection, and hard-knock experiences both on the streets of hell and in San Quentin. Though a role model I could never be, I could act as an African griot or Paul Revere, warning youths about what is coming down the crooked path.

Barbara liked how the book was turning out and managed to capture the interest of HarperCollins, a publishing company. Though they were interested, they preferred a book with stories of my past life, laced with blood, gore, and ghetto vernacular. They didn't want to hear about the refined Tookie; they wanted the beast, the Tookie of old. I told Barbara I wasn't that desperate. She wasn't sure whether my decision was the right one, but she respected my wishes and began looking elsewhere. Most other publishing companies considered my proposal to be too controversial, chiefly because I was on death row.

Barbara divided her time between looking for a publisher for the children's books, writing her own book, and assisting in the Hands Across Watts project. This was a program designed to promote peace between warring Los Angeles gang factions, initiated by the reformed P.J.s Crip commander Tony Bogard and a Blood named Ty-Stick. Bogard grew up on the Crip legends about me battling rival gangs throughout the West Side, Compton, P.J.s, and J.D.s. Bogard had told Barbara, "Every Crip knows that if you want to know the history of the Crips, contact Tookie on death row."

During this same period I received a letter from Jimel after fourteen years of complete silence. With no proper salutations or "long time no see," he launched into a propaganda campaign against Hands Across Watts and Jim Brown's AMER-I-CAN program, and with no explanation. Then he rattled on about Raymond, himself, and me starting the Crips, therefore he and I should stick together. I figured the man was intoxicated, delusional, amnesic, or all three. With his false claim, he was no different from other charlatans who claim to be cofounders of the Crips. Years later, I would read a book entitled *Uprising* that was read and ridiculed by every Crip and Blood on death row. One of the book's chapters, "Godfather Jimel Barnes," was riddled with misinformation, with Jimel's guilty conscience compelling him to defend against "a lot of people saying I [Jimel] didn't pay my dues," or saying that "he [Jimel] was a perpetrator." Those are Jimel's words. Although in that chapter there were numerous contradictions, I'll only address one example of misinformation. In the book (pages 152 and 153), Jimel states, "Later, after Raymond passed away, I wanted a twin brother, I wanted somebody to replace Raymond, so I went out and found this guy Tookie and built him up from a little small guy to be a gladiator like me." In fact, I was incarcerated on March 15, 1979, *more than four months before Raymond's death* on August 9, 1979. It was not possible for Jimel to have met me and "built me up" *after* Raymond's murder. Second, his misuse of Raymond's name to enhance his credibility, and elevating himself by minimizing me and others, does not agree with the facts. My memoir should decontaminate the misinformation by Jimel and others.

Though I had known Barbara for a short period, I was more inclined to value her judgment about the Hands Across Watts program than the ravings of someone I hadn't heard from in over a decade. Hands Across Watts was receiving positive coverage, particularly within the South Central community and from the press. During a regular prison visit, Barbara asked if I wanted to be a part of an upcoming Los Angeles gang summit for peace. This was Barbara's method, I learned later, of determining if I was still Crippen and whether I was sincere about promoting peace. How was it possible for me to participate from death row? Barbara said that she could have my speech videotaped and shown on a huge screen before an audience. After I agreed to compose two speeches, one for adults and a second one for children, she scheduled the taping the following week, to be held in a boardroom at San Quentin.

Sometime after I completed the videotaped speech, Barbara told me that certain prison staff had assured her I'd never show up to do a video that repudiated gangs because I was still the Crip Godfather. They told her, "That man will not even come out of the cell. You're wasting your time and money hiring a video production team." When I arrived to meet Barbara for the taping, I found the room was packed with a camera crew, guards, and other prison authorities dressed in suits—and wearing shocked expressions. How dare these strangers who knew me only by name, reputation, and documentation (that was false) try to second-guess my response to a given situation. I was not an institutionalized animal, trained and predictable.

Completing these two speeches allowed me to cast off a great burden. I could not foretell whether my speech would be taken seriously. I waited anxiously for the results. After a few days, an ecstatic Barbara told me that the moment the screen popped on with an image of me reading my speech, the entire audience became silent and watchful. After the speech ended, there was a standing ovation! In a display of hypocrisy, even Jimel—who had suggested I distrust the nonprofit Hands Across Watts organization—was happily nibbling on the event's hors d'oeuvres.

My appellate attorneys during that period had objected to the video being shown, but I overrode their disapproval. They acted as if I was a dirty secret that should remain unseen and unheard by the public. Their opinion didn't faze me. I was determined to get my message across to black youths about the perils of drugs, gangs, crime, violence, and prison life. What mattered most was the contribution I could make toward helping youths and Hands Across Watts.

On January 13, 1994, while in the P.J.s, not wearing his bullet-proof vest, Bogard was shot and killed by another P.J. Crip. May Bogard rest in peace.

1994 would be a year to remember. Barbara had it in her mind that I deserved Grade A and somehow she'd make sure I got it. Everybody on our yard figured my chances of getting to Grade A were slim and none, so for years I refused each scheduled classification committee. Barbara refused to accept the status quo. She was a delicate-looking woman but a tenacious fighter with a fierce drive. She initiated a support campaign that included a number of notable citizens from mainstream society. The warden and associate warden were bombarded with letters and e-mail messages from credible advocates expressing their concerns and their belief in my conversion.

Associate Warden Nelson was the chief arbitrator for the classification committee in the Hole at that time. It would be difficult to find a prisoner who would disagree that Nelson was deemed the meanest and most unmerciful person on staff. There was no way Nelson would allow me to have Grade A, but if by some miraculous intervention it did happen, everybody on the same yard had a shot.

The committee was composed of Caucasians with the exception of a black counselor, Hammond. Word had it Hammond was mean-spirited, antiprisoner, and an Uncle Tom, but I delayed my opinion. When I was summoned to Hammond's office for a C-file (central file) review, he expressed interest in the videotaped speech for the gang summit and the children's book project I was working on. After making copies of documents in my C-file and discussing my children's project, Hammond admitted that I was nothing like what he had heard or read about in my files. I let him know that the prison files are a mere caricature of who I used to be, not who I was today. He caught me off guard when he asked why I thought I deserved to be on Grade A? I told him, "I've committed no rule violations to be in the Hole. I'm no longer Crippen and haven't had a disciplinary write-up in years. I've undergone a personal transformation." Hammond didn't say much, just that he hoped to see me in classification. I left the office thinking that the man appeared to be up front with me. That was all I asked of anybody.

When I talked again with Barbara, she said I deserved Grade A because the speech I made for the Los Angeles gang summit was a public declaration of my repudiation of gang violence, gang membership, and my leadership and participation in gang life. That speech was truly my forever farewell to Crip: I had chosen another path. I felt that my videotaped speech from death row, though unprecedented, would have no effect on the committee. I agreed with Barbara that I would go to the classification, which occurred every sixty days—but I didn't believe a change in grade status was possible.

At the committee meeting, Hammond reminded the members that I hadn't had any disciplinary write-ups in years, and so he was therefore recommending I receive Grade-A status. Nelson, the associate warden, vehemently objected as did the others. One of them said, "The man's the cofounder of the Crips, for Christ's sake! His influence is too vast. He doesn't deserve a status change." Then another counselor proposed that I should "debrief." Hammond explained that debriefing was for *prison* gang members, not a street gang like the Crips. Another counselor said, "Well, since Mr. Williams wants Grade A he should have to debrief anyway." Hammond said, "I'm confident Mr. Williams would refuse to debrief or to submit to a polygraph test," then he looked over at me. Through clinched teeth I said, "Of course I refuse. I value my life and dignity too much to debrief." I left the room, steaming. Later, both Evil and Treach told me the committee brought up debriefing to them, which they too rejected.

Debriefing is a system used throughout the California Department of Corrections to barter the souls of prison gang members, revolutionists, or any prisoner, for information about their gang, its members, their hegemony, and any past and present criminal activities. Crips passing through the Hole used to talk about homeboys and other individuals in prison gangs who had debriefed like it was the thing to do. Rumor had it that the only way a man could get out of the Hole at Pelican Bay—a maximum security prison in California near the Oregon state border—was by being paroled, debriefing, or in a casket.

During a visit I explained to Barbara what debriefing meant. Offended by their suggestion that I should debrief, she said her next step would be to contact Hammond and find out what could be done. I told her it wasn't enough that I was facing execution; they also wanted to rip my dignity out of my chest. I didn't believe Barbara could get my speech videotaped—but she accomplished it. In time she convinced me never to doubt her abilities. It was rare for me to trust anyone in society other than my mother, but I found myself trusting this woman, when I didn't even trust my attorneys. I marveled at Barbara's trustworthiness and her dedication to follow through in a pinch.

Very few people in society are beating down these gates to go to bat for a death row prisoner. No other person on the face of this planet has offered to help me achieve a positive goal. But in a short time Barbara earned my respect and trust. Her energy was so infectious, I started thinking, "Well, perhaps there *is* a possibility of getting Grade A."

Moto Ndani (The Fire Within)

There was a fire kindling in my mind, a fire that drove me to write books for children. Its name I coined *Moto Ndani* (the fire within). The source of this fire was distinct from my usual rage. When I saw television or newspaper accounts of drive-by shootings with innocent children caught in the crossfire, I felt something that I am unable to articulate to this day. For the first time I was concerned not just for myself or those murdered children, but also for the welfare of other people's children, my children, grandchildren, nieces, and nephews. I found myself incapable of eating after viewing scenarios of children suffering in Africa, afflicted with disease, poverty, genocide, starvation, racism, despair, and death.

Decades ago I had built an emotional rampart against empathy for the hardships of others not close to me. But this new alien feeling of human compassion worried me. It was toppling one of the last bastions of the violent, misguided machismo that helped suppress my inner human feelings.

Maturation was occurring. I was becoming a person with a heart.

Gradually I began to gain fresh perspective on my unkind and puzzling life. It wasn't by chance I was born black in a world where my color made me a pariah by definition, long before I was able to determine the content of my character. Neither was it by accident that I was dys-educated, drug-addicted, enraged, bullet-riddled, pessimistic, Crippen-bound, culturally unconscious, and wrongly convicted. Tribulations such as my intimacy with the psychoses of this world could have damaged and defeated me, leaving me psychologically scarred, moribund. It was a belated effort on my part, but I was proving that even from the wretched abyss of death row, the impossible was possible. Perhaps merely demonstrating that this awakening was possible was my mission.

In the Hole nothing good is expected to happen. You enter the Hole without a fighting chance. And when you leave it, months or years later, a part of you remains there forever. The Hole extracts something you can never regain. It could be the loss of your mind, blood, time, dignity, conviction, or your life. As it stood, I could not rely upon charm or wit to finagle my circumstances. I had to confront myself with the deepest, most undeniable self-truth. No matter how many thousands of men were unsuccessful before me, I felt I'd somehow excel. I wasn't special—but my fighting spirit would not lie down. Since I no longer indulged in mind-stimulating drugs, there was nothing except death to thwart my intention to elevate myself.

As for the previous classification committee's recent rejection—well, I refused to worry about it. Like a man possessed I pushed forward to achieve what the authorities perceived to be unachievable: transition toward redemption. Armed with the radical evolution of mind, body, and behavior I was being reshaped by the disciplines of consistent willpower, knowledge, dedication, and spirituality. Serving as an ethical nutrient in my life, the "spirit act" of spirituality induced me to give beyond myself. Its cleansing effect introduced me to Ma'at (an Egyptian or Kamitic term that means truth, justice, and righteousness), and I discovered how to devote faith and praise to the one and only God.

In time I was able to deduce, through comparative studying of world religions, that no single person or religious sect has a monopoly on God or spiritual cultivation. I am not a Christian, Muslim, Jew, Buddhist, or any other religious indoctrination, category or doctrine. I have no qualms about being nondenominational. My intention is to connect with God based on my own merits, to obtain spiritual enrichment rather than focus on a particular church or religion. I will never turn away the spiritual knowledge of the Metu Neter, Qur'an, Bible, *Perennial Psychology of the Bhagavad Gita,* or any other worthy spiritual scripture. I construct my faith around facts that can best help me to redeem myself.

Over the years I have disciplined myself to fast, meditate, eliminate beef and pork from my diet, and wash up and purge prior to my own composed silent prayers. When I pray, I'm facing east, toward Africa, the holy place where God permitted humanity to originate. While standing, I recite several composed prayers, including the Prayer of Mercy, and then kneel on a prayer rug, pillow, or blanket. I recite other composed prayers that bestow praises and thanks to the Creator. Throughout each day and evening I pray seven times or more, depending upon the spirit that moves me.

In the beginning it was difficult for me to pray on my knees. Still lingering was the macho tripping. If someone approached the cell while I was on my knees praying, I'd jump up and pretend to be doing something else. But once I understood the importance of prayer to my spiritual growth, it didn't matter if the entire prison population marched in a line past the cell during my prayers. I wouldn't budge an inch.

If not for the spiritual cultivation that provided me with a principled edge, I would have succumbed to outside distractions. I was able to propel myself forward with a resolve never to give up regardless of the odds or circumstances. I tested my practice of thought in the desolate climate of the Hole. As a result I was able to stand among men from any walk of life, and be confident of who I now define myself to be. Prison is no friend of mine. Its objective is to torment my body with years of isolation and seek to damage my mind with constant distractions, violence, sensory deprivation, and other injustices. I'm not immune to the chaos of this prison setting, but I have been able to confront and counter the menace.

I warn black men and women everywhere: beware of these tombs for the living called prison.

I am now finding an inner peace that has cooled the vapors of suspicion and defensiveness born of years in this unpredictable place. In prison it's tactical to be a little paranoid; it keeps me spry and on my toes. I also find solace in talking with Barbara about my innocence, my gang past, and about the plight of black people. To protect Barbara I have always avoided discussing with her the details of my black gang warfare past. It is necessary to keep her safe and uninvolved. The attorney general's office subpoenaed Barbara once in an unsuccessful attempt to coerce incriminating evidence about me—evidence that did not exist. Barbara has become my intellectual sounding board when I choose to dwell upon the "psycho-philosophical" analysis of gangs, politics, religion, underprivileged children, and my life.

Though I discussed many of the same topics with Evil and Treach, we had been locked up too long. I needed an outside perspective. Feedback was important to me. I didn't want to be stuck in a time warp or be led astray by my own grand illusions. I was interested in how my book would fare in society, so I wanted bare facts to compare in order to form an analysis. I was determined despite Barbara's warning that I was exposing myself to the relentless stone throwers.

In reality I had too much *Moto Ndani* in me to be hindered by myopic opinions based on anyone's superficial knowledge of me. I have become a man who will never buckle under controversy; I now use controversy to fuel my motivation. Naturally, there are other prisoners who have undergone major personal change and can appreciate what is required to uplift oneself from the bowels of wretchedness. Through experience I knew the futility of trying to subvert or to outfox these existing conditions. I would have to bend it to the will of my determination, to rise above the madness. There have been numerous prisoners who have failed, but that didn't faze me. I knew of a few black men—one in particular, Malcolm X—who underwent a miraculous change from a seemingly permanent criminal to a reborn black man. To me it didn't matter how prominent the individual. His or her achievements were of earthly means and therefore attainable for me and anyone else with the audacity to step forward. Who am I to even try? Just another black man, grounded, reaching for the stars with soaring thoughts and dreams.

There was nothing outside of self-obstruction that could stop my progression. I discovered time and again while reading black history that regardless of a person's background, when one's mind, behavior, circumstances, and spirit are aligned with destiny, the impossible can be achieved. Likewise, for a lowly person such as myself, there was a harmonized order, a dimly glimpsed path I could take to alter my negative existence. The isolation designed to emasculate me and cripple my spirit had failed. I was not the same man they had marched through the entrance to the Hole years earlier. My rejection of the institution's contempt for humanity, and its pseudo-reform system—jumping through hoops to become a flunky or stool pigeon—was an affront to their mentality. For them my transition, my redemption, was bogus. I epitomized everything that they did not want a prisoner to be.

I was now neither burdened by the external chaos that surrounded me nor by my own miscarriage of thoughts. I was prepared to stand before the committee without the baggage of deception, doubt, or defeatism. During the next scheduled classification committee meeting, the dissenting members jockeyed with Hammond, who stood his ground in support of my receiving upgraded status. Prior to the meeting, unknown to me, Hammond convinced Associate Warden Nelson to support the transfer. It seemed like an unshackling of heavy chains when Nelson expressed his agreement with Hammond in front of the entire committee.

I can visualize Nelson's hard-eyed expression when he asked, "Mr. Williams, if you are given Grade A, do you plan to attack anyone in East Block?" I assured him I did not. "In spite of what everyone thinks," I said, "I'm not a rabid animal. I don't have any plans to attack anyone. However, I want this committee to know that I am not a pacifist, and that I will defend myself under threatening circumstances. Other than that, you [directing my words to Nelson] have my word as a man that I will not initiate untoward violence, nor violate my word." Then the associate warden, the man most blacks and

Mexicans in the Hole call the grand dragon of racism, approved my Grade A.

When Barbara next visited me, I expressed my gratitude. Without her determination, the committee's decision would not have shifted in my favor. I knew that it was her compelling presentation that convinced counselor Hammond. She smiled broadly and said, "You're welcome."

Later that day I learned there would be a delay in my departure due to an incident in East Block. For years on death row, there have been racial flare-ups pitting blacks against Aryan Brotherhood and their allies, the Southern Mexicans (*La Eme*). This time a black man named Pride had scuffled with a wannabe Nazi who wore a swastika but looked more like an Asian or Portuguese. As a result Pride, who was said to have had his back turned, was shot dead. He was neither Crip nor Blood but a black man of controlled rage, intelligence, and a willingness to assist other blacks. When he and I used to drive iron, his favorite topic was Afrocentricity and revolution.

The days of delay for my Grade A turned into weeks. There were rumors that I had ordered Pride to attack the Nazi. My transfer was suspended until the incident was investigated. (Some spineless inmates would say anything to prevent my arrival in East Block.) While I was exercising on the yard, the prison mouthpiece showed up, still styling a Jheri-curl 1970s hairdo. Standing outside the fence he said that there was talk of possibly allowing me to visit in East Block if I agreed to be fully shackled while the other death row prisoners roamed free in the visiting room. He smiled at me like a reptile about to swallow a dove. With the composure of a seasoned snake handler I declined the offer.

More weeks passed. Hammond said there was an East Block lieutenant who stated, "As long as I work in this condemned unit, Tookie cannot be housed here!" The lieutenant apparently believed the myths documented in my C-file. Hammond told me there were numerous "kites" (notes written anonymously to prison officials by prisoners) protesting my transfer to East Block. Inmates would sometimes try reverse psychology to avoid facing their issues directly. Instead they would "warn" the prison staff in a kite that I would be attacked the moment I set foot on the yard—which the San Quentin officials would want to avoid. Little did I know what kind of weakness I was up against.

Barbara, bless her heart, believed that death row prisoners stuck together—one for one, all for all, like a college football team. In time she realized this wasn't so. When she asked why so many prisoners were opposed to my being housed in East Block, I replied, "Fear— not fear of me per se, but of the old me and my peers, the return of the monster presence." My peers and I were depicted as ruthless individuals pushing a rigid, compulsory program of discipline, exercise, study, and with zero tolerance for snitches. Though the zero tolerance had been true for years, the other rhetoric was a tactic to keep the rank-and-file from associating with us. When I finally would enter the hornet's nest in East Block, my opposition was likely waiting to frame or fabricate incriminating statements then report back to their masters. Not once did the possibility of being physically harmed enter my thoughts.

Still, I remained Grade-A-housed under Grade-B rules. Unfortunately, more Confidential Information Disclosure Forms—with absurd allegations—were being added to my C-file. Supposedly I was in collusion to "hit" certain prisoners and guards in East Block. I found myself experiencing a flashback, a "visual reckoning." I again reviewed my cataclysmic past, in vivid color and in all its horror. The doomed life I had loved, praised, and was foolishly willing to die for began to fade with a farewell gesture into darkness. Sleeping one night, I saw a powerfully bright halo of light encircling enormous crowds of children of different ethnic backgrounds. I hadn't the faintest idea what was going on. I awoke drenched in sweat, wondering if it was another omen, and why? There was no need for a warning. I couldn't forget the earthly hell, and I surely did not wish to return to it. I had made a covenant with *Mwenyezi* (Almighty) to embrace a complete change. The fervor of my determination would not allow me to deviate from that goal.

More than a month later the lieutenant who had strongly objected to my being in East Block was transferred, but there were still inmates whispering dissent into Hammond's ears. Fed up with the chickenhearted controversy, Hammond announced that whoever felt uncomfortable with my being on the yard should request reassignment to another yard. I heard there were quite a few yard jumpers. When the day arrived for my departure I left a lot of books, food, and personal care items with Kerm to distribute among our peers. I wasn't worried about not seeing them again. I felt that once the prison authorities observed my behavior for a year or two, my peers would leave the Hole as well.

The moment had finally come. I could truly vacate the hellhole that had stolen a small part of me and vandalized so many other lives. As I exited the building, a committee member who was absent the day I received my Grade A was walking in. He hysterically questioned the escorting guards: "Where are you taking Tookie?"

One of the guards told him, "He's being rehoused in East Block."

The committee member's face contorted grotesquely. He spat out, "Tookie, you're very lucky I wasn't in classification that day. I would never have recommended Grade A for you!"

I responded, "Being lucky had nothing to do with it. Prayers work, especially when faced with the malicious minds of others."

Redemption ... Step Forward

A rriving in East Block after six and a half years in the Hole was an odd new experience. I actually felt a sensation of butterflies in my stomach. While I was being placed in a holding cell, Chico was being escorted out of an adjacent one. I asked him where was he going; his response, "To the Hole, Cuz!" Though rough around the edges with an explosive temper, Chico was cool. He was the flip side of Young Kerm, who had unmistakable rage in his voice, posture, and behavior. What I respected most about Chico was his appetite for learning. I jokingly called him "wild man." He was a gifted mathematician.

I was housed in 3-EB-106 next door to an Indian whom I befriended named Apache. He conveniently ended up being in charge of the phone. The following morning on the yard I was cheerfully greeted by Herc, Mad Dog, Hollaway, Cricket, Taco, Wimp, Little L, Ex-Lax, Ant, Louisiana Smooth, Ocean, Square, Silent (Kwesi), Doggs, and Grandpa. When the hoopla died down, I was embraced by an evolving brother named K.C. whom I've known for many years. Though he wasn't into the gang life, he was a personable brother with heart. In addition to sharing the fact of being black and battling this killing machine called "capital punishment," we both strove for knowledge and freedom.

Scanning the yard, I saw that some were nervous, those who had something to hide. There was apprehension in their little eyes and in their strained smiles. It didn't matter to me. I planned to associate only with a few who had proven to be stand-up men over the years. As long as I was left alone, nobody had anything to worry about. I was harmless. If my interest had been revenge, there were so many prison provocateurs and riffraff, I would have had to arm myself with weapons in both hands, and some strapped to other parts of my body, to make sure I didn't miss anybody. No matter how deeply I despised particular individuals, they were not worth my violating my spiritual resolve. I even gave the individual who had offended me the most my assurance, in front of God and everybody who could hear me: "You have absolutely nothing to fear from me, because violence is no longer an option for me."

Later that same day I received a visit from Barbara. I got to dine on vending machine food while we engaged in conversation about the children's books and other projects. I was aware of being closely monitored by guards, not just in the visiting room but also when I was on the yard, tier, and in the cell. Barbara noticed that I was under critical surveillance in the visiting area, and was surprised when I told her guards were making side bets about how long I'd remain in East Block. They had no way of knowing that I was no longer the same dolt they believed they were betting on. In spite of the controversy, Barbara and I prayed, as we always do near the end of our visit—and thank God for our surviving each day.

While those who opposed me were lost in their collusions and hypotheticals about my next move, I forged ahead with renewed enthusiasm. It was as though I was living in a subjective world impervious to their negative vibes. Having overcome my own ignorance, I can understand those who remain blinded by the same dense veil that once covered my eyes.

Returning to East Block was like jumping from the fire into the frying pan. I rejected its old pecking order struggles and the mind games. I had no plans to get caught up in its stagnant conditioning. I didn't believe in existing just because I have a pulse. There is more to life than steel bars, senseless barbarity, prisoners, guards, gun towers, and the other hokum. Though physically I could not separate myself from the disorder of prison, mentally I could escape to Africa or beyond the sun's distance, 93 million miles from earth.

Every aspect of my struggle was devised to overcome the elements that held me in bondage, beginning with myself, then working outward. I was beginning to understand that my experiences with these dysfunctional elements—the drug addiction, poverty, gangsterism, racism, and other roadblocks—these were excuses that had defined my life. No longer would my actions be dictated by blind ignorance. Nor would I ever again allow the excuse of circumstances to dictate who I should be. It was routine studying and questioning that prompted my soul-searching. I began to develop a sense of critical reasoning from which sprang the first stirrings of conscience.

This shocked me. This was the moment redemption fused with my life. Until then, I didn't have an inkling what was happening to me. There was no defining moment that marked my redemption, no voice of reason from the sky, no jolt of energy. The path of education and introspection enabled me to reason and to develop a conscience that rejects criminality, drugs, and senseless violence. Redemption allowed me to acknowledge and atone for my past indiscretions, vow never to repeat or create new ones—and extend an olive branch to youths and adults who desire peace.

My redemption is a continual process of change that promotes day-to-day improvement in my life. No one can give redemption to me; no one can intercede on my behalf. I have to earn it myself. Even now, attempting to clarify this experience, I fall short. I don't expect anyone who's not had this sort of experience to comprehend it or be able to relate to the redemptive struggle by a condemned man. I have swum in the gutter among the dead, but had the fortitude to step out of the filth, wash off, and walk among the living.

Redemption is not a discriminable commodity based on classism, elitism, political favoritism, gender, race, creed, or color. Redemption awaits everybody. God's mercy needs no defense.

Still, there are racists posing as liberals, conservatives, moderates, and religious folks who believe black men are inferior, are incapable of atonement and an overall change. I know I'm expected to languish in violent stupidity on death row until my execution, but I cannot. This prison environment is not a reflection of me, nor am I addicted to its deadening and vicious manipulations.

In 1995 a succession of arrivals entered East Block: first Chico, then Treach, Ghetto, Evil, and Kerm. Each of them entered the setting with an intention to function at the highest order of discipline. To have all of us on the same yard again was a joyous occasion and a proud moment for me, knowing I had held firm during this extended test of my discipline.

Meanwhile, Barbara attended the American Booksellers Association's annual meeting in Chicago. The convention center was larger than a football field, and with multiple floors. It took Barbara two exhaustive days to visit the six thousand–plus booths. Many publishers found favor with my work but shied away because of where I was incarcerated. One black man, Amos Wilson, was developing his own publishing company and showed an interest in my work. Wilson was a black psychologist and author of several books addressing the dilemma of black youth. But before we could connect, Mr. Wilson died suddenly and unexpectedly.

By walking the floors of the convention for two days, Barbara located a publisher at Rosen Publishing Group, whose books were aimed chiefly at schools and libraries. He agreed to publish my work. The publication process was tedious, having to meet the syntax standards of *two* editors, Barbara and the publisher's editors. After months of correcting and rewriting, the book was ready. Barbara told me that the numerous chapters in my single children's book had been transformed into an eight-book series. The series was published in September 1996.

The books quickly were accepted in poor black school districts, as well as in middle-class schools and libraries, because gangs had become a growth industry among white children as well as minorities. In

South Central Los Angeles at West Athens Elementary School, students asked if they could take the books home on their first day back at school after summer vacation. This sort of request was unprecedented. The West Athens school principal, Barbara Lake, is quoted in *The Los Angeles Times* (September 11, 1996) saying that she "could think of no other set of books that prompted parents to jam the school's switchboard, asking where they could buy their very own copies."

When the mainstream media got wind of antiviolence children's books authored by a death row prisoner, their curiosity triggered further investigation. NBC's *Today* show did a story on the books. After that, reporters and journalists across America and around the world scrambled for telephone interviews with me and with Barbara.

Some journalists thought I had a hidden agenda and set out to expose me to the public. Others, after meeting me for an interview, would comment on my sincerity and intelligence—and then in their articles stick daggers into my back to appease the gods of "balanced" journalism. But no one could ignore the books' power to capture the attention of those troubled youths who disliked reading, but chose my books over many others. Magazines and newspaper articles displayed beaming faces of children, parents, teachers, and librarians endorsing the books.

In 1997 Barbara and I came up with an idea for an educational website (www.tookie.com) that has had hundreds of thousands of Internet visitors from all walks of life. I wrote another book, *Life in Prison*, for junior and high school youths. Published in 1998, it has won two national book honors, including one from the American Library Association.

During this time I decided to embrace Swahili names. Treach and Evil chose several Swahili names that best depict the type of person I have become. Treach chose Ajamu, meaning, "He that fights for what he wants." Evil chose Niamke, "God's gift." The third name all three of us adopted is Kamara, "He who teaches from experience." In choosing names for one another Evil became Ajani, "He who fights for possession," and Treach became Adisa, "One who makes himself clear."

As part of my transition and redemption I'm extremely proud to have as my Swahili name Ajamu Niamke Kamara, which resonates with who I am. I feel no allegiance or kinship to my slave names despite their being patronymic (a name descended from the father). Although I am on death row, my life has new meaning. I no longer feel as if my existence is of no consequence. It was only natural that in my reawakening and cleansing I discarded the old and adopted the new. With the exception of my mother and Barbara, everybody else had written me off the moment I was sentenced to die. And I was mentally dead up to the precise second I made the conscious decision to redefine and redeem myself. And so . . . I am alive. The maze that once appeared to have no exit has been forced open for passage. Hear me, black man! Indian! Caucasian! Asian! Mexican! Jew! Arab! Others! There is a path out of desolation. Look within!

As my life evolved I was still doing interviews over the phone and face-to-face. One of the best and most enlightening visits was with Barbara, David Evans, an international peace mediator, and three South Africans: Joanna Thomas, Mohau Magkobeyana, and Penny Foley, from the Center for Conflict Resolution Youth Project and Johannesburg's Joint Enrichment Project.

The visit was unforgettable. Adisa engaged in a dialogue with Mohau, and Ajani and I talked with David, Barbara, Joanne, and Penny. I had read about the kindred spirit existing between blacks in America and the blacks in the Motherland, but I never expected to experience such a powerful feeling that drew me close to Joanne and Mohau. Other than our black faces and ancestry, we shared social blights: poverty, drugs, racism, disease, street gangs, illiteracy, rapid prison growth, Afrocide, and other madnesses.

I was taken aback by brother Mohau's humility and his congenial disposition. Here was a black man from the Motherland who had no misunderstanding about what constituted his manhood, nor did he display a violent air of toughness with a street thug swagger. His words were articulate without venom. His fortitude, humbled spirit, and absence of arrogance was in total contrast to what I saw in America. His inner warrior shined with reserved dignity. Not once did the words "nigger" or "bitch" enter our dialogue. Meeting Mohau pointed me toward a deeper learning of the art of humility while maintaining a resolute pride.

After taking a few group photos, we sat for thirty more minutes discussing our foundling project, the Internet Project for Street Peace. This program would connect kids in the United States and in South Africa to communicate, learn, and be mentored via e-mail and computer chat room. I wanted children on both continents to evolve into culturally conscious adults, bridging the gap that we adults have failed to mend. The encounter was refreshing, allowing me to reclaim the nexus severed since African slavery began to claim black lives, families, and psyches. As my visitors rose to leave, we made plans to keep in touch and explore other ideas to bridge and benefit our continents.

Later that year I received a visit from actor Mike Farrell, a star of the comedy sitcom, *M*A*S*H*, political activist, and chairperson of Death Penalty Focus, an anti-death-penalty organization. Barbara, Adisa, and an associate of Mike's were present as well. Our discussion centered on the possibility of creating a movie out of my memoirs. I listened intently to the conversation, aware that this was an embryonic stage in what would become a long and challenging project. Actually, I know of only one person capable of transforming our ideas into tangible realities: Barbara. I call her the human angel.

While walking with Barbara and Mike inside the visiting area, the topic of my redemption surfaced. I stressed that had I not undertaken a dynamic interior change, there would be no atonement for me. I was able to eliminate the vile nature of my past—the impulsive behavior, foul language, irrationality, vengeance, and a nonspiritual existence—through reflection and prayer. No longer do I possess defeatist dreams that kill my potential for envisioning hope and progress. But my redemption is small and self-serving if I fail to assist the violence-ridden communities from which I came. I wasn't sure Mike understood precisely what I was trying to verbalize. But a person doesn't have to understand the structure of a rose in order to acknowledge its beauty. As long as he recognized I was not the same person I had been—that was good enough for me.

I told Mike and the others that my redemption was not a hazy fantasy in which a street thug becomes a good guy and lives happily ever after. I said that my mind was no longer polluted, and that the decades of personal vice and of Crippen, of the deeply rooted psychological illness that drove me have been resolved. But the cruel, desolate reality of prison is unforgiving. As long as I remain imprisoned, I will continue to be challenged to remain a human being and not a beast. Just because I chose to readjust my thoughts and behavior, the small claustrophobic world of death row did not shift. Death row is constructed for punishment and execution, not for reform.

That reality is unchanged.

A Woman Called Mother Africa

In 1998 Barbara told me that Nobel Peace Prize winner Archbishop Desmond Tutu of South Africa had written to me in support of my children's book series. I responded with a letter of gratitude and enclosed my pencil-drawn portrait of Desmond Tutu. Nothing is sweeter and more humbling than being accepted by your own people, those who can relate to your personal triumph over self and the insidious tentacles of color prejudice. But without the dynamic urgency of my *Moto Ndani*, I would not have been able to overcome my past and the atrocious prison madness to move as far forward as I have.

Working on my memoirs, the children's books, and the portraits of Desmond Tutu and others while maintaining a low profile has not prevented prison authorities and their minions from lurking in the background. The day I was escorted by several guards after a visit straight to the Hole was no surprise to me. The following day I received a 115 Rules Violation Report and a Confidential Information Disclosure Form. It identified me in some off-the-wall conspiracy to provide inmates on East Block AD/Seg Yard-6 with a hacksaw blade (which never existed) to cut a portion of the AD/Seg Yard-5 fence to enter and attack the Aryan Brotherhood and the EME. Then authorities concocted a second story with a new twist: I was planning to use the hacksaw blade in my attempt to escape from death row. Utter foolishness!

No matter how many times I end up in the Hole, the initial shock of its rude solitude and feelings of helplessness can weary the mind. It didn't matter how tough, peaceful, transformed, brave, or confident I was. The Hole would confront me with an immediate reminder of my insignificance in the penal hierarchy. There was nothing I could do. I knew my refutations would fall on deaf ears, and to present witnesses on my behalf was meaningless. It was not unlike being in criminal court where I was presumed guilty and not about to be proven innocent. Literally, my hands were tied.

Barbara contacted Mike Farrell, who called Senator Tom Hayden and Jesse Jackson Sr. The four of them, with other signatories, drafted and signed a letter of appeal, which they mailed to the San Quentin warden and the director of corrections to question what had been done to me. I had been in the Hole for more than a month when I was taken to classification—and found not guilty. Though I was long since accustomed to the tactics used against me, Barbara was surprised by them. Here on death row, I explained to Barbara, I'm the bogeyman, ogre, or the sacrificial lamb, depending on the requirements of the prison authorities. As I detailed in *Life in Prison,* nothing changes here. I realize that it is difficult for someone to divorce his or her prejudices from their profession, but my past and the color of my skin are just too much of an irritant to the hidden racism of some of the guards and San Quentin authorities.

In 1999, Barbara and I developed the Internet Project for Street Peace. Officials from several countries with youth gang problems expressed an interest in setting up Internet Street Peace hubs and becoming a part of the network. To my astonishment, Winnie Madikizela-Mandela, Nelson Mandela's ex-wife and then-member of South Africa's Parliament, expressed immediate interest in our program. I had read articles about Winnie's struggle to free Nelson Mandela and to champion the people's cause for freedom. She was a beautiful queen warrior who proudly stood up and spoke out against the racist apartheid system. Equally amazing was that from San Quentin's death row the reverberations of my unchained words were heard by this woman called Mother Africa.

When Barbara told me Winnie was preparing to visit me in person—well, to say I was honored is an understatement.

On October 28, 1999, Winnie crossed the Atlantic Ocean to grace me with her presence at San Quentin State Prison, to address my youth work and children's books and to attend fund-raisers for the Internet Street Peace Network. Later I learned that our visit was delayed because Winnie's bodyguard didn't want the prison staff to touch her. The media awaited her arrival outside the prison walls. They were scrambling to interview her.

I wasn't certain how I should greet Winnie. Should I be formal or informal? But the moment I saw her, the ancestral ties were immediately felt, and instinctively we embraced with smiles and a kiss on each cheek. A black female guard had the entire visiting room rearranged to specifically accommodate Winnie. Yes, even the black guards working that day, male and female, couldn't play down the unprecedented reality that Mother Africa herself was visiting a death row prisoner.

With me, seated between Barbara and Winnie, were Betty R. Soskin, Adisa, Ajani, an Associated Press journalist, a deputy for a California state assemblywoman, Winnie's spiritual advisor, Reverend John Shaka, and Winnie's bodyguard. While we sat around the connected tables, we broached the subject of the death penalty. Winnie was curious about the statistics and about the treatment of blacks on death row. She expressed her profound opposition to the barbarism of America's capital punishment apparatus and vowed to visit whenever possible, until I regained my freedom.

I told Winnie about the time I was scheduled for execution in the late 1980s but my attorney was missing in action. I was approached by a San Quentin representative who asked me if I understood the execution procedures to be carried out. Infuriated, I rolled my eyes and responded, "What's there to know?" Then I launched into a rapid description of the macabre ritual of capital punishment. I said, "I know about the last meal, the priest's viaticum, the brand new state-issued clothing to die in, the warden's inquiry about the prisoner's final words, the march to the gas chamber, being strapped in the death chair, the voyeuristic white strangers peeking at their own mortality vicariously through me, cyanide tablets being dropped into a liquid solution; then silent cheers for one less dead nigger." When I finished answering the questions, as I told Winnie, I suggested that the representative and the guards could "all go to hell."

Winnie responded hotly, in her lilting accented English, "The death penalty should be terminated across the board, wherever it exists!"

Meeting Winnie was an enlightening moment. Her features, stature, mannerisms, and soft voice reminded me of my mother's.

When the conversation came around to gangs, I addressed the essentials and touched upon how a large percentage of blacks on death row were maintaining their own gang peace. I talked about the periodic eruption of racial wars in prisons that prompted blacks from diverse backgrounds and affiliations to band together to defend themselves. In prison blacks find themselves battling a discriminatory system, racist inmates, and guards who directly or indirectly support inmates' racial foolishness. It may astonish middle-class America to know that the Crips and Bloods, those eternal enemies, have gravitated toward an alliance with other black men against the prison opposition. Many of these black men, involved in the over-three-decades-long Crips-Bloods gang rivalry, have real esteem for one another. These days, that solidarity is what causes me to see only black *men*, and no differences between Crips and Bloods.

Talking to Winnie provided me with an opportunity to vent against the hypocritical, imprisoned "sick minds" that feel the need to despise blacks more than the institutional beast—the prison authority—that can devour us all. I explained that in prison, racial war is indifferent to whether a black prisoner is peaceful, wise, respected, young, or old. His color will pull him into the madness. He has no choice but to fight . . . or die. When the guard on the gun rail fires into a crowd, only a prisoner dies—and usually a black prisoner.

With time winding down I suggested we take some photos. While standing, waiting for the guard to take a picture, a tactful Barbara asked Winnie to convince me to keep my eyes open. I always close them before a photo is taken. I have done so for years; it is my way of blocking out the madness that surrounds me. After a few unsuccessful attempts, I managed to keep my eyes open to a degree. Though most of the pictures taken were of Winnie and me, everybody in our entourage was able to join in. There were several other black families who asked to take a photo with us. Among them were Fadh and his two daughters, and an elderly black couple. Winnie was gracious, but I inquired about whether she was tired of taking pictures. Her response: "This is your moment. I came to see you. I'll stand here and take pictures all day if you want."

After the photo sessions I asked Winnie if she wanted something to eat from the vending machines, to which she replied, "Just some bottled water." The machines don't stock bottled water—but to our surprise the San Quentin spokesman volunteered to locate water and paper cups. His gesture caught me off-guard. Perhaps there is salvation after all for this person, whom most prisoners and visitors privately refer to as an Uncle Tom.

How Barbara managed to overcome the political bureaucracy to bring Winnie to America, I can't imagine. God was working overtime through this woman. I was both grateful to and proud of her. It was a gracious gesture for Mother Africa to visit me in this despicable place, not unlike one that had held her former husband captive for so many years.

Time was running out. Adisa and I tried to cram many questions into the few minutes left with Winnie. Then the speaker crackled loudly with a female voice: "Visiting is over, visiting is over!" I was annoyed and wanted more time. Sensing my irritation, she lightly patted my hand and said, "Don't worry, Stan, there will be other times. I plan to give you a Swahili name too!" The 7,200 seconds I spent with Winnie were more than an acknowledgment and a show of support. Her visit also created an everlasting nexus that linked us in a circle of kindred spirits. After our warm good-byes—I thanked Winnie for the hundredth time—Adisa, Ajani, and I filed into a long line of prisoners waiting to be escorted back to the cells.

Talking to Barbara later on the phone, she told me what had happened when they left the East Block visiting room. They heard what sounded like a hundred voices singing in Winnie's native tongue. A throng of prisoners on the exercise yard who had heard through the prison grapevine that Winnie was on the grounds, though unable to see her, were serenading her as she left the visiting room. I extend my thanks to all those brothers, though I'm unaware of who they were. *Asante santa!* (Thank you very much!)

That same night I smiled to myself, recalling that Winnie had said the highlight of her trip was seeing me. Being able to visit and talk with the woman called Mother Africa was a spiritual experience that profoundly touched my life. That night I made a decision. Whether my demise is of natural causes, or my soul has been abruptly snatched out by unnatural causes beyond my control, I want my body buried in Africa underneath a yohimbe tree; or my cremated ashes scattered over Africa's Blue Nile river to feed the fishes and other organisms. Even in death, I can engender life. Peace and blessings to you, Winnie Madikizela-Mandela. I'm grateful and proud to have met you.

Black Phoenix Rising

ecause I am guilty of being black, I have learned to expect the
unexpected. After Winnie's visit I saw an increase in harassment,
surveillance, Confidential Information Disclosure Form documents, and cell searches. On April 19, 2000, I received a CDC 128-B
chrono falsely accusing me of gang leadership, and all of my peers
also received a chrono for associating with me. A particular black
lickspittle sergeant told Chico during a 602 hearing, "I don't care
about you or any of the others. It's Tookie we want!" After I filed an
inmate appeal 602 form, the chrono was supposedly rescinded and
destroyed.

On May 3, 2000, I documented an officer positioned on the gun
rail with a video camera focused on the exercise yard to which I am assigned. He was taping *only my movements and interactions.* Obviously
the video was meant to capture either a specific association or something untoward that could later be substantiated. I hadn't done anything improper for nearly a decade, and I associate with everybody on
the yard—black, Indian, Cuban, Iranian, Caucasian, Mexican, Greek,
Russian, and others.

On June 27, 2000, I received a Confidential Information Disclosure Form labeling me a Crip leader, and it included an illogical conspiracy theory. The form's allegation about me was as follows: "To
attempt to gather support of other Grade-A condemned prisoners of

gang affiliation [i.e., Crips, Bloods, and *La Eme*] to assault staff in retaliation for the death row contact visiting being discontinued." In response I filed another appeal form stating that while the warden and associate warden rejected the confidential informers' statements, they refused to remove the negative Confidential Information Disclosure Form from my C-file and were unwilling to acknowledge my charges of being falsely gang-profiled and harassed.

On October 11, 2000, I received another outlandish Confidential Information Disclosure Form accusing me of having a position in a disruptive Crip group. Again I countered with a 602 form. Truly, only staff members with vindictive and bigoted minds could imagine that I, a black with a violent gang past, could not change.

The California Department of Corrections has carte blanche with its inmates—to harass, set up, brutalize, lie, cover up, demonize, and murder any prisoner here, in addition to conducting sanctioned executions. There are prison guards just as inhuman and irrational as some prisoners. Case in point: the 1971 Stanford Prison Experiment, which divided students into two groups. One group posed as prisoners and the other as guards, both in a makeshift prison setting. The six-day experiment resulted in a barbaric transformation in attitude among those students role-playing as prison guards, resulting in termination of the experiment. This was a scaled-down version of the full-blown madness behind these walls where some of the most sado-masochistic minds belong to guards. Some of the males and females working in prison undergo a Dr. Jekyll and Mr. Hyde metamorphosis. Their family members and friends would be appalled to discover how odious, conniving, mendacious, perverted, insidious, and animalistic they can be at work. Or perhaps they would not.

It's an act of jujitsu, fighting an institution that not only protects its own, but even polices itself when charges of malfeasance are brought forward. Where is the accountability? To address an injustice, I use whatever resources are at my disposal within the prison's jurisdiction, and when that fails—as it usually does—I seek recourse outside the wall. But regardless of the prison's underhanded tactics, the power of faith and perseverance has taken me higher. With all the shoveled dirt used to try to bury me alive, it was faith that enabled me to rise up. The more I'm targeted with their madness, the more people in society come on board to support my children's books, other projects, and me.

On November 18, 2001, Barbara excitedly told me that Mario Fehr, a member of the Swiss Parliament, had nominated me for the Nobel Peace Prize. Barbara warned me to prepare for the naysayers to voice their opposition. That evening many of the major news stations on television and radio reported the nomination. Barbara was quickly inundated by print, radio, and TV reporters requesting interviews with both of us. The circus atmosphere treated the nominations as if I had already won the Peace Prize. I braced myself for the same media to flip their script and undercut the nomination. How dare a destitute black man, non–Ivy leaguer, co-founder of a notorious gang, and a death row prisoner, be nominated for the world's most prestigious award? It was an insult to racists, cynics, and sanctimonious people everywhere.

Coming out of the woodwork to vilify my nomination were law enforcement agencies, death penalty proponents, victims' rights groups, newspaper columnists, and San Quentin's official spokesman. In the media's one-sided mudslinging I've been referred to as a criminal beast; a moral coward; a serial killer (please note that the overwhelming majority of serial killers are *Caucasian*); an unrepentant thug; a black Hitler; and a few other unmentionable names reflecting America's embedded, toxic racism.

I have come to learn that criticism without a viable solution is nothing more than an arrogant show of words laced with barren self-importance.

Notably, a few people were hot under the collar that Mr. Fehr, a white European male, had the audacity to nominate a black face from America's death row. Overlooked in the wailing over my nomination was Fehr's courage in defying racism and the popular political slant that supports capital punishment. His stance enabled him not to prejudge me on the basis of color, race, allegations, or circumstances. Instead Fehr focused on the merits of my self-transition and the efficacy of my redemptive output to help underprivileged children. I'm grateful for his courageous action. It is humanitarian gestures such as Fehr's and others' that convince me not to stereotype all Caucasians as racist.

My life mirrors the lives of numerous black men on San Quentin's death row. Many have arrived here apathetic, distraught, fearful, enraged, and bent on further destruction. The intent to survive at all costs can be rerouted and channeled into an intent to rise above one's own madness. Though I was trained on violence, I've discovered that strength can be found in the might of the intellect, in spirituality, in creativity, and in constructive progress. I am not the violent genetic misfit incapable of change that the courts, society, media, law enforcement, and prison administration believe I am. None of these people really know me. They only know *of* me.

By consistent discipline and practice I developed what I call an "instinctual consciousness" that helps me to address a given situation with effective results. It was never easy to detach myself from the prison's procrustean efforts to render me an automaton. The odds never favored my continued existence, before I was imprisoned or after.

Neither my peers nor I could have anticipated the rising hunger for knowledge among both younger and older blacks who have been undone by the draining force of ganghood. I believe behind these walls there is a conscious awakening, an untapped treasure of black minds—Crips, Bloods, and others—capable of altering the mindset of a multitude. I have listened to their perspectives on life, politics, religion, and the plight of black people, perspectives communicated with keen perception and logic. Black society could benefit by studying those of us in prison, seeking creative perspectives to address ills that plague our communities. The crisis demands more than posturing from our black intelligentsia, think tanks, politicians, community leaders, religious sects, and the black citizenry. Whether in prison or behind the invisible bars of public society, no black face can run, hide, dismiss, or intellectualize the problem away. It requires more than theorizing, complaining, rapping, pointing fingers, or fighting among ourselves to make an impact.

Many black men have been criminalized. They are spiritually deprived, cultural iconoclasts, woman abusers, neglectful fathers, drug-ridden, violent, illiterate, and self-destructive. I suffered from these vices that finally morphed into psychological illness. The infirm state of my mind was not genetic, but rather psychological instability, a survival adaptation to an environment that promised much and delivered only degrees of failure. It wasn't too late for me to initiate my own self-therapy to make the transition into the realm of enlightenment.

I have forever awakened the true black man within me.

Burned in effigy with no regrets was my misconception of manhood, culture, education, life, and the world. Death row became the Gethsemane where I overcame my hypocritical conscience and my self-hatred. No longer the possessor of a radioactive mind polluted by self-destructiveness, I now exist with an analytical mentality and a thunderous heart that beats with inner peace, atonement, and truth. Whether I'm dismissed from this physical world today or tomorrow, I take pleasure in knowing I defied the odds to embody a process of change that produces a positive effect on me and other people.

It was in my hostile past that I strove for thug greatness; but now I am intent on helping children discover their inner potential. Black redemption is my *ankh*, in every form and fashion. I'm learning to "master self" while rising from the ashes of madness.

Sons of the Father

Because there are so many black fathers trapped within America's prison system, an entire nation could be grown from the roots of our abandoned children. Mass incarceration has become a divisive force that splits families and foments a son's resentment for his father. As a youth I often felt emptiness in my life, and not simply for lack of a father's presence. My biological father was a sad example of fatherhood. I yearned for an esteemed black male figure who projected a dynamic image I could strive to emulate or to surpass. In different circumstances my chances for success would have increased considerably.

My struggling mother was a true warrior for motherhood, but I could not absorb the male image from her. There are thousands of fatherless households where male youths grow up to become responsible adults. Perhaps I was just needier. In my early life, absent a strong fatherly presence, I launched a doomed odyssey in search of uncovering a maleness to fashion as my own. Although my mother and grandmother contributed fortitude, wisdom, dignity, and love, my psyche instinctively rejected their femininity as a base on which to build my manhood.

My defiance was not an attack against my mother but an effort to establish my manhood with no father around. I despised him for not being there to support our family. With my father gone, I picked up mixed messages about what constituted fatherhood. I promised my-self I'd never be anything like my father, but along the way I too be-came selfish, forgetting my vow, and was incapable of taking care of a single son, never mind a second one. I'm past my disdain for the fa-ther I never knew. I've forgiven him, whether he accepts it or not. But—could my sons forgive me?

Apart from my relationship with my mother, the closest family for me was the Crips. In the ultimate display of fatherly irresponsibility, I forsook my sons to barnstorm throughout South Central Los Angeles in the name of Crippen. I had only faint memories of Travon as a child when I periodically showed up to have sex with his mother, Bonnie. I was no more than a sperm donor: when that job was done, fathering wasn't necessary. From the moment of Travon's birth on Oc-tober 30, 1973, I can count on two hands the times I was in his pres-ence, and on one hand the times I held him in my arms before I was incarcerated six years later.

I didn't begin to become a father to Travon until he was twenty. That's when he began to accompany my mother to visit me, which she did once or twice a year.

I remember his first visit to San Quentin vividly. The visiting area resonated with the sounds of screeching babies, children's laughter, and vocal admonitions from parents, mostly black and brown fami-lies, visiting their loved ones. Many of these families had traveled long distances for just a few precious hours.

When I arrived, my mother was already sitting on the stool, using her handkerchief to clean the phone that usually smelled like bad breath. My hulking son stood impatiently behind her. Both my mother and my son Travon watched as the guard locked the steel-meshed door behind me and removed the modified handcuffs—a larger pair of handcuffs with a long linking chain in the middle to accommodate in-dividuals too large for the standard cuffs. With the handcuffs off I felt a momentary sense of freedom. Despite being imprisoned, I experi-ence other forms of freedom when I pray, type, meditate, exercise, shower, draw portraits, use the phone, study, assist youths—and during personal visits. I looked through the smudged, scratched window, marveling at the beauty of my aging mother as she began to pray with her head slightly bowed. Her soft voice and angelic smile masked the grief of having a son on death row. I know that under the cloak of darkness, back at home, the emotional camouflage disappears as she crumbles into a weeping mother, sharing tears with a huge number of other lamenting mothers throughout South Central, as well as California and the nation.

Maintaining control is a common discipline among black mothers everywhere. They are accustomed to bearing the brunt of their sons' or daughters' misfortunes. But my mother was genuinely happy to be talking with me face-to-face. Occasionally I'd glance at Travon, who kept throwing up his hands as if to say, "When's my turn?" I knew he was anxious, but I motioned for him to be patient.

Minutes later my mother handed the phone to Travon, who sat down on the stool. He was a mirror image of me, with thick black eyebrows, brown complexion, and massive size. It was awkward talking to my son, knowing I had neglected him for all of his young life. I told Travon I understood if he resented me, and I wanted to apologize for committing the ultimate sin, forsaking him to a fatherless childhood.

Back in the day, fatherhood scared me. I was an unfit father, too immature to enlighten him about life. I admitted to Travon that I was ashamed for not being there for him. I had been plagued with a corrupt concept of manhood that would have jeopardized his future. I told Travon that at that time, I was no good for him or myself, and that I wasn't living. I was dying. I would have brought him down with me.

I explained to my son that my maturity allowed me to present him with an olive branch and a message of wisdom. I gave him kudos for the wonderful job he was doing in taking care of his family. Though there was a lot for him to absorb during our visit, he appeared to appreciate my forthrightness. In between sharing the phone with my mother, I stressed to Travon that it was never his or Bonnie's fault, that the blame rested entirely on my shoulders. I wanted my son to know that I regretted not being there for him, that I would never forsake him again. My heart pounded, knowing I could hug neither my mother nor my son. But, I thought, one day it will happen. One day I will be able to say, "I love my son!" It was impossible to make up for all the lost time, but I hoped he and I could establish a new beginning.

When the visit ended, we said our good-byes and promised to keep in touch. Over the course of months and years of phone calls and annual visits with him and my mother, I tried my inexperienced hand at being a father from death row. Though I wanted desperately to assist Travon, I possessed nothing of material value. I had nothing but words—then again, what could I tell a son who was succeeding in life where I had blundered? In the back of my mind I often wondered, "Does Travon resent me?" He had every right to feel embittered, but one day he would have to give it up for his own sake.

Through Barbara I was in contact with Stan, another son whom I abandoned. His misfortune was in trying to follow the path I had trod. Stan was an Imperial Court Crip and had christened himself "Little Tookie" in my honor. Older Crips who knew Stan said his attitude was reminiscent of me at that age. Travon had told me that he had met Stan once, that they hung out for a while, and then parted ways. Other than being fathered by me, they seemed to be from different worlds. Stan was out there Crippen like his father had, masking his frustrations with intoxicants. Barbara offered to locate him so we could establish communication.

It was Tony Bogard who found young Stan for us. Barbara provided him with a place to rehabilitate. He seemed ready to start anew. I shuddered at the thought of my son Stan telling Barbara he wanted to end up on death row with his father just to meet me as an adult, even after she explained that it was possible for him to visit me face-to-face. Barbara had even lined up a job for Stan—but he faded back into the madness of the streets, gone just like that, and this time no one could find him. I knew we were at a critical point, with a son announcing he is willing to give up his life to be in prison with his father. I hoped he was just "jaw-jackin'."

Later I learned that Stan had been convicted of manslaughter. He was sentenced to sixteen years to life in prison. Prior to leaving the courtroom he addressed the jury: "My father, Tookie, will get every one of you!" Of course this statement triggered a report sent to San Quentin officials. I was in the Hole at that time and was allowed to view the document before it was placed in my C-file.

Stan and I started corresponding through the very slow prison mail system. In the beginning I found it difficult to decipher my son's street vernacular. In time I convinced him to clarify his communications so that I could understand him. Like Travon, Stan was enthusiastic about increasing his vocabulary. However, Stan doubted his ability to read legal documents and relied upon others to do it for him. He even tried to foist his responsibility on me by sending his trial transcripts—which were lost in the mail. His hard-headedness was an unpleasant reminder of how I used to be.

Throughout the years I received bits of information about how Stan was doing. While T.C., from the West Side Crips, was passing through San Quentin on his way to another prison, we talked about my incarcerated son. T.C. had met my son at Mule Creek prison, and he had nothing but respect for him. He confirmed that Stan looked exactly like me, and he was a low-rider, meaning he was quick to indulge in violence. Another East Side Crip, Scrappy, arriving on death row, told me he knew Travon and that Stan was his cellie—cell-mate—when they were in Los Angeles County Jail.

Although I began to receive letters from Stan via the internal mail system, our letters were often lost, destroyed, or confiscated. Missing are more than twenty irreplaceable photographs I sent to him over the years. After two decades of being trampled by the whimsy of the "goon squad" (a specialized prison gang unit) who have expropriated hundreds of pictures of me, I thought that they would have had enough by now. Still, it was a blessing being able to hear from both Travon and Stan. I hope that one day we can reconnect as father and sons in society.

On death row I have met numerous black men the same age as

my sons or younger, like Whack, Jamal, Shawn, Asikiwe, and Whiz. I didn't have to wonder why there were so many black men—young and old—on death row. Everywhere I turn, our black sons are milling around in this pit of death, waiting for a favorable outcome that may never be. Though ensnared in the web of the racist capital punishment system, I continue trying to set a noble example for my sons and others. My faith and discipline are the pillars of my resolve. I believe my sons can draw from those principles.

When I do talk with Travon or write to Stan, I try to embrace their viewpoint in order to familiarize myself with their interior lives and their aspirations, to encourage them. My efforts with them recall my own childhood, when my mother tried in vain to impress her wisdom upon me. During an early conversation with Travon I learned that though he works in the medical field, his ambition is in music, to be a rapper, producer, and lyricist. For a short period Travon had been influenced by his Crip legacy and had considered pursuing that disruptive life, but he spurned the enticements of the gang life. I applaud his triumph.

The situation was different with Stan. Both his mother and I were missing in parental action. He was raised by his mother's elderly grandfather and his grandmother, both of whom died while Stan was young. In spite of his grandfather's love, concern, and dedication, he went down this most unpromising road to imprisonment.

But Stan didn't wind up on death row. There are enough individuals here who *are* related by blood, such as Herc, whose Swahili name is Muata, and his cousins, Ghetto, Snipe, and Gangster Dee. It would have been cruel to find myself on death row with my son. After years of being shuttled between different prisons, Stan was sent to Pelican Bay, a state-of-the-art, often locked down prison of well-documented cruelties and racial riots. Occasionally in our correspondence he'd mention the names of Puppet, T.S., Double Life, H.B., Turtle, and many others who showed him the ropes. More than a year later I would meet Loco and Ken Dog from the East Coast. They expressed respect for Stan and had looked out for him. I humbly extend my gratitude to those black men and all the rest who provided my son the knowledge to survive these hellholes, chiefly T.S. and Puppet, whom, with his sister Linda, I've known the longest.

I'm not able to see Stan at all, and the few photos I have of him are not enough to substitute for his presence. But I am fortunate to receive visits from Travon and my mother, who once brought my grandson to visit me. When I first met my grandson he was six years old, clean-cut and well-behaved. He impressed Adisa, Ajani, Muata, and me with his ability to read exceptionally well. As we strolled around the visiting room with my hand on his shoulder, I'd point to a sign, and with enthusiasm he'd read every word. When he was confronted with unfamiliar words he would break them down into syllables.

Once he understood the patriarchal chain of command, he boldly asked, "Grandpa, since you are my father's father, will you beat him up for me?" He floored *everybody* with that question.

As four generations of us Williams posed for pictures, I thought about Stan's absence. I wondered if the day would come when I'd meet him face-to-face, and I yearned to have both Travon and Stan in a family gathering. In every letter I wrote to Stan, I wanted to gain his acceptance into whatever kind of life he had established in prison. In prison, each man has to confront the isolation with his best and strongest desire to survive. It's not a cakewalk. In many of my letters to him I tapped into his views on gangs, politics, religion, and black culture. There was a similarity in my sons' perspectives and mine. He was curious and asked a lot of profound questions.

I saw in Stan's letters a clear interest in shedding the self-destructive mentality in favor of becoming a culturally conscious black man. The respect he had for me enabled him to incorporate my hard-earned wisdom into his transition. I was proud when he cleared the first hurdle, abandoning cryptic gang vernacular for more comprehensible language, coupled with an interest in retaining new vocabulary words. As years passed and he acquired no rule violations, Stan wanted to transfer from Pelican Bay to another prison. He began to study law with the intent to fight for his freedom. My friend Benita obtained a copy of his trial transcripts. The next step was to locate an attorney willing to help emancipate him.

Certain events can be termed God's will or the destiny of divine tutelage. I believe it was both that made the following possible. On a Wednesday evening, March 13, 2002, at 3:40 p.m., I was abruptly awakened by my neighbor Adisa. He hollered over several times before I finally understood his urgency, "Ajamu, Ajamu, your son is calling you!" Groggily I asked, "What did you say, bro?" Adisa said, "Your son is downstairs calling you!" I jumped up, misinterpreting the statement as, "Your son is dead!"

From downstairs boomed a voice, "Baba ["father," in Swahili], Baba!" Since I had never heard Stan's voice before, I asked, "Is that you, son?" Stan responded, "Yes, Baba, it's me, your son! How are you doing, Baba?" I let him know I was doing excellently because I was able to talk to him. Briefly we engaged in a ritual of salutations. Stan said he was passing through overnight, on a bus headed for Salinas Valley State Prison. As much as I wanted to, there was no way for us to hold a decent conversation with me hollering from the fourth tier down to him on the first tier. And being able to see him seemed impossible.

Adisa suggested I try to get one of the sergeants to allow me to go downstairs to talk with my son. Minutes later, when the rookie tier officer passed by, I told him it was an emergency, that I needed to see the sergeant. Assuming I had a complaint against him, the officer wanted to know why I needed the sergeant. I explained that my objective was to get downstairs to talk with my son, whom I had not seen since 1979. "Is your son on death row?" the officer asked. I said, "No, he's just passing through on his way to Salinas Valley Prison." I was taken aback when the officer said, "Okay, no problem. As soon as the four o'clock count is over." After telling Stan I'd be seeing him just after count time, I began putting together a "care package" along with some photos.

I could hear the excitement in Stan's voice as he talked to Scrappy a distance away on the second tier. After count time, at 4:10 p.m., I descended the stairs. The tier officer asked, "How long has it been since you've seen your son?" I said, "Over twenty-three years!" When we reached a holding tank area, Stan hollered out, "Over here, Baba!" Fate smiled on me this day: all the cells were occupied except for one next to my son. As the officer placed me in the cage, I thanked him for making it possible. After being uncuffed, I faced Stan for the first time in more than two decades. His resemblance to me was striking. It was like looking in a mirror.

With a huge smile on his face, young Stan stood there with arms folded genie-style across his chest. He said, "Baba, you look good!" I reciprocated with the exact same words. Then we reached up to an upper corner where there was a gap between the cages to touch fingers in an ad-lib handshake. Standing with the mesh cage separating us was surreal. Styling a Kool-Aid grin, I told Stan, "This scenario in itself is a miracle!" He explained that about fifteen of his peers were supposed to go to C-section, but it was filled up. They were waiting in East Block's holding cages until other arrangements could be made. Stan said, "I figured no matter where I went, somebody would know who you are, so I just started asking."

When I handed Stan the photos, he thanked me profusely. I passed some food, candy, and personal care items to him through the gap in the upper corner of our cages. A guard passed by and offered food from a food cart. Instead, Stan made several sandwiches from the peanut butter and jelly I gave him. In between bites while he bombarded me with questions, I seized the moment, as we faced each other, to initiate a father-and-son dialogue we could build upon. We needed for our peace of mind to see and hear, to physically confirm our family connection. This moment did more for us than a thousand letters of correspondence could ever do. It was a validation of our biological connection and a new beginning for our relationship.

There was no making up for my paternal negligence of Stan but I could at least try, as I do with Travon, to discover a common ground in addition to the biological tie. Since time was limited I wanted to impress upon him what wisdom I possessed. I apologized for not being there for him. He smiled and said, "Baba, I've already forgiven you. There's no need to explain. I understand the life you lived because I followed in your footsteps. You were Tookie, my father, the most notorious Crip. In my eyes you could do no wrong."

I interjected, "I was wrong for not having the courage to be there for you."

"Fair enough, I accept your apology, Baba," he replied. This moment sent waves of intense feeling throughout my body. Not that I was looking for an acceptance of my apology from anyone else in this unmerciful world, but no one has ever said to me, "I forgive you"—other than Travon and Stan.

This expression of forgiveness was a huge boulder lifted off my shoulders. It was a cleansing that would allow me to reach out to the other sons and daughters of the world. It was atonement.

Staring at Stan, I saw that he projected the quality of thug arrogance I had once exhibited, an arrogance capable of getting him killed. That unsettling thought made it vital that I speak on self-transition. When I discussed the need for introspection, humility, and discipline, he mistook my emphasis on self-control as a pacifistic line, turning the other cheek. He said, "Baba, racial riots have broken out in every prison I've been in. I chose to fight rather than retreat or accept a beat-down." I had no argument with defending oneself. I would do the same. I told him I was referring to the senseless violence that is triggered without reflection on its consequences: the stupid behavior, the vicious canards, the thug stare-downs, the idle words of machismo that prick the ego. "Son," I told him, "just because we exist around madness does not mean we have to function like mad dogs."

Most new prisoners greet the negative prison conditions with open belligerence. When pitted head-to-head against the force of the gun tower, guards, barbed wire, steel bars, discrimination, duplicity, and double-standard prison rules—we lose. We must be motivated by our *Moto Ndani,* our fire within. We must rise above the grinding, rigid conditions by nourishing our intellect and spirituality. We must outthink negative situations with a commonsense approach that radiates masterful countermeasures.

Stan vowed, before he left, to incorporate into his life the disciplines of education, spirituality, exercises, redemption, and transition. He had heard that my peers and I had developed our own methodology to oppose the negative forces within and outside of ourselves. Since earlier in the conversation he had unabashedly admitted to following in my footsteps, I posed a question: "Son, are you willing to come anew?" Without hesitation he said, "I have infinite love for you, Baba, and I'm determined to do what is necessary to change!" I was pleased to know Stan had the gumption to seek victory over his inner demons and that he trusted my judgment. I let him know that my word to him would never deviate from the truth, and that I would assist him in any way that I could. "My love for you and Travon," I said, "is undying!"

I reminded him not to be apprehensive about undergoing a transition, that his heart, conviction, and determination would not diminish but would only increase.

It was nearly time for us to say good-bye. We briefly discussed the children's books I had written, which he thought was a courageous effort on my part. Stan said when he read in the newspapers about my nomination for a Nobel Peace Prize, it made him proud. In his words, "Everybody I know thought it was phenomenal that you were able to turn your life around, write children's books, get a visit from Winnie Mandela, and be nominated for a Nobel Prize. And you did it all from behind bars, on death row!"

Suddenly the guard appeared. He gave notice to Stan it was time to go. But before Stan departed we reached up and touched fingers once again, as our eyes locked in a father-and-son bond. He was put back in handcuffs and walked by the cage I was in, turning his body so we could shake hands. Then almost as one, we spoke two words: "Perfect love!"

To gaze at my son walking away was like watching myself fade into the unknown. My fiery heart cried out with each step he took away from me. I now know and love Travon and Stan equally. At last, with my two sons' forgiveness, I felt redeemed.

Still, at this writing, my journey continues . . .

Afterthoughts

In 2002 I was nominated for the Nobel Prize for Literature, a nomination made by William Keach, a Brown University professor of English literature. During that same year I was also nominated for a Nobel Peace Prize by Philip Gasper, Ph.D., chairman of the philosophy department at Notre Dame de Namur University. Dr. Gasper and others have repeatedly nominated me every year since then. Being nominated is a high honor, although I certainly do not position myself alongside Martin Luther King, Jr., Nelson Mandela, Desmond Tutu, or Toni Morrison—all Nobel Laureates. Each of these individuals rose above racist adversity, opposition, and predetermined outcomes to make an impact on the world.

On the other hand, I have emerged from a microcosm of fallibility, but as no less a human being than those esteemed individuals or any other person. Living under the duress of an impending execution, I daily withstand hostile conditions, limitations, confidential informants, racial stereotyping, and the self-appointed naysayers to achieve the impossible.

Throughout California's prison complexes and on death row, I am branded a black bogeyman, the Crip Godfather, and a whipping boy for any kind of prison controversy. Like other black prisoners, I'm automatically pitted against institutional racism, whereas black guards—regardless of rank—are defenseless. They have to turn a blind eye to these kinds of injustices. There are some racist prison staff, men and women, who function under a delusion of *Herrenvolk* (master race) grandeur. Their malice is so racially depraved they don't deserve eye contact. Odd but true, there are some menticided nonwhite staff members that ape their nominal cohorts with similar or worse mistreatment of prisoners. These nonwhite guards tend to forget that the racists here view them likewise as niggers who wear a badge. The exceptions—white and black staff who do try to treat a prisoner with dignity—are often ridiculed, ostracized, or pressured to change for the worse. Little wonder that television media are barred from bringing cameras into San Quentin to interview prisoners about conditions of incarceration and how they are treated—or, for that matter, about any topic. People who claim racism is nonexistent here—or anywhere in the United States—are in denial, or they live above the poverty radar. Racism is not an excuse, it's an obstructive reality.

Under these conditions, it is difficult for any man to overcome the odds, be he Indian, Asian, Mexican, Caucasian, or (chiefly) black. But like others, I dared to resist the institutional harassment, which continues to escalate. The emperor has no clothes in the prison environment. His skin is white.

In the latest twist of penal aggression, I have been targeted for a literary public lynching. On Tuesday, July 1, 2003, the *Los Angeles Times* printed an inflammatory front-page article entitled "Crips Target of Prison Lockdown" by Jenifer (sic) Warren and Dan Morain: "Authorities at Corcoran State Prison have locked 1,300 African American general-population inmates in their cells with limited privileges as they investigate whether incarcerated members of the Crips street gang are conspiring to attack prison staffers in retaliation for the anticipated execution of the gang's co-founder."

The spurious article goes on to say that correctional officers at Corcoran discovered a so-called "kite" (a written message sent anonymously to the warden) directing Crips to attack and kill high-ranking prison staff members. The article continues, quoting Corcoran officials: "The anonymous kite (may) have been sent on behalf of Williams, whose court appeals are winding down."

It is unprecedented that an anonymous, false prison kite can justify front-page coverage in a prestigious metropolitan newspaper and trigger the prison lockdown of thousands of prisoners in Corcoran, Pelican Bay, and Salinas Valley Prison.

I agree with many of the opinions expressed by those who have sent messages to me at www.tookie.com. They felt the *Times* article was a pretext hatched by the attorney general's office, the California Department of Corrections, and others to discredit my youth work, the Nobel Prize nominations, and primarily to influence the Ninth Circuit Court judges to ensure my execution. In fact, Russ Heimerich, a Department of Corrections spokesman in Sacramento, said, "Any time we have a Crip attack a staff member, we look for the link to Tookie." His words confirm that regardless of my transition, positive youth projects, peace initiatives, and more than a decade of committing *not a single disciplinary infraction,* I am always to be a suspect. The vindictive objective to destroy me is so irrational that the California Department of Corrections is apparently willing to incite potential prison bedlam under the guise of preventing violence by locking down hundreds of African American prisoners.

As a precautionary measure, to avoid potential administrative sabotage, it is necessary for me to speak indirectly on the phone about federal appeal strategies, book or youth projects, media interviews, or any other positive activities. There is so much intrigue surrounding me here that I'm overly circumspect and selective about whom I communicate or associate with in any form.

Nonetheless, I manage to rise above these malicious attempts to negatively portray me. Anxiety and defeatism are not an option.

In 2001, there was talk of a movie project. Barbara negotiated with Twentieth Century Fox to support a movie based on particular segments of my life, entitled *Redemption,* for its FX cable television channel. Emmy Award–winning Lynn Whitfield was chosen to play the role of Barbara. But when Jamie Foxx was signed to play me, I couldn't help but think that Fox executives weren't taking the project seriously. Most of my peers were scratching their heads, saying, "Bro, I don't get it. I can't see Jamie playing you!" Only Adisa believed the brother could pull it off.

No one doubted Jamie's talent for mimicry. The question was whether he could make a portrayal of me believable. I reasoned that he didn't necessarily have to *look* like me. I knew it was impossible for him to pack on huge muscles in a short span of time. Would he have to wear padded muscles?

I was humbled by the fact that someone was interested in trying to capture the redemptive phases of my life, when many people think I'm irredeemable, incapable of transformation. Several months later Barbara and I met with the intended writer of the movie. In a few hours we covered many of the necessary topics. At the conclusion of this meeting, the writer promised I would not be demonized or misrepresented for melodramatic purposes. However, when Barbara and I read the first draft of the script, it was littered with black stereotypes. I had little faith in either writer or producer, or their ability to compose a realistic script. I thought Fox executives might eventually kick them off the project.

It was some time after reading the script that I received a visit from Barbara, who came with film producer Rudy Langlais and his sidekick, both of whom tried to assure me that the movie would represent me in a redemptive light. Having viewed the rejected scripts, it was difficult for me to believe. I mentioned to Barbara later that all we could do was to pray that these Hollywood characters would not develop acute amnesia about their announced intentions to me.

On July 12, 2003, I entered the visiting room to meet Vondie Curtis Hall, Jamie Foxx, and Jamie's manager, Marcus King, for the first time. We talked about everything: street gangs, prison, politics, religion, families, entertainment, and my life. I could see Jamie studying my mannerisms. When I brought up the subject of my youth mentoring program, Jamie expressed his willingness to participate. Jamie mentioned that he and rapper and producer P. Diddy often exchanged thoughts about helping youth and about the plight of black folks. He talked about how they had kicked around ideas for building a school for inner-city youths. Though there were comedic moments, Jamie was mostly observant and serious.

The conversation shifted to my thoughts about those in society professing to be Crip godfathers and cofounders. I assured them that my memoirs would put into proper perspective the facts, and mentioned my distress about those who come forth making claims of being originators of this legacy of death. Too many black lives have been lost—and will continue to be lost—until the cycle is reversed. I am not proud of my role, the roles that Raymond and I played, nor should anyone else be proud of their roles.

After two hours, there was a break. I went to the restroom while the others purchased more vending machine food. When we reentered the visiting cage, Vondie asked how I was able to maintain my sanity. I responded, "With extreme difficulty. I maintain my sanity through prayers, studying, exercising, drawing, reading, meditating, typing, visits, and using the phone."

Jamie and Marcus wanted to know what was it that kept me motivated. "Faith in God," I replied. *"Dum spiro spero.* While I breathe, I hope."

Near the end of the visit I asked Jamie if he was planning to visit me again. Both Jamie and Marcus said that they would be back the following Sunday and assured me that they were committed to the youth projects. During a brief conversation with Vondie, he vowed to represent me in the film with justice. I told him that I would definitely need it.

Following the visit, I was escorted back to the hellhole. That night prior to dozing off, I revisited the moments of the day. Vondie and Marcus were extremely persuasive about Jamie's having the talent to play the role. Jamie had proven to be down-to-earth, personable, and attentive to the slightest detail of my concerns. He amazed us all by mimicking my voice and gestures with uncanny exactness. I thought perhaps this man *could* work his magic.

Jamie and Marcus were men of their word. They showed up the following Sunday to visit me. Jamie talked extensively about the need to portray me as I am today. During the break, Jamie and Marcus had to leave to prepare for the trip to Canada where the movie set was being constructed. We paused to take more pictures, which Jamie signed, and I did likewise for him and Marcus. After they had left, Barbara, as usual, asked what I thought. I said, "If the script is rewritten well, I believe Jamie can deliver an excellent performance."

During August and early September, as the movie was being shot, I talked on the phone with Barbara, Jamie, Marcus, and just about the entire movie crew. Prior to the close of shooting, I composed a taped message thanking the team for the dedication they had shown to the project. Several times I was able to converse with Lynn Whitfield, who was playing Barbara in the movie. Amiable and kindhearted, Lynn promised to visit me despite her hectic schedule.

Barbara had traveled twice to Toronto, staying for a week each time. While there, she and Lynn established a strong rapport. On her final trip to Toronto, Barbara was accompanied by her mother, Lillie, who came to watch the filming and enjoy the sights. Usually when I called, they were on the set, watching the goings-on. Even with Barbara present at the filming, I knew with all the executive testosterone unchecked, her prudent suggestions might be patronized and ultimately neglected. Neither of us had any legal control. I remained concerned about the producer's "creative freedom" that permits him and others to embellish and put words in my mouth. Jamie, I learned, refused to do the original movie promo because he considered it to be uncharacteristic of me. Without Jamie's having my back, the promo would have been filmed in a way that misrepresented me. I doubt that any other black male actor would have gone out on a limb for a man who is condemned to death.

I have great respect for Jamie Foxx.

Returning from Canada, Barbara told me that Lynn and Jamie had been exceptional in their roles. While imprisoned, I will not be able to see the movie. But I pray the movie has revealed to all who saw it that even the lowest of the low-life—despite their circumstances—can transform and redeem themselves.

Daily I face life's challenges with relentless faith and resolution. Now I'm a fighter of a different kind. I fight for the poor and wretched among us, of all ethnicities. My redemption has enabled me to appreciate and respect myself, my culture, women, and other people as well as other cultures.

Though it may be viewed by many as illogical on my part, I envision freedom outside these forbidding walls . . . if not tangible freedom, then certainly in spirit.

For me there are felicitous moments, even here on death row. These occur during conference calls to schools, as I am answering letters and e-mails, and during face-to-face visits with underprivileged youths. I can still hear their inquisitive voices and envision their innocent faces. Indeed, the brightest instances are when the youths (myself included) pledge to avoid gangs, drugs, crime, and other pitfalls in life. I believe them! These same beautiful children are the future stars of the universe. I am not a hero, nor am I a role model. My former image is unworthy of emulation. I only reflect an undying determination under fire.

This is why I find comfort in knowing that these children can triumph over adversity—and that they *will not follow* in my footsteps.

Epilogue

By Barbara Becnel

Stanley Tookie Williams's daylong march toward death—to his own execution—was the most courageous act that I have ever witnessed. It was also the most horrific experience of my life.

On Monday, December 12, 2005, the day before Stan, fifty-one, was killed, we all still had such hope that he would live to continue his violence prevention work; that California governor Arnold Schwarzenegger would make history by granting Stan clemency and, thus, would remove him from death row; that Stan would be able to finish the book he was writing for girls who were tempted to join gangs. San Quentin prison authorities, however, had a very different focus: they were steadfastly preparing for Stan to die at their hands, on their terms, at a designated time—December 13, 2005, starting at 12:01 a.m. To visit Stan at San Quentin State Prison during the last days of his life was like stepping into a tilting room at a House of Horrors. Prison rules kept changing to accommodate the protocols associated with staging a state-sponsored death.

During the thirteen years that I knew and visited Stan at San Quentin he was allowed to see me and others without handcuffs and so was free to move about within a randomly assigned visiting cubicle. Thirty days before his execution Stan was moved to a transparent visiting module that allowed everyone who entered the room to see him. His handcuffs were still removed prior to his entering this visiting booth, but he and his visitors were put on public display. Since Stan's story was on television every day, he was easily recognizable. I remember how difficult it was to keep my eyes focused on him as he spoke to me, because there were so many people staring at us, pointing their fingers at him, and lingering around the cage we inhabited. It was unnerving for me to feel like a rare animal caged at a zoo. But Stan sat with perfect posture throughout those visits and never acknowledged the indignities of the situation in which he was placed. And he could still embrace his visitors with bear-like hugs, where he would use his legendary 250 pounds of muscle to lift you off the floor and grin, as if he had just engaged in mischief.

On the fifth day before Stan's scheduled execution, the rules changed once again. This time, Stan and his visitors were moved to a large enclosed room. There was now privacy from strangers, but no privacy from prison guards. From that day forward an officer was in the room with us throughout our visits because this change in protocol had relegated Stan to a new status: he was now a "pre-execution watch prisoner," which meant he could no longer experience even one minute alone. The assumption by prison authorities was that Stan—like any prisoner soon to be executed—had to be watched twenty-four hours a day to stop him from committing suicide. The State of California wanted to be the entity responsible for killing him. If Stan managed to take his own life, that would be an unacceptable outcome.

As a pre-execution watch prisoner, he was also required to be manacled in the most inhumane ways. A chain was wrapped around his waist and handcuffs placed on each wrist, then those handcuffs were connected to the right and left sides of the chain so that he was positioned in a penguin-like stance, with his elbows forced to bend. Shackles were placed on his ankles, causing him to walk without being able to raise a foot; he had to shuffle along, dragging his feet to keep from falling. Still, he stood as upright as possible, given the conditions, as he entered the new visiting room. In the middle of this room was a steel chair that had been bolted to the floor. Stan was instructed to sit there. He was then chained to the chair like Hannibal Lecter so he could barely move in any direction throughout our visits. Moreover, it took so much time to get unchained from that chair to use the bathroom, Stan would forgo eating and drinking for eight hours or more so that he did not have to urinate and, thus, did not have to leave his visitors and lose precious moments with them.

Meanwhile, the rules had drastically changed for Stan within the prison. He was moved from the East Block Condemned Row cell where he had resided for many years and into a cell directly across from the San Quentin death chamber. All of his belongings were taken from him, including his toothbrush, television, and linen. The television was placed outside of his cell for him to view through the bars and grate. If he wanted his television turned on or the channel switched, Stan had to ask whatever guard was present and seated in a chair next to the television to adjust it for him. He was being watched twenty-four hours a day during those last three days, so a different guard sat in that seat during each of the eight-hour work shifts covering a full day. When Stan wanted to brush his teeth, he had to ask the guard to provide him with his toothbrush and toothpaste. To prepare for bed, he had to ask for his linen and return it in the morning when he awakened. Stan was no longer permitted to use his typewriter to work on his book for girls, which was a great blow to him since, in the last days of his life, the thing that he loved the most—to write—was denied him. So Stan denied himself television, denied himself all but the basic necessities needed to maintain his personal hygiene, so as not to have to ask the guards for what should have been his right to have.

What became clear to me was that these prison protocols were designed to make the last few days of a death row prisoner's life the very worst days of what had already been a life of many thousands of days residing in hell, many years of being treated as a "dead man walking," many nights of wondering what it would feel like to look directly into the face of your executioner. This sudden recognition of what Stan was experiencing caused me to be seized by an overwhelming sadness I could not hide. Stan, in turn, saw my distress and though chained to a steel chair, hardly able to move, he told me, "You represent me. And if I can stand up to this abuse and not break down—and they're trying to kill me—you can stand up to it too and not break down." His words became my motivator, which later helped me through the most terrible time in my life: the morning Stan was executed.

On the last full day of Stan's life, I arrived at San Quentin at about 10:30 a.m. Everything was different yet again from what it had been before. There were media trucks with satellite antennae on their roofs lining both sides of the mile-long winding street that begins at the San Quentin freeway exit off the Richmond–San Rafael Bridge and dead-ends at the prison. But it was so quiet. It felt as if no one wanted to break the silence, become a disruption, interfere in any way with what would finally signal Stan's fate. That day the governor's decision—clemency or no clemency for Stan—would be announced. There could be no more delays.

Stan had a roomful of visitors on that last day. Besides me, two other friends were present, Shirley Neal and Rudy Langlais. Stan's lawyers were due to arrive shortly. Civil rights leader Jesse Jackson also stopped by and promised that he would return tomorrow when Stan had *not* been executed. Stan managed to laugh in support of that statement. But Reverend Jackson had not been gone an hour before we were notified by prison guards that the Reverend wanted to come back inside to visit Stan. We all knew that a clemency decision must have been announced to cause Reverend Jackson to return so quickly. But we could not know for certain because we had no access to a television, radio, or telephone. When Jesse Jackson reentered the visiting room he was, in fact, the bearer of bad news: Governor Arnold Schwarzenegger had denied clemency. The execution would proceed as scheduled. Stan had less than twelve hours to live.

Stan was quiet for a moment. He was obviously processing the news. But soon he began to organize the remainder of his day, which was, of course, the remainder of his life. He would talk with all of us for a while and then meet individually with each one of us. When those one-on-one meetings were over he wanted all of his visitors to join him to say our last good-byes. Stan talked about the indestructibility of his soul. He talked about his redemption and how that redemption had confounded the prison authorities, but had given him great peace. Stan said that those authorities had expected him to remain an uneducated, angry, and troubled man. However, Stan told us that he had great joy in his heart because of the children's books and Street Peace Protocol that he had written to steer kids away from gangs, drugs, and prison. He repeated that he was innocent of the crimes that had brought him to death row and that he could not apologize for something he had not done, even though it appeared that his refusal to do so was likely to cost him his life. He talked about his love of God and that he was not angry at the Almighty for Arnold Schwarzenegger's decision. He even turned to smile and thank a guard in the room for giving him a little privacy to shower earlier that day. "You don't know what those ten minutes did for my dignity," he said.

So Stan was calm. As he assessed the way he had spent the last fifteen years of his life, Stan was pleased that he had transcended his former thug life and had become a man of peace. He said that he could not go back to feeling the rage that had consumed his youth and first years at San Quentin. No, he said, he would never allow himself to go back to that place of anger in his head nor would he ever again isolate his heart.

I asked Stan if I could stand with him in the death chamber because earlier he had said that he did not want me or anyone who knew him to be there. He was prepared to die alone. But I argued that he would not be alone. There would be a roomful of prosecutors, victims' family members, and others in the San Quentin death chamber, people who were there because they *wanted* to see him killed.

These same people could be expected to project a great deal of hatred and vengeance toward him in the death chamber. And hatred and vengeance should not be the last thing that he saw in this world. I told him he deserved to look into the face of someone who cared about him during his final moments. I said *that* should be the last thing he sees. I asked Stan to let me do that for him. Eventually he said okay. Stan then said he would find a way to lift his head and smile at me at some point during his execution, no matter what was being done to him. And that is exactly what he did.

At 6:00 p.m. prison guards rushed us out of the large visiting room with the steel chair for the last time. The thick chain connecting Stan to that chair was removed before we could get out of the room. Though still shackled at the ankles and handcuffed to the manacle around his waist, Stan immediately stood up, causing the chains that engulfed him to rattle, noisily. As he rose from the chair, his huge muscled chest expanded to its full width and Stan's head tilted slightly upward. I remember walking backward out of the room, trying to take in this powerful upright image of Stan for as long as I could, knowing that the next time I saw him he would be in a prone position on a gurney, waiting to be killed.

Five of us entered the death chamber in support of Stanley Tookie Williams the night of December 13, 2005: I was there, as were Shirley Neal, Rudy Langlais, and two of his clemency attorneys. About thirty-five other people also witnessed the execution, all of whom were people who did not know Stan, including the print and television media, prosecutors, some of the victims' family members, and, it was explained to us, a group of strangers who were there to represent the People of the State of California, though their identities were to remain forever sealed.

At about 11:45 p.m., all five of us were driven in a van to San Quentin's death chamber by a prison guard who did not speak until we arrived at our destination. We were then told what we should expect—"the thing" (Stan's execution) would only take a few minutes—and we were told the rules—we could not speak above a whisper; we could not "sob loudly." I asked, "What happens if we break the rules?" The answer: immediate ejection from the death chamber.

We waited in silence.

In front of the entrance to the building was a double line of armed prison guards who faced each other, leaving just enough room between them to allow a person to walk through. The gauntlet that they formed was about fifty feet long. As midnight approached, our group was instructed to leave the van and enter the death chamber by walking past those guards. We were the last to enter the chamber, which was very much like a dungeon. Virtually everything was made of concrete—the walls, the floor, and the tiers that were to serve as our appointed place to stand throughout the killing ritual. The other witnesses were already assembled, including one victim's family member and representatives from the Los Angeles District Attorney's Office, who were the only witnesses allowed to sit on folding chairs. They sat directly in front of the large octagonal-shaped execution room within the larger room that had large glass panes covered by white curtains so that we could not see inside. We were directed to stand on a tier to the left of that curtain-enclosed room. But I refused to step onto the tier until I was assured by the guard that I would be able to see Stan from my designated spot.

We had been warned by guards that we should remember to flex our knees while standing because it was not uncommon for a person's knees to lock, causing the person to collapse in the death chamber. We were also told to expect it to be very hot in the chamber. I do not remember becoming either hot or faint. I do remember feeling the coolness of the concrete on the left side of my face as I pressed my entire body against the wall to angle myself to see as much of Stan as I could once the curtains were opened and he was strapped onto the gurney.

When he turned to his left, he could see me, Shirley, and Rudy. So we started to mouth messages to Stan, since we were not permitted to speak above a whisper and he was enclosed by glass. But he was close enough—about ten feet away—that he could understand what we were trying to convey and we understood the messages that he mouthed back to us. We told him that we loved him, that we would miss him and that God would bless him tonight. Shirley and I kept blowing kisses to him and he smiled. At one point, Rudy extended his arm and balled his fist in the black power salute and Shirley and I immediately joined Rudy, saluting in the same way so that we three stood in unity, symbolizing black defiance of these terrible circumstances. Stan actually chuckled, for the briefest of moments, at our rebellion.

His laughter was short-lived because he was being hurt by the nurse, who we later learned was having great difficulty inserting the catheter into Stan's left arm—the catheter that would carry the poison to kill him. At one point Stan displayed his frustration with this nurse's inability to prepare him for death by lifting his head and making some sort of statement to her. A tall guard, who stood next to him, touched Stan's shoulder as if to give him comfort. It would be reported some nine months later that two of Stan's veins had collapsed during this nurse's effort to hook him up to the chemicals of death. And that a second catheter, which should have been connected to his right arm to allow for extra chemicals—if needed to speed up his death—was never attached, as required by San Quentin's lethal injection protocol. So Stan's death, which was supposed to take only a few minutes, according to the guard that brought us to the death chamber, took a total of thirty-five minutes, the last ten minutes of which were slow, ugly, and torturous.

Once the nurse walked out of the execution room—after Stan was trussed up, both hands wrapped about three inches high with white gauze—the guard who only moments before had comforted Stan now quickly swung the gurney around so that Stan, tilted up and on display, was facing everyone in the room. Stan raised his head one last time and looked at me, Shirley, and Rudy, then, abruptly, his head fell back. He had lost consciousness after being injected, through the catheter, with what prison officials refer to as a "three-drug cocktail." The first drug—sodium thiopental—puts the prisoner to be executed into a state of unconsciousness. Pancuronium bromide, the second drug, is a paralytic agent that causes the prisoner's face, lungs and most other parts of his body to become immobile. The final drug—potassium chloride—provokes a massive heart attack, which succeeds in ending the death row prisoner's life. But for Stan, the process did not work entirely as planned. The midsection of Stan's body did not stay still. It began to contort, caving in to the point of distortion—his stomach appeared to have been sucked dry of all internal organs, as it sunk so low it nearly touched his spine. And his convulsing continued for a while. At the sight of Stan's monumental struggle to die, I thought that I heard an audible and collective gasp fill the room. But perhaps the noise came only from me.

I do know that my prayers shifted. Instead of asking God for a miracle that would stop the execution, I began to pray for God to take Stan. Over and over I demanded: "Take him now, God. Take him now." It was clear that Stan was dying a very painful death, though his paralyzed face did not reflect his suffering. The grotesque irony was that Stan's facial features were frozen into the very normal expression of a person who had just fallen into a deep and restful sleep. After what felt like a slowing of time—seconds became the same as minutes for me and minutes became like hours—the curtains closed and a disembodied female voice announced over a speaker system that the execution of Stanley Tookie Williams was over and stated his time of death. Thus far, San Quentin's theater of death had gone unchallenged. This so-called civil ritual of state-initiated killing had commanded our silent attention. So I leaned to my right and whispered to Shirley that we should shout a protest, in unison, before we left the death chamber. She nodded her head in agreement. I asked her to tell Rudy. He too nodded yes. I assumed that we, Stan's witnesses, would be made to leave the building first—and I was right. So as we stepped down from the tier, all eyes on us, and our feet touched the concrete floor of the San Quentin death chamber, we turned toward everyone and yelled: "The State of California just killed an innocent man."

Because the room was windowless and the walls were concrete, our words reverberated like bullets, bouncing off those walls and assaulting the order that had, until that second, characterized the execution of Stan, my friend of thirteen years. We then were instructed to leave the building by the route we entered: walking through the narrow space provided by the double line of armed prison guards who had formed the fifty-foot gauntlet. Of course, I had no idea what those guards might do to me, might do to us, given our loud and unexpected protest. Would they drag us to jail? Would they point a rifle at us? Would they march us off the prison grounds? I did not know. But I walked out of the San Quentin death chamber as erect as ever that night, remembering my friend's request several days earlier. "I represent Stan," I said to myself. "I represent Stan."

The execution of Stanley Tookie Williams was a symbolic moment in California's history. It has also proven to be a revelatory moment of unintended but historic consequences.

For some who wanted him dead, Stan symbolized a "trophy kill." He was the cofounder of the Crips gang. So "Tookie deserved to die," as many angry e-mails sent to him—and to me—stated. The writers of those messages did not care if Stan was, in fact, innocent of the crimes that put him on death row. They made him culpable for every criminal act committed by any gang member located anywhere in the United States. Stan became the symbolic black-man-as-criminal stereotype. (Few people knew that Stan had *never* been to prison in his life prior to being sent to death row.) Others who rejoiced in his execution considered his death a "must-win." Those e-mails often linked him to O. J. Simpson, writing that "we didn't get O.J. so we need to execute Tookie." That was how justice could best be symbolized for them. But the majority of e-mails were simply racist with no other pretense. Those folks wanted Stan dead because as one wrote:

"Just think for a second if your son or daughter was killed by this nigger. You might change your tune. I say kill the fucking nigger. Kill him graveyard dead." Another one wrote, after Stan's execution: "Why don't I run over a nigger riding a bike? Because it's probably my kid's bike. What would you call the first black president? Nigger. What would you call Tookie if he were white? Alive." Following the execution someone else stated: "One down and many more to go . . . What no riots? You niggers get some sleep or something?"

Meanwhile, the rally in front of the prison, composed of people who came from all over the state and nation to protest Stan's execution, was the largest in San Quentin's history, with five-thousand-plus participants. Elders and children stood side by side, black, white, brown, and yellow people converged to stand in support of the idea of redemption and in support of the life of a redeemed man. More than four thousand people, including international human rights leaders as well as national civil rights leaders, attended Stan's memorial service held in Los Angeles on December 20, 2005, most of whom had to stand outside for over four hours, watching the long ceremony on a big-screen television in the Bethel A.M.E. church parking lot. The day before the service, the opportunity to view Stan's body drew crowds of people, lined up and extending around the corner and down the street, for seven straight hours from 2:00 p.m. to 9:00 p.m.—and even then, many people were turned away because the funeral home's staff had to leave. Children as far away as New Haven, Connecticut, reported their public school teacher, questioned the idea of an eye-for-an-eye punishment regarding Stan's execution. They did not want him to be killed. Some of these students wore blue bandannas to school on December 13, 2005, to acknowledge Stan. In Philadelphia, the prison system screened his movie, *Redemption: The Stan Tookie Williams Story*, to more than two thousand inmates. The day after the memorial service, a small group of gang members in Los Angeles determined that "the Governor didn't give our homeboy clemency, but we have the power to give each other clemency by stopping the killing of one another," which they did by forming a

Cease Fire Committee. In just a year's time this committee grew to include some three hundred Crip leaders who vowed no longer to hurt each other. They continue to use the Street Peace Protocol created by Stan. So for those who wanted Stan to live, he became—and remains—a symbol of hope and inspiration.

Stan continues even in death to support life in yet another way: an unintended consequence of the state's killing of Stan has been a de facto moratorium on executions in California. In February 2006, two months after Stan's death, another execution was scheduled, this time to kill prisoner Michael Angelo Morales. However, his attorneys filed a brief that opposed his execution based on the use of the lethal injection method. They claimed that lethal injection was cruel and unusual punishment and cited the prolonged execution of Stanley Tookie Williams as one of several examples of a prisoner who could possibly have felt excruciating pain in the process of being killed by the State of California. Federal Judge Jeremy Fogel eventually allowed this claim to be investigated and stopped all executions from occurring in California until he was satisfied that prisoners were not suffering at the hands of San Quentin execution teams. The results of his investigation were shocking to those who were not in the execution chamber the night Stan died. I had been speaking publicly for months concerning what I witnessed—that Stan had been slowly tortured to death. Law enforcement authorities had referred to my comments as "hysterical." They also wrote a document describing any person who would question the painless nature of Stan's death as someone with an "untutored eye."

On September 26, 2006, in a San Jose, California, courtroom, Judge Fogel held hearings about these matters. Specifically, he wanted to know whether California's lethal injection protocol, as actually practiced, created an unnecessary risk that a prisoner would suffer pain so extreme as to rise to a level of unconstitutionality by causing cruel and unusual punishment, a violation of the Eighth Amendment. I attended the first day of those hearings. I heard a pharmacological expert testify that the drug used at San Quentin to put prisoners to sleep was a very unique drug that made a person immediately lose consciousness, but had a rapid "half-life." The judge asked what that meant and was told that this drug does not keep you unconscious for very long. The average person, this expert said, would begin to awaken within two and a half to three and a half minutes from being administered this drug, given the dosage dictated by California's lethal injection protocol. Stan lived a full ten minutes *after* being given this drug, so it is highly likely that he was awake when the other poisons were shot into the catheter. Those poisons—the paralyzing agent and the drug that stopped his heart from beating—would have caused Stan to have awakened unable to scream out because of his paralyzed lungs, but also unable to breathe. So he would have been aware of slowly suffocating to death at the same time the heart-attack drug was coursing through his veins, causing all of his blood vessels to feel as if they were on fire. In addition, his massive heart failure, induced by that drug, would be like having a ten-ton truck dropped on his chest.

A respected veterinarian also testified before Judge Fogel that day. The veterinarian said that he would never euthanize a dog or cat using the lethal injection protocol California had approved for use on humans. When asked why, he said: "Because I have ethics and standards." He went on to say that he would never use drugs that he was virtually assured would cause an animal great pain and suffering as it died. The packed courtroom fell silent at that moment. A high-level representative from the California State Attorney General's Office was also there and he admitted that mistakes had, in fact, been made during the execution of Stan. But one of the members of the San Quentin execution team assigned to kill Stan expressed on the record his opinion about those mistakes: "Shit does happen. . . ." This quote, referring to Stan's botched execution, so bothered Judge Fogel that he later included it in a footnote of his December 15, 2006, ruling that continued to uphold the moratorium on executions in California.

Since Judge Fogel's actions, many state governments throughout the country have introduced moratorium bills as well as undertaken investigations of their own lethal injection procedures.

During my last hours with Stan, he made two requests of me: he asked that I scatter his ashes in South Africa and that I continue his work to steer marginalized youth away from involvement with gangs, drugs, and incarceration.

On June 25, 2006, Shirley Neal and I traveled to South Africa to fulfill his first request. His ashes were released in a lake at Thokoza Park, located in Soweto, South Africa. Stan and I chose Soweto because of its important history with the youth of that township. On the morning of June 16, 1976, the black students of Soweto decided to leave school and protest, peacefully, the apartheid-era conditions they faced—overcrowded school rooms, high dropout rates, the racist content of their curriculum, inadequate facilities, and the fact that they were being forced to learn Afrikaans, the language of their oppressors. The children were fed up and, in large numbers that day, decided to march down a main road with signs of protest. But as they marched, these defenseless children were shot down and killed—a total of 172—by South African police. The willingness of those Soweto youths to stand up for themselves and for the betterment of their community personified what Stan had hoped his work would instill in the youngsters who reside in urban America. So that is why Stan's desire to end up in the Motherland led him—and me—to the township of Soweto.

My plans for responding to his second request include keeping all of his books in print, starting with this book, *Blue Rage, Black Redemption*, and publishing once again the eight-book violence prevention series for elementary students that Stan and I co-authored more than a decade ago. The many essays that he wrote will be released over the years and his educational website, www.tookie.com, will be redesigned and maintained for many years to come. Stan made numerous audiotaped recordings—messages to youth, incarcerated adults, teachers, and parents—which will be released over a five-year period. I have also created a Stanley Tookie Williams Legacy Fund to provide grants to nonprofit groups working to help at-risk youths stay out of trouble and improve their literacy through encouraging the reading of books, as well as supporting advocacy groups intent on ending the death penalty and removing race and class bias from the criminal justice system.

My heart and mind were hugely enriched by my friendship with Stan. I know that I am stronger for the tragedy that his death represents for me. The worst day of my life—watching Stan die so painfully and too soon—has put steel in my spine because of the courage Stan displayed on that same awful day. But I am most pleased to see that Stan's street peace work, his death, and his story have become a living legacy that supersedes the annihilation of his body, because now his spirit soars. I am proud to have worked with him. I feel privileged that he was my friend. And I know at least one other thing: I would do nothing differently; I would be there again in that San Quentin death chamber to stand with him and bear witness to what was done, which inspires the truth that I will speak and the fight against injustice that I will champion until my dying day—or until capital punishment ends and major criminal justice reform occurs in this nation. Why? Because I represent Stan, I will always remember. I represent Stan.

Special Acknowledgments

It is necessary to acknowledge individuals I neglected to mention within the body of my memoirs. This is in recognition of individuals in society and on death row who, despite their history, are true friends, are involved in progressive organizations, youth projects, and self-evolutionary journeys, and provided invaluable feedback for my Peace Protocol. This is also for the ancestors in spirit form who continue to support our efforts.

Adisa	Blue	Geronimo Pratt	Little Ace
Ajani	Boon	Ghetto	Little Bruce
Ajene	Bopete	Grandpa	Little Dee
Amin	Chico	H.B.	Little Money
Angela Davis	Chief	Haki	Louis Farrakhan
Apache	Chunga	Half Pint	Louisiana Smooth
Asikiwe	Clint	Hollaway	Lynn Whitfield
Assata Shakur	Cool Breeze	J. King Puppet	Magic Johnson
Bahari-Ku	Cricket	Jamie Foxx	Malcolm X
Barbara Becnel	Cutes	Jay Dog	Malik
Barbara Lee	David Madden	Jesse Jackson	Marcus King
Barefoot Pookie	Desley Brooks	Jessie James	Mario
Big Al	Dr. Renee Garrick	Jim Brown	Melvin Hardy
Big Alton	Eddie H.	John Shaka	Michael Christen
Big Cane	Elu	K. Dog	Monkeyman
Big James	E-Moe	Kerm	Monster
Big Reg	Eric and Derrick	Khalifa	Mouse
Big Time	Fat Rat	Kiilu Nyasha	Muata
Big Tony	Frederick Douglass	Kwesi	Mumia Abu-Jamal
Big Vertice	Gerard Boccacio	Lisa Demberg	Mustafa

My mother	P.R.	Shirley Neal	Tony Robbins
My sons	Peewee	Side Winder	Vondie Curtis Hall
Ndio	Philip Gasper	Skull	Walt
Nelson Mandela	Pointblank	Snoop Dogg	Warlock
Nkpume	Romeo	Steven G.	Wayne Holiwell
Nthato Robin	Rudy Langlais	Stockton Mike	Will Rock
Shaka	Rusty	T. Stacy	William Keach
Oatmeal	Scrappy	Ted Chung	Willie Herb
Ojare	Shoes	Tony Muhammad	Winnie Mandela

May you all continue to promote self-transition, redemption, self-reliance, and above all, peace.

The Tookie Protocol for Peace

A Local Street Peace Initiative

Stanley Tookie Williams

Peace Protocol Contents

Signature Agreement
Community Peace Accord

A Final Note from Tookie

Create a Street Peace Kit

Introduction

To address the social state of emergency regarding urban violence, I have prepared this protocol for street peace—a comprehensive strategy for peace and reconstruction within the community. The design can be modified to meet the needs of a particular situation.

The United States government's approach to urban violence is often to launch one of its intermittent "wars" on crime and then trumpet success by pointing to wholesale incarcerations, measures which fail to deter or to rehabilitate the criminal mentality. Meanwhile, for a generation of disgruntled youth and adults, living the thug life and going to prison have morphed into an underdog aspiration.

But placing blame is irrelevant. We must concentrate on a workable solution.

The approach to resolving an epidemic begins with understanding the origins of it, the causes and effects. To broach this issue I draw on my life and gang experience as the cofounder of the infamous Crips. I grew up in South Central Los Angeles amidst poverty, street gangs, pimps, prostitutes, police tyranny, illegal drugs, criminality, and other social injustices. Here was a social vacuum without paternal guidance, without career-oriented programs, and without a nurturing village or community to support the male rite of passage toward becoming a responsible adult. Violence, gangs, and street-level socioeconomic crimes (selling drugs, robbery, prostitution, and theft) were—and continue to be—direct results of living in these conditions.

This social vacuum has spawned black urban nihilists like the Crips, the Bloods, and many other street gangs. Gangs serve as a weapon of rebellion against parental authority, culture, religion, community, law enforcement, the world, God, and other gangs. The muscular irrationality of a gang's instinct to survive is used to justify any wrongful act, even at the expense of a family member, stranger, friend, or foe.

The phrase "by any means necessary" serves as a destructive rationale for street gangs to fend for themselves in society, without regard for anyone else. Each faction operates as an independent, lawless body that has no difficulty recruiting among the disenfranchised.

The absence of access to affordable housing, health care, quality education, secure employment, and other necessities produces social instability. Any efforts to establish a peace policy will be doomed unless there is tangible social progress. Peace cannot be sustained without it. Poverty, racism, and hopelessness foster an environment that supports the growth of toxic conditions.

Understanding Retaliation

From an illusory elitism of gang membership, a pattern of retaliation has emerged that perpetuates the pattern of murder-for-murder. In this scenario there are no winners. And the losers are too often buried in graveyards, maimed by gunfire, or incarcerated for their crimes.

Like a pendulum, retaliation swings back and forth with its inevitable, brutal payback.

Trying to stop belligerent gangs from retaliating against each other is difficult. Retaliation brings a sense of machismo and an earned street "reputation." Society sees only a cycle of senseless murders, an unending tragedy. It would amaze both gang members and others in society to hear that conflicts between Crips and Bloods on death row—where I live—are rare. These sworn enemies engage in nonhostile dialogues, banter, share food and books, study, and exercise together on the same prison yards without controversy.

If notorious rivals who have been exterminating one another for more than three decades can establish a truce in prison, then a ceasefire is surely possible in society. Throughout California prisons, Crips and Bloods coexist for the purpose of survival. That simple philosophy can be transmitted to rival gangs in society. Instead of our killing each other, that energy can be harnessed to oppose poverty, illiteracy, unemployment, discrimination, and other social and judiciary injustices.

There are many reasons why warring factions should avoid this cycle of violence and retaliation, of *lex talionis* (an eye for an eye): innocents are injured or killed, and the psychic and social scars on adults and children are handed down to next generations.

Conclusion

There is no quick-fix remedy for the gang epidemic.

Here on death row I have discussed a street gang truce with individuals from different age groups, geographical locales, gangs, and mentalities. I discovered that my ideological and philosophical outlook on peace was in step with perspectives of the newer and the older generation. I also realized it is illogical to create a peace not based on an individual and collective improvement of the lives of community members. Failure to establish a truce that includes a social agenda will cause any negotiation for peace to relapse into war.

I am convinced that peace *is* possible, despite the many lives that have been lost from years of youth gang warfare. This document is designed to assist those whose aspirations are to create a cease-fire, end gang violence, and restore social order. Pessimistic individuals may quote the English translation of the Latin phrase, *si vis pacem, para bellum*—if you desire peace, prepare for war. But I strongly disagree.

Real peace will conquer war.

Perpetual Peace Accord for Opposing Gangs

Acknowledged here and now on this month _____, day _____, and year _____, is a perpetual Peace Treaty between the warring parties: _____ and _____. This word-of-honor agreement binds the aforementioned rival factions to put aside their differences, be they ideological, political, religious, philosophical, racial, economical, geographical, criminal, material, personal and collective retaliation, or any social reliance on violence or murder. This document is an oath of responsibility for the parties involved to coexist in peace and reconciliation for the security of their communities, residents, and offspring.

Signatory: _____

Date: _____

Observing Witness: _____

Point I:
Proclamation

A-1: WE THE INVOLVED PARTIES WILL immediately cease fire and end any verbal, written, or physical violence against one another.

A-2: WE THE INVOLVED PARTIES WILL cease and desist the perpetuation of drive-by shootings, walk-up shootings, setup shootings, ambushes, murder, drug deals, robbery, vandalism, kidnapping, rape, extortion, female and child abuse, illegal profiteering, or any other kind of violence or criminality.

A-3: WE THE INVOLVED PARTIES WILL use every nonviolent measure to resolve all past, present, or future conflicts between us.

A-4: WE THE INVOLVED PARTIES WILL learn to respect one another and coexist in peace within the community and elsewhere.

A-5: WE THE INVOLVED PARTIES WILL help to restore order and to rebuild the community.

A-6: WE THE INVOLVED PARTIES WILL NOT disrespect, instigate, or taunt each other or family members, relatives, wives, girlfriends, and acquaintances of the opposite parties.

A-7: WE THE INVOLVED PARTIES WILL NOT encroach upon each other's community or neighborhood without prior notice, to avoid suspicion or conflict.

A-8: WE THE INVOLVED PARTIES WILL help individually and collectively to keep the community safe from any improprieties.

A-9: WE THE INVOLVED PARTIES WILL NOT use the Peace Accord as camouflage to commit mayhem against each other.

A-10: WE THE INVOLVED PARTIES WILL neither seek out nor plot with acquaintances or outsiders (defined as parties not obligated to this Proclamation) to carry out vendettas against each other.

A-11: WE THE INVOLVED PARTIES WILL NOT allow mistreatment or harm to befall any individuals appointed as Peacekeepers or others involved in the peace process.

A-12: WE THE INVOLVED PARTIES WILL put forth effort to become educated, computer-literate, and to learn a trade that will enable us to become productive in the reconstruction of our community.

A-13: WE THE INVOLVED PARTIES WILL eliminate any self-destructive behavior and personal vices—illicit drug usage, drug dealing, abuse of alcohol, inhalants, etc.—that would intoxicate our minds, impair our judgment, and jeopardize the peace negotiations.

A-14: WE THE INVOLVED PARTIES WILL work side by side to do whatever is ethical to uphold the Peace Accord and Proclamation, and we vow to live in harmony.

A-15: WE THE INVOLVED PARTIES recognize both the Peace Accord and Proclamation as being fair and attainable. We agree to its entire contents.

Signatory: _____

Date: _____

Observing Witness: _____

Point II:
Violations of Proclamation Clause

This written clause is designed to maintain fairness in the determination of possible violation of Point I: Proclamation, and to determine what, if any, will be the punitive measures. Violations committed by parties from either side will be adjudicated (via monetary fines, community labor, expulsion, etc.) ONLY by a selected nonpartisan Peacekeepers Committee, to avoid possible hostile reactions by a violator from either party. Violations will be recognized as followed:

 I: To violate the cease-fire in any form;

 II: To violate any of the provisions in the Proclamation, including A-1 through A-15;

 III: To assist another party member to violate the Proclamation;

 IV: To alter or rewrite the agreed-upon Proclamation to favor one party's interest over the other party's;

 V: To obstruct any of the appointed Peacekeepers from performing their duties to maintain peace.

Signatory: _____

Date: _____

Observing Witness: _____

Point III:
Peacekeepers and Monitoring Committee

B-1: Mediators, who may be members of local faith-based groups or other community-based organizations, initiate an outreach process to begin establishment of a Peacekeepers Committee. In the beginning they play a crucial role in identifying the founding members of the Peacekeepers Committee. Once this core group of founders is established, their outreach abilities are used to further expand the Peacekeepers Committee, and the founders become members of that Committee.

B-2: Members of the Peacekeepers Committee will consist of several—preferably former—local gang leaders or influential gang members; church leaders or influential members of the church congregation; local political representatives; grassroots community leaders; concerned parents; and other reliable and interested people within the community.

B-3: The Peacekeepers will assemble daily or less often—depending upon the severity of the situation—until there is peace and community stability. Meetings can be held in a specific home, basement, garage, church, gymnasium, or in any enclosed facility. To provide safety for all the people involved in the peace negotiations, implement "pat searches" and metal detectors.

B-4: Selection of Peacekeepers Committee members can be held annually or biannually.

B-5. All Peacekeepers will wear a specific-colored armband and insignia of peace to identify them. Any vehicle driven by a Peacekeeper will have a visibly attached white flag prior to venturing into any recognized area of either party participating in the transition to peace.

B-6: All decisions related to peace strategies and/or violations of peace among either party must be voted on by the Peace-keepers Committee before any such measures are enacted.

B-7: Each Peacekeeper is required to allocate his or her time to monitor specific communities and war zones. Moreover, he or she is expected to keep in touch with members of both parties.

B-8: Any Peacekeeper Committee member can be voted off the Committee if he or she is neglectful of duties or guilty of any wrongdoing—be it criminal or otherwise.

B-9: To prevent Peacekeepers from involvement in law enforcement issues, they are to leave the investigation of serious crimes to the authorities.

B-10: The Peacekeepers obligation is to implement and maintain peace and *not* to play the role of a police officer, a member of the FBI, the Central Intelligence Agency, or any other law enforcement agency.

B-11: The Peacekeepers Committee is expected to create Buffer Zones (see Point V: Buffer Zones) within the community to meet the needs of either party. These Buffer Zones are necessary for the provisions of peace meetings, socializing, sharing information, and providing sanctuary.

B-12: All Peacekeepers must recite and sign a written oath regarding their responsibility to establish peace.

B-13: No Peacekeeper will act as a vigilante or enforcer through means of violence, nor will any Peacekeeper suggest or rely upon representatives of either party to act as vigilantes or enforcers.

Signatory: _____

Date: _____

Observing Witness: _____

Point IV:
Peacekeepers Oath

I, _____, do solemnly swear to uphold all the obligations of being a Peacekeepers Committee member. Throughout the course of my appointed duties I promise to be truthful and fair with either party. As a Peacekeeper my responsibility is to establish and maintain peace within the community. I vow to adhere to everything required of me within the Peacekeepers Committee, Point III: B-1 through B-13, and the Peacekeepers Oath.

Signatory: _____

Date: _____

Observing Witness: _____

Point V:
Buffer Zones

Both parties agree to designate neutral areas called Buffer Zones that are monitored by the Peacekeepers Committee. These Buffer Zones will be set up to provide either party with a safe haven for peace talks, intermingling, relevant information sharing, meetings, etc. Such Buffer Zones can be established in a church, office, home, recreation center, building, or any kind of structure or territory, including a block or entire community. All members from either party will agree never to violate the sanctity of the Buffer Zones, which are created to assist in peaceful negotiations.

Signatory: _____

Date: _____

Observing Witness: _____

Point VI:
Gang Membership Renunciation

The long-term objective is for an eventual dismantling of all disruptive parties (gangs, sets, 'hoods, groups, organizations, empires, etc.) that are prone to create havoc within the community. There will be party members from either side interested in changing his or her lifestyle. Point VI is written to protect any person who decides, or is encouraged, to give up his or her membership from any disruptive group.

1. All parties agree to allow any member who chooses to disassociate himself or herself from membership or association with any disruptive group representing either party to do so without threat or enactment of ridicule, violence, or retaliation.
2. Former members of a disruptive group representing either party will be allowed to continue helping to establish peace without fear of repercussion.
3. Counseling and reorientation will be offered to any individual who decides to quit membership in a disruptive group representing either party.
4. For whatever reason, if any ex-member of a disruptive group rejoins his or her group, he or she will be excluded from the ongoing peace initiative.

Signatory: _____

Date: _____

Observing Witness: _____

Putting the Theory of Peace into Practice

Establishing Peace

The process for creating peace among hostile factions requires a neutral mediator or mediators. The following is a process mediators should use to initiate a peace process:

Have as many supporters as possible on board prior to contacting either of the warring parties.

Schedule a meeting separately and together with local churches, mosques, synagogues, temples, community-based organizations, violence prevention programs, schools, veterans groups, Masons, businesses, and local politicians to discuss their participation in the grassroots struggle for peace. Present a proposed peace document to each of these entities that illustrates the critical role of each of these groups to the community peace process.

If a mediator (or mediators) is not familiar with either of the parties, then that mediator should seek assistance from a reliable source who is acquainted with both sides and is capable of setting up separate meetings with each of the most influential representatives of the opposing parties to recruit their participation in the development of the community's peace process.

Prior to the meeting, the mediator should learn as much as possible about the individuals the mediator is scheduled to meet.

Whenever the mediator (or mediators) determines that positive gains have been made during the dialogue with both sides, then the leaders of the opposing parties should be invited to attend a joint meeting in a neutral setting. Make it known that for security purposes, pat searches and metal detectors will be implemented.

During those joint meetings, encourage both parties to express themselves while the mediator (or mediators) observes and listens carefully. Since both sides are protagonists in the peace process, make sure to embody their most reasonable suggestions in tandem with your ideas about peace.

Present both parties with a comprehensive peace strategy that is viable and attainable.

Seek assistance in the peace process from the parents, family members, relatives, and other associates of the leaders and members of the opposing parties. With both parties aware that people they care about will also be present at each peace meeting, rally, march, and other social functions, potential hostile actions should be avoided by all participants.

To effectively address urban warfare the peace plan should address situations within a community, block by block, and expand as the project prevails.

Draw from influential sources such as Original Gangsters who are incarcerated from within either party. Redemption, integrity, and aspirations can be found among the most wretched.

Do a background check on members of the Peacekeepers Committee to prevent possible infiltration and sabotage to your process by agent provocateurs. (There *will* be attempts by internal and external sources to disrupt the peace protocol. A viable peace policy supported by a staunch community can overcome its detractors' obstacles.)

Initiate study groups to familiarize both parties with the origins of their ancestors and culture. Help them to develop pride in themselves and in their heritage. Teach them to renounce their self-hate that produces violence, and show them how to cleanse themselves with dignity, honesty, justice, and righteousness.

With peace as the objective, fear or flight is not an option. When you reduce the human factor to its bare essentials, we all want to live.

Everyone's life is on the line. It will require instinct, intellect, sponsors, and absolute courage to bring together a tractable peace agreement. With the majority of the community on board, peace can prevail.

Maintaining Peace

To establish peace is one reality, to maintain it is another. To preserve peace will require consistent discipline, upkeep, interaction, and monitoring. Here are a few suggestions:

In addition to the Peacekeepers, select a Community Watch Group organized with video cameras to monitor activity in the community. This is a precautionary—and interim—method to let police and everyone else know that they're being observed. Post large, visible signs to forewarn that these areas are being video-monitored.

Both the Peacekeepers and the Community Watch must work in shifts, around the clock, to monitor behavior and maintain peace. Their availability is critical to uphold order.

Communal communication is necessary to supervise the war zone areas. Strategic points can be established throughout a neighborhood provided with computers, cell phones, walkie-talkies, etc., to monitor social activities. During the day, at-home mothers and elderly folks are suitable candidates for Community Watch Groups. Whenever there appears to be improper activity, Watch Group members should contact the Peacekeepers to address the situation. The most serious incidents (shootings, murders, etc.) must be left up to law enforcement agencies. Peacekeepers and Community Watch members are not police officers.

All Peacekeepers and Community Watch Groups should interact with all people in the community. Throughout the neighborhood, go door to door to discuss the peace policy or to distribute peace fliers. If there are people who refuse to discuss peace with you, leave a flier in their mailbox or underneath the windshield wiper of their car. *Let no community resident be ignorant of your peace initiative.*

Follow through on every policy that will create peace.

Maintain contact with all parties under the peace accord. Keep them abreast of progress being made, and/or any concerns, suggestions, etc., concerning the truce.

Remind all individuals participating in the peace process that they will be held accountable for their inappropriate behavior. Established and agreeable guidelines for punitive damages will be enforced by Peacekeepers. Damages can range from monetary fines, community work, expulsion, or other requirements of the peace agreement. Maintain a written report on the progress of the peace negotiations.

Always encourage all individuals involved in the peace process.

To preserve a truce, children must be educated about the premise of peace. The knowledge of peace combined with their direct participation will help to create a generation of peace idealists.

To disarm is the ultimate gesture of peace and a true moment of reckoning. Disarmament is not a coward's way out, but rather a wise person's way *in* for peace. However, for me it would be a disservice to suggest to anyone that they disarm themselves when peace is still a theory and not a living practice.

It is a myth that manhood and womanhood can be defined through the barrel of a gun. Realistically, the majority of people who do possess weapons will not surrender them under any circumstances. Moreover, if a self-hate mentality is maintained among community residents, violence will continue, with or without the presence of guns.

For people to disarm themselves, they must first disarm their minds with education and enlightenment in support of an ultimate peace. Dare I entreat every man, woman, and child to lower the barrels of their weapons in honor of peace?

Social Agenda for Peacekeepers

It is unrealistic in any attempt to establish a peace policy without including a social agenda. History has shown that communities and nations have either prospered or perished depending upon the viability of their social agenda—which is an orderly system that promotes prosperity for all its residents.

Throughout history, we see that the absence of peace and a workable social covenant can give rise to nihilistic settings. Here in America, the subculture of gangsterism and criminality continues to devastate communities with its lawless agenda. This social agenda, in the paragraphs below, has been designed to help reintegrate the so-called gangbangers, criminals, ex-cons, and other incorrigibles into society.

Education and Career Trade Programs

This process is geared to provide each individual with the opportunity and information to earn a high school diploma or a General Equivalency Diploma.

In addition to this fundamental education and certification, individuals with scholastic ambition are encouraged to pursue further education: in politics, socioeconomics, computer technology, architecture, sociology, psychology, mathematics, history or law. Their education and skills will be valuable assets in the redevelopment of both themselves and their communities.

Establish a relationship with local schools, colleges, youth centers, and technological centers to request their assistance in bringing the students' education to fruition.

Create your own study groups and computer classes to be held in a home, church, garage, basement, youth center, or other places.

Political Awareness

Stress the importance of being politically conscious. Encourage individuals to read relevant materials (newspapers, magazines, books, websites, etc.) to become politically literate, recognize their rights and the power of their votes.

Educate them on the duties and obligations of each local political representative to further their community involvement.

Teach residents to be alert to political dynamics that affect their lives. Impress upon them that if the politician representing their district has not improved their lives by helping to develop jobs, livable housing, health care, quality education, no addicts/drugs/homelessness, safe, clean neighborhoods, and reduced poverty, violence, and crime—then something is wrong.

Employment Placement

When an individual has completed an educational process, he or she will need to find a job. An Employment Placing Panel can be created to help find a suitable job for each individual. This will require phone calls, e-mails, and footwork to locate available jobs. This "recruiting" process is itself a useful skill.

Teach each individual etiquette and mannerisms: how to speak well, dress properly, maintain good personal hygiene, be prompt, patient, and develop a good work ethic. The objective is to gain employment, then to begin to build a solid employment record.

Socioeconomic Commission

Establish a Socioeconomic Commission consisting of entrepreneurs, bankers, economists, stockbrokers, and other business professionals. Contact people whose resources can be a valuable asset.

Your presentation to these business-oriented people must be cogent, reasonable, and doable. Remember that the Peace Protocol and the Social Agenda is a unified package that includes the specific role of Socioeconomic Commission members.

The Commission's mission is to help create a system of small businesses that in turn promote ownership, local employment expansion, and overall community economic development. In addition, the commission's mission is to teach a grassroots individual how to administer a small business enterprise.

Encourage individuals to reduce their consumer spending and debt.

Peace March

Beginning with the famous August 28, 1963, March on Washington (climaxed by Martin Luther King's "I Have a Dream" speech), there have been numerous other peaceful marches that have momentarily seized our focus on relevant issues. The march of peace is akin to the march of war, because both are predicated on the notion of overcoming obstacles to success.

When we march in the name of peace, let us march with a strategic purpose that will produce tangible results: peace, employment, housing, health care, education, property ownership, and other amenities.

Community Cleanup

Another important reality is the need to clean up the community, block by block. I can already hear people moaning at the thought of having to clean up the community. There are run-down neighborhoods that should be a priority and need immediate addressing, much as a person cleans his or her own home. Knock on every door on every block and ask for everyone's participation in the cleanup project.

Street by street, groups of adults, children, and youths can clean up filth, abandoned cars, graffiti, and other refuse. Naturally, to refurbish homes and apartments may require financial assistance from committed sponsors and others who have an interest in the community's development. But funds are not necessary when we can rely on our own hands and a little footwork. The cleanup project benefits everyone, because the area is clean and no longer an eyesore—and it raises property values!

Armed with brooms, trash cans, plastic bags, paintbrushes and rollers, and water hoses, residents can purge their own communities. Upon the completion of the cleaning process, post fliers that emphasize the need for cleanliness and no littering. The rise or fall of any neighborhood can be attributed to the residents' concern with keeping the community clean, alive, and well—or to continued indifference, lack of pride, and neglect.

Community Peace Accord

We the people of the community named here, _____, do solemnly swear to participate in the Street Peace Protocol to restore decorum and to provide safety for all residents. We agree to work side by side with all other people whose goal is the pursuit of peace. We are not a vigilante group or militia, nor are we working in the capacity of a law enforcement agency. We function as an independent peace group and as concerned citizens of our community. We believe that peace can be established and maintained through dedicated work.

We agree to adhere to the standards of this document, without fail.

Signatory: _____

Date: _____

Observing Witness: _____

A Final Note from Tookie

There are no books or manuals on how to create a peace policy for street gangs. I have drafted this peace protocol to serve as a prototype or framework on which to build. It is a commonsense approach that beckons the heart and invites your strong intention to assist those who live in chaos and fear, both children and adults. I hope that my insight will move society—and gang members—to draft from this peace protocol and make it work.

As you move in this direction, you will learn to construct a peace policy that will meet the necessities for peace in your neighborhood, in your city, in your nation. There is much serious work ahead, and the entire community will depend upon each and every one of you. Keep in mind that even the warring souls of gang members yearn for peace but are blind to its path. Your faith, wisdom, concern, and guidance can help show them the way. Never allow yourself to be distracted or discouraged by detractors and dissenters whose views are counterproductive.

Finally, I call upon the pure energy of human beings and institutions—gangs, ex-cons, parents, churches and mosques, schools and universities, youth centers, think tanks, university professors and other educators, entrepreneurs, entertainers, human rights agencies, social organizations, politicians, rappers, newspapers, media broadcast outlets, the employed and unemployed, the wealthy and the poor, the young and the elderly, and anyone else who is interested in promoting street peace—to help create a new community of safety and well-being. This peace protocol is not the solution. Look in the mirror. There is the solution.

Create a Street Peace Kit

Help the children in your community by creating a Street Peace Kit that you can donate to your local school, church, nonprofit youth agency, or community policing program. The kit should include:

1. The Tookie Protocol for Peace. This peace protocol provides a detailed process a community can use to create peace, block by block and neighborhood by neighborhood. The document can be obtained at no cost: simply go to www.tookie.com and click on "Protocol for Peace" to print the pages from this important document. Already 92 Indiana gang members—Gangster Disciples and Vice Lords—and 150 Crips and Bloods in New Jersey have signed truce documents based on the Tookie Protocol for Peace after watching *Redemption: The Stan Tookie Williams Story* and printing Tookie's protocol from his website.

2. *Redemption: The Stan Tookie Williams Story.* This ninety-three-minute cable television movie about Stanley Tookie Williams's life was aired April 11, 2004, on FX cable in the United States. The movie received numerous accolades after its telecast, including the honor of its premiering at actor Robert Redford's Sundance Film Festival in Park City, Utah, in January. *Redemption* also won the highest award at the Pan African Film Festival in Los Angeles in April 2004 and screened in May of that same year to a standing ovation at the International Cannes Film Festival in Cannes, France. *Redemption* is now available on DVD at Blockbuster,

Target, and other stores throughout the United States and the rest of the world. This movie has inspired thousands of people to give up their gang membership.

3. *Blue Rage, Black Redemption: A Memoir.* Stanley Tookie Williams's autobiography fills in all the detail not seen in *Redemption,* the movie. Tookie talks about the origin of the Crips youth gang and his long, steady process of self-rehabilitation initiated during the late 1980s while he was housed in solitary confinement for six and a half years on San Quentin State Prison's death row. With this memoir, Stanley Tookie Williams offers profound insight into the causal relationship between the socioeconomic conditions of South Central Los Angeles (or virtually any low-income city or township in the world) and the youth gang culture embedded with self-hate and self-destruction often spawned by those conditions. The messages and observations Tookie writes about create a primer for what needs to be studied in public policy, law enforcement, and youth program development.

About the Author

In the early 1970s, many young people of South Central Los Angeles were members of small gangs. The youngsters roamed South Central, taking property from whomever they chose, including women and children.

Stanley Tookie Williams, seventeen, was then a high school student with a fearsome reputation as a fighter and leader of South Central's west side neighborhood. To protect family members and friends, Tookie—with Raymond Lee Washington, also seventeen years old, who lived on the east side—created the Crips street gang for black teenage males.

By 1979, the Crips had grown from a small Los Angeles gang of boys to an organization with membership of boys and young men who claimed the streets in many cities throughout southern California as their "territory." They had become like the gang members they had once sought to protect themselves from—they had become gangbangers who terrorized their own neighborhoods.

A rival gang member murdered Raymond in 1979. That same year, Tookie was arrested and charged with murdering four people. In 1981, he was convicted of those crimes and placed on death row.

Over the coming decades, to Tookie's surprise, the Crips gang would spread across the nation and around the world.

Since 1989, Tookie worked to redeem himself from a Crips legacy of black-on-black crime and community destruction. He authored nine antigang books instructing youth how *not* to follow in his footsteps. These books are in schools, libraries, and juvenile correctional facilities in the United States and Europe as well as parts of Africa and Asia. Tookie also created the Internet Project for Street Peace, an international peer mentoring program for children. He regularly provided "live" mentoring via the telephone, calling schools and juvenile correctional facilities to steer kids away from gangs, crime, and violence. He was also nominated five times for the Nobel Peace Prize and four times for the Nobel Prize in Literature.

Tookie's accomplishments were made from his nine-by-four-foot prison cell, without a chair, without a table.

Tookie was executed by the State of California on December 13, 2005.

To the end, he maintained his innocence of the crimes for which he was convicted.

To learn more about how the legacy of Stanley Tookie Williams's work will be sustained, visit the STW Legacy Network at www.STW Legacy.net<http://www.stwlegacy.net/>.

The following questions serve as a foundation for your exploration of
Blue Rage, Black Redemption.

1. What are your initial impressions of the author's style, tone
   of voice, and perspective? How does he manage to capture
   and hold your interest in his story? Do you trust his
   retelling? Why or why not? How does Stanley's use of fore-
   shadowing affect your reading of his story?

2. Although Stanley is quick to defend his mother and ac-
   knowledges her love for him, he believes that he and his
   mother's mindsets about the world and the best way to live
   life differ and are in conflict. How would you characterize
   Stanley and his mother's views? How do they develop? Can
   you foresee a middle ground between their perspectives?
   Do you gravitate toward one more than the other? Explain.

3. Stanley's mother sought to help her son adjust to life in
   South Central Los Angeles in a number of ways. Identify
   the strategies she took. Why are her methods unsuccessful
   in changing Stanley's troublesome behavior? Why does
   Stanley believe her efforts failed? Can you envision other
   methods that may have been more successful to help deter
   Stanley from the gang life he followed?

4. What does Stanley mean by the term "dys-education"?
   Who or what provides opportunities for dys-education?

5. What are Stanley's initial perspectives on gangs? What strategies does he employ to deal with gangs? How and when did his view of gangs begin to change?

6. Define the purpose and the value of the Crips for Stanley. What are some of the metaphors that Stanley uses to illuminate his relationship to the Crips? Discuss the values, codes of conduct, and rites and rituals within the culture of the Crips gang.

7. Discuss the differences between Stanley and his alter ego, Tookie—his real middle name and the name he was called by his gang friends as well as enemies. What does this alter ego provide for Stanley? Is one more real than the other? How so? Does the exploration of these values change your perspective on the Crips?

8. Stanley and Buddha's time at Banning High School and the boys' camp outside of San Diego stand in stark contrast to their lives in South Central Los Angeles. What do their experiences in both locations allow us to see about Stanley and his friend Buddha? What does it reveal about their lives and the roles they either choose or are forced to play?

9. What impact does Buddha's death have on Stanley? How does Stanley come to view his own mortality in light of Buddha's death? How does Stanley's perception of death evolve throughout his story?

10. Stanley's bus to trip to San Quentin reminds us of his fateful trip to South Central Los Angeles with his mother. How does the world he encounters in prison differ from the world he leaves behind in South Central? How are they similar? What approach does Stanley take to deal with the prison world?

11. Stanley leaves the Hole as if with new eyes. Describe his perceptual shift. What role does compassion play in his awakening?

12. What does Stanley mean by the process that he calls "instinctual consciousness"? Have you ever used such a process? Discuss occasions when this process may be necessary or useful.

13. Stanley's transformation reaches its zenith when he is given the name Ajamu Niamke Kamara by his peers and is acknowledged by others as a changed man. What is the significance of naming in Stanley's story?

14. What do you believe it means to be redeemed? Do we have commonly accepted ways of evaluating or talking about redemption? Do you believe in Stanley's redemption? Why or why not?

Enhancement to Your Book Club

1. Read one of Stanley Tookie Williams's children's books and discuss his approach to writing about gangs for children. Does the book reveal new insights about the author? What do you believe is the appropriate age for the book? If any members of your group have children, discuss whether they would share this book with their child. Consider reading the book with a child you know and discuss the relevant themes. Were there challenges to raising the topic of gangs with the child? What did you discover about gangs based upon your discussion with the child?

2. Reading a memoir provides ample opportunity to envision our own lives and the choices and paths we took or failed to take to arrive at our current state. Stanley conceived of his life in two parts, Blue Rage—and later, Black Redemption. Try to locate a significant event or series of events that similarly divided your life into a before and an after period. Who did you believe you were before the event(s)? What were your values? What were your hopes and dreams? How did they change? Could others notice any of your changes? Why or why not? If you could name your before and after periods, what would you call them? Create your own memoir book cover with a brief introduction and bring it to share with your group.

3. Visit Tookie.com and print out his Protocol for Peace. Review the document prior to meeting with your group and

make two concrete additions to any section of the document. Write each addition on separate 3-x-5 index cards. Bring your two index cards to the meeting and place them in a bowl. At some point in the meeting, perhaps during a snack break, have the group leader read all cards aloud. Discuss the merits of group members' suggestions. Stanley calls on all of us to participate in helping to create a safe and healthy community. How did it feel to contribute to the Protocol? What were your challenges to imagining a way to create peace? Which elements of the Protocol seemed doable?

Author Questions and Answers

Responded to by Barbara Becnel

1. **Stanley discusses that various institutions, most notably the education system, failed him as a child. Since most children have to go through the education system, how would you supplement their learning?**

   Stan believed in rigorous academic preparation for the most disenfranchised youth of this nation. So he supported longer school days, which could include after-school-tutorial programs, and involved parents. Further, Stan wanted parents to sign a contract with the school that their child attended, a contract detailing their commitment to assisting in the child's education.

2. **Stanley struggled with the lack of black images in religious imagery, yet his own transformation was aided by spiritual practice. How is he able to make that leap?**

   The adult Stan did not ascribe an ethnicity to God.

3. **Stanley's mother tried desperately to steer him in the right direction when he was a child. What strategies does the individual parent have at their disposal to assist their child in navigating the streets?**

   Stan repeatedly stated that parents must help a child identify the interests unique to that child and for which that child has a special talent. Once that is determined, the parent should help that child become very engaged in the development of the skills and resources needed to realize that interest, for example, becoming a chef, firefighter, teacher, carpenter, nurse, plumber, writer, actor, musician, singer, coach . . .

4. **You point to the underlying punitive rather than rehabilitative nature of the penal system. Can you envision a time when we will conceive of justice in a different manner? Are there any notable systems that we can take inspiration from and try to emulate?**
I do not have a great deal of faith in the politics behind the growth of this nation's criminal justice system buttressed by a law-and-order mentality based, I believe, on class and race bias. So I cannot envision a time that I will live to see justice delivered equitably and without regard to the ability to pay for qualified legal representation and the skin color of the accused. I am impressed, though, by the penal philosophy and practice that informs Switzerland's corrections system. That European nation genuinely believes in rehabilitation and devotes considerable resources to assisting their incarcerated prepare for a return to mainstream society. I've visited their youth prisons and have spent time talking to the psychiatrists and psychologists they employ to work closely with prisoners, including rapists and child molesters. Also, Switzerland has no death penalty and there is no such concept or punishment identified as "life without the possibility of parole." So *all* prisoners in Switzerland will, at some point, be allowed to return home.

5. **Some individuals have challenged whether Stanley had really abandoned the codes of the Crips and his redemption, because he did not approve of snitching. How would you answer these critics?**
First, Stan was not required to debrief—otherwise known as snitching—at San Quentin because California State

Prison rules only demand that members of *prison* gangs, not street gangs, have to debrief to be released from the Hole. Since the Crips was founded on the streets of South Central Los Angeles, instead of in one of California's prisons, Stan was never really confronted with the requirement to debrief. However, even if he had been asked to do so, he would have refused: debriefing is a very dangerous choice to make in the prison environment. To debrief—point a finger of guilt at another inmate—not only puts your own life in danger. Debriefing, more important from Stan's point of view, puts in jeopardy the life of the person on whom you have snitched. Stan's pact with himself and with God, once he decided to rehabilitate himself, was to never again take any action that could knowingly hurt another human being. So Stan was not driven by the "codes of the Crips" in his stance against debriefing, he was driven by his own code of ethics inspired by his relationship with the Almighty, which is the name Stan used to refer to God.

6. You continually recognize the potential and the underutilized talents of Stanley's fellow inmates. How would you like to see society incorporate both current inmates and former inmates in addressing social injustices?

    Stan's voice proved to be the credible voice for a large population of young people who were on the verge of following in the gang-member footsteps of Stanley Tookie Williams. These are young people who often would not listen to the same antiviolence message from you or me: we would have little or no credibility with them. So, to the extent that there are other prisoners or former prisoners who are willing not only to proclaim a message of peace, but are willing, as was Stan, to live the life of a peacemaker, those are prisoners and former prisoners who should be sought out and used by local government and community-based organizations to become our ambassadors of peace on the streets of urban neighborhoods throughout the country.

7. **How do you continue to maintain hope when individuals who are not even incarcerated succumb to hopelessness and despair? How do you keep the flame of hope burning within?**

   What Stan conveyed to me about the origin of his hope was that it was inspired by his gratefulness to the Almighty for allowing him to discover his raison d'être and for guiding him to help so many young people by steering them away from gangs, violence, drugs, and criminality.

8. **Stanley gives situations his own name, like the terms "dys-education" and "instinctual consciousness." What does it do for you to have these codified in such a way?**

   I considered Stan a remarkably original thinker. These phrases helped me and, I hope, will help all those who read *Blue Rage, Black Redemption* to become aware of what is no longer examined in mainstream culture: the varied, complex impacts of long-term oppression on those who have been oppressed.

9. **This book is more than just a memoir; it is imbued with a passion for real social transformation both for the individual and society at large. How would you like for people to receive this book? What do you want someone who has never heard of Tookie to take away from reading this memoir?**

   Stan insisted on including his Street Peace Protocol in *Blue Rage, Black Redemption* because he wanted to provide people with a definitive plan of action after reading his book. Also, Stan wanted the readers of *Blue Rage, Black Redemption* to understand on a gut level what it means to be raised as a child in a neighborhood like South Central Los Angeles. He wanted a reader to accept some measure of individual responsibility for that knowledge by taking steps to make such communities life-enhancing places in which to grow up as opposed to spirit-breaking neighborhoods.

10. **What drew you to Stanley and this project? What will your next work be?**

I was drawn to Stan and his work because I recognized the tremendous potential his redemption and willingness to work in support of humankind could have on many thousands of at-risk youth. As I got to know Stan better over the years, I was also drawn to his integrity and his strength demonstrated by his lack of bitterness about the injustice and corruption that he faced in trying to get the truth of his innocence revealed. Stan's integrity and strength were further demonstrated by his ability to be such a prodigious worker for street peace despite residing on death row in a nine-by-four-foot steel-and-concrete cell for nearly a quarter of a century. My next work will be a book that I alone am writing. Its title is *Bear Witness: The Execution of Stanley Tookie Williams*. In this book I will tell the complete, untold story of the fight to save Stan from execution. I will also provide an analysis of the political as well as historical factors that led to Stan's capital murder conviction and his killing by lethal injection on December 13, 2005. This book will lay bare the institutional and legal machinery that grinds slowly toward the state-initiated death of a human being, whether that person is guilty or innocent—or has redeemed himself completely.